# GREENSPAN

# GREENSPAN
## The Case for the Defence

Edward L. Greenspan and George Jonas

A COLLINS PAPERBACK
TORONTO

First published 1987
by Macmillan of Canada
This edition published 1988
by COLLINS PAPERBACKS
100 Lesmill Road, Don Mills, Ontario

## Canadian Cataloguing in Publication Data

Greenspan, Edward L.
  Greenspan, the case for the defence

Includes index.
ISBN 0-00-215437-4

1. Greenspan, Edward L. 2. Trials - Canada. 3.
Criminal justice, Administration of - Canada. 4.
Lawyers - Canada - biography.  I.  Jonas, George, date.
II. Title.

KE416.G74A3 1988   345.71'0092'4   C88-094819-1
KF345.Z9G74 1988

Printed and bound in Canada

To the memory of my father, Joseph H. Greenspan

*I trust that no one will understand me to be speaking with disrespect of the law, because I criticize it so freely. I venerate the law, and especially our system of law, as one of the vastest products of the human mind. But one may criticize even what one reveres.*

— Oliver Wendell Holmes

# Contents

# Foreword

Arthur Koestler pointed out that a man should write his memoirs before he's fifty; if he waits much longer he runs the risk of passions cooling, recollections fading, and memory turning stale. I can confirm this. I'm only forty-three, and I have already forgotten everything. Since I can't remember my life, this book could not have been written without assistance from a number of friends. I list their names in the acknowledgments.

Of course, this book could not have been written without my enemies either, but I see no point in thanking them here by name. In any event, I named names throughout the book whenever possible, except as noted. The exceptions have nothing to do with libel laws. When I resorted to pseudonyms, it was for one of the following reasons:

One, in deference to a court order where a publication ban was or appeared to be still in force. Two, in deference to the compassionate practice of not mentioning the names of certain bystanders or minors whose involvement in a criminal matter is purely peripheral — including in this category, more chivalrously than fairly I think, complainants in cases of alleged sexual assault. Three, in deference to clients, whether acquitted or convicted, whose names had not appeared in print before. (It would be ironic for a client whose involvement in a criminal case had never been made public to find his name for the first time in his own lawyer's book.)

In addition, I did not name some people whose conduct might expose them to criminal charges. My job is to defend, not to denounce or prosecute.

Some people may wonder why I have omitted discussing in this book two extremely well-known murder cases, *Regina v. Peter Demeter* and *Regina v. Helmuth Buxbaum*. In the case of Peter Demeter, I was the junior counsel at the trial and there is nothing I could add to my co-author's book, *By Persons Unknown*, which exhaustively analyses the murder of Christine Demeter. The case of Helmuth Buxbaum is before the courts in two separate ways. Mr. Buxbaum's appeal from his conviction has not yet been heard, and I have a dispute with him awaiting resolution. I did not think, under these circumstances, that it would be appropriate for me to comment on his trial.

I alone am to blame for all omissions and errors in the entire book, but in point of fact I have not written, selected, or edited anybody's comments or recollections about me. These appear in passages written in the third person. While I do not necessarily remember the anecdotes or endorse the views, I take responsibility for their inclusion. The way in which other people see me or my work is part of the record.

ELG

When my friend Eddie Greenspan asked me to collaborate with him on this book, he outlined his position on the working method he wanted us to follow. "I've done my bit by living my life," offered Greenspan. "You can do yours by writing it."

It did not turn out as Greenspan had hoped. Reluctant as he was, he had to talk at length about his work and his life. When he could no longer stand the sight of me, he had to speak into a tape recorder. He was even forced to put pen to paper, much as he may have kicked and screamed about it.

As a result, the first-person sections in this narrative are by Greenspan. However, they are not about him; they are about other people or the law. The rest of the book is about Greenspan by other people.

GJ

# Acknowledgments

I wish to express my gratitude to a number of people who contributed to this book.

Guy Gavriel Kay, a distinguished author in his own right and a dear friend, edited the manuscript with intelligence and skill.

My partner Marc Rosenberg read every chapter and made constructive suggestions. He also wrote a number of the footnotes. My partner Chris Buhr carefully reviewed those cases in which he was involved with me for accuracy, and recalled some anecdotes that I had long forgotten.

I want to thank my friends Philip Epstein, Q.C., and David Greenspan, Q.C., for permission to reprint certain letters. Gary Siskind, a lifelong friend and a true baseball fan, made an invaluable contribution in the chapter involving Fergie Jenkins. Alan Borovoy, general counsel to the Canadian Civil Liberties Association, kindly recalled some anecdotes.

I received special assistance and encouragement from my brother Brian, my sister Rosann, my mother Emma, and my dear friend Harvey Strosberg, Q.C. He and his partner Robert Barnes, Q.C., were kind enough to read the manuscript and make helpful suggestions.

Whatever success I have had is due to the most important partnership in my life. My wife Suzy is not only my best friend but has been one of my most important advisers. At the risk of exposing her to a charge of practising law without a licence, she has read all my jury addresses, has corrected them, and has invariably improved them. She has stayed up with me many a night, encouraging me and assisting me in my trial preparations. She is my thirteenth juror.

I want to thank my daughters, Julianna and Samantha, for no other reason than that life would become intolerable for me at home if I did not thank them.

The only reason I am not going to thank my literary agent, Stanley Colbert, is that I believe it is probably inappropriate for a lawyer (a) to have a literary agent, and (b) if he does have one, to thank him. It it were not for these two factors, I would say that I am very grateful for his help.

Finally, I want to thank a number of clients who kindly permitted me to talk about certain aspects of their cases.

ELG

PART ONE

# NO LITTLE CLIENTS

# 1. Babies Don't Fly

In the morning of March 8, 1982, Edward L. Greenspan was driving to Niagara Falls, Ontario. A few weeks earlier he had turned thirty-eight. He was a married man, the father of two children. A criminal lawyer and senior partner of his own law firm in Toronto, he was on his way to defend a woman charged with manslaughter at a preliminary hearing in the Provincial Court at Niagara Falls.

It was a tragic case; if it ever came to trial, it was likely to be a high-profile case as well. The prosecution accused the woman of tossing her baby into the Horseshoe Falls on the Canadian side of the Niagara River.

By 1982 Greenspan had many high-profile trials behind him. The newspapers had been calling him "a leading criminal lawyer" for years — since 1974, to be precise, when he acted as junior counsel in the murder trial of the wealthy Toronto developer Peter Demeter. However, driving along the Queen Elizabeth Way that morning, Greenspan didn't feel like a leading criminal lawyer at all. He was feeling as though he were about to make his very first appearance in court. Even more irritatingly, he felt as if he were thirteen years old again.

Niagara Falls had been Eddie Greenspan's home town. In one sense, he always regarded this as other people might regard an affliction. He could be absolutely scathing about the gaudy-seedy little tourist trap on the shores of the world-famous waterfall. In another sense, his sarcasm was always tinged with an element of nostalgia. Speaking objectively, he had mainly happy memories about the small town of middle-class honeymooners on the American border where he was born and raised, and where he eventually graduated from the Niagara Falls Collegiate Vocational Institute, as had his uncles, his aunt, and his father before him.

Eddie had adored his father. Joseph H. Greenspan had been hoping to become a lawyer himself, except that his father's illness had forced him to take over the family business. So he became a scrap dealer in

Niagara Falls, and the small enterprise provided his wife and children — Eddie, his sister Rosann, and his younger brother, Brian — with an adequate living.

Then Greenspan's father himself died at the unforeseeably early age of forty-two. The business collapsed. There was no insurance. Mrs. Emma Greenspan had to raise her three children (Eddie, the eldest, was only thirteen at the time) on her salary as secretary for a local public school. The years that followed were grim, but they were not the reason for Eddie's ambiguous feelings about his home town. Nor was it, as some friends suggested, an association of Niagara Falls with early death and unrealized hopes.

The much simpler fact was that Greenspan fit the town of Niagara Falls like a battleship fits a swimming-pool. He was unsuited to his birthplace in spirit and in intellectual ambitions. He had only dreams at that point, but they were big dreams. Some people enjoy dreaming big in a little place; Eddie did not. He knew that a number of eminent people came from Niagara Falls — his own school could boast of having educated William Francis Giaugue, who won the Nobel Prize for chemistry in 1949 — but the whole point was, these people came from Niagara Falls, they didn't stay there. It was (as the writer Morley Torgov was to say later of another little Ontario town, Sault Ste. Marie) a good place to come from.

It was in Niagara Falls that Eddie — as well as his younger brother, Brian — first decided to choose criminal law as their careers. They both decided it at the age of nine or ten, when most children have no idea what they might wish to do in life. Even more unusually, they both followed through with it without any of the stops and starts characteristic of young people, especially in the turbulent sixties.

It seemed that neither of the two Greenspan boys needed to "find themselves". They knew exactly what they wanted, and what they wanted was what their father would have liked to do. There was nothing subconscious about it, but it was an interesting psychological reversal just the same. Usually it is fathers who insist on their frustrated ambitions being fulfilled by their sons. In the case of Eddie and Brian Greenspan, it was the sons who insisted on fulfilling the frustrated ambitions of their father.

Eddie Greenspan had been away from his native town for nearly twenty years by that Monday in March 1982. He had proved himself in a number of significant ways. He had become a defence lawyer of some *national prominence; he had argued cases in Ontario, British Columbia, Quebec, and Manitoba, and in the Supreme Court of Canada. His legal business had taken him around the world from France to Pakistan.*

*As it happened, he had never before contested a case in Niagara Falls.*

*There was absolutely no reason for him to feel nervous about it, and of course he didn't. The very idea was ridiculous. He was no longer a child; there wasn't anybody he had to impress any more. He tried telling himself that Niagara Falls had meant nothing to him for years. It was just a little town he could hardly wait to escape from back then, and the greasy spoon — for some reason he remembered the greasy spoon, where he used to feed quarters into the jukebox with his friends — was no doubt a parking lot by now. Most of the kids he used to know, the kids he had grown up with, had probably left town themselves long ago.*

*He would go to court and do his best, which was all anyone could do. It was what he'd try to do whether he was in Niagara Falls or at the other end of the earth. The rest was just — well, it was just the kind of self-indulgence he abhorred. This trip was a job: it wasn't a homecoming in any sense. He wasn't making a sentimental journey.*

*Greenspan floored the accelerator — probably his costliest single habit. He had always collected speeding tickets as if they were going out of style and sometimes his licence was only a couple of points away from suspension. He had often promised to reform, but this time he couldn't help it. Memories came flooding back. He was being sentimental, and he was furious with himself.*

I happen to know the spot where 2½-month-old Hesham Sayegh fell into the west Niagara River. I know it intimately. It is a place just a few yards north of the Horseshoe Falls, almost at the lip of the immense cataract. When I was a child I used to spend hours standing there, in the early autumn evenings when most of the tourists were gone, looking down at the darkening, swirling, hypnotic waters. It was a perfect spot from which to see the Falls, because the prevailing winds would usually blow the chilly clouds of mist the other way.

It was the height of the tourist season on August 29, 1981, when a self-employed Toronto limousine driver named Rafic Sayegh took his family to look at the great gorge. Visitors stood packed at the railing in long, unbroken lines. It was a perfect Saturday, the kind of day that keeps the economy of Niagara Falls going. People who wanted to catch a close glimpse of the waterfall would often have to wait for a place to open up at the low cement wall which had a curlicued iron railing on top of it.

The cement wall would come up to just about the knees of a five-foot-two adult. The railing would be at approximately the right height for most people to lean on.

Dunia Sayegh, Rafic's twenty-seven-year-old wife, was five feet two inches tall. She came to see the Falls with her husband, her three children, and her younger sister, Nada Nasrallah. The Sayeghs' little girl, Hela, was eight years old then, and their elder son, Haissam, was twelve. Rafic and Nada were looking after the two older children; Dunia was carrying her infant son, Hesham, in her arms.

Rafic and Dunia Sayegh, along with two of their three children, had immigrated to Canada from Lebanon almost eight years earlier, in 1974. By religion they belonged to the Druze sect of Shi'ite Islam, a small and closely knit group of about 250,000 adherents, living mainly in Syria and Lebanon.

On August 29 the family did what most visitors do at the Falls: they looked at the sights and took pictures of each other. One of the photographs turned out to be the last one of little Hesham, held by his mother. In the picture they were both smiling. After about an hour, at around 1:45 p.m., Rafic Sayegh and his daughter went to the Table Rock Restaurant to buy more film for their camera.

It was at this point that Dunia Sayegh became separated from her older son and from her sister Nada. While the two were looking at something else, Dunia, holding Hesham in her arms, approached the iron railing at the edge of the water.

An American visitor named Alan King, who was standing at the low cement wall about six feet away, saw Dunia as she stepped up to the rail. She was cradling the baby in her arms and looking at the waves rushing below. There was nothing unusual about what she was doing, so Mr. King turned his attention elsewhere. In any case, another couple were standing between Dunia and Mr. King. A period of time — at least two minutes, maybe three or four — elapsed before the woman standing next to King started screaming that someone had dropped a baby.

King looked — down at Dunia's feet first, because he did not expect the baby to fall over the rail. It was then that the woman next to him screamed that "the baby went over the Falls." King saw Dunia backing away, also screaming hysterically: "My baby, my baby, I dropped my baby." Then, describing a little circle, she started back towards the railing. Worried that she might try to climb over it, King restrained her. Dunia collapsed, saying, "I'm so dizzy," and King, along with some other people, helped her to the Table Rock Restaurant. The police arrived about fifteen minutes later.

There was no reason for believing that whatever happened at the railing was anything but a tragic accident. There were no witnesses to say otherwise — indeed, there were no eyewitnesses at all. Alan King had not looked at Dunia in the critical two- to four-minute period, and the couple standing at the railing between King and Dunia never came forward. They may not have seen anything, in any case, until after the baby fell.

The Sayeghs loved their children, and there was ample evidence that they took meticulous care of them. Hesham had been a planned baby: both parents looked forward to having him. Dunia and Rafic were part of a culture that took the family seriously; more so than most contemporary cultures. As individuals, Rafic was a devoted father and Dunia a very concerned mother.

Ironically, the fact that Dunia may have been a little too concerned with her baby for Canadian tastes (perhaps for male tastes in general) contributed to the suspicions of the police when they found out about it.

Hesham had suffered a minor birth trauma when he was born. The umbilical cord had been wound around his neck, which caused the infant some breathing difficulties at first, and later required four days of observation and treatment at the Sick Children's Hospital in Toronto. After that period the doctors released Hesham as perfectly healthy.

Dunia, however, remained anxious about her baby — more anxious than the baby's condition warranted, in the opinion of her family physician, Dr. Cyril Press. According to his later testimony, a couple of weeks before the tragedy he had to treat Dunia for some dizzy spells, which he thought might have been hysterically induced because of her anxiety about Hesham. Apparently, after the baby came home from the hospital, Dunia had fainted a few times for no medical reason that Dr. Press could see. When the police arrived at the scene in Niagara Falls, a distraught Rafic, speaking in poor English, also said something to them about Dunia's having been worried about the health of the baby, though he had kept telling her that there was no need to worry.

Still, this would have been hardly enough to make the police suspicious. Since they had no evidence of any wrongdoing whatever, it's impossible to tell how or why they became suspicious of Dunia initially; it's only possible to say that they did. Within an hour of the incident the investigating officers were to tell a psychiatrist that the baby's fall "may not have been accidental."

Dunia, of course, was in a state of great emotional distress. She kept alternately fainting and reviving in the restaurant to which she was taken. She was pale and sweating; her hands and feet were jerking in spasmodic movements. At intervals she repeated that she had been clutching Hesham to her chest at the railing, and then she got dizzy and could not remember anything else.

From this, possibly coupled with Rafic's remarks, the authorities seemed to glean some notion that this might be the case of a woman whose earlier anxiety about her baby had affected her own mental health. At the Greater Niagara General Hospital, to which she was taken in an ambulance from the restaurant, they had her examined by a psychiatrist named Dr. Wallace Mitchell. He formed the opinion that, while Dunia wasn't psychotic, she was suffering from post-partum depression.

The police noted certain things that Dunia said in the presence of various nurses and physicians at the hospital. They included "My baby doesn't want me" and "God doesn't want me to have the baby." Clearly, the suspicion was rising in the police's mind that an overly emotional mother, needlessly or hysterically worried about her baby's health, might have deliberately decided to do away with him.

Right after the event, distraught as she was (and difficult as she found it to communicate in English), Dunia did appear to say that she had been clutching the baby to her chest as she was going up to the railing — before she became dizzy, that is, and could no longer remember anything. She even demonstrated it by gesture. This, indeed, was the way in which the witnesses Alan King and a lady named Mae Fragale saw her holding the baby when they noticed Dunia approaching the retaining wall, a few minutes before the incident. If this was what she did, if she was holding the baby cradled in her arms — the police asked themselves — how exactly could the baby have fallen into the river?

The officer in charge of the investigation, a Sergeant Cornelis Vandermeer, decided to conduct an experiment the following day. He found a woman, a twenty-one-year-old typist from the Niagara Regional Police named Carol Berry, who was similar in height and build to Dunia Sayegh. The police gave Mrs. Berry a "Rescuci" doll, normally used in demonstrations of life-saving techniques. They instructed her to stand at the spot where Dunia had been standing, hold the doll cradled in her arms, then drop it.

The experiment was repeated, with Mrs. Berry assuming slightly different positions at the retaining wall two more times. Each time the doll fell on the cement sidewalk *inside* the railing. "As a result of the re-enactments," Sergeant Vandermeer was to state later, "I concluded that the baby could not have fallen into the water as described by Dunia Sayegh."

Having so concluded, Sergeant Vandermeer arrested Dunia Sayegh on a charge of second-degree murder on Tuesday, September 1. She virtually had to be carried by her brother and a lawyer friend of the family from her apartment, where she had been lying under sedation, to the waiting police cruiser. Dunia, apart from repeating that she did not kill her baby, that she was holding him in her arms as she was standing "beside the cement" and couldn't remember anything else, made no further statement to the police.

*After* Dunia's arrest (no doubt concerned that their impromptu re-enactment with the Rescuci doll on Sunday might have been insufficiently scientific), the police had Mrs. Berry repeat the experiment on Thursday, September 3, under the supervision of Eric Krueger from the Engineering Department of the Toronto Centre of Forensic Sciences. Mr. Krueger also expressed the opinion that "an unintentional accidental fall of the baby over the fence into the river could not have occurred."

Mr. Krueger saw fit to say this. Later, reading his statement, I was fit to be tied. In my view, to offer this experiment as "scientific" evidence was a shocking misuse of the term. It was one thing for the Niagara Regional Police to play with dolls, but quite another for a renowned institute such as the Centre of Forensic Sciences to lend its name to such antics.

To begin with, Mrs. Berry was holding a doll, but Dunia Sayegh was holding a *baby*. Dolls do not move or wriggle; babies do. Even at two and a half months they can arch their backs and flail with their hands and feet.

Second, what possible conclusion could anyone draw from the fact that the doll didn't fall into the river when dropped from those two different positions that Mrs. Berry happened to assume at the railing? Dunia Sayegh could have stood there in a variety of positions. No one knew what her position was. She couldn't remember, and no one saw her. Even the marginal validity of a doll as a stand-in for a live baby is nullified unless it's dropped from exactly the same position, and no one could tell what that position was. A scientific experiment? Evidence to be offered in a court of law on a charge of murder? It was pure speculation.

By 1982, when I was retained by Dunia Sayegh's family to defend her, I was no longer surprised at speculation masquerading as science in court. However, I could still be outraged by it. Not only some police officers, but quite a few experts, come to court with instincts better suited to authors of detective mysteries. Useful as such instincts are for writing fiction, they are next to irresponsible when exhibited on the witness stand. Yet there's no field of human endeavour, from engineering to psychiatry, that would not have spawned its quota of frustrated novelists in court.

Nothing demonstrated this more clearly than the second "scientific" peg that the prosecution attempted to hang its hat on, namely that Dunia had been suffering from post-partum depression, an emotional illness that in extreme cases might cause a mother suffering from it to kill her baby.

The Crown's only evidence in support of this theory was Dr. Mitchell's psychiatric opinion. (Spouses were still not compellable witnesses in 1982, so Rafic Sayegh could not be forced to repeat in court his remarks to the police at the scene about Dunia's anxieties regarding Hesham's health — remarks probably made in an attempt to explain to the officers how good and caring a mother his wife was.)

Dr. Mitchell's opinion was based on an examination conducted within hours of the incident. It was made after some police officers expressed their suspicions to him that the baby's fall "may not have been an accident.'' Before Dr. Mitchell dictated his diagnosis, the Sayeghs' family physician, Dr. Press, had also communicated to him his view that Dunia had appeared to be needlessly concerned with her baby's health.

Because of these factors, I was singularly unimpressed with Dr. Mitchell's report. In my view, any psychiatrist would have to conduct his examination under less tainted conditions than those obtaining immediately after a woman had dropped her baby into a waterfall, if he were to form any conclusions about her prior mental state. At least, any conclusions deserving to be called scientific and offered in evidence as such. In fairness to Dr. Mitchell, he expressed some caution about this himself, but he still stood by his conclusion.

My views about the value of opinions formed under these circumstances would have been the same even if Dr. Mitchell's diagnosis had eventually been confirmed by other medical findings, but in point of fact no such evidence was ever offered by the Crown. I've often wondered since the Sayegh case if a psychiatrist (or a policeman) would care to be diagnosed, let alone judged in court, on the basis of how he might appear to someone a couple of hours after his infant slipped out of his hands and fell into Niagara Falls. Yet policemen, doctors, and some other witnesses are constantly appearing in court to offer assessments of defendants on the basis of their words or behaviour under circumstances almost as extreme as that.

One of the problems with all such speculations is that they can influence the public, from whose members, if a case comes to trial, a jury will be drawn. At a preliminary inquiry, which is the procedure at which a judge decides whether there is enough evidence to commit the case for trial, the court usually prohibits the attending press from publishing the evidence adduced. The defence's dilemma in this instance was that the preliminary hearing was to be held in Niagara Falls. The incident was big news. Members of the eager American media from across the river would be in attendance, and the nonpublication order of the Canadian court would be unenforceable on the American press.

As I knew from personal experience, people in Niagara Falls often read American papers. We've always watched U.S. television and listened to U.S. radio from Buffalo. A prohibition binding on the Canadian press alone would be meaningless under such circumstances. If a potential jury is prejudiced by what they see, hear, or read in the media, it makes little difference whether such information comes from Ontario or the state of New York.

Accordingly, when the court opened on March 8, 1982, I began by making an unusual motion before His Honour, Judge D. J. Wallace. I asked for the exclusion of all members of the public, including the press, at the preliminary inquiry. The judge was reluctant (properly so, because closed trials are in neither the public's nor the defendant's interest on the whole), but under the circumstances he agreed with my submissions. From that point, only the parties to the proceedings were allowed to stay inside the courtroom.

By the time of the preliminary hearing, the Crown had reduced the original charge of second-degree murder to one of manslaughter. This was an act of rare prosecutorial generosity. At the same time, in order to secure a conviction on this reduced charge, the prosecution had no need to prove that Dunia Sayegh had intended to kill her baby. The Crown Attorney, Allen Root, had only to satisfy a court that Dunia performed some unlawful act that resulted in the death of her infant.

But what was the unlawful act? Going to Niagara Falls was a perfectly lawful act, as far as I could remember. The Ontario Ministry of Tourism encouraged people to go to Niagara Falls.

Once in Niagara Falls, it was also a perfectly lawful act to approach the retaining wall and view the gorge. Most people who ever went to Niagara Falls went there for no other purpose.

And there was simply no evidence that Dunia Sayegh did anything else but go up to the railing with the baby in her arms and look at the Horseshoe Falls. The rest was only speculation and a lot of grown-ups playing with dolls.

Yet the Rescuci doll remained the main basis on which the prosecution was asking the judge to commit Dunia to trial. No evidence emerged at the preliminary, except as outlined above. In his final submissions to the court, Allen Root argued on behalf of the Crown that there were only two positions at the retaining wall in which Mrs. Sayegh was known to be standing. Those positions were known by her own words to the police as well as by the evidence of the American visitor, Alan King. From those two positions the doll, when dropped by Mrs. Berry, did not fall into the water. This being so, in the Crown's theory the doll (and therefore the baby) would have had to be tossed.

"We don't know what position [Mrs. Sayegh] was standing in," Judge Wallace interrupted at this point.

"We have it from her own lips: 'I was beside the cement,' " replied the Crown.

"Well, that could be anywhere, could it not?"

"Well, your Honour, to my knowledge babies don't fly," said the prosecutor. "If she is anywhere other than against the wall, if she is anything further than that, [the baby] must of necessity drop to the ground."

There was one fatal flaw in this argument. According to the evidence, Dunia's last "known" position was two to four minutes before the baby dropped from her hands. In two to four minutes people can assume an awful lot of different positions at a railing. But, for some reason, the Crown Attorney thought that this supported his position. "That is all the evidence, and this court is not allowed to speculate," he said to the judge.

I was grateful for this remark. It just about summed up the case for the defence. Judge Wallace saw it immediately. "*That's* your problem, Mr. Root," he said to the prosecutor.

However, since the charge against Dunia had been reduced to manslaughter, it gave the Crown an opportunity to rely on a secondary position as well. It went like this: going to the railing with the baby in her arms, knowing that she had been suffering from dizziness or fainting spells in the past, Dunia exhibited gross negligence. Such gross negligence and "reckless abandonment", the Crown argued, also amounted to manslaughter in law.

I thought that this was really trying to get Dunia Sayegh coming and going. If a woman worries about her baby's health, and faints or suffers dizzy spells for which her doctor can't find an immediate physical cause, then she must be afflicted with "post-partum depression", giving her a motive to throw her baby into Niagara Falls. If, however, she accepts her doctor's and her family's reassurances that there is nothing wrong with her and, feeling fine, goes on a Saturday outing with her family, doing whatever any normal, healthy woman would do at Niagara Falls, then she exhibits "gross negligence" or "reckless abandonment" in the view of the authorities.

I felt that if there was anything reckless going on in that courtroom it was the charge against Dunia and the arguments supporting it. Minimally, it was very, very unfair.

If anything unlawful occurred at Niagara Falls, it *had* to occur in those two to four minutes for which the prosecution could offer no evidence, because up until that point, on the Crown's own evidence, Dunia had done nothing unlawful whatever. In effect, the prosecutor was asking the court to judge a case from *before* the period during which anything that might have turned Hesham's fall from an accident into a crime had to happen. Why? Because that was the best he could do. "If that's the best [the Crown] can do," I said in my closing submissions to Judge Wallace, "it doesn't make it a case."

His Honour took a day to consider the matter. On March 12 he delivered his judgment. "The case before this court may be summarized as follows," he said. "If a reasonable jury, properly instructed, accepted the utterances of the accused, it could only conclude that the death of the infant child was the result of a tragic and unfortunate accident.

"If the jury were to reject the utterances of the accused, then it is left with no evidence whatever as to how the death of the child occurred. . . . The jury cannot fill in the 2 to 4-minute gap through conjecture or speculation. . . . The result is that in my opinion the Crown has made out no case for the accused to answer, and there is no triable issue for a jury to consider. Accordingly, the accused woman must now be discharged."

Dunia's legal ordeal was over. Her personal ordeal, obviously, could only be healed by time. One question remained in my mind, though: how could a tragic freak accident have escalated into a charge of murder?

Dropping a baby into Niagara Falls was, of course, headline news, but the Sayeghs themselves were not headline-makers. They were what many lawyers would refer to as "little clients". They were ordinary, hard-working people, immigrants from a distant land and culture, neither seeking nor, in the normal course of events, prone to receiving attention. They had undergone a horrendous experience in this country. The experience would have been terrible, needless to say, even if it had not been followed by criminal charges. Facing an accusation of homicide in court must have made it truly unimaginable for Dunia Sayegh and her family.

How could it have come about?

I must engage in some speculation myself to answer this question. I have the excuse, though, of doing it only in a book and not in a court of law.

In the aftermath of the accident, however it happened, Dunia was in a state of psychological shock. So was her entire family. Rafic was standing in the manager's office at the Table Rock Restaurant, at times hitting the wall with his fist, at other times directing emotional questions at his wife in Arabic. Their eight-year-old daughter was allegedly overheard by one of the waitresses saying to her mother, in English: "Mommy, I told you not to put him in the water." (The prosecution actually tried to introduce this in evidence against Dunia, but Judge Wallace ruled it inadmissible, as there was no evidence that Mrs. Sayegh had heard the child's remark at all.) This was the scene that confronted the police officers who arrived about fifteen minutes after the event.

What they saw was a distraught, barely coherent family, who could not explain anything to them. There were no eyewitnesses. A baby had been dropped into Niagara Falls, apparently for the first time in living memory, and no one could tell the police how or why.

Dunia, drifting in and out of consciousness, was obviously feeling "guilty" about what happened. Who wouldn't? Any normal mother would "blame" herself if her baby slipped from her hands into Niagara Falls. A recognition of this feeling of abstract "guilt" in her may have translated itself into a suspicion of *legal* guilt in the police officers' mind.

It must have. They had no other evidence against Dunia, then or later, to support their suspicion. Their suspicion, of course, was not "evidence" either, but it was enough to set a legal machinery into motion. It was enough to create a frame of mind in Sergeant Vandermeer and his colleagues which, with the tenuous support of a snap diagnosis by a psychiatrist and a doll being bounced off the ground by a group of policemen playing at "science", resulted in a charge of murder.

Once that charge was laid, the machinery became almost unstoppable. That's the way our system works in Canada.

The Crown prosecutes in this country, but in practice it runs with the charges laid by the police. The prosecutor may make technical adjustments in a charge before a case comes to court, sometimes even major adjustments such as reducing murder to manslaughter, as in Dunia's case. But these changes, when made, are often made only for tactical reasons. In essence, the Crown generally feels obliged to follow the police theory of an event, even when it has to employ the most tortuous and far-fetched reasoning to prop up the evidence available in court.

Nothing illustrated this better than a discussion I had with Allen Root before the preliminary hearing. (Crown and defence often meet for private, semi-formal talks concerning such matters as plea negotiations, procedure, or sentencing.) "Why don't you just drop the charges, Allen?" I asked Root when I saw him in his office. "It's the right thing to do. It was just an accident. This woman loves her children. She lives for her children."

"Well, there's another side to this, Eddie," Root replied. "What about reincarnation?"

I actually knew what he was talking about, though I could scarcely believe my ears. In preparation for Dunia's trial, the Crown had a university scholar prepare a study on the Druze religion to which the Sayegh family belonged. A belief in reincarnation was, apparently, among the tenets of the Druze faith. In light of this, Allen Root was considering arguing to a jury that Dunia might have killed the baby she thought was ill in the belief that it would come back as a healthy infant in another life.

"You can't be serious," I said to the prosecutor. "Over half the world believes in reincarnation. You don't see them going around killing their children. There are more people with birth-defects in countries like India than just about anywhere else. According to your theory, they should all have been killed as babies."

But the Crown Attorney was speaking in earnest, at least during our discussion. The police had apparently considered Dunia's religion as being part of the prosecution's case against her. The matter did not come up at the preliminary hearing, but, had the case gone to trial, an attempt might have been made to introduce it to the jury in the form of yet another bit of "expert evidence" by a university professor of Islamic studies. Along with, possibly, the suggestion (which was also mentioned in the study prepared for the Crown) that the jury shouldn't believe whatever members of Dunia's family might say on the witness stand, because Druze people do not consider lying a sin if it is to protect a member of their own clan against outsiders.

I would certainly have argued against such gravely prejudicial evidence being admitted in court. My protests might or might not have been successful. "Experts" are permitted to give opinion evidence on a wide range of subjects. The prosecution might well have attempted to introduce the notion of reincarnation to support a flight of fancy by the Niagara Regional Police.

For Crown attorneys to play straight-man to the police, to scrape the bottom of the barrel for evidence to prop up fanciful theories, is not a necessity. It is far from being the only way to bring cases to trial. In fact, Ontario is one of only a handful of jurisdictions within the Anglo-Saxon system of law where charges are laid by the police, or by the police alone. In most other jurisdictions — including Quebec and New Brunswick, and in the United States — the police merely bring information to the prosecutor on the basis of which charges may or may not be laid at the Crown (or District) Attorney's discretion (or as a joint decision of the prosecutor and the police).

In such jurisdictions a prosecutor is not obliged to run with any ball (or Rescuci doll) dropped willy-nilly into his lap by a police officer. Chances are, he will not pursue a case unless, on the face of it, it's supported by enough admissible evidence to survive a preliminary hearing.

In theory, of course, prosecutors can drop truly unwarranted or legally insupportable charges in our system, too. Or they can go to court and call no evidence. Crown attorneys may do so in some extreme cases, but not in others. The weight of our system goes the opposite way. In most provinces of Canada, the tone is set by the police. The Crown often — at least, often enough — becomes a mere adjunct or mouthpiece for police suspicions.

The systems employed in most other jurisdictions seem wiser to me. Being lawyers, prosecuting attorneys are generally better judges of the legal merits of a case than policemen are. Leaving the decision to lay charges up to the Crown may reduce the chances of frivolous or inhumane (and very costly) prosecutions. It may also reduce the needless overcrowding of the courts.

In terms of recent Canadian legal history, such a system might have prevented the well-known and, in my opinion, frivolous prosecution of nurse Susan Nelles — a case in which, according to later testimony before a Royal Commission, a homicide officer made the ultimate decision to charge Nelles with the murder of four babies at Toronto's Hospital for Sick Children because she had asked for a lawyer. Police officers' not being empowered to lay charges on their own might, I believe, also have prevented the lesser-known but equally frivolous prosecution of Dunia Sayegh.

NOTES

p.9, 1.25: The evidence of a forensic expert, described in the Allen–Lorenz murder case later in this book, provides another revealing illustration of this point.

p.14, 1.10: Ordinarily, what some other person has said out of court is excluded by the hearsay rule. However, where an accusation is made in the presence of the accused in circumstances where it is reasonable for the accused to have denied it if it were untrue, then, if the accused makes no reply, she is said to have "adopted" the statement or accusation, and it becomes evidence against her.

Since Mrs. Sayegh was *not* shown to have heard her daughter's remark, it was obviously not reasonable for her to have made a reply or a denial. So the little girl's remark was simply inadmissible hearsay.

p.16, 1.30: I'm using the word "frivolous" here in a sense often employed by the courts, not in the way it is used in common parlance. I don't mean that people are being prosecuted as a kind of practical joke, only that they may be prosecuted on the basis of evidence unworthy of serious consideration in a court of law.

p.16, 1.38: At the time of writing, Susan Nelles had accepted a sum of money offered by the Attorney General, *ex gratia*, for legal expenses. This is without prejudice to her civil suit for malicious prosecution, which she is still pursuing against the Attorney General.

# 2. A Gift from the Crown

*When Greenspan was first asked to write a book, he wanted to know what such a job might entail. The answer was that he would have to (a) tell about some of his cases, and (b) tell something about himself. The first of these tasks presented no problem for Greenspan, but the second one seemed to. Though he never said so, it was evident that he considered talking about himself soppy, and somehow intrinsically in bad taste. It was something actors did, or maybe poets, but not criminal lawyers. He tried to solve the problem by postponing it as long as he could. The view he expressed was that he was much too busy to do it in Toronto, anyway.*

*"Vienna," he said to his friend George Jonas, who was to be his collaborator. "We'll talk about my early life when we meet in Vienna."*

*"Why Vienna?"*

*"You'll see. Vienna is the perfect place to talk about early lives."*

*In Vienna, Greenspan became busy with a law conference. There was a whole group of lawyers and judges there from Canada, and it seemed that Eddie simply had to have a business meeting with every one of them. "Salzburg," he reassured Jonas. "Wait till we get to Salzburg."*

*The problem was, Greenspan had apparently said this to a number of people, who all turned up in Salzburg. He even invited his unsuspecting collaborator's eighty-year-old mother. The gang spent a fruitful and enjoyable time in the ancient Austrian city. Greenspan was especially fascinated with the well-equipped torture chamber in the castle of Salzburg's bishop — the good cleric used to rule his little music-box of a town with scant regard to due process — but talking about the bishop's law did not leave much time to talk about early lives.*

*"Zürich," Greenspan said. "Zürich is the place."*

*In Zürich it was raining. Jonas conceded that it was too depressing to talk about people's early lives in the rain. "You know," Greenspan said, "in a sense my youth really has to do with Paris. True, I was born and raised in Niagara Falls, Ontario, and it is also true that I don't speak any French. But Paris has always had a special place in my heart."*

*This statement seemed surprisingly confessional. Jonas had never doubted that Greenspan had a heart, but normally his friend would have considered making such revelations far too personal. Maybe they were getting somewhere. Now that he actually agreed to put a private matter like having a heart on record, Paris held out possibilities for opening up a reluctant Greenspan even more.*

*However, as if afraid that he might have said too much already, in the French capital Greenspan clammed up altogether. "Never mind your early life," Jonas offered as a compromise. "According to some discreet inquiries I have made, your early life is pretty dull stuff anyway. What about your later life?"*

*Greenspan agreed to discuss the matter in Phoenix, Arizona.*

*And so it came about, in the isolation of the Biltmore Hotel in Phoenix, surrounded by no one but Greenspan's wife Suzy, their two children, his sister Rosann (a California criminologist), and perhaps seven or eight of Greenspan's friends and acquaintances — with their children, grandchildren, and baby-sitters — that Jonas had an opportunity for a series of almost-secluded conversations with Greenspan about his private life. He didn't find out much that he would not have guessed over the previous twelve years of their friendship:*

Greenspan is a hard taskmaster. His associates and law students have to keep pace with his tempo, his hours, and the rigour of his case preparation and legal research. Though the students in his office are not required to walk Greenspan's dog (he doesn't have a dog), they are pretty much required to do everything an apprentice to a crafts-master would have been required to do in the eighteenth century.

Some articling students relish this, and some put up with it for the experience. Most end up with stories to tell.

The writer and lawyer Guy Gavriel Kay remembers the following episode from his articling year with Greenspan. Shortly after lunch one day, Greenspan, who was preparing to take an afternoon flight to New York, stopped Kay in the hallway of the court. "These four clients are due to be released from the Don Jail on bail," he said, handing Kay some papers. "Will you see to it right away?"

It was already 2 p.m. Bail in the four cases amounted to over a million dollars. The administrative procedures involved were complex enough for Kay to say that he might not be able to get the clients released until the next day. Greenspan looked at him coldly.

"Guy," he said, "listen to me carefully. In a few minutes I'll go to the *airport, where I will take a plane to New York. In New York I'm going to stay at the Carlyle, which is an excellent old hotel. After I've concluded a business meeting there, I will have a short rest in my suite.*

*"Then, I will go to a Broadway show which I've wanted to see for some time. It has had great reviews and I expect that I will like it very much. When the show is over, I'll have dinner at a first-rate restaurant where I've booked a good table. I want you to know that the chef at that restaurant is one of the finest in North America.*

*"After I've enjoyed my meal, I will take a taxi back to the hotel. As I enter, the doorman will say to me: 'Mr. Greenspan, there's a message for you under your door.' I will nod, and go up to my room. I will open the door, and under it I will find a message.*

*"The message will be from you, Guy. It will consist of two words: 'They're out.'"*

Greenspan is a clumsy man. This is not apparent to the casual observer, as his lack of co-ordination does not affect his bearing. His movements are dignified, even graceful, and he never bumps into things. What he finds difficult is to make objects obey him.

Guy Kay recalls sitting at the opposite side of a table from Greenspan in a conference room. The meeting was going on and on; Kay's coffee cup was empty, and the pot was in front of Greenspan. When Eddie started pouring himself a cup of coffee, Kay, reaching over, held out his own cup to him.

"Will you?" he said to Greenspan.

Greenspan looked up, hesitated briefly, then proceeded to pour the coffee in a stream arcing neatly about a quarter of an inch away from the lip of Kay's coffee cup. He kept pouring it for a few seconds, soaking the tabletop and the documents on it with the steaming liquid. When he finally noticed what he was doing, he slammed down the pot, splashing more coffee on everything.

"Don't ever," he said to Kay, "ask me to do something like this again!"

Kay had only started working for Greenspan at the time, and he actually misunderstood the situation. He thought that, as a young student, he had committed a faux pas by asking his law principal to pour coffee for him. He felt terrible. It wasn't until he got to know Greenspan better some time later that he realized this wasn't Eddie's problem at all. He didn't care about ceremonial matters; what he couldn't cope with was the physical act of transferring coffee from the pot to the cup — or, sometimes, from the cup to his own lips.

*Greenspan is a shy man. This is none the less true for not being evident to those who see him in court or on a speaker's platform. He enjoys being "high-profile", he enjoys talking in public — but only at one remove, about legal issues or topics. He is the very opposite of a confessional personality. Getting him to discuss any subject that seems to him to be of a private nature (with the exception of funny stories) has always been an uphill struggle.*

*During his interview sessions with his collaborator in Arizona, Greenspan was loath to talk about his early years even as a lawyer. He didn't want to describe his first case. "It was important to the client, naturally," he said, spilling a quantity of coffee on his shirt. "It was important to me. But who else would give a damn?" In the end, however, he agreed to submit the question to a jury of readers.*

It has been nearly twenty years since I graduated from law school, and twenty years is a fairly long time. By nature I have always concentrated on the case I happen to be doing at the moment, pretty much to the exclusion of everything else. Whatever advantages this cast of mind brings with it, it does little for the development of memory. I retain relatively little of the past. I cannot always recall the faces of major clients; I can no longer remember the details of many headline-making cases. Obviously I remember legal points from cases that stood for important principles in law, but I do not invariably recall the human stories and facts.

The case of James Dombie is an exception. It made no headlines. It stood for no ground-breaking principles in law. Dombie himself was a boy of sixteen in 1970, who came from a working-class family in the Regent Park development of Toronto. Most lawyers would not have thought of him as an important client.

Yet I remember James Dombie. For me, he was the most important client I've ever had or ever will have.

Dombie's was my first case: the first I argued in any court. As it happened, I argued it in the Ontario Court of Appeal. The appeal succeeded, and then Dombie's case became the first for me to lead — and win — before a jury.

The young boy from Regent Park had given me the first two

victories of a legal career. There was no reason why this should have been of the slightest importance to him and his family — the important thing to them was that James, a totally innocent boy, should be acquitted — but it was of much importance to me. It confirmed me in my choice of profession. No matter how confident a person may appear to other people — or, on some days, even to himself — the doubts are always there. Decent marks in law school, victories in academic debates or exercises, are nothing but drills. For a litigation lawyer the only test of fire comes from successfully arguing a case in court.

I was a junior lawyer in the offices of Joseph B. Pomerant, David Pomerant, and Julian Porter when the Dombie case was handed to me. Another young lawyer in Pomerant's office around that time was my contemporary at law school, Bob Reilly. Dombie's appeal file landed on my desk because it was a very minor matter.

Dombie had been convicted in Provincial Court of having in his possession "without lawful excuse, instruments of housebreaking, shopbreaking, vaultbreaking or safebreaking". He was convicted in a short trial, without being represented by a lawyer. He received a suspended sentence and probation for one year.

The sentence was mild enough, but that wasn't the point. The conviction gave Dombie a criminal record — and Dombie had done nothing criminal. Also, his ambition was to become a policeman, which is impossible with a criminal record. Unlike many such cases, his was not a matter of a basically good but misguided or high-spirited youth, a youth from a troubled background, making one mistake. No. Dombie wasn't in the least misguided. He wasn't even particularly high-spirited. He was simply innocent. He came from a modest but quite untroubled background, his father being an ex-policeman and his mother a former schoolteacher. They lived in a happy family unit together with their daughter and three of their four sons.

What happened was that Dombie, who had a job as road manager for a rock group playing at high school dances in Ontario, came back to Toronto after being on the road for a few days. In his absence his car, a Mustang that he liked, had undergone some repairs. Dombie decided to test the car on his return, and went for a ride with a couple of friends. On the way back, around midnight, they stopped at the empty parking lot of the suburban Dorset Park Plaza because one of Dombie's friends needed to find a washroom. A police constable named Tunney saw the three youngsters, and he decided to investigate. He looked over the Mustang, and had the boys open the trunk. He found certain items in the car that seemed suspicious to him, and promptly laid charges against Dombie, the car's owner, for the possession of housebreaking instruments.

The "instruments" in the Mustang consisted of a screwdriver, a crowbar, a sheath knife, a flashlight, bolt-cutters, a pair of gloves, and two walkie-talkies. In other words, there wasn't a single item among them that did not have a legitimate use, or that any ordinary person of mechanical inclination might not have in his car. Ironically, even most of these rather innocent items did not belong to James. The bolt-cutters and the crowbar were his older brother's (who was doing some electrical work, and had used the Mustang in Dombie's absence), while the walkie-talkies belonged to his little brother, a boy of about eight.

It is difficult to describe how a young lawyer feels when he appears in the Court of Appeal for the first time. Maybe I shouldn't say "a young lawyer", because there may be young lawyers who can take it in their stride; but I felt intimidated beyond belief. The hushed, vaulted courtroom, the elevated, distant bench, the formidable, robed judges entering one by one — it was the stuff of nightmares. (The Supreme Court of Canada is worse, because there the full court consists of *nine* judges, and they keep coming at you from both sides in their great medieval robes until you feel like screaming "Stop! Close the door! It's enough!") The Ontario Court of Appeal had only three judges sitting in this instance, but they included the fearsome Mr. Justice Aylesworth. When he walked in I could feel my legs turning to jelly. I didn't think of myself as a baby, but for a moment I seriously doubted if I could rise to my feet to address the court.

Mr. Justice Aylesworth made no effort to ease the experience for me. He started out by calling me "Greenspoon". When I mentioned that my name was actually Greenspan, he responded that he did not care for my name any more than he cared for my arguments. He meant it, too, because he continued calling me Greenspoon.

It was tempting to throw in the towel and sit down, which was, as Mr. Justice Aylesworth made it abundantly clear, what he wanted me to do. But I had come with some solid legal points. The trial judge had made insufficient allowances for the fact that Dombie had been unrepresented; he had admitted evidence that was clearly hearsay and therefore inadmissible; and he took judicial notice of things that were not proper subjects of judicial notice. Like any citizen, Dombie ought to have received a fair trial and he did not. I may have found it difficult to rise to my feet in the beginning, but now I found it impossible to sit down.

One of the other justices on the court, Mr. Justice McGillivray, who had just as keen a legal mind as Mr. Justice Aylesworth, happened to be a much kinder human being. His personality was not in the least abrasive. I would glance at him occasionally, hoping that he might intervene on my behalf — which I believe he would have, had he been able to hear the argument. Unfortunately, by 1970 he was so hard of hearing that he seemed to miss most of what was being said. This was something I hadn't reckoned with. I always knew that justice was blind, but I didn't realize that sometimes it could also be deaf.

Then an interesting thing happened. Since he couldn't get me to sit down, Mr. Justice Aylesworth started listening. Being an acerbic and tough man, but by no means an incompetant or unfair judge, he saw that I had a point. Having seen it, he proceeded to give the unfortunate Crown counsel as rough a time as he had given me. No one could ever accuse Mr. Justice Aylesworth of playing favourites: he would demolish any lawyer in his court whose position didn't impress him.

The appeal was allowed. The only thing about which I could not change Mr. Justice Aylesworth's mind was my name. He called me "Greenspoon" to the end.

If, once in a while, I'm impatient with those who dump on the "system" in vague and general terms (I'm never impatient with valid criticism on specific points), it may be because of my first experience. I find that the "system" is criticized in such general terms mainly by lawyers who are not good or persistent enough. Had I sat down when Mr. Justice Aylesworth first growled at me, perhaps today I would also be convinced that ours is a terrible system.

In any event, Dombie had now won the right to a new trial, but unless we won the trial itself, the exercise would remain academic for him. The original notice of appeal — filed by David Pomerant before I was admitted to the bar — did not ask for a jury trial in the event the appeal succeeded. It seemed to me that Dombie's case should be heard by a jury, so I decided to file a supplementary notice of appeal. I was much less certain whether I could deal with a jury on his behalf, having never argued in front of one before.

One can't be a lawyer without going to law school. However, one can't become a lawyer just by going to law school either. Law schools teach a great deal about the theory of being a courtroom advocate. They teach much less about the craft, and almost nothing about the art.

Remarkably, they teach next to nothing about the nuts and bolts of courtroom work either. In fairness, perhaps courtroom practice cannot be taught in a classroom. It must be acquired through experience.

For example, far-fetched as it sounds, I didn't know how to express an objection in court to a question or statement by my opponent. I thought that there may be a proper, formal way to do it, but I had no idea what it might be. As Dombie's trial began, a couple of minor matters came up almost immediately to which I would have liked to object. But what should I say? I did not want to interrupt the Crown or address the bench; I thought it might not be the right thing to do.

I stood up, hoping that the judge would recognize me. His Honour glanced at me, but said nothing. The trial continued. I was standing there, feeling exceptionally foolish, and I could see the jurors' eyes beginning to turn toward me. Finally I reached over to the water jug and, as if I had been meaning to do it all along, poured myself a glass of water. I don't do that sort of thing too well, but I managed to get the water into the glass. I drank it, too, though I wasn't the least bit thirsty.

During the first recess I saw in the hallway a seasoned Crown Attorney, Frank Armstrong, whom I happened to know. Needing advice desperately, but too ashamed to admit that I wasn't familiar with such a rudimentary procedure, I said to him: "Frank, I know there are many individual ways of objecting in court, but, as a matter of interest, how do *you* do it?"

Armstrong seemed a bit surprised. "Me?" he asked. "I guess I just say: 'I object!' What else?"

What else, indeed. Back in court I had to resist the impulse to test my new-found expertise every five minutes. When the Crown asked the next witness what his occupation was, I felt like saying: "I object!"

The Crown was Ken Chasse, a very able counsel. However, as a prosecutor he was zealous enough to inadvertently hand me a little gift at Dombie's trial. In spite of my inexperience, I sensed that it was a gift, and instinctively made the most of it.

Dombie's eight-year-old brother had testified at trial that the two walkie-talkies in the car belonged to him. In his address to the jury Chasse said: "What kind of man would get his little brother to lie for him?"

The small boy was sitting in the courtroom, and he was devastated by Chasse's remark. Though he tried to control himself, he started crying. I could see his shoulders shaking and the tears rolling down his face. The boy's reaction wasn't surprising; quite apart from the fact that in his case it happened to be undeserved, being called a liar by the high dignitary of the Crown in the formidable atmosphere of a courtroom can be a trauma of almost Dickensian proportions for an eight-year-old child.

I wanted to be sure that the jury didn't miss it. I stood up, walked over to the boy, sat beside him on the spectators' bench, and put my arm around his shoulder.

It is never possible to be certain why a jury reaches the verdict that it reaches. However, as I sat next to the crying little boy listening to the rest of Chasse's jury address, I'd have felt safe betting any amount of money that there would be an acquittal. In this instance I was right, too — but being right in such matters is a mixed blessing.

Winning a bet with yourself the first time out may give you the illusion that you will be able to call it every time, which is a dangerous illusion. It may create in one's mind that hubris, that pride that comes before the fall, which is the inescapable but risky side-effect of having been right too soon or too often. Still, as there isn't a third choice, I prefer winning to losing and being right to being wrong.

I've never ceased to be grateful to zealous prosecutors, though. With very few exceptions, they almost always overreach. When they are seen doing it, it's invariably a gift from the Crown to the defence.

I remember walking back to the office, elated. When I arrived, there was a little party in progress. Bob Reilly, who started working for Joe Pomerant in 1970, the same year as I, was regarded as the golden-haired boy of the firm. Justly so, because he was very good. Pomerant had given him a fraud case, with the highly experienced Robert Carter as co-counsel, and the team had won an acquittal. They were celebrating in Pomerant's office with a glass of champagne.

When Bob saw me passing in the hallway he called out:

"Come in Eddie, I just won my first case!"

I walked in with a grin. "Me, too," I said, proud as a peacock. Sitting behind his desk, Joe Pomerant looked up.

"Have you billed it yet?" he asked.

"Well, no," I replied, taken aback.

"You don't come in here," said Pomerant, "until you bill it."

Joe Pomerant, for whom I worked through law school and whose office I joined upon graduation, was a second cousin once or twice removed, about ten years my senior. The Second World War made us close relatives, since most of his family in Europe, along with mine, had perished in the Holocaust. It may have been my sensitivity, but I always felt that Joe resented the family duty of having to take me on. I felt like a poor relation — I was one, in fact — and perhaps there was nothing Pomerant could have done to make me feel otherwise. At the same time I admired him. He was a very able and highly experienced criminal lawyer. To me he appeared to be fully at home in the field to which I wanted to gain admittance more than I wanted anything in the world. He seemed to know everything about matters that I was desperate to learn something about. For that reason, especially in the beginning, he could have lashed me with a bullwhip every day and I would still have stuck around him.

Pomerant used no bullwhip; he only called me an "unmade bed". Perhaps he was right. Certainly at that time I wasn't even aware of the things that were uppermost in his mind. Such as billing, for instance. The practice of law had no other meaning for me but dealing with cases. If I had thought about anything else, it would have been about questions of jurisprudence or social issues (along with watching a good baseball game or spending a week in Paris with my wife). I knew nothing about retainers or accounts receivable; I had no real notion of disbursements. I realized, of course, that someone had to pay rent, utilities, secretaries, juniors, or private detectives; I knew that the furniture in the office must have cost money; I understood that there were funds involved in trial transcripts, travel, hotels, and long-distance telephone bills; and I also knew that some clients couldn't or wouldn't pay. But it was an abstract kind of knowledge. Far from preying on my mind, it generally did not even enter it.

Years had to pass before I would have the slightest understanding of what must have kept Pomerant awake at nights. In fact, I had to become a senior partner myself before I would understand it fully.

However, understanding it changed nothing. More precisely, it changed only the uncomprehending and judgmental attitude I developed towards Pomerant at the time. That attitude was due only to ignorance — some of the problems that concerned Pomerant were real enough — but even when, years later, I came to realize this, my own concerns remained unchanged. The case still continued to be the thing in my practice.

What I did learn eventually was that there is a middle ground between the blissful fiscal vacuity of my early years, and a preoccupation with money. The first is due to inexperience and idealism, and even more to the luxury of having senior partners around to keep the wheels rolling. The second, however, is destructive. Chasing the chimera of financial success can literally affect a person's mind. In extreme cases, worrying too much about being cheated can turn someone into a cheater of others. It can change ordinary prudence into grasping dishonesty. It can make one lose all sense of proportion and turn a good lawyer into a careless megalomaniac. In the end, it can ruin his life.

It can also have a very detrimental effect on the lives of people around him. In Pomerant's case the signs were present from the mid-seventies. By 1976 it caused two of my colleagues and me to split up the firm of Pomerant, Pomerant and Greenspan and establish the new firm of Greenspan, Gold and Moldaver. Six years later, in 1982, Joe Pomerant pleaded guilty to four counts of forgery and one count of attempted obstruction of justice, and received a sentence of five years' imprisonment.

My feelings about Pomerant are ambiguous to this day. He caused some of the worst moments of my life. He was often a cruel and humiliating man to work for, and on the break-up of the firm he saddled my colleagues and me with an almost unmanageable financial burden. But I cannot sink him into some Orwellian memory-hole. He gave me my start. I learned a great deal from him. In his best years he was a first-rate criminal lawyer. Not to acknowledge this would leave the record incomplete.

## NOTES

p.21, 1.24: A pseudonym. The case was never reported elsewhere.

p.23, 1.11: The harshness of this law has been somewhat relieved as the result of amendments to the Criminal Code which require proof that the items were possessed "under circumstances that give rise to a reasonable inference that the instrument had been used or was intended to be used" for breaking into a place. Under the previous legislation, the courts had held that proved possession of even "neutral" tools capable of housebreaking cast the burden on the accused to prove his innocence.

However, under the present law a young man walking near a shopping centre late at night while in possession of such common items as vice grips and a flashlight could still find himself before the courts and required to explain himself.

p.24, 1.4: A detective was allowed to testify about what he had *heard* from an employee of the company that employed Dombie's older brother; Dombie was given no opportunity to cross-examine the detective; and the judge noted without evidence the location of washrooms of the area in question as well as the use of walkie-talkies in similar offences.

## INTERLUDE: **THE BARRACUDA**

*It was a Saturday in October 1966. A twenty-year-old girl named Suzy Dahan was invited by friends to go to a party somewhere in the St. Clair Avenue–Bathurst Street district in Toronto. In truth, she was not particularly looking forward to the event, but it was the weekend and she was feeling lonely.*

*She did not know a soul at the party except the girlfriends who invited her. She knew very few people in the entire city, having recently come from Montreal to take a teaching job at the Toronto French School. For that matter, Suzy did not know too many people even in Montreal. With her parents, her younger sister, and her brother, she had come to Canada only about a year earlier from French Morocco, where she was born. Her family had not been poor while she was growing up there, but now they had nothing left.*

*For the first half-hour or so, Suzy just sat on a sofa looking at the other people. At twenty, she was an exceptionally striking girl, with immense dark eyes and a figure that could only be described as voluptuous. She was bright; she was well educated. As a realistic girl, she was quietly aware of her own assets and liabilities. It was this calm recognition of her own good and bad points, without illusions but also without false modesty, that was one of the most unique things about Suzy. It went hand in hand with a sense of humour, containing an equal mixture of pride and self-deprecation. ("Was I beautiful?" she'd say later, with some irony but also quite matter-of-factly. "I was* gorgeous.*")*

*While not exactly shy, Suzy was a private person and more than a little reserved. Also restless, perhaps, having lost interest in the world she knew well — it was she who had cajoled her parents into leaving Morocco — but feeling somewhat out of her element in a world she did not yet know. North America, with its tastes and preoccupations, seemed very peculiar to her. She hadn't been too impressed with young Canadian men, who, on hearing that she came from Morocco, seemed to evince nothing but a desire to discuss the movie* Casablanca *with her.*

Inwardly Suzy had resolved never to date a man who brought up the names of Humphrey Bogart or Ingrid Bergman in her presence.

Coming from a Sephardic Jewish family in Casablanca, Suzy had had an upbringing quite uncommon for a middle-class girl of her background in colonial French Africa. Naturally she spoke no Yiddish — that language was not used by Jews in that part of the world — and, since Sephardic women did not take part in religious services as a rule, she spoke no Hebrew. But, except for a few phrases, Suzy spoke no Arabic either. (She knew English only slightly better than Arabic after a few months in Toronto.) Suzy spoke, read, wrote, thought, and enjoyed life only in French — Parisian French, as spoken in the private Catholic girls' school of the Carmelite Sisters to which her parents had sent her to be educated.

Even though her family had deep roots in North Africa, having settled there after the Spanish Inquisition had made life intolerable for Jews in medieval Spain, Suzy simply wasn't raised as part of the Moroccan Jewish community. Her mother had encouraged, and her father had acquiesced in, her being raised as a French girl.

Peculiar as North Americans seemed to her, Suzy wanted to find out more about them — but this did not seem to be the party for it. The small apartment appeared to be filled with nothing but Moroccans. No doubt the girls who invited her wanted Suzy to feel right at home. They had no way of realizing that Suzy was in Toronto precisely because she had never felt quite at home in North Africa.

There seemed to be only two Canadians in the apartment. One was a student named David Pape, a very handsome young man, who soon asked Suzy to dance. For some reason, however, Suzy could feel her eyes wandering back to another young Canadian who had been lying on his stomach on the floor ever since Suzy had entered the room. Being a little short-sighted, she could only see him as an enormous silhouette, outlined against a low coffee table laden with a mixture of Moroccan and Jewish-Canadian dishes from couscous to chopped liver. Suzy thought he must weigh around three hundred pounds. Somewhat like a sea lion resting on a rock, he would raise himself on one elbow from time to time to pick at the food.

Suzy had noticed him as soon as she came into the apartment. "Look at that guy, he's the only one eating," one of her girlfriends had whispered to her. The young man seemed not to glance at Suzy even once, but when the music stopped and David Pape left the room to get some drinks from the kitchen, he suddenly rose to his feet and moved in on Suzy. "He moved in," she was to recall later, "like a barracuda." By the time Pape came back with the drinks, he was already dancing with Suzy.

In total contrast to his bulk, the young man was dancing easily and well. He was leading Suzy around the floor with a light, commanding grace. He made her confused and a little resentful. "When he put his arms around me," she remembered, "it was like nothing before." The problem was, Suzy did not come to the party in a receptive mood and had no intention of being swept off her feet by a three-hundred-pound silhouette.

When the young man asked her her name, she told him that her name was "Pink". To this day Suzy doesn't know why. "I'd never done that before and, God knows, I liked him a lot." But she had said "Pink", it being the first English word that occurred to her. She did not ask him his name. In fact, they hardly talked; the music was too loud, the party was too noisy, and Suzy could barely understand anything the young man was saying to her anyway. As the party broke up, they somehow lost sight of each other in the street, and Suzy did not think that she would ever see him again.

He called her the following Monday, having spent Sunday tracking her down. As Suzy found out later, his sole information had been that Suzy shared an apartment on Bathurst Street with a girl named Green. It was enough. Though Green, Suzy's room-mate, was not listed in the phone book, he apparently went from apartment lobby to apartment lobby until he discovered the name shortly after midnight on Sunday. He got the number from information, but by that time it was too late to call, so he decided to wait until the following day.

On the telephone he said that his name was Eddie — which meant nothing to Suzy — but she immediately knew who he was because he asked to speak with "Pink". To Suzy's utter astonishment, Eddie said that he had called to take her to a hockey game. A hockey game? Suzy thought for a moment that he must be joking. She was even more astonished to hear herself say yes.

If Suzy still had a lot to learn about the courtship habits of young Canadian men, Eddie was giving her a crash course. He was certainly not smooth, attentive, or romantic — at least not in any sense that would be so understood by a girl raised in a French culture. In his dress, speech, and manners, in his preoccupation with spectator sports, she thought that he was probably typical of the small Canadian town of Niagara Falls, Ontario, where he said he had been born. But it also occurred to Suzy that in another sense Eddie was typical of no one but himself. He was like no other man that she had ever known.

For instance, when he first came to pick her up, he stayed in the apartment for about half an hour chatting with her. He was a law student, a rather penniless law student as he explained to Suzy, living pretty much from hand to mouth on a student loan. He didn't even have a car. But when they finally left the apartment to go to the hockey game — Suzy being totally reconciled to the idea that they would take a bus — she discovered that Eddie had come for her in a taxi, which had been standing outside the door, meter ticking, while they were chit-chatting upstairs.

The taxi was not to impress her — Eddie could not have made it plainer that he was as poor as a church mouse — nor was it an expression of reckless gallantry. He was simply not the dashing cloak-across-the-puddle type; even ordinary gallantry seemed rather outside his make-up, Suzy thought, let alone the reckless variety. He was not rude, but it was evident that opening doors or helping a woman with her coat would never occur to him. Clearly he had kept a taxi waiting only because it was easier than trying to get another one. As for the cost, well, it was only money.

Suzy liked that. She always felt somehow demeaned in the company of men who appeared to worry about money, even if they appealed to her in other repects. Money was not an end in itself, only a means for making life more convenient. If, at the beginning of a relationship, every person has to pass some magic hurdles, Eddie had just passed the second one for Suzy. He passed the first hurdle the minute he moved in like a barracuda and put his arms around her.

From that moment they saw each other every day. For Suzy the magic persisted, though she often felt bewildered by her own feelings.

At first glance the two of them would not have seemed compatible to anyone. They barely had a language in common: Suzy, at least, was willing to give English a chance, but Eddie's disinterest in all languages except the one used in Niagara Falls was firm and abiding. (At one time he tried taking Spanish in school, thinking that the "BL" mark he had earlier received was a low "B" — in fact it meant "below the line".) They were both Jewish, but they came from such different branches of Jewish culture that it made the link between them almost meaningless, especially as neither of them was observant. The rest of their interests appeared to be just as divergent. She rather liked classical music and belles-lettres for instance, both of which put Eddie to sleep. They shared a taste for good restaurants, but they could only indulge that taste when in funds, which wasn't very often. Suzy certainly had no interest in football, basketball, or gambling — the kinds of things that would absorb Eddie's interest in so far as anything could absorb it outside of the criminal law.

There was one major thing in Eddie's favour: he said he had never seen the movie Casablanca.

Suzy later remembered that first year as a time of hanging around and waiting for Eddie. Waiting at hockey games; waiting while he endlessly chatted with his friends; but mainly waiting while he was lying on his stomach with his law books spread out before him on the floor. Eddie was not a model student; he might cut classes for the racetrack or a game of gin rummy, but then at Suzy's he would read law, non-stop and voraciously, with his features set, his attention totally fixed, until finally he fell asleep on the floor of her living-room. Usually she would be asleep long before him, curled up in an armchair.

He could hardly be called conventionally handsome, though, as Suzy noted, there were always a surprising number of girls trailing him who seemed to think of Eddie as a "boyfriend", despite the fact that he paid absolutely no attention to them. He was charming — very charming, in fact — but only when he remembered that there were other people around him. Just as often, no matter who he was with, his eyes might glaze over as he began to think of something else, and he might even suddenly rise to his feet and walk out of the room. He could, in company, pick up a book and start reading, or just lie down and fall asleep as if he were all alone.

As for his prospects, Suzy could not make up her mind if he had excellent prospects or none.

Eddie seemed to be an unusually difficult person to make predictions about. When she was listening to him talk about the law, about public events, about his fellow students or professors, it appeared to Suzy that Eddie's prospects were limitless. He was quick, incisive, and tremendously witty. No one had ever made Suzy laugh so much. But when she considered his preoccupations and interests, not to mention his lifestyle, he seemed a toss-up between a legal scholar and a riverboat gambler: a strange and not very promising mixture.

*None of which would have caused Suzy to move back to Montreal. She did move back, though, fourteen months after they had met. She returned because she had overheard Eddie say to someone at a party that he'd never get married until he was thirty years old. Two months later Suzy was back in Montreal, enrolled at McGill University.*

*As far as Suzy was concerned, it wasn't a question of taking a chance. If Eddie knew what he wanted out of his life, by that time so did she. What she wanted was Eddie — but it was up to him. "I was very rational, even though I was young," she would say later. "This was a new country, and I was not going to muck around."*

*When she told Eddie that she was moving back — without telling him the reason — he said nothing. He gave no indication that he did not want her to go. He simply started driving his car — by that time he had acquired an old broken-down Skoda, an awesome specimen of East European automotive chic and reliability — to Montreal every weekend. He'd drive the 350 miles to see her throughout the winter of 1967, often taking sixteen hours or more to make the trip, with time out for repairs. After the first couple of months, as Suzy thought of it in retrospect, "I knew that I had made an impression."*

*She couldn't be absolutely sure, however. True, Eddie came every week. He even monitored Suzy's political science lectures at McGill. (He took notes, compared his notes with hers, shook his head, then, in a clear demonstration of taking charge of her life, made arrangements with another student to lend Suzy his notes because "my girlfriend can't speak English.") But he did not once discuss the subject of marriage.*

*He did not use the word even in May when he telephoned Suzy from Toronto. His proposal, if that's what it was, consisted of one sentence: "What's your ring size?"*

*"I don't know," Suzy replied, taken by surprise.*

*"Well, find out and call me back in a couple of hours," Eddie said, hanging up the phone.*

*They were married in August 1968 in the backyard of one of Eddie's aunts in Niagara Falls. It was decidedly not an affair of many frills, though his aunt's backyard gave Eddie the opportunity to call it "a garden wedding". Suzy's parents were happy: Suzy had assured them that they were in love, and they took her word for it that Eddie was a decent fellow. They had to take her word for it, beause they had never been able to exchange any words with him. (When Suzy first introduced Eddie to her mother and father, in French of course, he gave his future in-laws a charming smile. Then, somewhat to their consternation, he lay down on the floor and started reading a newspaper.)*

*The Canadian branch of Eddie's family was equally delighted with Suzy. She was beautiful, classy, intelligent, and, most importantly for Eddie's mother, obviously in love with her son. However, some members of a distant branch of Eddie's family in Israel — to Eddie's innocent and very Canadian astonishment — would later walk out of the room when he tried introducing his new wife to them. Suzy was not astonished, knowing more than Eddie about the tensions that exist in the Middle East between Oriental and European Jews.*

*So Suzy and Eddie were married, making their commitment at a time when the institution appeared to be on its way out, especially for bright, ambitious, unconventional young people. Their honeymoon hardly amounted to an auspicious beginning. They had made the mistake of accepting a friend's offer of a cottage for a weekend in Northern Ontario — not that they had much choice, being totally broke. The problem was that Eddie viewed the outdoors as others might regard outer space, infested with strange, alien shapes (such as trees or rocks, for instance) and bizarre, frightening creatures as manifested by daddy-long-legs. They spent one night in the wilderness before escaping back into civilization — cooking scrambled eggs and making no attempt to turn down the bed upon which Eddie had earlier seen something shiny, black, and unquestionably animate. (In Toronto they did not stir from their apartment for another two days for fear of bumping into their friend whose kind offer they had spurned.)*

*They did resolve to travel, however, as soon as they could remotely afford it, and to travel to the one continent that exclusively fascinated both of them: Europe. Within Europe, their special focus was France, and within France, Paris. They made their first trip the year after they were married, returning to Europe afterwards at least once a year and invariably spending a few days of each trip in the French capital.*

*The circumstances of the first visit, however, were vastly different from those of later journeys. For one thing, they still had absolutely no money. Eddie had graduated from Osgoode Hall Law School in 1968, the year of his marriage, but he was working as an articling student and had not yet been called to the bar. Their only choice was to stay at the house of Suzy's aunt and uncle just outside Paris, with Eddie determined to do the Michelin guide's full tour of Paris in the eight days that they could afford.*

*Suzy's uncle would give them a ride into town every morning, after which they walked (sometimes all the way back to the suburbs at night if they missed the last train). Eddie, a born leader, was determined to show Suzy the city she already knew quite well — and which he, at that point, did not know at all. It made no difference. Turning out to be as methodical a traveller as he was a law student, Eddie believed in preparation and in leaving nothing to chance. He'd lead the way, with the Michelin guide under one arm and the Criminal Code under the other, in case he had some time to read a little law during lunch. Two days before the end of the trip Suzy collapsed. From then on Eddie practically carried her all the way, terrified that they might not finish seeing the sights on schedule.*

*Suzy was gradually discovering the man she had married. The first thing she learned was that this bulky figure, whose movements, though graceful, were so slow as to be almost ponderous, whose weight fluctuated between 250 and 300 pounds, whose physical indolence made him invent a method of flicking ashes from his cigarette two or three feet into an ashtray because he was too lazy to bend forward — that this man was, in fact, possessed of boundless energy. He never got tired. He hardly slept at night. After a catnap now and again during the day, he could wake up thoroughly refreshed. He made his plans, then executed them calmly, steadily, inexorably, missing no detail. Suzy had to admit that she did not really know her favourite city, Paris, until Eddie showed it to her.*

*Eddie never hectored anyone (except as a joke). He did not seem highstrung or intense, he gave off no nervous sparks — at times he seemed barely awake. Only he was unstoppable. He'd regard no hour as too late, no task as too big, no defeat or frustration as acceptable. He would simply persist until he got his way.*

*Suzy found it impressive. She also found it irksome. She did need her eight hours of sleep. She was not at all tireless. Her energy level was merely normal, and she tended to regard any hour after 11 p.m. as much too late. At the same time she was also a perfectionist, also intolerant of frustration, and equally determined to arrange her life as it suited her.*

*In the beginning Eddie was as unsophisticated in the ways of Europe as Suzy had been in the ways of North America — the difference being that Suzy trusted Eddie's knowledge, but Eddie could not conceive of Suzy's understanding any practical matter. In fact, as he would say later, "I married Suzy because I didn't think she could survive alone. The world was just outside her grasp."*

*As a result, for instance, Eddie would insist on turning up in a Paris restaurant for dinner at 6 p.m., just as the amazed waiters were about to set up the tables. He would not believe Suzy when she told him that people in France seldom dine earlier than eight, and fashionable people tend to dine at ten. This, after all, was not what people did in Niagara Falls. Another example was Eddie's first glimpse of the huge cement walls on the shores of the English Channel, opposite the Channel Islands. When, back in Toronto, Suzy had told him about the swimming-pools of Casablanca which are filled by the sea at high tide, Eddie thought: "Poor thing, she has these fantasies. You can't have a swimming-pool filled with sharks and octopus. I must marry her." Now, seeing the seawater swimming-pools of St. Malo, Eddie wondered if Suzy had married him under false pretences. She seemed to know more about the world than he did.*

*Their first visit to London was equally memorable. Eddie had been dragging Suzy through town, grimly determined to explore the fine print in his Michelin guide and show his bride everything in the historic capital and cradle of British common law. The problem was that it was raining, Suzy could hardly move her feet, and Eddie did not have enough money even for bus fare. Suzy was pinning her hopes on Eddie's being able to borrow a few pounds from a travel agency on his Diners Club credit card, but it was a Sunday, which made the transaction impossible. After being turned away, they were walking on opposite sides of the street, no longer talking to each other. When Eddie bumped into a Toronto acquaintance he had to point to the wet and miserable figure on the other sidewalk: "And that is my wife."*

*Suzy did not think that it was possible to be as desperately tired and hungry as she was at that moment. Though Eddie did not have a cent in his pocket, he was the possessor of that one single card — his first, offered by Diners Club to graduating law students. Considering their finances, they agreed not to use it for anything as frivolous as dining except in emergencies. Looking at Suzy, Eddie now declared an emergency.*

*However, scan as they might the doors of the restaurants they were passing, they could not see the welcome symbol on any of them. Finally, as they were about to give up, they discovered one. It was a restaurant called Mr. Chow's. The name meant nothing to them, but it looked fine. Perhaps too fine, Suzy thought, as they gratefully allowed a deferential maître d' to relieve them of their dripping overcoats. She wasn't sure, as* she glanced at the other diners, if the two of them were really dressed for such a place, but at that point she was past caring.

Suddenly Eddie nudged her. "Look." She followed his glance, and saw at the next table Faye Dunaway dining with Marcello Mastroianni. Some of the other diners, though she couldn't recognize them, looked equally familiar. Eddie, as relaxed as if he had suddenly found himself in his own living-room, ordered everything in sight. The food was superb, the service flawless. From one moment to the next, the shivering, humiliating, exhausting gloom that was London turned into an enchanting evening. All it took was one small plastic card. Afterwards, of course, it was a long, chilly trudge in the rain back to their hotel, but Suzy didn't mind. Nor did Eddie care that it took him several months to pay off the Diners Club card on his salary as an articling student for the Attorney General's Department.

Before her marriage, Suzy sometimes wondered what the routine of daily life might be like with a husband. Being married to Eddie, she soon discovered that it was one question she would not have to worry about. There never was any routine. Eddie was not a nine-to-five lawyer, or a nine-to-five person. He would work as required, or as the spirit moved him, including evenings, midnights, Sundays — and in any case seldom less than twelve hours a day. They would travel, entertain, dine out, or see their friends in the same haphazard fashion. Even the birth of their two children — Julianna in 1972 and Samantha in 1977 — introduced nothing that would be viewed as routine in most other households.

The only exception, Suzy thought, might have been their quarrels. Those were routine enough, in that they almost invariably centred around two subjects: Eddie's eating habits, and Suzy's requirements for sleep.

Eddie, always overweight, had an unfortunate family history of heart disease. His grandfather had had his first heart attack in his early forties; his father died of a massive coronary when he was forty-two (and Eddie only thirteen). Deeply as his father's death affected Eddie in other ways, it did nothing to change his ideas about what constituted a satisfying meal. "When we were first married," Suzy would recount later, "I'd buy a week's supply, and it would be gone in two days." It wasn't as if Eddie didn't try; he'd start out by eating a very light supper, but then, working late into the night and getting famished, he'd go into the kitchen to raid the fridge. Suzy's solution was to attach big cow-bells to the refrigerator door. She knew that Eddie, never too handy with physical objects, could neither remove nor neutralize them.

It still wasn't a very happy solution, because it led directly into the second conflict. The bells would wake Suzy — and Suzy, wakened from her sleep was not a person to trifle with. A sensible man would not have cut short Suzy's sleep even to give her a present of a diamond necklace, let alone to exhibit himself with his face stuck into a refrigerator. But Eddie, though he knew that his wife deprived of her sleep was simply not the same human being as his wife rested, still couldn't resist. By mutual agreement the cow-bells were soon abandoned. The marriage could not have withstood them.

Suzy eventually realized that Eddie was not being merely self-indulgent. (She always knew, of course, that he was not stupid, and was fully aware of what over-eating, over-working, and over-smoking might do to anyone, let alone a person with his family history.) Nor was it simply a question of Eddie's being fatalistic. The reason lay deeper, and it had to do with Eddie's essence, which was not amenable to doctor's warnings, cow-bells, or tearful scenes. Eddie was a person who did not want to meet life on its own terms. He wanted life to meet him on his terms — though without illusions, and in full knowledge of the penalty that such a philosophy may extract. Restrictions offended him. He liked to play the long odds and was ready, if necessary, to pay the price. He would sooner live as he liked for forty years than for seventy as prudence demanded. He did not want to tiptoe around his own existence.

This resulted in a rule on which Eddie insisted. In Suzy's words: "We decided at an early stage that we'd never sleep separately after an argument. No matter how much we hated each other's guts at the moment, we'd always sleep in the same bed." Unspoken, this had to do with Eddie's inner conviction that, like his father, he would die young. Suzy believed he did not want her to have the burden of this ever happening on a day when the two of them were not reconciled with each other.

The first rule was enunciated before the wedding. "They say the law is a jealous mistress," Eddie said to Suzy, "but in fact I'm married to the law. You are my mistress. No matter how much I love you, the law will always have to come first in my life. It is a condition of our marriage. It is the only condition. Do you agree?"

Suzy said yes. During the years that followed, she lived up to her end of the bargain. As she was to acknowledge, perhaps a little ruefully, so did Eddie.

NOTES

p.34, l.3: Greenspan finds this passage offensive. His difficulty with languages, he points out, has nothing to do with disinterest or disdain; it is
simply a disability. There is a scientific word for this condition but, as it is
in Latin, he can't remember it. As for *belles-lettres*, he reads a wide variety
of classical and modern literature with interest and enjoyment. He agrees
that poetry puts him to sleep.

# PART TWO

# NOT ABOVE THE FRAY

# 3. Walking the High Wire

Some large urban courtrooms are like a stage: they have several entrances. The judge comes through one door, the witnesses and the public through another. There may also be separate entrances for jurors, lawyers, and defendants. Entering through different doors symbolizes the different roles these actors play in the judicial drama.

Ideally, in our system of justice, judges (and jurors) are totally above the fray. As triers of fact or interpreters of the law, they are, in legal jargon, "indifferent" between the Queen and the accused. This does not mean, obviously, that they are indifferent between right and wrong but that, unlike Crown attorneys, they do not represent the state. They take no sides in the contest between the prosecution and the defence. Judges referee the fight to make sure that it is fair; then they (or the juries with whom they sit) render their decision on the outcome.

In some ways even the lawyers representing the two sides are above the fray. A barrister for the defence is an officer of the court in the same way as the barrister for the Crown. Like the Crown counsel, the defence lawyer performs his assigned role within the adversary process as a servant of justice. The courtroom duel of these two legal gladiators may *be* the fray, but it is only a fray by proxy. This means, first, that the thrusts of the two lawyers should never be personally aimed at each other and, second, that the duty they owe to their respective clients, the Crown and the accused, should never exceed the duty that they owe to their real master, the law.

The Crown is said to "neither win nor lose as long as justice triumphs." (Her Majesty, of course, is not at any great risk. She loses cases all over the Commonwealth every day, yet, for her, life goes on as before.) Such lofty sentiments could hardly be expressed on the defendant's behalf, because for him justice triumphing may mean spending the rest of his life in jail.

Still, as people have often pointed out, while the defence lawyer's *side* has an obviously higher stake in the outcome than the side represented by the lawyer for the Crown, a defence lawyer himself need not have a greater sense of personal involvement than a prosecutor. Having done his best, and having made sure that his best meets the highest standards of advocacy, he is under no greater obligation to win his case than his opponent. The Law Society may discipline him for incompetence or negligence, but not for losing. In fact, his peers are more likely to punish him for trying to win, should his attempt to do so bring him into conflict with the law or with the rules of professional conduct. Except for not being able to say to his client after a guilty verdict: "Think of it this way, Charlie, justice has triumphed," no potential consequence of losing a case is greater for a defence lawyer than for a Crown counsel. And, at the end of the day, wherever his client is going, the defence lawyer will be going home.

I dispute none of this. Nevertheless, even though I walk into court through a door marked "lawyers' entrance", there is a sense in which I have never felt myself to be above the fray.

I *am* an officer of the court and a servant of justice, and there are very strict limits beyond which I would consider it unthinkable to go in anybody's defence. As a defence lawyer I am only an accused person's counsel, not his partner, let alone his partner in crime. A lawyer acts for his client to the full *legal* limit of his client's endeavours and interests, not beyond. The things that no defence lawyer can legitimately do for his client would fill a book (and have, in fact, filled many). They include suppressing, or tampering with, the evidence. They include calling a witness to testify under oath to something that the lawyer knows to be a lie. No lawyer can mislead a court for a client; no lawyer can obstruct the administration of justice. Strictly speaking, in Canada he can't even instruct his client, as American lawyers on TV seem to be doing all the time, to "say nothing to the police". (If circumstances warrant it, a lawyer can advise a client only that he has a right to remain silent, and that it would be in his best interest to exercise that right.)

However, conscious as I am of limits, I do not think that for a defence lawyer those limits are set by his own moral imperatives. They are not set by his personal judgment of good and evil (as some lawyers seem to believe) or by the requirements of "good citizenship". I think that those limits are set strictly by the law. What's more, I would consider it wrong for a lawyer not to explore those limits. I would consider it wrong if a lawyer stopped short of doing whatever the law *might* permit him to do for a client, or stopped short of claiming the benefit of any legal protection or safeguard that *might* be available to his client. It would make no difference to my opinion about this whether the lawyer stopped short because of timidity, ignorance, or laziness — or because of conscience, moral judgment, or considerations of some "higher" civic duty. The real social and moral obligation a defence lawyer has, in my view, is to do everything permissible in law for his client, and to resolve any honest doubt he may have in this regard in his client's favour. Even if this means, as it may at times, walking a high wire without a net.

I am far from being the only lawyer to hold this view. The fact is, though, that those of us who hold it are seldom "above" the fray. Once in a while we can, in fact, be no more certain than our clients are whether we will be going home at the end of the day or not.

One such day was April 21, 1980, when Nick Coluccio walked into my office.

Nick was a man of thirty-six, who had been born in a small village in the Calabrian region of southern Italy and came to Canada with his family at the age of six. He had been living with his sixty-nine-year-old father, a widower, in a small house in Downsview, a quiet, middle-class suburb of Toronto. Nick's widowed sister, Rosa Albanesi, and her twenty-year-old daughter, Carmela, had shared the home with Nick and his father. Sitting in my office on April 21 Nick told me that the police were looking for him because of a shooting incident that occurred at their house a month earlier, on March 23, 1980, claiming the lives of Carmela and Rosa.

The facts (as they were eventually agreed to by the defence and the Crown) were that Carmela grew up in her grandfather's house, her own father having died a few weeks after she was born. This was the house to which her widowed mother, Rosa, moved with her, and it was also the home of Carmela's uncle, my client Nick Coluccio. Nick, never having married himself, treated Carmela as his own daughter. The whole Coluccio family did, according to Nick's elder brother, Giuseppe, who lived with his own wife and children only a few blocks away. In Giuseppe's words, "Carmela was the pet of the family. She was spoiled by everybody. Anything she wanted she could have."

Unfortunately what Carmela wanted as she grew up turned out to be young men. More precisely, it was a style of life which, natural as it may have seemed to a Canadian girl in the 1970s, seemed wholly unnatural to Carmela's Calabrian family. In fact, to the Coluccios, Carmela's ways seemed immoral and dishonourable. She did not want to bring her boyfriends home and introduce them to her family in a proper, respectful manner. Carmela wanted to date boys, hang out with boys, talk on the telephone with boys, and even stay out with boys overnight.

Her mother, Rosa, viewed this as shameful and simply could not cope with it.

The first time Carmela failed to spend a night at home happened two years before the shooting. At that time, worried about his niece, Nick called the police. The police found the girl almost immediately, but could do nothing to help: eighteen-year-old Carmela said that she did not wish to return home. Rosa responded to this news by attempting to commit suicide. She was taken to hospital, where she refused all medication. A week later Carmela came to her mother's bedside, after which Rosa allowed the doctors to attend to her.

Two months later the entire sequence was repeated. Carmela stayed away overnight; Rosa spent four weeks in hospital after her second suicide attempt.

The third incident occurred about a year later when Rosa began suspecting that her daughter was not working late at the office as she claimed, but wasn't coming home in the evenings because of some other engagements. One day Rosa went to Carmela's office before quitting-time and created a scene, which resulted in the police being called. Nick and Giuseppe took their distraught sister to Toronto's Mental Health Centre on Queen Street and had her admitted.

Nick did his best to mediate between mother and daughter. While sharing many of his sister's values and regarding his niece's ways as rather shocking and shameful, Nick did consider Rosa's reaction overly sensitive and old-fashioned. Perhaps because he had grown up in Canada himself, Nick attempted to find a modern solution to the problem. He tried talking to Carmela; he tried to get her to see a psychiatrist. He was as gentle with his niece as he knew how to be;

he never once laid hands on her. He was, as his brother Giuseppe put it, "like a father with a problem child".

Of course, the "problem child" maintained that it was not she who needed a psychiatrist but the rest of the Coluccio family. In this she may or may not have been entirely right. For one thing, a clash of cultural values need not be a mental problem on either side. For another, Carmela did more than stay out of the house overnight. Apparently she also forged her grandfather's signature on some cheques, embezzling in this manner nearly $1,200 from the old man. A family need not hail from southern Italy to find this extremely upsetting — or sick.

Carmela's forgery came to light only a few days before the shooting incident. Nick actually tried to cover up for his niece, telling his father that it happened only once and it involved only $75. The old man, who had worked in the same job all his life, spoke no English, and was almost completely deaf, loved Carmela. He kept giving money to her all the time. Knowing the shameful truth about his granddaughter's repeated forgeries would have, in the family's view, "broken his heart".

The last quarrel between mother and daughter occurred on a Saturday. It involved, once again, Carmela talking on the telephone with someone. She told her mother it was only a girlfriend but in fact it turned out to be a boy. The quarrel also involved Carmela's little address book, which, as Rosa told Nick when he came home that night, was "filled" with the names and phone numbers of young men. Nick told his sister to go to bed, promising to have a talk with his niece the next day.

Apparently Rosa did not sleep all night. Then, Sunday morning, she discussed the matter with her older brother Giuseppe, who came over for a visit. Nick and Carmela were still asleep. Rosa was distraught, and Giuseppe promised to come back later in the afternoon. Grandfather Coluccio, being not only deaf but busy renovating the upstairs kitchen, was largely unaware of the tension in his house. When Nick woke up he talked matters over with his sister for about an hour, then Rosa served lunch for everyone. It was a strained and silent meal; Carmela, who had a slight weight problem, ate nothing and drank only some black coffee. After lunch, Nick called his niece into the living-room for a talk.

Carmela came out of her own room in a combative mood. "You are not going to start like this again, are you?" she asked her uncle. Her position was that she was twenty years old and could do whatever she wanted. Nick replied that she could leave, but as long as she stayed in the family's home with the family paying her way she had to abide by the family's rules. It was a standard argument. Arguments of the same kind were probably taking place between parents and children in hundreds of Canadian homes that very Sunday.

The difference in this case was that in the Coluccio home Carmela told her uncle that she did not have to answer his questions. Not about boys, not about what she did with her grandfather's money, not about anything else. Then she flew at him and pushed him. Physically. She had never done that before. It is probable that few nieces in southern Italy had ever raised a hand against the uncle who had brought them up. Nick went to the closet where he kept a gun in a shoebox. The next few moments were a blur of incoherent words, passion, hurt, and confusion, at the end of which both Carmela and her mother Rosa were dead. The pathologist's report would later establish that Carmela had been six to eight weeks pregnant.

It was, of course, not for me to pass judgment on my client. It wasn't for me to judge the dynamics of a particular family or the moral and cultural values of Calabria (or of contemporary Canada, for that matter). In any case, sitting at my desk after that first interview, I only had the barest outline of the whole tragic story. At that point I knew very little, except that I had to advise Nick to give himself up to the police. (He knew that himself: if he had wanted to escape he would not have consulted a lawyer. The police had not been able to find him for nearly a month, and he had more than $900 in his wallet when he came to my office. The fact was, Nick wasn't a criminal and he wasn't cut out to be a fugitive. He came because he wanted to surrender.)

While Coluccio was telling me his story, I noticed that he was holding a brown paper bag in his hand. I thought, frankly, that it contained his lunch. After he finished, I pointed to the bag: "And what's that?" I asked him.

"Thatsa da gun," he replied matter-of-factly.

I think I was silent for a full minute after Coluccio said this. His statement had plunged me straight into one of the classic, textbook dilemmas for a criminal defence lawyer. The word "textbook" may be misleading, because textbooks only pose such problems, they do not resolve them.

Whatever a client tells his lawyer in connection with his case is protected by the confidentiality of the solicitor-client relationship. This is an absolute privilege, from which a lawyer can only be absolved by the client. It's not just that a solicitor is not *required* to reveal to the authorities something he heard from his client: a solicitor is not *permitted* to reveal it. If he did so, he could be disbarred.

However, it goes without saying that the law does not permit the suppression of evidence — physical evidence or evidence of any other kind. You can't stab someone, then go to your lawyer, saying: "Here, put this knife in my file." A lawyer who concealed potential evidence would risk not only disbarment but criminal charges for interfering with the administration of justice.

At the same time a lawyer's duty is to defend his client, not to act as an investigator for the prosecution. Since the law puts no positive duty on an accused to assist in his own conviction, how can it put such a duty on his defence counsel? Everyone is presumed to be innocent. Everyone has an absolute right to stand mute and let the prosecution come up with the evidence, if there is any, to prove him guilty beyond a reasonable doubt. If an accused is not required to produce evidence against himself, how can his lawyer, who is supposed to defend him, be required to do so? Why should anyone seek the advice of a lawyer if, by doing so, he might put himself in additional jeopardy — if, say, a defendant could be forced to reveal something through his lawyer that the law could never force him to reveal on his own? If there *were* such a legal requirement, some accused persons would be better off going to court unrepresented by legal counsel — an obvious anomaly.

Yet concealing the existence of the weapon in Nick's paper bag would have been clearly unlawful. There was absolutely no way in which I could say to Coluccio: "Skip the gun. Hide it, throw it away, forget you've ever told me about it." If I said anything like that to him, I would be breaking the law.

I had no intention of breaching the Criminal Code — but at the same time I couldn't see myself advising Coluccio to surrender to the police with a gun in his little paper bag. At that point I didn't know what evidence there was against him, or if there was any evidence against him at all. I knew nothing but a story he told me, and that the police were looking for him. I had no idea if he was guilty of any offence in law — that's impossible to know until after a trial. Guilt or innocence can't be determined until a court has weighed all the evidence for the prosecution as well as for the defence. I had no idea, as I was sitting in my office, what Coluccio's defence might be. Whatever he told me could have been true or a fantasy; he could have been sane or crazy; and whatever was in his bag could have been the gun involved in the shooting or not. I didn't know. It was not up to me to tie my client to any gun by having him hand it over to the police.

Helping to convict someone is the very opposite of a defence lawyer's function. As potential evidence, the gun had to reach the police somehow: there was no doubt about that. But was the defence under any duty to interpret the evidence for the police by telling them that the gun was connected with Coluccio?

For me to say to the prosecution: "This is Coluccio's gun," would be to offer my own interpretation of the evidence. An interpretation, moreover, that might be detrimental to my client. How could I do that? How could I tell if this *was* Coluccio's gun? Because he said so? At that stage, how could I know if Coluccio wasn't trying to take the blame in the death of his sister and niece only for some reason of family honour or expediency — say, because, unlike other family members, he had no children of his own? If guilt or innocence could be determined after an interview in a lawyer's office, it would be a waste of money to have judges and juries.

That was certainly my view — but my view doesn't govern in such matters. The views of the courts (and of the Law Society) do. I couldn't be sure how they would look at the dilemma.

It was around 11 a.m. when I finished my interview with Coluccio. He sat and waited patiently in the outside office for my student to take him to police headquarters. The police asked me, when I telephoned them, not to surrender Nick until 2:15 p.m., because the officers in charge of the investigation were tied up in a meeting.

Meanwhile my associate Marc Rosenberg and I were canvassing other lawyers and the Law Society for second opinions. We got opinions — but they were, to put it mildly, conflicting. Everyone had a different idea of what would be the right thing for a lawyer to do in the hypothetical case of a client's showing up in the office with what might be a murder weapon in a brown paper bag. (Or a bag of any other colour, which, as all the lawyers agreed, had no bearing on the matter. It was the only thing they all agreed on.)

Marc and I were telephoning our colleagues in our separate offices, occasionally reporting to each other the results. "Well, X.Z. feels there is no choice. The lawyer must surrender the client to the police with the gun." "Oh, really? Well, X.Y. wonders what the fuss is all about. The lawyer should just tell the client to throw away the gun and forget about it." "So-and-so is of the view that if the lawyer tells the police about the gun, he could be disbarred for breaking solicitor-client confidence, and if he doesn't, he could be charged with a criminal offence for concealing evidence. So, first of all, the lawyer must cover his own ass and tell the client that he has no advice on the gun. Then, let the client do whatever he wants."

By 12:15 p.m. I had made up my mind. I retained a lawyer for myself — Richard N. Stern, who had an office in my building. Ricky Stern used to be my articling student and I retained him for one specific purpose, which was to immediately deliver a large plain envelope to the office of the Crown Attorney of North York, preferably placing it in the hands of the senior Crown, Stephen Leggett. As Ricky's client, I instructed him to tell the Crown that he, Ricky Stern, had been retained by a client to deliver the envelope to the Crown, as its contents were the subject of an investigation by police officers within his jursidiction. Ricky was to add only that the envelope itself was not evidence, but that its contents probably were.

Having been instructed by his client to tell the Crown nothing else, as a lawyer Stern would not be required to say anything more. *He* had no personal knowledge of what was in the bag — he didn't see it. Whatever else he may have been told by his client would be privileged information (including his client's identity). That took care of the legal side of things.

However, I felt an obligation not to have a bunch of people accidentally shoot themselves by placing a loaded gun into their hands — or, more precisely, a loaded paper bag. To protect Stephen Leggett and anyone else who might be in the vicinity when the envelope was being opened, I also instructed Ricky that, subject to an undertaking from Leggett that such information would not be used against him, he could further advise the Crown that the envelope contained a bag. The "bag" might be loaded and it could go off, though we believed it had the safety catch on.

Leggett, a very experienced and fair-minded Crown with a quiet, dry, no-nonsense air about him, was at lunch in the cafeteria behind the courts at 1000 Finch Avenue as Ricky, whose attitude to potentially loaded bags is one of infinite caution, approached the prosecutor's table. He held the large envelope gingerly in his hand. At that point, not having seen the gun and knowing only what I had told him, Ricky could not be entirely sure if the whole matter was not some elaborate practical joke. He suspected that it might be serious business, but he couldn't be certain.

The thought might have crossed Leggett's mind as well. In any case, not being a man easily perturbed, he finished his lunch at a leisurely pace, then bade Ricky to follow him upstairs to his office. Putting the envelope on Leggett's desk, Ricky spoke his piece, adding that he would tell him something else in exchange for an undertaking that it would not be used against him.

Leggett frowned. Clearly, whether it was a joke or a serious matter, he was not going to give any undertakings without finding out something more. "Why don't we just look inside it," he suggested, grabbing at the envelope.

Ricky also grabbed it and held on. He had visions of everybody being blown to pieces in the office. It seemed more important at that moment than any undertaking from the Crown. "Off the record, watch out, there's a bag inside and it's loaded," he said quickly. "That's all I've been told. The safety's on."

Leggett looked at Ricky with raised eyebrows. He took the envelope and started opening it carefully. "Oh, and another thing," Stern said. "There may be fingerprints on the contents."

Leggett abandoned the package. "I think we'd better get a copper," he said.

In the meantime my student took Nick Coluccio to the police. He was clutching about a dozen copies of a document in his hand, drawn up in my office. It is a document I give to all suspects who are about to be arrested. It said, in part, "I, Nick Coluccio, hereby confirm that I have instructed my counsel that I do not wish to be interviewed by the police in connection with this matter and I do not wish to give any statement whatsoever at this time. . . . After instructing my counsel of my wishes this document was drawn up so that any and all officers who attempt to take a statement from me shall be given a copy of this document. . . . . I confirm that if any statement is made by me, it shall be without my consent and will not be free or voluntary."

Many years ago I saw a cartoon pinned to the wall of a police station. It depicted a small man in handcuffs facing two large police officers. The caption said: "You came in here with a pretty face and some information. You can't leave with both."

The cartoon was just a joke, and I chuckled at it myself. Still, legal safeguards exist to make sure that such cartoons remain jokes, not everyday reality. It is not some smart lawyer but the *law* that gives accused persons the right to remain silent. Lawyers only ensure that the law is actually observed by those whose job it is to enforce the law. By every one of them, not just the most decent and the best.

Nick Coluccio was charged with two counts of first-degree murder. He made no statement. On May 2, 1980, the Centre of Forensic Sciences in Toronto reported that a gun, noted in the records only as "F22; Source: Turned over to Police", was found to have been the weapon that fired the bullets that caused the deaths of Carmela and Rosa Albanese. There was no evidence as to who the gun belonged to.

Neither this nor anything else about the case became a contested issue. The Crown and the defence agreed on a set of facts, and the Crown agreed not to persist with the murder charge. On Wednesday, June 11, 1980, Nick Coluccio pleaded guilty to the lesser and included offence of manslaughter. He was sentenced to six years in prison.

A crime had been committed, and crime must not go unpunished. For the next number of years Nick Coluccio would be paying his debt to society. At the same time his rights and legal safeguards had been meticulously observed. By that stage, it was all society could do for him or for the Coluccio family. Their tragedy could never be undone.

No sentence could "deter" or "rehabilitate" Nick better than any other sentence: he knew as well as any person in Canada that killing was wrong. He surrendered himself to society's judgment because he was already suffering from guilt and remorse. Beyond that, no person can be rehabilitated. The law must be enforced, but it would be arrogant to suggest that we should "rehabilitate" people from their own moral values or culture. In a case like Coluccio's there was no question of either the Crown or the defence winning or losing. I believe, though, that in the end justice had triumphed.

## NOTES

p.44, l.7: There are other judicial systems, such as the civil or inquisitorial systems of continental Europe, in which judges and assessors play an entirely different role. In those systems the judges, representing the law, take part in the fray on the side of the state. In such systems the defendant's adversaries and judges are the same. The difference is that they do not regard themselves as adversaries but merely as inquisitors, trying to find out the truth.

Which is the better system? The glib statement has been made that "innocent" defendants fare better in an inquisitorial system, while "guilty" defendants fare better in an adversary system such as ours. I do not agree. I would say that how a defendant, guilty or innocent, fares in the inquisitorial system depends entirely on the wisdom and integrity of the examining magistrate who happens to be in charge of his file or *dossier*. While the inquisitorial system can be no better than the human beings who administer it, the adversary system can be and is.

I find it revealing that while the various inquisitorial systems have been capable of adoption by tyrannies, no tyranny has ever adopted the adversarial system for its judicial model.

p.47, l.36: In modern Canadian culture we may consider a mother's repeated attempts at suicide because of a loose-living daughter more than just overly sensitive or old-fashioned; we may consider it "hysterical" or "sick". It only goes to show how difficult it is to judge individual behaviour by the standards of a different culture. In many cultures distant from us in time or geography, suicide for a proud and decent person could be a perfectly "normal" response to a perceived loss of family honour.

p.50, l.7: The law provides that, generally speaking, what a client says to his lawyer in seeking or obtaining legal advice is privileged, and neither the client nor the lawyer can be compelled to disclose it. The client may, however, waive the privilege by voluntarily offering his testimony, or that of the lawyer, concerning the communication. The client may also be deemed to have waived the privilege by, for example, attacking his lawyer's conduct of the case in such a way that to defend himself the lawyer must disclose the communication. Finally, there is a broad fraud or crime exception.

Communications made to the lawyer which are criminal in themselves, or are made for the purpose of committing some future crime, are not privileged.

# 4. Clients Play Hardball

In 1971 I was applying for leave to appeal the murder conviction of a man I will call Cain. My client wasn't a Canadian, but it was in this country that he was convicted following an incident in which a man was punched to death in a small Canadian town. After his conviction Mr. Cain was incarcerated in Kingston Penitentiary.

In 1971 I had been out of law school for three years. I had been called to the Ontario bar only the year before. In an abstract sense, like most young lawyers, I probably knew as much about "the law" then as I know now — maybe more, because it was fresher in my mind. However, I certainly did not know much about lawyering. I knew nothing about colleagues or clients, for instance. There are no courses called "Clients 205" or "Colleagues 302" in university. I very much doubt if any could be set up. Colleagues and clients may play as large a role in a lawyer's practice as the law itself, but you must learn about them as you go along.

Knowing about the law, I thought that I might have a slight — very slight — chance of getting leave to appeal Cain's murder conviction. (He had been unrepresented at his trial, and the judge let in some evidence that may not have been admissible.) I wasn't too optimistic. I would have been even less optimistic had I known that the victim happened to be the brother of a lower-court judge, who was also a regular bridge partner of one of the Supreme Court justices — a fact I only learned about later.

I would not dream of suggesting that a strong case for an appeal would ever be denied for such a reason — not because it would be disrespectful to suggest it, but because I do not believe it to be true. However, I agree with the nineteenth-century French novelist Honoré de Balzac that the highest appointment and the greatest personal integrity are powerless to suspend human nature entirely, and I also believe that things do blur at the margins. The merits of Cain's appeal *were* marginal.

In any event, Cain seemed not to have a great deal of confidence in my ability to get leave for his appeal, because on the day I was arguing his case in court he became involved in a riot at the penitentiary. Some prisoners took a few prison workers as hostages, possibly hoping to bargain their way to freedom. Cain and his friends weren't successful — but then I wasn't successful in court, either, on Cain's behalf. My request for leave to appeal his conviction was unceremoniously denied.

It had been a violent riot; it claimed the lives of a number of people. After it was all over, I went to Kingston, where my client was facing new charges because of his involvement in the hostage-taking incident (though not in any of the killings). Having talked with Cain and having reviewed the evidence against him, I advised him that a plea of guilty to a charge of unlawful confinement was the best course of action on the basis of the facts. (Perhaps this is a good place to mention that about three-quarters of a criminal lawyer's practice consists of such pleas, followed by sentence submissions. Contrary to popular belief, trying to "get people off" by hook or by crook is not what criminal lawyers do for a living.)

So Cain pleaded guilty to this charge along with the rest of the prisoners accused of being involved in the hostage-taking — all except one, the main co-conspirator. He pleaded not guilty. To everyone's astonishment, the former hostages couldn't identify him at the preliminary hearing. There being no other evidence against him, naturally he was discharged.

The Crown asked for a three-year sentence for Cain, to be served consecutively to the life sentence he was already serving for murder — that is, to be served *following* his life sentence, rather than concurrently with it. Such a sentence had the potential of adversely affecting Cain's eventual chances for parole. This, I believed, was wrong. As I said to the court: "You have only one life to give to your penitentiary system." (This was not settled law then. A couple of years later, following a case called *Sinclair*, the point I argued in 1971 was accepted by the Court of Appeal and it did become the law in Ontario.) In any case, my client received a sentence of three years, concurrent.

Cain was still furious. Here he was pleading guilty like a sucker, while the leader, the main guy, got off by simply pleading "not guilty". It seemed to Cain that if pleading not guilty is all it takes to get off, anybody can do that — and his lawyer ought to have known it. He called me down to Kingston to tear a strip off me, and I could only hope that this would remain a figure of speech. A man convicted of murder for having punched someone to death never lacks lethal weapons.

Cain was not about to use lethal weapons; he only wanted to fire me, then appeal his conviction for his role in the Kingston riots on the only ground available to him, namely that he was incompetently defended by me. He wanted to swear in an affidavit to a set of facts which, if true, might indeed have resulted in any competent lawyer's advising him not to plead guilty. The plain fact was that Cain had told me too much about what he had done. Now he wanted to hire another lawyer — and tell him less.

Cain was naturally entitled to do this. I didn't think that he would succeed (and, as it turned out, he didn't), but it was certainly something he could try.

Many people believe, as Cain might have, that your lawyer is there "to get you off". That's what you hire him for, they think; that's his function. But that's not quite so. Your lawyer's function is to *defend* you.

Unlike Cain, most professional criminals are likely to appreciate the difference more than ordinary citizens who happen to be charged with some offence once in their lives. Full-time crooks are likely to know better than to say to their lawyers: "Sure, I made this illegal U-turn, but who is to know? I'll deny it, so you can get me off."

Ordinary citizens are sometimes surprised to hear that their lawyer can't put them on the witness stand to say in court that they didn't make an illegal U-turn when, in fact, they made one. Why can't he let them say it? Because it's not true.

A lawyer can't assist his client or anyone else in misleading a court — on the witness stand or in an affidavit. All a lawyer can do is to advise his client of his right to say nothing in answer to a charge. He can advise him to stand mute, then make sure that the prosecution discharges the burden of proof placed on it by law. Sometimes the prosecution can't, as in the case of the man charged with being the main co-conspirator at Kingston; and if the Crown can't prove its charges beyond a reasonable doubt, then of course the accused must go free.

It is a lawyer's duty to put the Crown to the most rigorous test, but no lawyer can assist a client in the commission of perjury. Accused persons are always presumed innocent, but, even beyond this general presumption, if a lawyer leads an accused's denial of guilt in the witness-box as part of the defence's evidence, then the lawyer himself, in his own mind, must be in a state of doubt about the defendant's guilt. He can't say this to a jury, of course, because a lawyer's state of mind is irrelevant. But though he can't say it, it has to be so, for the simple reason that no lawyer can knowingly allow a client to state falsehoods or deny true facts under oath.

But while a client can't tell one set of facts to his lawyer, then expect to swear in court to another set of facts, he is always free to change lawyers. He is also free to accuse his ex-lawyer of incompetence. Cain did that, and when his appeal was eventually turned down, he wrote me a letter to say: "No hard feelings."

There were no hard feelings on my part — even though I don't like being accused of incompetence any more than the next person (and in 1971, being as insecure as any young lawyer, I liked it even less). But Cain still taught me a valuable lesson. I learned from him that clients will give you no quarter. Nor should you expect them to, because it is their liberty at stake.

Most people, having never had their liberty at risk, can't really fathom how high the stakes are for a person in prison, or one facing imprisonment — that is, for the majority of the criminal lawyer's clients. People can't really imagine a prisoner's state of mind, with nothing but endless time stretching before him, and no thought except to somehow regain his liberty. (Incidentally, that's why there is no such thing as an escape-proof prison. Guards and prison authorities have many different concerns, while certain inmates have only one: to escape. No guard can ever concentrate as hard on keeping such a prisoner inside as the prisoner can on getting away.)

Even some criminal lawyers can't fully appreciate this. I couldn't myself, in the beginning. I always knew it, but I didn't appreciate it. It was clients like Cain who brought home to me that, with so much at stake, a client can't worry about trifles such as his lawyer's reputation. How could he, when he often no longer worries about his own life. It is much more amazing that once in a while, even with so much at stake for him, a client will exhibit much concern for others, including his lawyer. I have seen examples of that as well.

As a rule of thumb, though, clients play hardball. I don't like it, but I can't blame them. That's the game. As to what a lawyer can do to safeguard himself (in addition to getting the best possible results for his client), there is a long, involved, technical, partial answer. The short answer is more honest and more accurate. Nothing.

## NOTES

p.57, l.10: Law, somewhat like medicine, is highly specialized. A young ear, nose, and throat specialist relatively fresh out of medical school may know more about "medicine" in general than he will ten years later. However, ten years later he's likely to know much more about ears, noses, and throats. If you tell him at that time that your foot hurts, he might say: "*Foot?* A foot is an organ down there at the opposite end some place, isn't it?" In the same way a criminal lawyer might say: "Sue for *divorce*? I vaguely remember the word from law school, but I don't really know what it means. Should you be charged with killing your spouse, however, I will be happy to act for you."

p.60, l.6: A defence lawyer, unlike a jury, need not be in a state of *reasonable* doubt. He has a duty to give the benefit of even the slightest doubt to his client, as long as it is an honest doubt and does not run counter to his factual knowledge. But if, say, he knows for a fact that his client was in Toronto on the night of the robbery, he can't let him (or any other witness) testify under oath that he was in Vancouver.

# 5. The Crown Plays Hardball

It was a Saturday, just after 11 p.m., on March 18 in 1972. Constable Ian Leslie was walking his beat in the Dufferin Street–St. Clair Avenue area, the heart of Toronto's Italian district. Suddenly the policeman saw a flash. It was almost as if, by some mistake, the sun had come up for an instant in the middle of the night. The flash was immediately followed by the sound of two explosions, so close together that they sounded very nearly like one. The first was a small bang, but the second one was shattering.

Turning the corner of Earlscourt Avenue at St. Clair, Constable Leslie saw that the building on the corner of the next block west, at St. Clair and Greenlaw Avenue, had collapsed and was on fire. The ground floor of that building had been occupied by a grocery store, called the Conte Supermarket. The building next door had also partially collapsed, with the travel agency on its second floor sliding into the rubble of the grocery store. For half a city block the pavement was covered with shattered glass, as the windows of nearly thirty neighbouring stores had been blown into the street.

On the sidewalk outside the collapsed building Constable Leslie noticed a five-gallon container of gasoline. There was about a pint of liquid left in it.

A woman's body was found in the ruins. She was soon identified as Maria Simone, a cleaning lady who had worked in the offices of the travel agency next door to the Conte Supermarket. She had died of blast injuries and thermal burns.

In the basement of the supermarket there was another body, later identified as Pietro Moretti, a young Italian man. He, too, had died in the explosion, which had torn off his clothes, including his shoes and socks. There was a black olive left imbedded in his body.

However, even before these two corpses were discovered, Constable Leslie had pulled a third person out from under some bricks and plaster-boards at the rear of the Conte Supermarket. The clothes of this person had also been torn to shreds by the explosion; he had been badly burned and was in great agony, but he was alive. His name was Paolo Quaranta, and I was eventually retained to act for him on a charge of non-capital murder.

It was to be my first murder trial. When I was retained, I didn't know that it was also going to be the first (and, so far, only) trial in my life in which I would risk entering the courtroom as an accused even before entering it as a lawyer. If the "Cain" case had taught me something about clients, the Quaranta case would teach me something about prosecutors.

In a sense it would be the same lesson. Both clients and prosecutors mean business. I'm saying this with no sense of resentment, just as a statement of fact. I am a defence lawyer, and I mean business too.

Quaranta had been born in Italy in 1951. He spoke virtually no English. Before he retained me, he gave several statements to the police. While under sedation in hospital, drifting in and out of consciousness, Quaranta told an Italian-speaking policeman that he had done it "for my friend Santo. Santo was the one who planned everything. We got a thousand dollars for it."

"Santo" was a man named Santo Presta. The Crown later alleged that he, along with one Giuseppe LaGamba and Pietro Moretti, the dead man found in the rubble, conspired with my client, Paolo Quaranta, to burn down the Conte Supermarket. The Crown's theory was that the four men were going to torch the supermarket for its owners, Raphael Bencardino and Giuseppe De Carlo, in an insurance-fraud scheme. These allegations were based largely on the statements of the badly burned, sedated, and semi-conscious Quaranta in hospital, and as a result Bencardino and De Carlo were also charged with non-capital murder.

The story that emerged, partly from Quaranta's statements to the police and partly from what he said on the witness stand at his own trial, was that he entered the Conte Supermarket shortly after 8 p.m. on Saturday with Presta, LaGamba, and Moretti. The plan was to set fire to the store at 11 p.m., but first they went down to the basement because "we thought we might as well get something to eat." This accomplished, Quaranta drove with Presta and LaGamba to a gas station, while Moretti stayed inside the store. After the three men returned with several containers of gasoline, Quaranta and Moretti went upstairs to the empty apartment above the store and lay down for a rest. Shortly before 11 p.m. Presta woke them, and the four men spread the gasoline around the basement. Then Presta and LaGamba left the premises. The alleged plan was for Quaranta and Moretti to burn down the store while Presta and LaGamba were going to collect "the money" for the job from the supermarket's owners. They were to meet at the Impero Bar afterwards, then take a plane to Brussels the next day. (There was evidence that the four men held tickets on Sabena Airlines for Sunday, March 19, the day after the explosion.)

After Presta and LaGamba had left, Quaranta and Moretti chatted for a few more minutes in the Conte Supermarket's basement. The fumes were rising from the gasoline that had been spread around earlier, making Quaranta dizzy. He went upstairs, telling Moretti to throw a match and run out. "I was only a step away from the door," Quaranta told the police. "I think I fainted because of the fumes, because I don't remember what happened."

What happened, of course, was an explosion levelling two buildings and substantially damaging several more. It came close to killing Quaranta, and it did kill his friend "Pierino" Moretti, along with a totally innocent bystander, Maria Simone, next door. It was her death that resulted in the charges of non-capital murder against Quaranta, as well as against supermarket owners Bencardino and De Carlo, along with Santo Presta and Giuseppe LaGamba, both of whom had left Canada by that time. They were being held by the police in Italy pending extradition.

It was this last factor that resulted in a threat of criminal charges against me.

In order to extradite Presta and LaGamba, the authorities needed an affidavit from Quaranta. In the meantime, Quaranta had retained me to defend him, and I naturally advised him that he had a right to remain silent. Possibly as a result of my advice, Quaranta refused to swear out an affidavit for the authorities.

While Quaranta could do whatever he wanted, my judgment was that it was in his best interest to say and do nothing, and as his lawyer it was my duty to tell him so. The rest was up to him. There may be such a thing as "doctor's orders", but there is no such thing as "lawyer's orders", even as a figure of speech. A lawyer can only advise. He can't do anything more — but he must do nothing less.

I would probably have given Quaranta the same advice even if I had known that he had already given statements to the police implicating Presta and LaGamba, but as a matter of fact I had no idea that he had done so. The reason was simple. My client, as he was to testify later, couldn't remember talking to the police in the hospital at all. He was under sedation and semi-conscious when he said whatever he did say to an Italian-speaking officer. He obviously couldn't inform me of something that he didn't remember himself.

The Crown Attorney in charge of the case was the veteran Frank Armstrong. He was, and is, a straightforward, dedicated, incorruptible prosecutor. He is uncompromising and tends to see matters as black-and-white. When he telephoned me, on a Saturday morning, he presented me with what he saw as my choice in equally black-and-white terms. Either Quaranta comes up with an affidavit for the extradition of Presta and LaGamba — or *I* face a charge of attempting to obstruct justice.

It was interesting. In a sense, it was my first introduction as a very young lawyer to the fast lane. My wife, Suzy, and I were wondering how, if it came to that, we were going to raise the bail. We didn't have a penny. I was not looking forward to my mother's reaction to a request to put up the family home in Niagara Falls as surety for her son, the lawyer. (Come to think of it, she didn't even have a family home by then.) Maybe, I thought, the judge might release me on my own recognizance until my trial. After all, I had fairly decent roots in the community.

Jail? I knew that come it might, but it wasn't going to come easy. I didn't think that the Crown could put me in jail without trying very hard, and I didn't think that he would try hard enough. However, I couldn't be sure of that. I could only be sure of one thing: no prosecutor would force me to give my client any advice that I believed to be contrary to the client's interest. In a country where the Crown could do that, there would no longer be any point in being a lawyer.

Within ten minutes of receiving Frank Armstrong's phone call I retained counsel myself, the very experienced and respected Robert Carter, who had often helped me with his friendship and advice in the past. Armstrong had actually phoned me from the hospital, where, along with the late Judge Joe Addison, he had been standing by at Quaranta's bedside expecting Quaranta to sign the affidavit in the judge's presence. Armstrong wanted me to come down to the hospital right away and advise my client to co-operate or else.

Carter and I went to the hospital together. (The minute Judge Addison saw us coming, he walked out of the room; he clearly didn't want to be around for a brawl between Crown and defence.) Carter told the Crown Attorney that, as my lawyer, *he* was now advising me not to advise my client Quaranta to make any statement.

This did not settle the matter, but it did create an interesting dilemma for the Crown. It seemed to be the prosecution's position that I was obstructing justice by my advice to Quaranta. Was Carter also obstructing justice, in the Crown's view, by his advice to me — and if not, why not?

Inciting someone to commit a crime may well be a crime itself, but standing mute is not a crime. On the contrary, it is a person's fundamental right in our system of law. Advising a client about the law is a lawyer's duty, whether his client is an accused arsonist or another lawyer. Can anything lawful a lawyer ever does in the discharge of his duties amount to an obstruction of justice because it may frustrate the Crown's purpose? (Obviously not, because anything short of a plea of guilty may frustrate the Crown's purpose.) But can certain things amount to that, at certain times?

Carter and I didn't think so, but we couldn't be sure because it hadn't been tested in these particular terms. Nothing is sure in law until it has been tested and has become "settled law". Frank Armstrong seemed fully prepared to test his proposition. When, after our conversation, Quaranta continued to refuse to sign an affidavit, Armstrong recommended in a memo to the Senior Crown, Peter Rickaby, that I should be charged.

Cooler heads prevailed in the Attorney General's Department, where I had spent my articling years. Clay Powell, at that time the Assistant Deputy Attorney General of Ontario, had sufficient doubts about the legal merits of the Crown's position to withhold his assent — much as he may have enjoyed seeing one of his former clumsy articling students in jail. As a result, no charges were laid against me. I was on my way to losing my first murder trial unhindered.

There was no doubt about what Quaranta did — he told it to the jury on the witness stand himself. There was also little doubt that, since his unlawful act of arson resulted in the horrible death of an innocent woman next door, he may well have been guilty of manslaughter.

I did not think, however, that he was guilty of non-capital murder. The crime of manslaughter does not require specific intent in law; the crime of murder does. You can "manslaughter" someone without meaning to kill him or her, but as a rule you cannot murder anyone without the intention to kill.

Quaranta and his accomplices obviously didn't mean to kill Mrs. Simone or cause her bodily harm reckless of whether death ensued or not — which in law is one definition of murder. Nor did they kill Mrs. Simone by mistake while meaning to kill somebody else, which would also amount to murder in law. Quaranta meant to kill no one; he only meant to burn down an empty building. The murder charge against him resulted from paragraph 212(c) of the Criminal Code. This section defines as murder a situation where an act is done by a defendant for an unlawful object, if such an act causes somebody's death and if the accused knew or ought to have known that it probably would.

The Crown contended that Quaranta knew or ought to have known that creating a huge explosion that nearly levelled four houses was likely to cause someone's death. In talking to the Italian-speaking policeman in hospital (his sick-bed statements were ruled admissible by the trial judge), Quaranta apparently used the melodious phrase "*saltare in aria*", which would translate "to blow up" rather than "to burn". But it seemed evident to me that, while *saltare in aria* was what happened, all Quaranta meant to do was to start a fire in the basement of a building he knew to be empty. He and his late friend Moretti would hardly have stuck around if they had expected an explosion.

A fire in the basement is what would have happened, in fact, had Moretti and Quaranta thrown a match the minute they finished pouring the gasoline, instead of standing around chatting until the rising fumes had actually made Quaranta feel sick. It was the fumes that exploded; the gasoline would only have burned. Whether Quaranta knew or ought to have known that a fire in an empty building was "likely" to cause anybody's death seemed much more questionable to me.

The question wasn't whether or not Quaranta committed a very serious offence. Of course he did; but did he commit *murder*? A conviction for manslaughter is not a parking ticket. Just like a murder conviction, it can also mean a life sentence in jail. To me, it seemed the appropriate result in Quaranta's case, but it did not seem so to the jury. As I was looking at the twelve men and women in the jury-box listening to the dead cleaning lady's husband testifying about the moment of the explosion — Mr. Simone happened to be talking with his wife on the telephone about ordering in a pizza just as the building blew up — it did not appear to me that this group of good citizens would be in any mood to weigh fine points of law. As it turned out, they weren't. During my jury address I experienced for the first time what it is like to talk to an unresponsive jury. It's all in a day's work, of course, and defence lawyers are supposed to be big boys — but it is a lonely feeling.

So Quaranta was convicted of non-capital murder, but that wasn't the end of the story. The trial of Raphael Bencardino and Giuseppe De Carlo was coming up. The two owners of the Conte Supermarket were also facing a charge of non-capital murder. The prosecution's case against them, led again by Frank Armstrong, rested almost entirely on the evidence of my client, Paolo Quaranta.

Bencardino was defended by one of Canada's greatest criminal lawyers, the late Arthur Maloney, Q.C. Acting for De Carlo was the equally eminent David (now The Honourable Judge) Humphrey. Until the mid-seventies many if not most of the so-called "Italian cases" were being handled by Arthur Maloney and David Humphrey, and it was Maloney who first referred a few Italian clients to me. For instance (as it emerged at the Bencardino and De Carlo trial), Quaranta consulted Maloney first before being referred to our office.

As an aside, it's worth noting that a particular lawyer may end up handling a disproportionate number of cases from a given ethnic community or social stratum. There is nothing sinister about this; it just happens this way. People frequently retain lawyers by word of mouth. When clients send along other clients, they are often from the same national (or interest) group, which is where the clients have their own affinities and associations. An anti-war protester is likely to send you a fellow-protester; a society lady another society lady; a Chinese client another Chinese client. That's why, for instance, ten per cent or fewer of all lawyers may end up handling ninety per cent or more of all "political" or "civil liberties" cases.

When it comes to certain groups, however, a lawyer runs the risk of becoming known as a "Mafia lawyer" or a "lawyer for extremists" (or even "terrorists") simply because of this word-of-mouth process which may bring him many cases from the same ethnic or interest groups over a relatively short period of time. I dislike the connotation, because it is a totally unwarranted slur on the lawyer. (In the case of the so-called "Mafia" or "Chinese gangs", I also find it an unwarranted slur on the Italian or Chinese communities, something I will discuss in more detail in the next chapter.)

In any case, Quaranta started out by testifying at Bencardino's and De Carlo's joint trial as the Crown expected him to do. Substantially his evidence was that both owners were present in the supermarket before the fire was set, and one of them even said, "Do a good job, boys," before leaving. However, after the Crown had closed its case, Arthur Maloney informed the court that a client of Dave Humphrey's, a man by the name of Bruno Pisani, had sent word to him that Quaranta had told him (Pisani) in jail that he (Quaranta) had "lied at certain points" in giving his evidence against Bencardino and De Carlo.

Maloney further informed the court that Humphrey then contacted "Mr. Greenspan about the matter" as Quaranta's lawyer. (By that time I was no longer acting for Quaranta, in fact.) In any event, eventually Quaranta gave a statement to his court-appointed solicitor in which he denied that the owners had been in the store on the night of the fire or had said anything about doing "a good job".

Naturally Maloney and Humphrey now wanted the trial judge, Mr. Justice Haines, either to compel the Crown to recall Quaranta or to call him as the court's own witness. This was vital to the defence. The prosecution's theory about Bencardino and De Carlo rested almost entirely on Quaranta's original evidence. If he was now saying that he had lied earlier, and if the jury believed this or was left in a state of reasonable doubt as to whether he had lied or not, they might have no choice but to acquit the two accused.

After listening to Quaranta's new evidence in the absence of the jury, Mr. Justice Haines decided not to call him from the bench or compel the Crown to do so. But he pointed out that Maloney and Humphrey could call him as a defence witness if they wished. They did, and Quaranta told the jury his new version of the events. Naturally he was cross-examined on it vigorously by Frank Armstrong, who suggested to Quaranta that he had changed his evidence because of threats conveyed to him by Bruno Pisani and others.

"As long as you tell that [new] story they will let you live to at least rot in jail; isn't that true?" Armstrong asked Quaranta.

"Not true," was Quaranta's reply.

Armstrong had a problem. He had no evidence that Quaranta had ever been threatened. His mere suggestion to Quaranta was not evidence, while Quaranta's denial was. The judge was bound to warn the jury that they couldn't consider any suggestion put to a witness as evidence, while they must so consider the witness's reply. The jury *could* reject Quaranta's reply, but they had to weigh it as evidence; they couldn't even weigh Armstrong's question.

It was then that Frank Armstrong decided to call me as a witness for the prosecution. By that time Frank appeared determined to have me in his courtroom in some capacity other than as a lawyer. If he couldn't put me in the accused's dock, then at least he was going to put me on the witness stand. In hindsight it turned out not to have been a good decision for the Crown, though in fairness to Armstrong it came close to being one. In a slightly different form it would have been a bold and potentially winning move.

The facts were that, well after Quaranta's conviction, my client communicated with me from jail. As soon as he did that, I met Armstrong and told him that Quaranta had been in Collins Bay Penitentiary, where he seemed content; when, however, he was transferred for some reason to Millhaven Penitentiary he had received threats on approximately six different occasions with respect to the evidence he was to give at Bencardino and De Carlo's trial. He was also approached at Toronto's Don Jail. I made the specific request to Armstrong that, after testifying, Quaranta should be returned to Collins Bay Penitentiary rather than to Millhaven for his safety.

This was what *I* had said to Armstrong. I doubted if a judge could possibly let it go to a jury. Anything I may have told a Crown Attorney was evidence of nothing; it was just inadmissible hearsay. Whatever Quaranta had said to me, on the other hand, may have been relevant evidence of his state of mind — a possible fear of threats, as the Crown was alleging — except I didn't think that I could be called to reveal it without my client's permission and against his wishes. It was, I thought, as privileged as any other solicitor-client conversation. I certainly had no intention of testifying about it unless ordered by the court.

Mr. Justice Haines wrestled with the question. He listened to the submissions made by Arthur Maloney, Dave Humphrey, Frank Armstrong, Quaranta's new counsel Frank Fay, and the lawyer addressing the court on my behalf. It was a thorny problem. Mr. Justice Haines did not want his ruling to give either side grounds for a successful appeal — no judge ever wants that — and solicitor-client confidentiality is a privilege most jealously and properly safeguarded in law. At the same time the matter was vital for the Crown. In the end the trial judge decided that I must tell the jury what I had told Frank Armstrong, but that I couldn't speak about anything that Quaranta might have told me.

So I did. I testified as ordered, telling the jury that I had said to Armstrong that Quaranta's life had been threatened, and that I had made a request to have him returned to Collins Bay after giving evidence at the Bencardino and De Carlo trial.

I told this to the jury for what it was worth. As it turned out, it was worth nothing. The jury did convict Bencardino and De Carlo of manslaughter (the very verdict that, on the same grounds, I had unsuccessfully sought for Quaranta), but the Ontario Court of Appeal quashed the convictions and ordered a new trial for both men. The main reason was the evidence of "one G., a barrister" as the head-note described me when the judgment was published in the Canadian Criminal Cases. Their lordships held that "what Mr. Greenspan said to Mr. Armstrong is not evidence of anything." It should never have been admitted.

This did not surprise me; it was the point that Maloney, Humphrey, and I had urged on everyone concerned at the time. More surprisingly, however, the Court of Appeal also expressed the opinion for the guidance of the new trial judge that he should "conduct a *voir dire* as to what Quaranta said to Mr. Greenspan and if it appears that Quaranta was not seeking legal advice but rather relief from intimidation in prison or if it appears that he expressly or impliedly authorized Mr. Greenspan to divulge his plight to the authorities," then his communication to me would no longer be privileged and I could be required to repeat it to the jury.

The Ontario Court of Appeal rendered its judgment "with commiseration for the learned trial Judge in a very difficult and unusual trial." Still, in plain words, the higher court said that Mr. Justice Haines let in from my evidence precisely what he should have kept out, and kept out what he might have been able to let in. I could have predicted the first conclusion but not the second. It seemed that, even though it cost him the trial, Frank Armstrong had come very close to having the right idea.

There was no second time for me on the witness stand, though. During Bencardino and De Carlo's new trial, the trial judge, Mr. Justice Fraser, became sick. When he eventually died, a mistrial was declared. The case later came to court again before Mr. Justice Samuel Hughes and a jury, and the defendants were acquitted.

Quaranta never testified at that trial. In fact, he escaped from prison after a year and some months and has never been apprehended. I can truthfully say that I had a client once who served less than two years for murder.

I have had many trials with Frank Armstrong since 1972. He has always been the same: skilled, honest, fair, uncompromising, and very, very tough. He still sees things in the same black-and-white terms. It is a polite custom to call counsel for the opposing side "my friend" in court, and in the case of Armstrong I have regarded this as more than just an empty courtesy. Yet I'm sure that if he ever felt he had to do what he tried to do to me fifteen years ago, he would, without a moment's hesitation, do it again. He might visit me in jail, though.

NOTES

p.67, l.35: Not every death caused during a fire will lead to a murder conviction. If the perpetrator meant to cause bodily harm to facilitate arson, the offence is murder under s. 213 of the Criminal Code. If he set fire for some ulterior unlawful purpose, then, as in *Quaranta*, s. 212(c) applies even if he did not intend bodily harm. Thus, if he set fire for the purpose of unlawfully destroying someone's property, s. 212(c) applies (*R. v. Vasil*, S.C.C., 1981). In *Quaranta*, it would apply if he was a party to an alleged insurance fraud/arson conspiracy. In such cases it is sufficient that the accused ought to have known that death could result from his unlawful and dangerous conduct.

p.69, l.35: The difference is considerable. If the Crown is compelled to call a witness unfavourable to its own case, the impact his evidence is likely to have on the jury is much greater. Also, the side that calls a witness cannot ordinarily cross-examine him on his evidence, at least not without declaring him a hostile witness.

p.70, l.10: This wise rule inhibits both the prosecution and the defence from flinging about wild accusations, without unduly restricting the latitude counsel must have in effective cross-examination. As Lord Radcliffe put it in *Fox v. General Medical Council* (1960): "An advocate is entitled to use his discretion as to whether to put questions in the course of cross-examination which are based on material which he is not in a position to prove directly. The penalty is that, if he gets a denial or some answer that does not suit him, the answer stands against him for what it is worth."

p.71, l.23: Kelly, Jessup and Martin, JJ.A.; (1973), 15 C.C.C. (2d) at page 342.

# 6. Everybody Plays Hardball

*1* In November 1980 a self-confessed enforcer and member of the Satan's Choice motorcycle gang made up his mind to turn over a new leaf. One obvious way in which a criminal can accomplish this is to become a police informer. Since he didn't have many alternative skills, this was Cecil Kirby's choice.

Kirby became an informer in exchange for immunity from prosecution for what he would later describe as "a hundred offences", as well as interim support by the police during his separation from his former life of crime — and the promise of a lump-sum settlement after his divorce from his criminal past became final.

It was not a bad deal for someone whose offences, on his own admission, included arson, bombings, aggravated assault, and culpable homicide. As Kirby put it on the CBC public-affairs program *fifth estate* in 1984: "Well, we all have got to live somehow." Kirby was clearly determined to challenge the proposition that crime doesn't pay.

Naturally, Kirby was not getting his deal for nothing: he was obliged to give value for money. As he said on the same television program: "I have succeeded in helping [the police] put fourteen people in jail for over seventy-five years." Therein lay a problem, though. The police were continually hoping to get a few more people and a few more jail-years out of Kirby for all the money, protection, and adverse publicity the deal was costing them.

Blackmail victims and police informers have one thing in common. As they quickly discover, a blackmailer's demand for more money is never-ending, and so is the authorities' demand for more information. It is very difficult to give the police a few choice tid-bits, wear a body-pack once or twice, tape some incriminating conversations with ex-associates and testify about them in court, then pick up a lump-sum cheque and new identity papers and walk away. That's just not the way it works.

As a rule, you can't "quit" being a police informer any more than you can "quit" being a spy for an intelligence service. There is always one more job, one more assignment, before that promised big pay-off and final handshake. The authorities always have a few more files to close.

The informer may not be able to stop talking just because he has run out of genuine information. If he tries, he might suddenly find himself in a very cold place. Not only is the big, final cheque late in coming (along with that brand-new birth certificate and driver's licence), but even the ordinary expense-money and protection may stop. Police officers may suddenly become unavailable to guard informers who have nothing more to tell them. As to immunity for past crimes, well, the authorities don't exactly go back on their word — but what about that one assault or one burglary that hasn't been covered by the original deal? Say, a crime committed at an earlier or a later date? That, the police might say to their star snitch, should still be good for a couple of years in jail — and you know what happens to people in jail who are known to have "ratted" (to use Kirby's own word) on their fellows.

These are the facts of life. They add up to a lot of pressure on an informer (or any accomplice-witness) to keep talking even after he has run out of things to say. The media often analyse the moral ambiguity of making deals with people like Cecil Kirby but seldom mention the problem of reliability, which, to my mind, is just as worthy of note.

There *is* a moral dilemma involved in offering immunity, protection, and money to someone like Kirby — who, among other things, claimed to have bombed two Toronto restaurants, killing one person and injuring several more — in order to secure the conviction of other criminals who may be as bad as, but are scarcely worse or more dangerous than, Kirby himself. Still, it has been argued that such deals are not wrong because they are necessary. Fine; but it's surely wrong to risk convicting people of crimes they may not have committed just because the pressures of the deal compel informers like Kirby to keep coming up with stories even after they have had to switch from facts to fantasy.

In fairness to the police, the pressure does not invariably come from them. The informer may also acquire a taste for talking. He may become a media celebrity of sorts, getting offers from TV programs and publishers. After a while he may talk "for the book" that he says he is planning to write — as Kirby eventually did, with co-author Thomas Renner. (In 1987 I was faced with the prospect of having to hand Kirby an award for his book, *Mafia Assassin*, as it was nominated for a Canadian Crime Writers Association award, which I was to present to the winner. Since the Kirby book did not, in fact, win, I did not have to say anything undignified.) In any case, far from having to pressure a certain type of informer, the police may have a hard time stopping him from coming up with yet another story.

It is in the interest of informers to keep accusing other people of crimes. Their living, and at times their lives, depend on it. When they stop, so does the money and perhaps the protection of the authorities (or the money and the attention from the media in a few high-profile cases). This does not mean that informers never tell the truth about their former associates; it only means that they lie about them often and easily. They lie about them for profit, and they lie about them to save their own skins. As a defence lawyer I have always been concerned with anyone having to face a charge based on the evidence of a former criminal associate, without corroboration or at least confirmation by some independent evidence. Someone like Kirby may tell the truth at times, but I wouldn't take a dog to court on Cecil Kirby's word alone.

In the spring of 1981 this abstract proposition took a very concrete form for me. That was when, on the basis of Cecil Kirby's evidence, supported by some surreptitiously taped conversations, three of my clients, the brothers Cosimo, Rocco ("Remo"), and Michele Commisso, were charged with a variety of serious offences, including conspiracy to murder a Toronto man named Paul Volpe.

2   My clients (as well as their intended victim) had frequently been described in the press as "Mafia bosses" or "members of organized crime". This is central to the story I am about to tell, so I must enlarge on why I have always found such designations dangerous and unfair.

The Commisso brothers as well as Paul Volpe had had criminal convictions. They had friends or associates who had had criminal convictions. Some of these friends were, like Volpe and the Commisso brothers, of Italian birth or extraction. These factors, taken together, have generally been sufficient for the press, the police, and the prosecutors in North America to label some people as members of organized crime.

I have always had a problem with this label. For one thing, I have found it redundant. In my years as a criminal lawyer it has been my experience that crime, like many other forms of human activity, is generally "organized". The planning or execution of crimes often involves two or more people. With the exception of a few lone muggers, embezzlers, or rapists, most crime is organized in this sense. Burglars have receivers of stolen goods; fraud artists have accomplices; loan sharks have enforcers. From bank robbery to gambling, from price-fixing to insider trading in stocks, crime is frequently characterized by a conspiracy of several individuals.

When criminals conspire, they most often conspire with other criminals. After all, who else would they conspire with? They can't conspire with priests or philosophy professors. They can't conspire with law-abiding people in any walk of life. So, as a rule, they will conspire with contacts they have made during a previous stint in prison, or maybe with childhood friends (or relatives) from the old neighbourhood. They conspire with people they think they can trust. One needs an introduction to the world of crime in much the same way as one needs an introduction to high society.

It is also common for all people who organize activities, in the spheres of both legitimate business and crime, to give some preference to associates of their own ethnic and social roots. Many, in fact, will give a preference to members of their own families. It will not be an exclusive preference — what people need is like-minded associates first of all, persons of like skills and interests — but once that requirement is met, the second most important factor in the selection of confederates is usually a shared background. The less legitimate an organized activity is, the more important kinship becomes. A shared background implies confidence.

This holds true for all nationalities, so it holds true for Italians. It is a factor in legitimate business, and it's a factor in crime.

When non-ethnic criminals conspire with each other in this manner — when they make agreements to receive stolen property, pass counterfeit money, take gambling bets, lend money at usurious rates, and so forth — the word "organized crime" is rarely used to describe their activities. But let southern Italians conspire with each other in exactly the same fashion and the words "Mafia" or "organized crime" will immediately appear in the language of the authorities and the press. Allusions to a big, sinister "mob" or "Cosa Nostra" — implying some centrally directed criminal network — will be made even in the absence of the slightest evidence that the criminal conspiracy has involved anything but three or four like-minded individuals who may have some ethnic, linguistic, or family ties with one another going back to the old country.

The point is, many allegations of crime heard in our courts involve such criminal conspiracies, yet the term "organized crime" will be attached to only a few — mainly to conspiracies comprising, or at least including, Italians. Three Torontonians of Anglo-Celtic background accused of passing counterfeit money are likely to be described as three alleged Toronto counterfeiters. Three Torontonians from Calabrian backgrounds accused of doing the same thing are likely to be described as the Mafia.

In all my years of practice I have yet to see any cogent evidence of a "Mafia". I only saw alleged or convicted criminals who consorted or dealt with some other alleged or convicted criminals — some of whom were described as members of organized crime by the prosecutors and the press. They were selected for this "honour" in such an arbitrary fashion as to be almost whimsical. Criminals so described appeared no different in their case or life histories from other alleged or convicted criminals who were never described as members of organized crime by anyone. Both groups did exactly the same things, for the same motives and with the same frequency. The only difference I could ever see was that the first group was Italian (or had Italian associates), while the second group wasn't or didn't.

There may have been one other difference. Those described as members of organized crime were luckier or more successful in eluding the police for a while. They may have been suspected for a longer time before sufficient evidence could be gathered against them for a criminal charge. Then, when finally brought to court, they would be labelled "mobsters" or "mafiosos" almost as an act of prosecutorial revenge. (Or, as a colleague suggested, as a kind of explanation on the part of the police for taking longer to catch them: "They were the Mafia, that's why.")

Objecting to this is not a mere semantic quibble. "Mafia" and "organized crime" are emotionally loaded terms. A person described as a "mobster" or a "mafioso" can virtually forfeit the ordinary protections, safeguards, and presumptions of the law in the eyes of the police, the public, and sometimes even the courts. The label creates an emotional atmosphere in which a fair investigation, fair prosecution, and a fair trial become very difficult to conduct.

An appreciation of these two factors — the nature of police informers, and the label of "organized crime" — is vital for understanding the events that follow. The story of the Commisso deal came to pass in this context, and would probably not have occurred in any other.

3 In May 1981, after a complicated sting in which Cecil Kirby had been acting as an undercover agent for the police, the Commisso brothers were arrested and charged with having plotted to kill a Connecticut woman named Helen Nafpliotis, a Toronto man named Peter Scarcella, who was one of Volpe's friends, as well as Paul Volpe himself. Kirby's own evidence about the conspiracies was backed up by some body-pack tapes of statements made by the Commisso brothers to Kirby while he was posing as a hit-man supposedly carrying out the murders on the Commisso brothers' behalf.

On examining the Crown's material, it appeared to me that the evidence was strongest against the eldest brother, Cosimo Commisso. In his case a trial (as Judge Arthur K. Meen would comment on the matter later) would "almost surely" have resulted in a conviction.

The case against Remo Commisso was much weaker. Borrowing Judge Meen's words again, he "might have been acquitted" at trial. The case against Michele, the youngest of the three Commisso brothers, was substantial enough, but the charges themselves were much less serious. He might well have been convicted of these lesser charges but would not have faced anything like the potential life imprisonment his eldest brother Cosimo faced in the event of a conviction.

The Crown regarded Remo, the middle brother, as the leader of the Commisso conspiracy — yet the prosecution had the least amount of evidence against him. This created an interesting situation. The prosecutors felt that they "had" Cosimo and Michele, but they did not want them quite as much as they wanted Remo, whom they didn't think they "had" quite as firmly. This gave me some room in the upcoming plea negotiations which the interests of my clients clearly required.

Cosimo Commisso was married and had dependent children, while Remo was unmarried and had no dependants. After I began discussions with Crown Attorney Howard Morton, it became apparent to me that there might be a potential conflict of interest between Cosimo and Remo, since the prosecution seemed willing to consider a lesser sentence for Cosimo only in exchange for an assured and possibly increased sentence for Remo.

I felt that Remo should have separate legal counsel. As negotiations continued, I turned to Robert Carter, Q.C., once more to ask if he would act for the middle brother of the Commisso family. He agreed. I continued acting for both Cosimo and Michele, whose cases had no potential for a conflict. Some time in August 1981, a little less than three months after the Commisso brothers had been charged, the prosecution and the defence came to an agreement.

Howard Morton and his associate Murray Segal representing the Crown on one side, and Robert Carter and I representing the three accused on the other, agreed that Cosimo Commisso would plead guilty to all charges, with the understanding that the Crown would join with the defence in a recommendation to the court that he be sentenced to eight years concurrent on each count. Remo Commisso would plead guilty to all charges on the same basis, while Michele Commisso would plead guilty with the understanding that our joint recommendation in his case would be a sentence of between two and two and a half years.

Such agreements between Crown and defence attorneys form the heart of the plea-negotiating process. It is a process in which each side comes away with some advantage it otherwise could not be certain of securing (and at a fraction of what a contest in court would cost both the clients and the taxpayers). In this instance, the Crown would be assured that Remo did not go free, while the defence would ascertain the limits to which all three defendants would be exposed.

None of these agreements, incidentally, are binding on the courts at this stage. For instance, having come to an agreement on the proposed disposition of the Commisso case, the lawyers for both sides would first have to meet in chambers with the trial judge, Chief Justice Gregory Evans of the Ontario High Court, to see if his Lordship felt that the proposals were appropriate. The Chief Justice, even if he considered the general framework felicitous, would still not be bound to impose the precise sentence recommended when the case came before him in open court. Such judicial supervision safeguards the integrity of the plea-bargaining process. In practice, however, a disposition jointly recommended by senior counsel for the Crown and the defence is rarely varied by a judge.

I'm outlining this not simply to describe the process, but because it played a major part in the case as it developed. The meeting in the Chief Justice's chambers took place on August 19, 1981, with the case scheduled to be heard in open court two days later. Knowing that an agreement had been reached, but discovering that the August 21, 1981, court date before Chief Justice Evans would conflict with a prior commitment for me to make a speech in Montreal, I asked Michael Moldaver, a partner in my law firm at the time, to represent me in court. His Lordship as well as Robert Carter and the two Crown Attorneys were busy men; an alternative court date would not have been easy to obtain, and my presence was no longer vital. Since I had come to terms with the Crown on all relevant details, Moldaver, a very able lawyer, could represent the defence before the Chief Justice as well as well as I could, at this stage.

This Moldaver did, along with Robert Carter. Chief Justice Evans weighed matters and, in evident agreement with the joint recommendations of the Crown and the defence — having accepted guilty pleas and registered convictions against all three accused — he imposed a sentence of eight years' imprisonment on Cosimo and Remo Commisso, and two and a half years on Michele Commisso, concurrent on all charges. In the normal course of events the matter would have rested there.

In the Commisso case, however, events did not take a normal course.

By custom and tradition criminal lawyers negotiate with each other in a very informal manner. Often there are just two lawyers talking in a room, with no secretaries, no minutes, no witnesses. The "room" may or may not even be an office — it could be a room in a restaurant where an agreement is reached over lunch. A Crown and a defence attorney may bump into each other in a courthouse corridor or a cafeteria, or in a hotel lobby at some legal conference out of town. If they have an outstanding case that happens to be simple or routine, they may reach an agreement on it while waiting for the bus to take them to the airport. I once settled a case in the service bay of a gas station outside a courthouse.

Deals are sealed with a handshake or a nod. Unlike members of the civil bar, criminal lawyers tend not to write confirmatory letters to each other. Some, myself included, do not even write "memos to file" (as a rule). Many agreements, or the reasons behind them, are too amorphous ever to be reduced to writing. If they had to be written down, some agreements would never be reached. Many additional cases would have to be contested in court to the bitter end — and the administration of justice would grind to a halt.

In spite of, or perhaps because of, this, disputes are very rare. If we could not rely on each other's verbal undertakings, members of the criminal bar could not deal with each other at all. Once two criminal lawyers agree on something, they seldom change their minds or go back on their words. A plea bargain, once struck, though it may be disallowed by a court, is hardly ever rescinded by the agreeing parties.

In the Commisso case, Robert Carter and I entered negotiations with the Crown in that spirit. Howard Morton, Q.C., the Director of the Crown Law Office, Criminal Division, had carriage of the prosecution. He was also Crown consultant to the Special Enforcement Unit (a joint venture of the RCMP, the Ontario Provincial Police, and the Metropolitan Toronto Police) investigating "organized crime". Morton was not only an able and senior prosecutor, but an old schoolmate. He and I went to law school together. I regarded him as a man of integrity, and I still do. I had (and have) the same view of his associate, Murray Segal. Neither Carter nor I thought that in discussing a case with lawyers such as Morton and Segal we would have any reason to depart from the usual, informal practices of the criminal bar. We did not go to the negotiating table with note-pads and tape recorders. Frankly, I would have felt foolish doing so — or needlessly confrontational.

At one point in the course of the discussions, Howard Morton mentioned that the police were investigating numerous other matters involving our clients on the basis of evidence vouchsafed by the Crown's star witness, the indomitable Cecil Kirby. These investigations, Morton said, might result in additional charges at some future date.

Although these matters were unrelated to the current charges against the Commissos, both Carter and I became concerned. Very concerned, in fact. We knew about pressures on informers, as outlined at the beginning of this chapter, and we wanted to make sure that the Crown would never proceed against our clients on Kirby's word alone.

In the current case it was not just Kirby's word against the Commisso brothers': the informer's testimony could be supported by taped conversations and some other evidence. This made the charges fair ball. What both Carter and I wanted to avoid was having Cosimo, Remo, or Michele Commisso stand in court one day facing *unsupported* allegations by someone like Kirby who had a direct interest in continuing to accuse other people of crimes.

Unsupported allegations from a self-confessed Satan's Choice enforcer wouldn't give most persons much cause to worry. If Kirby suddenly said to the police: "Oh, by the way, I just remembered that Mr. Solid Citizen wanted to hire me five years ago to break his competitor's legs — and I guess you owe me another thousand dollars for this information," the police might investigate, but, unless they turned up an awful lot of corroborating evidence, they would be most unlikely to lay a charge. (If they did, the Crown would be even more unlikely to get a conviction.)

But once people have been labelled "mobsters" and "members of organized crime", they can be vulnerable to even the most unsupported allegations. The police may be ready to charge them on the worst pathological liar's unlikeliest story — and, having been hauled into court, they may easily get convicted. Though the law requires proof of guilt beyond a reasonable doubt against organized criminals in the same way as it does against disorganized ones, the phrase "reasonable doubt" acquires an entirely different meaning in their case. An accused "mafioso" may have to show pictures of himself in outer space before his alibi would raise a reasonable doubt in many people's minds.

Charging the Commisso brothers on Kirby's word alone would have been simply unfair, I felt. As part of our plea negotiations, I wanted an undertaking from Howard Morton that no further charges would be laid against them just on Kirby's say-so, without corroboration. Morton and Segal didn't like the word "corroboration" — which has a very narrow legal meaning — and preferred the less specific word "confirmation". We discussed the matter at some length. Whether or not we succeeded in clearly defining what an acceptable *degree* of support for Kirby's evidence might be, both Robert Carter and I were absolutely certain in our own minds that Howard Morton agreed to the principle.

"You've known me long enough to know I wouldn't proceed on Kirby alone" was how I remembered Howard Morton's operative phrase. In substance, this was Robert Carter's recollection as well: "You know me," Morton said, as Carter remembered his key line. "I will not prosecute on the evidence of Mr. Kirby alone. Trust me."

As far as Carter and I were concerned, that was it. We certainly trusted the Crown. Once Morton had said that, nothing else was required. That's how deals are made between members of the criminal bar. Carter and I had concluded dozens and dozens of plea negotiations on the same basis — as, no doubt, had Morton and Segal. This deal was not as good as we would have hoped for — strict corroboration, as the word was then defined in law, would have been better — but the undertaking seemed clear to us. Kirby's word alone would not suffice to lay further charges against the Commisso brothers. Both Carter and I communicated this understanding to our respective clients.

Important as the matter was, it was not directly related to the current charges, so neither Carter nor I thought of it as anything that needed to be placed before Chief Justice Evans. It was simply something that might or might not arise at a future date, and we did not view it as having an immediate impact on what the Chief Justice had to weigh in connection with the plea negotiations. Accordingly, when I outlined the deal to Michael Moldaver before his appearance on my behalf before his Lordship, I did not include it in my briefing. There was no point in burdening Moldaver's mind with what then seemed an unnecessary detail. I never did that when asking him (or any other junior partner or associate) to deal on short notice with a relatively complex matter for me.

Carter was clearly of the same view. He did not bring up in court this part of our agreement with the Crown either.

Neither did Crown Attorneys Morton and Segal mention the matter before the Chief Justice — but for an entirely different reason. On their understanding of the terms reached during our plea negotiations they couldn't possibly have mentioned it because, as we would find out later, *they did not regard it as something on which we had come to an agreement at all.*

I would not learn about this for another year, though — until October 25, 1982, to be exact. On that day my associate Chris Buhr bumped into Howard Morton in a courthouse. Morton gave Buhr a handwritten note for me — a humorous message, in the tone that old schoolmates often employ with one another. The note simply said: "It's Chicken Little time."

I understood the message. It meant that the sky was falling. New charges were coming down on the Commisso brothers.

*4* One reason I understood Morton's note so quickly was because of a newspaper story quoting Cecil Kirby that appeared on the same day, written by Cal Miller in the *Toronto Sun*. Kirby was claiming that there were "a hundred" further charges against the Commisso brothers, but the police were just "sitting" on them. This was followed by a statement from a somewhat miffed police department spokesman essentially to the effect that Kirby was just trying to sell books and couldn't be relied on, but that there *would be* further charges.

At that point, of course, I didn't know whether these new charges would be based on Kirby's word alone, on Kirby's word supported by other evidence, or on some evidence that had nothing to do with Kirby at all. I expected to find out about the new charges on November 2, which was the date Morton and I set up for a meeting after I received his "Chicken Little" note. The truth is, by that time the nature of any new charges against the Commissos was not the focus of my primary interest. In the meantime I had devised an entirely different defence strategy to protect the interests of my clients.

This strategy was based on my conclusion that the Commisso brothers had no future in Canada. It wasn't just that the investigative, judicial, and penal authorities would never give them a break: I had no confidence that they would give them an *even* break — in other words, a fair deal. The system had come to view them as mobsters and public enemies. As far as the police and the prosecutors were concerned, they were lynchpins of organized crime. This was a view that simply precluded the presumption of innocence, or even that presumption contained in the very name of the institution to which the Commissos were sentenced: a penitentiary. That word implies that all incarcerated people are capable of penance — a view the authorities might never take of my clients.

It was not a question for me whether the authorities' view of the Commisso brothers had any merit or not; whether it was a somewhat justified or a wholly unjustified assessment of three human beings. I am neither a judge nor a Parole Board official. I'm a defence lawyer. No doubt there are people in our society whose legitimate function is to address their minds to these questions, but my task is different. My only legitimate function is to look out for the interests of my clients within the limits of the law. As long as I'm a defence lawyer I cannot and will not put my mind to any other question in connection with any person for whom I act.

I knew that so-called criminal "lynchpins" can get lynched in our system, at least metaphorically speaking. Their designation as "mobsters" puts them in a different ball game. They can no longer count on the protections or benefits of our judicial institutions. I fully expected, especially with new charges pending against them, that there would be no parole for the Commissos. They would have to stay in prison until the last day of their current sentences — by which time they might be required to begin serving some consecutive sentences for new convictions. If they ever got out of prison, they would be under suspicion and surveillance for the rest of their lives, with the authorities ever ready to harass or pin new charges on them, deserved or otherwise. Without a fundamental change in strategy, their lawyer could do little for such clients but collect his fees and watch them languish in jail.

So, addressing the only question that was for me to address as a defence lawyer, I concluded that the Commissos' best chance for a normal life outside a continual merry-go-round of courtrooms and prison lay in some arrangement whereby they would give up their Canadian citizenships and return to Italy, where they had been born. Such arrangements are quite complex, but there are precedents for them. Under some countries' laws a native-born person never loses his citizenship. At the same time, by our laws Canada is entitled to deport an alien. Therefore, if a naturalized Canadian renounces his Canadian citizenship, in theory it becomes possible for him to be deported to the country of his birth, provided that his native country accepts him under the requirements of *its* laws. Italy is one country whose laws do not exclude the possibility of such a deal.

International arrangements of this kind require lengthy and delicate negotiations. First of all, they require the co-operation and goodwill of the authorities, beginning with the office of the Attorney General. At a breakfast meeting with Ontario's then Attorney General, Roy McMurtry (which I mention mainly because, at a later point, the Crown would insist on questioning me about it in court), I discussed the matter and received his blessing to pursue it further within his department as well as at other levels of government.

Without the co-ordinated assistance of many government agencies such deals are impossible to set up. My argument to the authorities in Canada had to be that, *if* their view of the Commisso brothers as incorrigible mobsters was correct, Canada would be better off without them. Such an argument, of course, would hardly persuade the Italians to welcome them home with open arms: there the emphasis would have to be on why the Canadian authorities' assessment of the Commisso brothers was as exaggerated as I, as their defence lawyer, believed it to be.

This was the subject that I wanted to explore with Howard Morton on November 2, 1982. The new "Chicken Little" charges were secondary in my mind, whatever they were and whatever evidence supported them. If the Commissos were going back to Italy after serving some more time of their current eight-year sentences — which would be the essence of the new deal I was trying to put together — it would automatically dispose of all additional charges. In this context, my main concern on November 2 was not on whose evidence the new charges were being based, but that they should *not be laid at all until after Christmas*. It was for this that I wanted to secure Morton's co-operation. It would have given me two months to negotiate a deal between Canada and Italy, at least in principle, without burdening the Commissos' case with more outstanding charges.

In view of this, I listened in silence as Howard Morton told me that the new charges were being laid on Kirby's evidence alone, contrary to what I understood our deal to have been. I listened in silence when Morton explained that the initial reservations with which the police had viewed Kirby's stories were now replaced by full confidence in the veracity of the informer's evidence, so that they no longer had any hesitation about laying charges on Kirby's unsupported word. I listened in silence as Morton explained that since our last conversation the *Vetrovec* decision in the Supreme

Court of Canada had changed the legal requirements for corroboration (which was quite true, only it had little to do with what I understood our agreement to have been).

I listened in silence. I wasn't going to yell and scream at someone with whom I wanted to conclude a much more fundamental deal. When you're trying to sell a car, you don't yell at the potential buyer for having broken a headlight on a test drive — even assuming that you'd yell at him in any case, which is simply not my style. I don't believe in yelling: I believe in justice. If a dispute arises that can't be solved by negotiations, you solve it in court.

So, while I was dismayed at what I regarded as Morton's repudiation of our agreement, I said nothing. If that was the position he was taking, there was nothing for me to say — certainly not then and there. Instead, I concentrated on pursuing the Italian scenario with him. If that could be arranged, it would solve all other problems at one stroke.

Important as it was, Morton's co-operation would not have settled the Italian arrangements; his opposition, however, could have scuttled them. So, in the coming months, far from picking a fight with Morton over what I regarded as his reversal of our plea bargain, I did not even bring up the issue with him. (Later I'd be asked in court if I didn't feel hurt or betrayed. I found it an irrelevant question. What if I did? Clients do not retain a lawyer to feel hurt or betrayed over what he perceives as the injustices of the world. Clients retain lawyers to act in their best interests.)

Therefore, when the new charges were eventually laid against the Commisso brothers on Kirby's unsupported word, I decided to continue concentrating solely on arrangements for their possible repatriation to Italy — and I continued to be silent on what I believed to be a breach of the Crown's undertaking. Anything I might have said would have amounted to a declaration of war.

However, under the circumstances, it seemed best for both Carter and me to withdraw from actually acting for the Commissos on the new charges. We knew that we might have to testify in court in connection with the original plea negotiations, and it would not have been possible for us to be both defence lawyers and witnesses in the same case. On the new charges, Cosimo, Remo, and Michele Commisso would be defended by two very experienced lawyers, Louis D. Silver, Q.C., and Irwin Koziebrocki.

At the same time I was still keeping my fingers crossed that the issue of the plea negotiations would never have to come to court. What I wanted was not a dispute but a solution. Even a judgment favourable to our side on whether or not proceeding against the Commissos on Kirby's word alone amounted to a breach of an under-taking on the Crown's part — and therefore to an abuse of process — would have meant, in my view, winning a battle and losing the war.

The last thing I wanted was to have to stand up in court and say about Morton: "Yes, he promised," while he was saying: "Oh no I didn't." Even with an assurance of winning on the issue, I found the prospect of such a contest fruitless and childish. More importantly, while it might have achieved a short-term result for our clients, it was more likely to hurt them in the long run. It would certainly have meant saying good-bye to the Italian deal.

In fact, I was very dubious of winning in any case. Once I said, "He promised," and Morton replied, "I didn't," what could I say except "Yes, he did too"? Where would such an argument take a judge? The plea negotiations consisted of four lawyers talking in a room. There was no record of what was being said. There wasn't, as there almost never is, any *proof*.

Needless to say, the absence of proof in such disputes always works to the detriment of the party that brings the allegation. It can hardly be otherwise. We would be the "accusers", so the burden of proof would be placed on us. We would have to satisfy the court on the balance of probabilities that there *was* an undertaking given by the Crown to the defence, and that the Crown did not live up to it. If Morton and Segal made a similar allegation against Carter and me, the *onus probandi* (as this burden is called in law) would, of course, be on the Crown, but as long as the allegation was being made by Carter and me the onus would have to be on the defence.

How could the defence possibly discharge such an onus? When two eminent and respectable lawyers say one thing, and two emi-nent and respectable lawyers say something else, how could a judge determine whom to believe or whose recollection to prefer? And if he believed the four lawyers equally, he would have to find against the two who were alleging the breach — in this case Carter and me. That's what having the burden of proof means.

Going into battle from an untenable position is not my idea of a good time — but sometimes it cannot be avoided. On March 3, 1983, an information was sworn out against the Commisso brothers alleging twenty-five new charges based (mostly) on Cecil Kirby's unsupported evidence. The Italian deal — I was still somewhat hopeful about it — was far from being settled. Louis Silver and Irwin Koziebrocki, as the Commissos' new counsel, felt that they had no choice. They immediately entered a motion asking Judge Arthur K. Meen — who was to begin the preliminary inquiry into the new charges — to quash the information on the grounds that, because of the terms of our earlier plea bargain, the Crown's charges against the Commisso brothers amounted to an abuse of process.

"The die is cast," Caesar said crossing the Rubicon — in a rather dubious tone of voice as it seemed to his contemporaries. I was feeling equally dubious. Carter and I were going to be witnesses in a highly publicized, highly unusual (if not entirely unprecedented) court action between the defence and the prosecution: we were asking a judge to hold the Crown to what we believed was its word.

Frankly, I didn't think it could be done. The papers tagged the hearing "the battle of legal titans", but I felt titanic only in the uneasy sense of sailing into an iceberg.

The evidence on the motion was taken in the course of four days in August and September 1983. The Crown was represented by a young lawyer, Harry Black, an associate and friend of Howard Morton's. The rather aggressive, accusatory style in which he cross-examined me on the witness stand somewhat surprised me: it seemed an unnecessary exertion for the Crown, which held, from the outset, most of the cards. However, it was Black's case and he was certainly entitled to lead it in any style he wished.

Essentially, Black kept asking me why I did not complain or protest to Morton right away if I thought that the terms of our agreement were being breached. It was true that I didn't, and I gave Black my reasons. It's not a witness's place to make comments, so I resisted saying that such questions were a little disingenuous for a Crown counsel who ought to understand the process as well as anybody. It's like asking someone why he didn't get into a big fight with a policeman just when the officer was at the point of considering whether or not to give him a parking ticket.

Black also did a thorough job of establishing that Carter and I did not have any written proof of what we understood our agreement to have been, not even some memos to file. This, too, was absolutely true — and just as disingenuous. With rare exceptions, as Black knew well enough, that's not how plea negotiations are conducted between criminal lawyers. In any case, it wasn't how I preferred (or found it necessary) to conduct them in the past, and I said so on the witness stand.

All this was par for the course. Had it not been for Black's tone of voice, I would not even have considered it hardball. Once a case of this nature comes to court, one can expect nothing else.

The hardball came from a surprise witness called by the Crown after the hearing had been recessed for a few days. The witness was Michael Moldaver. By that time he was no longer my law partner.

There's little doubt in my mind that, had Moldaver still been my partner at the time, the Crown would never have approached him to appear as a witness. The reason was simple: Black, Morton, and Segal could not have known what Moldaver's evidence was going to be. They were not privy to how much I might have told my ex-partner about the terms of our plea agreement when, back in August 1981, I asked him to appear on my behalf in front of Chief Justice Evans. Had the Crown asked him privately, it would have been perfectly open to Moldaver to say: "If you want to know what I know, subpoena me and I'll tell it in court." As my partner, it would have been unthinkable for him to say anything else.

In that case, of course, the Crown would never have called him. You don't call a witness unless you expect his evidence to be favourable to your side. For all the Crown knew, I could have briefed Moldaver on everything about our plea agreement, including my understanding that the Crown was not going to proceed on any new charges on Kirby's evidence alone. In fact, Moldaver didn't know this: it had been totally unnecessary for me to brief him about it for what he was expected to do in court that day. But ordinarily the Crown could not risk calling him as a witness, having no idea what his evidence would be.

As it happened, since Moldaver was no longer my partner, a policeman was sent to him to ask. At that point Moldaver told the officer — truthfully — that I had never told him about that aspect of the deal.

A very able lawyer, Moldaver was aware of what he could have said to the Crown. As a matter of fact, he used that very expression with the new defence counsel of his former clients in the hallway just before he went into the courtroom to testify. When Louis Silver asked him what his evidence was going to be, Moldaver replied: "You'll hear it in court."

In fairness to Moldaver, he was suckered by the Crown. As he later explained to me, he had spoken to the policeman, a Sergeant Sandelli (who happened to be his friend) off the record and in confidence. He never expected the Crown to use this information to drag him into court and give evidence to the potential detriment of his former clients. Moldaver told me that he "yelled" at Harry Black when he found out about it, but by that time it was too late. I believed Moldaver; I could even picture the scene. Still, as he ought to have known, everybody plays hardball.

Howard Morton (as his evidence was later summed up by Judge Meen) "categorically denied ever having made any statement to the effect that he would not proceed on the evidence of Kirby alone." Morton's point was that with the police investigation still being "in an embryonic stage" he couldn't possibly have included the new charges in his original negotiations with us. Murray Segal supported his colleague's position in all essentials.

For our part, Robert Carter and I remembered what we remembered, and said so on the witness stand.

The result was a foregone conclusion. "This Court," ruled Judge Meen on January 11, 1984, "does not for one moment question the intellectual and genuine integrity of either Mr. Greenspan or Mr. Carter, nor for that matter does it question the integrity of Mr. Morton, Mr. Segal and Mr. Moldaver." Nevertheless, his Honour concluded, "I find that the applicants have not made their case on the balance of probabilities."

It was, as far as I was concerned, an impeccable ruling in law. On the evidence, given the burden of proof, Judge Meen could not have concluded otherwise.

After it was all over, Harry Black was quoted in the press as saying that, given the result, I ought to apologize to Howard Morton. It was a remark that intrigued me. True, we said that the Crown had reneged on a deal and we couldn't prove it, which is why the Crown won and we lost. But it was news to me that contestants ought to apologize to each other after an honest fight. In light of a judgment that confirmed our mutual integrity, I would not have thought that Howard Morton ought to apologize to me. Or Black himself, come to think of it.

About two months earlier, on November 15, 1983, the body of Paul Volpe was discovered at Toronto airport in the trunk of his BMW sedan. He had been shot twice in the back of the head. For the Commisso brothers in prison, who had in 1981 been convicted of a murder conspiracy against Volpe — and who in November 1983 were still waiting for Judge Meen's ruling — Volpe's death could not have occurred at a worse time. As even James Dubro, a journalist given to an uncritical acceptance of all myths about organized crime, was moved to remark: "the Commissos were naturally trying to keep out of trouble at the time . . . they seemed genuinely disconcerted by the timing of Volpe's murder." This had not prevented either Cecil Kirby or various police sources from being quoted as speculating — in the complete absence of any evidence — that the Commissos were responsible for Volpe's death.

What did my experience teach me? Nothing. I still refuse to initiate an exchange of written documents with the Crown concerning a negotiated agreement. I hold with Earl Levy, the president of the Ontario Criminal Lawyers Association, that requiring written memoranda of plea negotiations is a needless insult to fellow members of the bar.

Other than the Commisso case, I have had only one brief disagreement with a prosecutor about a negotiated plea in my entire practice. It happened about ten years ago. My childhood friend, Crown Attorney Harvey Frankel, remembered one number for a proposed jail term for a client, and I remembered another. We agreed to abide by the recollection of the investigating police officer. As it happened, the policeman went with my number. If I did not believe that, on the whole, it is possible to practise law in this manner, I would have no desire to practise law any more.

*When Greenspan finished his story, George Jonas felt that his friend's inside account of the famous Commisso deal needed an outsider's postscript. There is virtually no legal procedure that is so little understood as the plea-negotiating process. Nor is there one surrounded by so much controversy. Even members of the legal profession, including some judges, seem more than a little embarrassed by it. They are reluctant to explain it in plain language, or perhaps even to face it realistically themselves.*

*In 1971, appearing in a case called* Draskovic *before the Ontario*

*Court of Appeal, Greenspan brought up the dread word before the then Chief Justice, George Gale. In those days, even more than today, plea bargaining as a concept was supposed to knock only at the tradesmen's entrance of the law — yet there was Greenspan, boldly ringing with it at the front door.*

*"Hold it, Mr. Greenspan," said his Lordship, frowning. "What do you mean by this . . . this expression? What is this 'plea bargaining' supposed to be?"*

*"I'm just a year out of law school," replied Greenspan, "and I don't want to be the first to break the news, but you, my Lord, talked about plea bargaining before the Law Society of Upper Canada."*

*The Chief Justice turned purple. "If this is brought up in court," he said, "I'll never go to those lectures again."*

Not surprisingly, the Chief Justice of Ontario was perfectly aware of the concept and practice of plea bargaining. Everybody is. Everybody does it, but not everyone is prepared to acknowledge or talk about it. There is considerable reluctance still to give plea bargaining official status.

In civil cases, of course, no one quarrels with the idea of negotiated settlements at all. On the contrary, people consider it wiser to settle a case out of court whenever possible than to contest it. There is much agreement about a negotiated deal being not only more prudent and efficient, but perhaps even seemlier than two parties fighting like fishwives to the bitter end. This view — which is probably quite correct — permits all negotiations between the two sides to be conducted openly and proudly, as it were, and without the slightest reluctance to document the process every step of the way.

To some extent, this is true even of quasi-criminal or regulatory offences. Most municipalities will print their offer of a plea bargain, proudly and openly, right on the face of a parking ticket. "Plead guilty within so many days," the city fathers say in effect, "and we'll reduce your penalty by half. Hesitate or fight us, and we'll double it." (No one talks about "discount justice". No one says — though perhaps someone should — that giving a fifty-per-cent discount for prompt payment makes illegal parking half as expensive for the wealthy as for working people who may not be able to spare ten or twenty dollars until the next payday.)

But when it comes to alleged breaches of the Criminal Code, suddenly everyone becomes shy about negotiated settlements. Not so shy as *to refrain from making them, only shy enough not to spell them out. Very few lawyers would reduce a plea bargain to writing. Very few lawyers would even admit why they wouldn't want to engage in written agreements.*

*The real reason is not just some custom hallowed by time. It's not that criminal lawyers are so gentlemanly and old-fashioned that putting pen to paper would seem intrinsically offensive to them. Nor is the real reason simple hypocrisy. The real reason is that plea bargaining, like politics, is the art of the possible. Plea bargains are often based on utility. The trouble is, when it comes to criminal law, visible utility may appear to run counter to visible justice. Since "justice must be seen to be done," most people in the administration of justice prefer to keep utility invisible.*

*Negotiating settlements can be as prudent and efficient in criminal cases as it is in civil disputes: that's why plea bargaining continues to flourish. But criminal cases are not merely matters of prudence or efficiency. They involve moral issues in a way that most civil cases do not.*

*When Mr. A and Mr. B settle a contract dispute, they can pretty much settle it any way they find mutually expedient; the public doesn't really care. In a sense, it's none of the public's business. The public does care, though, if "guilty" Mr. A gets away with it — or "innocent" Mr. B goes to jail. Yet, as the Commisso affair illustrates, that's what plea bargaining is all about: Remo agrees to spend eight years in prison so that Cosimo won't have to spend his entire life in jail. Most instances of plea bargaining are not so extreme, but they all involve some measure of utility for both sides. The Crown's original charge, which is often far more serious than warranted by the evidence, also has this end in view: an end rooted in utility rather than in justice. Where is the lawyer who would be willing to spell out the terms of this process in writing? Where is the lawyer who'd want to face up to its full implications even in his own mind?*

*At the same time we all know that plea negotiations are in the public interest. We know it instinctively. We know that without them costs would skyrocket and the court system would bog down. We know that some genuinely guilty people would go free while other defendants, over-charged by zealous prosecutors or policemen, would run the risk of a wrongful conviction (or a vengeful penalty) without an opportunity to bargain for a reduction of their charges (or sentences) in exchange for a guilty plea.*

*There is a public interest in pure, abstract, maybe even "poetic" justice which plea bargains do not necessarily serve. But there is also a public interest in utility, which could not be achieved without plea bargains. While justice and utility need not invariably clash, they do not invariably coincide. This, in turn, is probably the main reason — a far bigger reason than some gentlemanly fastidiousness on the part of the criminal bar — why plea bargains can seldom be reduced to writing. It is also the main reason why the process is unlikely to survive if the people involved in it can't trust, or won't honour, a nod or a handshake.*

## NOTES

p.74, l.20: From a *fifth estate* program transcript as quoted in *Mob Rule* by James Dubro, pp. 220-1 (Macmillan of Canada, 1985).

p.75, l.19: For instance, during the controversy that erupted in connection with Kirby's case, in a letter to the editor Ontario's Attorney General Roy McMurtry emphasized that Kirby had immunity only *vis-à-vis* certain of his crimes; he could still be charged with others.

p.75, l.29: In 1977 the Wah Kew Chop Suey House was bombed in Toronto's Chinatown. The explosion killed a cook by the name of Chong Yin Quan. In 1980 an explosion in a fashionable Toronto restaurant called Napoleon injured three women.

p.76, l.20: In the period prior to the 1982 S.C.C. decision in *Vetrovec*, corroboration had come to have a very technical meaning. In summary, the jury had to be warned that they ought to view with caution the evidence of an accomplice unless it was corroborated by other evidence — meaning testimony that affects the accused by connecting or tending to connect him with the crime. In other words, this had to be "evidence which confirms in some material particular not only the evidence that the crime has been committed, but also that the prisoner committed [it.]" (From *R. v. Bakersville*, 1916.)

p.77, l.35: I'm using "non-ethnic" in the colloquial sense. In Canada, it usually means people of Anglo-Saxon, Anglo-Celtic, French, or maybe northern European background.

p.82, l.17: In fact, the defence couldn't really rescind a plea bargain even if it wanted to. If, for instance, a defendant changed his mind and pleaded not guilty at the last minute, the Crown would simply contest the case as if no negotiations had ever taken place. Only the Crown could change its mind by, say, arguing for a stiffer penalty than the one agreed upon *after* a guilty plea — but it just wouldn't. If a Crown Attorney made a habit of doing that, not only would he face censure by the courts, his superiors, and his peers, but he would very quickly run out of defence lawyers with whom to deal.

p.83, l.12: In addition, at that point Carter and I still had the tactical choice of waiting until the police completed their investigation. The Commisso brothers didn't have to go to trial on any of the matters relating to Kirby until the Crown finished gathering all the evidence. Going to trial on all matters would enable a jury to separate those of Kirby's allegations against our clients that were supported by other evidence from those that were not. However, by pleading guilty on the current charges, and then facing a new set of unsupported allegations, the Commisso brothers would be put in a highly prejudicial situation. If they testified in their own defence at a subsequent trial, the Crown could bring out that they had pleaded guilty on Kirby's allegations before — but the jury would never know that those allegations were supported by other evidence, and not Kirby's word alone.

p.90, l.12: *Yacta alea est* in Caesar's own language. I mention this to prove to Mr. Callaghan of Niagara Falls that his considerable patience in teaching me Latin had not been an utter waste of time.

p.92, l.31: Judge Meen's reasoning in his judgment seemed to indicate that he was more inclined to credit Morton's and Segal's memory than Carter's or mine. (He asked rhetorically if we did not "delude" ourselves in thinking that we had a deal when we didn't.) Judge Meen is a former cabinet minister, with ample experience with the civil service but much less at the criminal bar. He appeared to find it significant that Carter and I wrote no memos, either to each other or "to file". Still, this was not Judge Meen's ruling; his ruling was merely that the defence did not discharge the burden of proof on a balance of probabilities. Some other judge who came to the bench from a criminal law practice might have been disinclined to employ Judge Meen's reasoning, but any judge (unless he positively disbelieved the Crown) would have had to make the same ruling as Judge Meen.

p.93, l.11: Dubro, *Mob Rule*, p. 234.

p.94, l.27: As Harvey Strosberg, Q.C., points out, the civil rules in Ontario may penalize a winner in a civil suit by requiring him to pay the loser's costs if the winner did not accept a reasonable written offer of settlement.

*The one-time Provincial Court house in the town of Milton, Ontario, had always been referred to by local people as the "Pigeon Palace on Brown Street". Judge Douglas Latimer recalled that in winter it was next to impossible to hear in the courtrooms because of the pigeons: "[They] were all crowded against the windows to get warm and they were cooing like mad."*

*The pigeons, in fact, were not the worst creatures in the courthouse menagerie. Shortly before the 121-year-old building closed its doors forever in May 1978, Greenspan had been arguing a case there in front of Judge William Sharpe. Suddenly a movement caught his eye near a corner of the false ceiling.*

*Aghast, he turned to the judge.*

*"There are hornets there," he said.*

*"Yes, I know," said Judge Sharpe. "The hornets have been here for years."*

*It was true. As Burlington* Spectator *reporter John Burman was to note later, the Milton hornets' victims over the years had included, in addition to various clerks, constables, and journalists, such members of the judiciary as Judge M. J. Cloney from Toronto and the late Judge James Black.*

*"Your Honour doesn't understand," said Greenspan. "I can't stay here. The hornets are going to bite me, I can't concentrate, and I can't stay in the courtroom with them."*

*Saying this, Greenspan dashed outside, with a somewhat surprised judge following him a few minutes later. A bit calmer by then, Greenspan apologized and explained that he was allergic to hornet stings. "I can't do it," he said to Judge Sharpe. "They make me very, very sick."*

*It was the truth, though Eddie's allergy was at least partly psychological. The fact is, Greenspan is afraid of anything that crawls or flies; any creature that does anything other, as he puts it, than "act like a human being". This includes cats, horses, dogs (and, as Guy Kay remarked once, occasionally articling students). It need not even be fauna, as Eddie's discomfort embraces grass, bushes, and trees. For Greenspan, a rose by any other name is prickly and to be avoided at all costs.*

*Of all manifestations of nature, Eddie is at home only with human nature. Like Terence, the ancient Roman playwright, he finds that nothing human is alien to him — but virtually everything else is, whether animated by organic forces or technology. Greenspan looks at microchips with much the same suspicion as he does at animals or crystals, and is no more at home with a home computer than with a lap-dog. He writes in longhand, having never mastered the mechanical complexities of a typewriter, and he shaves with a safety razor, not having the patience required to operate an electric shaving-kit.*

*In view of this, it is not surprising that Eddie had not been a marked success as a Boy Scout.*

*As a small kid Eddie had never been to camp, until, at thirteen, the summer after his father died, his mother sent him and his younger brother Brian to Camp Shalom, near Gravenhurst, Ontario. Camp Shalom — "peace" in Hebrew — was not exactly a wealthy camp. It was, as Greenspan would describe it later, more like the camp in the movie* Meatballs. *In fact, the year Eddie was sent there was the first year that the camp could finally afford to buy a few canoes. They celebrated the occasion by immediately organizing a canoe trip.*

*The group of kids canoed along the system of lakes in Algonquin Provincial Park, Eddie serving as what he termed "the middleman" in one of the vessels. This meant that the others seated Eddie as a passenger in the middle of the boat, well away from the paddles, in a spot where he was less likely to do significant damage. Wise as the precaution was, subsequent events proved it to be insufficient.*

*The first day passed without incident. Eddie was sitting in the canoe, knowing that the North did not suit him and he did not suit the North — assuming that he was in the North now, about which he wasn't sure, though he rather suspected it. Still, he kept canoeing, portaging, and carrying supplies bravely (or, as he put it later, "doing all the things that the original explorers in this country did so that I wouldn't have to do this").*

*Then the night came. With the night came the bears.*

*Eddie had been huddling near the campfire, shivering with cold, wondering what he was doing there in the wilderness, when the shouted warning came that there was a bear in the nearby garbage dump.*

A bear! Eddie became hysterical. He remembered once seeing a bear in the zoo, and being nervous in spite of the iron bars between them. Now there was a bear running free less than fifty yards from him. His mind was not eased when he noticed that the two adults accompanying the kids, though making reassuring remarks, were also sticking close to the campfire.

The sounds of the bear rummaging in the garbage gradually subsided, but Eddie didn't sleep a wink that night. "I couldn't believe that my mother," he said later, "my mother, would send me to a camp."

Daylight came. Things began to look a little less menacing as the sun rose in the sky, until someone shouted: "They're back!" It was "they" because this time it was not only one bear, but two bears, or (according to Eddie's estimate) a whole flock of bears exploring the delights of the garbage. This was evidently not the spot for camping. The group decided to make a break for the canoes.

Eddie reached his canoe uneventfully. It was the one that was supposed to carry supplies for the entire group. The food itself had been packed into a huge bag, which was still on shore. As Eddie stood up in the canoe, one of the boys picked up the bag and pitched it at him.

This, in retrospect, was a mistake. As Eddie fell out of the canoe, the bag went sailing by him. There was a big splash, frightening the bears. After a few seconds the rings of water subsided and everything became quiet again. Eventually Eddie bobbed to the surface. The bag of food did not. It went straight to the bottom of the lake.

This was the end of the canoe trip. Camp Shalom could not afford to lay in new supplies. "Instead of the bears," Eddie remembered, "they decided to blame me. Scarred me for life." In fact, Greenspan could probably have coped with the trauma of being blamed if at least it had meant that he would not have to return to the wilderness again.

It was not to be, however. Mrs. Emma Greenspan, having hardened her heart, kept driving Eddie back to Camp Shalom year after year. In the end he was actually made a camp counsellor, proving the axiom that sooner or later everyone is promoted to the level of his own incompetence. One year when the Scoutmaster failed to show up in camp, his duties were entrusted to Greenspan.

Greenspan knew nothing about being a Scoutmaster, in keeping with his earlier tradition of not knowing anything about being a Scout. He had no trouble, however, reading the literature in which the mysteries of tying knots were adequately explained. This way, by carefully staying *one lesson ahead of his young charges, the new Scoutmaster's summer was progressing to what seemed to be a satisfactory conclusion.*

*Then a devastating incident occurred. It was caused by the author of one of Eddie's Scouting books, who, abandoning the safety of knots, proceeded to provide instructions on how to cut down a tree.*

*For reasons not easily analysed, the idea appealed to Greenspan enormously. It seemed to him that the education of his Cubs would not be complete without their witnessing a tree being chopped down. Emboldened by his success with knots, Eddie read and made careful notes on the new chapter about trees. The next morning, with an axe over his shoulder and followed by a group of excited ten-year-olds wearing their little white T-shirts and their "Young Judea" kerchiefs around their necks, Eddie set out for the nearest object on the horizon which he could recognize as a tree.*

*The project began promisingly enough. The tall growth of vegetable matter by the roadside was, in fact, a tree, and Greenspan started chopping away at it with his axe, explaining to the Cubs what he was doing every step of the way. The cut in the trunk became deeper and deeper. The cream of Young Judea watched with fascination as Eddie gave the tree a final whack, whereupon it twisted and fell. It fell, moreover, exactly in the direction Eddie had expected it to fall, well away from the road and the children. That was not the problem.*

*The problem was that Greenspan, whose attention had been riveted on the tree itself, had not looked up before starting to chop it down. Had he looked up, he might possibly have noticed the hydro wires running alongside the road. As it was, the first thing he noticed was a curious sizzling sound as the falling tree hit the wires. This was followed by a puff of smoke and a shower of sparks as the tree continued shivering, sizzling, and bouncing up and down.*

*The wires ran along the road to a small hydro station a few hundred yards away. It was easily visible from where Eddie and his Cub Scouts were standing. For this reason they were treated to a spectacular sight as the transformer blew up and burst into flames.*

*The electricity was cut all around the lake. The lights went out from cottage country to Gravenhurst.*

*At this point Greenspan did an extremely sensible thing. He turned on his heel and started running back to Camp Shalom, followed by about twenty-five utterly delighted Cub Scouts. That morning's outing with their Scoutmaster had proved to be the highlight of their summer.*

The director of Camp Shalom also reacted sensibly to what had taken place. He packed Greenspan some lunch, then sent him through the woods to a nearby area called Lionshead. From this high ground, Eddie could watch all day the black-and-white cruisers of the Ontario Provincial Police stopping by the camp to investigate cottagers' reports that they had seen a group of tots with kerchiefs around their necks running away from the site of the explosion that morning, led by a big guy carrying an axe.

After this youthful incident, Greenspan continued his uneasy coexistence with life on earth. His first trip to the Loire Valley with his bride Suzy was marred by an encounter with an enormous fly. The fly dwelt in one of the châteaux beside the historic French river, and its favourite chamber happened to be the one in which Greenspan and his wife decided to spend the night.

This guest-chamber was formerly the château's library. It was large and impressive, with solid oak beams running along its high-vaulted ceiling. It was on top of one of these beams that the fly had been sleeping when Eddie and Suzy entered the room. Hearing their voices, the dipterous insect woke up. Annoyed by the intrusion of the Canadians, it started flying around the room. Greenspan (as well as Suzy, who shares Eddie's outlook, not just on dipterons but on wildlife in general) froze.

The fly was sailing through the air with a deep, majestic rumble. According to Eddie, it sounded like a buzz-saw, though Suzy thought that it was more like an operatic baritone clearing his throat: Beh-beh-beh-beh-beh.

"Do something," said Eddie to his wife.

"Me?" Suzy asked. "Moi? You do something yourself!"

But there was nothing to be done. Discerning the murderous intentions of the foreigners, the Loire Valley fly kept its distance. Once in a while it would feign a diving attack, scattering its foes, then punch in the afterburners to regain the safety of altitude provided by the vaulted architecture of the Gothic period. Eddie's boldest strategic move was to mount the table, brandishing a rolled-up copy of Le Figaro. Though not devoid of tactical imagination, this proved inadequate to the task. To the end the fly retained its mastery of the airspace over the battlefield. Neither of the Greenspans slept easy that night.

It would serve no purpose to relate similar incidents, of which there are many, from Greenspan's life. It might even be needlessly depressing. Though one or two of the encounters ended in the paying of the ultimate *penalty by the odd incautious bug, on the whole Eddie could not fight the insects even to a draw. In an entomic sense, Greenspan's existence has been a disaster.*

*He has had much better luck with earthquakes.*

*Relative to other nations, earthquakes have not been a major part of the Canadian experience. Greenspan has devoted a certain part of his life to remedying this apparent lack. The first opportunity beckoned to him in Athens, and he took it.*

*This was in the late seventies, when a number of illegal immigrants from Greece living in Toronto were being defrauded by a man who told them that, for a sum of money, he could get them landed-immigrant status in Canada. The Greeks were to meet him, with the money in hand, in the building of the immigration department. When the illegal immigrants came, the man would take their money, then denounce them to the authorities on the spot.*

*The racket worked for a while. The immigration department would ship the illegals back to Greece, leaving no witnesses in Canada for the prosecution.*

*Finally Bruce Shilton, the federal prosecutor in charge of the case, decided to take commission evidence in Greece from the victims. He asked Greenspan to go to Athens and act as commissioner. This is a quasi-judicial function, somewhat like a referee, and it involves sitting in a courtroom while lawyers for the prosecution and the defence examine and cross-examine the witnesses.*

*The problem was that, at that particular time, no one was sitting in a courtroom in Athens. The law courts were closed. All public buildings were closed, because successive waves from a continuous earthquake kept hitting the city. Much of the population of the Greek capital was living in tents in the streets. The shifting plates of earth lay along a fault extending to Rumania in the north, having recently devastated that country's capital, Bucharest, with a loss of 10,000 lives.*

*Greenspan knew this, like other readers of the daily press, but while he had strong views on hornets and flies, he had no particular views on earthquakes. If anything, he suspected that reports about the devastation of earthquakes might be grossly exaggerated. To some extent he attributed such reports to the phobias and hysterical reaction of overly sensitive people in Europe and the Orient. They always tended to go on about earthquakes and tidal waves, neither of which had given Greenspan the slightest concern over the years. Hornets, yes. Eddie could* understand how a strong man might quail before hornets. But earth-quakes, no.

Having persuaded the rest of the Canadian lawyers that there was nothing to fear, Greenspan checked into his Athens hotel with them. The sight of the tents in the streets did not bother him. Greeks were known to be excitable. The fact that their hotel was nearly empty did not concern him either. Foreign tourists were notoriously excitable, too.

What gave Eddie his first pause was the crack in the bathroom wall at the Canadian Embassy, where the commission evidence was being taken. Not immediately, because it was just an ordinary crack, such as one may see in the plaster of any bathroom. Except that, only a couple of hours later, it became bigger. In fact, it became twice as long. No crack that Eddie had ever seen before had behaved in this particular fashion.

His colleagues noticed Greenspan becoming thoughtful and intro-spective over dinner.

By the second day the crack had gone right around the wall. It appeared to Greenspan that the entire top part of the bathroom was becoming separated from the bottom part, perhaps even tilting slightly. Occasionally the fissure would emit a strange crackling noise.

Eddie began looking at the people of Athens in a different light. They seemed to be possessed of a maturity he had overlooked before. The Greeks were a sturdy people, he felt, with a measure of common sense. On reflection, it appeared to Greenspan that common sense might be the Greeks' strongest feature. They seemed positively awash in common sense. Eddie started wondering what it would be like to live in a tent.

Healthy, without question. Quite comfortable, too. Under the blue skies of Greece a tent was definitely the place in which to live. These Athenians were very, very smart. "They live in these beautiful tents," said Eddie on the third day to the Toronto lawyer Al Bickerton, "while we're sitting in a tilting courtroom like a bunch of schmucks. What are we doing here?"

As he flew out of Athens after the fourth day, Eddie became con-vinced that earthquakes were pointless. They did not make for a good story. If nothing happened to one in an earthquake, the story about it would lack a punch line. If something did happen, the opportunity for telling the story might no longer arise. In that sense, hornets were better.

Notwithstanding such considerations, Eddie encountered another earthquake in St. Catharines, Ontario.

This was towards the end of the famous trial of the Ontario million-aire Helmuth Buxbaum for the murder of his wife, Hanna. Questionable as Buxbaum's life may have been in some other respects, he had always been a highly religious man. He was an elder of the Baptist church, and his home outside London, Ontario, was plastered from top to bottom with biblical quotations and religious sayings.

Greenspan began his jury address. He was in the middle of telling the court about Buxbaum's innocence when the earth started shaking. Later it crossed Greenspan's mind that it might have been something he had said.

At the time, however, Eddie was much too involved in his jury address to even notice the earthquake (which registered a respectable five points on the Richter scale). All he saw was the horrified look in the jurors' eyes, and that, for some reason, the journalists were getting up and running out of the room. Then he heard the trial judge, Mr. Justice John O'Driscoll, saying: "Mr. Greenspan! Mr. Greenspan!" Looking around, he noticed that the chandelier in the courtroom was swinging to and fro.

Greenspan stopped talking and, somewhat annoyed at the interruption, left the courtroom along with the judge. When the earth was no longer shaking, Eddie started thinking about the long and notorious trial. It occurred to him that bringing the jury back immediately might not be a good idea. He couldn't be sure if the jury was in any mood to listen to suggestions about Buxbaum's innocence even under ideal circumstances, let alone following an earthquake. But Mr. Justice O'Driscoll wanted the proceedings to continue right away, so Greenspan had no choice.

When court resumed, he stepped up to his lectern to face twelve fidgeting jurors. What could he possibly say to them to recapture their attention?

"For my next trick," he said, "I'm going to part the waters of Lake Ontario. . . ."

There was only one known example of Greenspan's exhibiting a friendly attitude to a creature of the natural order. It occurred one evening in 1977.

Earlier that day George Jonas had had some business in the offices of Bob Schulz Productions, the well-known makers of TV commercials, who were engaged at the time in shooting a television spot for a popular beverage known as "Baby Duck". The star of the commercial was, predictably, a baby duck. The shoot had started out with several crates of the little yellow ducklings, but, in spite of the studio personnel's best efforts, only a few aspiring starlets remained alive at the end of the arduous shooting day. The dry air under the hot studio lights proved to be too much for most.

Jonas, who is possessed of a sentimental streak, decided to rescue two of the survivors. He gave them some water and took them home in a box. That evening Greenspan saw the ducklings in Toronto's Sutton Place Apartments, where Jonas was living at the time. To his friend's utter amazement, Eddie not only showed a keen interest in the fluffy little creatures but actually asked Jonas to let him take them home for his daughter Julianna, then about three years old.

Jonas was only too glad to oblige. Earlier he had given the ducklings some breadcrumbs, which they had lustily devoured. Ducklings have a habit of trotting after any large, moving object, and, having decided that Jonas must be Mother Duck, they had been following him around the apartment. That would have been fine, except that, anatomically, a duckling is nothing but an oesophagus, eager at one end and irresponsible at the other. Jonas had a brown carpet, which clashed with the ducklings' favourite colour, green.

Gingerly, Greenspan claimed the box with the recaptured ducklings nestling inside, and took them home to Julianna.

It would be an exaggeration to say that Suzy Greenspan received the ducklings into her home with any degree of enthusiasm, but, somewhat to her husband's surprise, she actually accepted them. The enthusiasm came from Julianna, who adored the ducklings and started petting them right away.

Alas, baby ducks are delicate creatures. They can only stand so much petting from an enthusiastic three-year-old. By the next day one of the ducklings was dead. It was obvious that the life of the remaining duckling could only be saved by removing it from the Greenspan home — but where?

Eddie summoned up all his knowledge of the great outdoors, and he came up with Grenadier Pond in Toronto's High Park. He could recall seeing other ducks in Grenadier Pond — in fact, he could remember them beyond a reasonable doubt, to a point of moral certainty. Grenadier was actually an effluence of Lake Ontario. Surely the ecology of such a great lake could support one more baby duck.

Greenspan drove to High Park with the duckling in the front seat *beside him. It happened to be a cold, windy day. There weren't too many strollers in the park to observe a portly gentleman in a well-tailored overcoat alight from his car, carrying a small yellow duck. Greenspan carried the duckling into the bushes, and over to the near shore of the lake.*

*He had remembered it correctly. There was a bunch or a swarm of other ducks swimming away out in the middle of the pond. He had clearly come to the right place. "Go, duck," said Greenspan, placing the little duckling gently into the lapping waves. "Go and join your friends."*

*Eddie turned and walked back to his car. He unlocked the door, got in, and started the engine. However, he could not put the car into gear. Something was troubling him. Perhaps it was only his imagination, but those other ducks, the ones in the middle of the pond — well, somehow they did not quite look like his duck. They seemed to be ducks of a different feather. They looked like — that was it — they looked like wild ducks.*

*Perhaps a domestic duck could not make friends with them at all. Perhaps they would never take a fluffy middle-class duckling under their wings. An ex-showbusiness, Bob Schulz Productions duck-baby; a baby duck who had, after all, come close to making it on the silver screen.*

*Greenspan switched off the motor. He got out of the car and began walking back to the pond. The wind was chilly, and he became convinced that, apart from everything else, the duckling must be cold. It seemed to him that when he put the duckling into the lake it somehow did not take to it like a duck is supposed to take to water. No: he was now certain that the little duckling had looked back at him with a despairing glance of abandonment on its face.*

*Greenspan started running.*

*The duckling was still there, bobbing in the waves, when Eddie reached the shore of the pond. The wind and the current, however, had carried it just beyond arm's reach. Eddie knelt down by the water and stretched his hand out as far as he could, but it was useless.*

*"Duck!" Eddie said. "Swim, duck! You can make it if you try."*

*The duckling kept bobbing. It was drifting farther and farther away.*

*"You don't understand, duck," Greenspan shouted. "You can't stay in this place all by yourself. I've come to take you home."*

*He could hear voices behind him. Some people had evidently noticed* him and had stopped to watch. Greenspan felt very foolish, but by then he didn't care. He took off his shoes, rolled up his trousers, and stepped into the water. For a second he thought of turning around and telling the onlookers that he really didn't like animals at all, only this was a special case, but then he just kept wading into the pond.

The people on shore cheered anyway. They weren't quite sure what was happening, but they could see a very large man in a three-piece suit standing in knee-deep water on a very cold day, triumphantly holding up in his hand a very small yellow duck.

The duckling lived out its days on a friend's farm. When it grew up it had many ducklings of its own. On quiet evenings it may well have told them a new children's story about an ugly lawyer who also turned out to be a swan, in his own fashion.

PART THREE

# AND NOTHING BUT
# THE TRUTH

# 7. And Nothing But the Truth

In the late fall of 1985 I happened to be at a dinner party with John I. Laskin. A fine lawyer in the tradition of his father, the late Chief Justice Bora Laskin of the Supreme Court of Canada, John is counsel to a large Toronto law firm. At dinner he told me a puzzling story.

A month or so earlier, in October 1985, a senior partner of another downtown law firm was charged with dangerous driving, a fairly serious offence. According to the Crown's summary statement, the lawyer was driving from the garage of the Commerce Court Building in the heart of Toronto's financial district to the top of the parking ramp leading to Wellington Street. At the time there were a number of VISA workers engaged in a labour dispute with the Canadian Imperial Bank of Commerce. The strikers, said the Crown, were walking in an orderly picket line on the sidewalk in front of the exit ramp as the lawyer's Buick emerged from the garage.

The lawyer in his car, apparently without honking his horn or warning the strikers in any other way, suddenly "lunged" at the picket line. He stopped for one second, then lunged again. The strikers scattered, but not quickly enough. In the words of the police officer reporting the incident:

> The accused . . . suddenly excellerated [*sic*] quickly towards the picket line whitch [*sic*] was still moving in a very orderly mannor [*sic*]. . . . The accused vehicle moved into the picket line without warning causing once stricker [*sic*] to jump forward to avoid being struck by the accused vehicle, the victim who was behind the first stricker [*sic*] was unable to get clear of the accused vehicle was struck in the left leg and thrown up onto the hood of the vehicle and off the hood over the left fender.

This was the police version of the "stricker struck". The report-

ing officer represented himself as being at the scene and witnessing
the incident. Policemen may not be able to spell, but they should
have no trouble seeing. On the officer's story we had a very senior
lawyer who, apparently for no reason at all, aimed his car like a
missile at a line of peaceful pickets and scattered human bodies into
the air.

Senior law partners rarely make a game of running down striking
workers. For this particular lawyer to have done so made the story
more puzzling still. I knew Mr. Worthmore (as we'll call him here),
and he seemed to me just about the last person on earth who would
act in this manner, provoked or unprovoked. But people are capable
of acting in uncharacteristic ways, and judges encounter such people
every day in court. After a few years on the bench, it doesn't even
surprise them. It isn't a hot defence strategy to contend that someone didn't do something just because he isn't the kind of person
who'd do a thing like that.

Not only was Mr. Worthmore's version of the incident different:
his version was that there was no incident at all — at least not until
the police stopped and charged him. He had driven his Buick to the
top of the ramp. There were about a dozen pickets standing — not
walking — in front of the exit, deliberately obstructing his passage.
There were also three policemen. Mr. Worthmore rolled down his
window and asked the nearest policeman to "please move these
people". The policeman replied, "When I'm ready," after which all
three police officers turned on their heels and walked away.

Mr. Worthmore waited for more than a minute. The pickets continued standing there. The policemen were gone, or at least gone
from his line of vision. The lawyer was not involved in the labour
dispute. He was, however, on his way to an appointment. Eventually
he started inching his car forward. Not lunging, but inching. As he
kept inching forward, the pickets kept inching back. Then, slowly,
they moved out of his way.

No one had to jump. No one did jump. No one was hit. There were
no bodies flying over the hood in the air. There was no incident.
There was only a senior lawyer peacefully exiting a garage onto
Wellington Street. The incident began only when he reached the
street and — in the words of Mr. Worthmore's own memorandum —
"policemen were climbing all over the car."

There was a witness present, a tenant in the Commerce Court

Building, who expressed objections to the police's conduct. Unfortunately he was a man "whose name I did not get (brilliant)", as Mr. Worthmore recalled in his memo. This left him with his word against the police officer's word.

Let me indulge in a little aside here. Journalists often talk about the uphill battle an ordinary, poor, unsophisticated citizen faces when it's his word against a policeman's. They are right to talk about it because it's true. However, they're wrong if they're implying that a sophisticated, powerful member of the community would have less of a battle in a similar situation. In fact, quite wrong. A senior partner of a downtown law firm would have just as much of a battle, or an even worse battle, for one simple reason.

Crown attorneys and judges could be terrified that someone might accuse them of making a sweetheart deal, or of catering to special privilege, if they extended to a prominent citizen the same benefit of a doubt, or exercised the same discretionary powers in his favour, as they might for any other citizen.

Another problem a prominent person faces may be illustrated by a non-criminal parallel. A marital indiscretion coming to light nowadays, while uncomfortable and embarrassing, is virtually without professional or public consequences for most people. An engineer's or a businessman's career need not be disrupted by it. However, the same mistake would still devastate a politician or a television evangelist.

In a somewhat similar vein, while being wrongfully or innocently accused of a crime is horrible for any person, the fact is that being accused of some relatively minor offence — which carries no other penalty than a fine or maybe a brief jail term — need not irrevocably disrupt an ordinary person's life. For such a citizen, the consequences don't have to be completely shattering. Hurtful, yes; inconvenient, certainly; but fatal, no. Win or lose, an ordinary person can generally return to his everyday occupation, lick his wounds, and become restored to his previous position in his career and in his life.

Such restoration is not as easily available to a prominent or high-profile professional or business person. He may never achieve it if he's convicted, or it may take him much longer. Since he is much more exposed, his status is much more fragile. His social position, his business associations, even his friends or his family, may oblige him to standards that do not allow for a single mistake.

Or, assuming he is innocent, the *appearance* of a single mistake.

All this, incidentally, is hardly a novel discovery. Traditional wisdom has always warned that "the higher they rise, the harder they fall." I'm not bringing it up to elicit sympathy for the powerful and the prominent, only to do my bit for accuracy in the media. Also, to underline that Mr. Worthmore was in a bit of trouble.

He would have been in more trouble, in fact, if John Laskin hadn't been such a resourceful lawyer. Thinking about the matter, he and one of his colleagues remembered that there was a continuously operating security TV camera in the vicinity, and that it might have been positioned in such a way as to capture the entire incident. This, in fact, turned out to be the case. After some negotiations, Laskin got hold of the relevant section of the video tape.

The tape for October 4, 1985, 15:55 hours, showed that everything had happened exactly as Mr. Worthmore described it. Not only was there no incident with bodies flying off the hood of the car, there was hardly even a confrontation. The lawyer waited for more than a minute, then inched his way through the picket line, with the strikers slowly moving out of his way. No one was hurt; no one was endangered.

A police officer, however, was getting ready to tell in court a blatant, unmitigated lie.

When John Laskin retained me to act for Mr. Worthmore in the matter — a trial date was set for the late spring of 1986 — the temptation was great to simply walk into court and wait for the Crown to present its case. We could have let the policeman lie under oath, and even encouraged him to embellish his lies during cross-examination. We had reason to believe that, while senior police officials were aware of the video cameras, this knowledge had not filtered down to the cops on the beat. If some of the other policemen at the scene also perjured themselves to support their colleague, fine; the more the merrier. At the conclusion of the Crown's evidence, the defence could simply play the video tape. End of case; also end of the careers of one or more police officers.

I resisted the temptation. Such grandstanding is great for a Perry Mason episode on TV, but it's rarely in the best interest of a client. In criminal matters, whenever possible, the defence's best result for a client is to call the Crown's attention to the fatal flaw in the prosecution's case — if there is one — so that the Crown can quietly drop the charges. Any case coming to trial in a criminal court, even one that ends in complete acquittal and vindication, has the potential of damaging the defendant's reputation, and it cannot but damage his pocketbook and his nerves.

It is, incidentally, also in the best interest of the tax-paying public to avoid wasting a court's time. I'd suggested to Laskin that he try talking to a senior Crown attorney about the matter before I'd become involved in the case. He did so, but to no avail. A senior and very fair-minded Crown considered the matter but felt that there was nothing he could do. The police allegations, as set out in the Crown's summary statement, were much too serious.

At this stage Laskin had not told the Crown about the video tape. He'd only acquainted him with Mr. Worthmore's version of the event, saying that, considering the lawyer's blameless reputation, there was good reason to believe his story to be accurate and truthful.

This is fair warning. The Crown knows that an officer of the court — which all lawyers are, whether they work for the prosecution or the defence — wouldn't make such a statement frivolously to another. Once the statement is made, it puts the ball into the Crown's court. Disclosing the heart of the defence evidence at an early stage would be a grave tactical error. Having retained me, Laskin wanted to leave it to my judgment when, and under what circumstances, to play the defence's trump card.

I repeat, had Mr. Worthmore been a simple, decent citizen rather than an establishment lawyer, it's possible that Laskin's assurances to the Crown might have done the trick. Serious as the charge was, in labour disputes tempers fray with notorious ease, and in spite of all allegations of flying bodies there was no evidence that anyone got hurt. As it was, however, I had to consider that even disclosing the existence of the video tape might be insufficient to stay the prosecution's hand. A Crown counsel might be so jittery about the appearance of playing favourites as to prefer bringing even the weakest matter into court. That would have been fine with me; litigating matters in court is my business. I enjoy winning, and it would also have satisfied me to see a lying witness face the consequences of his lie.

At the same time I couldn't see dragging a client through a court procedure that could be avoided. In the end I opted for going to the Crown and not just telling them about the tape but actually playing it for them. That, of course, ended the matter. The charges were immediately withdrawn.

We can only speculate on why a police officer was prepared to bear false witness against an innocent man. The police themselves happened to be in a labour dispute with the Police Commission at the time; they were working "to rule" and walked about wearing baseball caps instead of their regulation hats. Possibly some officers developed a misguided sense of solidarity with the striking VISA workers. There was some suggestion that the strikers might have worked out some informal — as well as irregular and illegal — deal with the police to let them obstruct traffic in front of the Commerce Court Building for five to ten minutes at a time, after which the pickets would agree to obey the police and let the traffic pass. (A policeman saying "When I'm ready" in response to Mr. Worthmore's request to clear a path for him could be some evidence of such a deal.) The officers may have charged Mr. Worthmore simply to uphold their end of the bargain with the strikers.

All this is speculative. None of it would serve as the remotest excuse in law for making a false accusation against an innocent fellow citizen. Putting the cop's case at its highest, he was taking a tremendous chance on his own life and career for a pretty thin reason. Unfortunately, this happens far more often than people would like to believe.

I would not dream of suggesting that police officers are inveterate liars. I will only suggest that police officers are inveterate human beings.

It is not a shattering revelation to say that all human beings are capable of lying. Some people hardly ever tell a lie, while some tell lies most of the time. But all human beings can lie sometimes, regardless of occupation or social position.

Regardless, also, of whether they are in a courtroom testifying under oath or not. The difference is that when people lie outside a courtroom they do not necessarily commit a crime. When they lie under oath, they invariably do. They commit the crime of perjury, or some variation of it, punishable under the Criminal Code by imprisonment up to fourteen years.

This penalty has no doubt reduced the number of lies told in court, but it has not eliminated lying. It has stopped some police witnesses no more than it has stopped other kinds of witnesses, and no more than any other penalty has ever stopped human beings from committing any other crime.

It is a further fact that people sometimes commit very serious crimes for what would appear to other people very frivolous reasons. It is important to remember this. No day passes in our courts without someone pleading guilty to an offence the penalty for which far outweighs any possible gain or satisfaction for the offender.

Middle-class people have been known to shoplift items worth less than a couple of dollars; young professionals to risk a criminal record for the momentary euphoria offered by a fashionable drug. Being a few minutes late for a movie has been sufficient for some architects or scientists to chance a charge of dangerous driving. Many crimes make very little sense. Perhaps most crimes would not withstand a meticulous cost/benefit analysis. It is common for major offences to be committed for minor reasons — or for no reason at all.

It is important to remember this, because a police officer's credibility in court is generally enhanced by the assumption that, on the face of it, he has no reason to perjure himself. It doesn't "pay" him to do so.

It is true, of course, that while anybody may give false evidence, a witness is more likely to give false evidence for a reason than for no reason. He is more likely to do it when he has something to gain by perjuring himself than when he has nothing to gain. It is also true that a policeman has nothing to gain by lying — in theory ever, but in many cases also in fact.

A policeman is not necessarily accused of any wrongdoing by the defence in a trial; he may not even be criticized. There is nothing for him to deny or cover up. All he has to do is to tell the court truthfully what he saw, found, or heard — if he heard it from the accused — along with the circumstances under which he saw, found, or heard it. That's all. His task is to gather evidence to the best of his ability, then present it in court honestly and accurately. Once he's done that, he's done his job. His performance is not determined by the outcome of the proceedings. He is on salary. He is to be promoted on the basis of the general quality of his police work and cannot expect to receive raises, medals, or bonus points for a conviction. Needless to say, he suffers no penalties for an acquittal.

Under these circumstances, we might ask, why shouldn't the policeman tell the truth? And whenever it's his word against an accused person's word, why shouldn't the court prefer the officer's version? The officer is a disinterested witness, while the defendant has an obvious personal interest: he wants to be acquitted. Unlike the constable, the defendant invariably has something to gain by lying.

I must interject here that some people have long called a policeman's "disinterest" a myth — a myth accepted by juries who don't know any better and by judges who ought to know better but wilfully close their eyes to reality. Police officers do have things to gain or lose by the outcome of a case, according to those who hold this view. Their careers are very much affected by the conviction or acquittal of the defendants they've helped bring to trial, at least in a cumulative sense.

There may be some truth in this, but I consider it beside the point. Even if police officers have things to gain by the Crown's success in a given case — tangible, material things, from promotions to medals — it would be difficult to argue that they have enough to gain to offset the risk of being caught in a lie on the witness stand. Any criminal charge of interfering with the administration of justice would be sufficient to damage or disrupt a police officer's career, even if he were acquitted, and the consequences of a perjury conviction would be grave beyond measure. On any cost/benefit analysis it would make no sense for a policeman to be anything but truthful in court.

The real problem is more subtle and more insidious. It is that a strict cost/benefit analysis is an inadequate test for the behaviour of human beings. People do things for an infinite variety of reasons, and an objective stock-taking of advantages and disadvantages is only one of them. It may not even be the most important one.

The real danger comes from the assumption — the popular assumption, and also the assumption of many judges — that a police officer is telling the truth simply because he has no obvious or sufficient motive for lying, or has no demonstrable personal interest in the outcome of a trial. We make no such bland assumption about any other class of witnesses. We simply note their apparent lack of interest and weigh it as one factor among many others in deciding whether they're telling the truth or not.

That's all that real or apparent "disinterest" is ever worth: one small, single factor. Common experience proves every day that human beings, caught up in the swirl of events, entangled in their own prejudices, ideas, egos, or fantasies, can lie for no reason and even against reason; disinterestedly, and even against their own interests. They can lie for such relatively benign or altruistic motives as team spirit or misplaced idealism. They can lie under oath, as easily as they can shoplift or go through a red light, even when it doesn't "pay" them to do so.

Simple fairness also demands that we should not over-emphasize "disinterest" but should view it merely as one factor among many. Why? Because a *defendant* can never be disinterested. He is facing criminal sanctions if convicted. Whenever we make apparent "disinterest" the biggest test, the supreme factor in weighing the evidence, we're sending the only person who is at risk — a person still presumed to be innocent — into the ring with one hand tied behind his back.

If some police officers can tell lies about a defendant they know to be innocent, they find it easier still to tell lies about a defendant they believe to be guilty. My guess is that the most common example of false testimony in court — second only, if at all, to the possibility of a defendant's giving false evidence on his own behalf — is a police officer perjuring himself to secure the conviction of an accused he honestly believes to be guilty of the offence charged.

In 1971 I defended a man named Julian Anthony Werynski, a bank accountant who was charged with helping others to defraud the Bank of Nova Scotia of some $52,000. It was a sad case. On Werynski's evidence, for which there was considerable (though legally inadmissible) support, he had been coerced by some people into giving them inside assistance while they had perpetrated the fraud. Werynski was afraid for his life and for his family's lives, and his total benefit turned out to be a $500 loan from one of the men who had coerced him. He was eventually sentenced to the rather harsh term of four years in penitentiary.

At trial, the evidence indicated that at the time of his arrest Werynski had been seriously ill. His condition was such that he literally did not know what he was saying. This being the case, the oral and written statements he had given to the police were clearly inadmissible against him.

Statements made by a defendant are never admissible unless they have been voluntarily made. There is a simple reason for this: such statements may not be true. When a person is scared out of his wits by threats; when he's swayed by promises; when he's barely conscious because of medication, drugs, sleeplessness, or hypnosis, he might say anything. The courts cannot rely on what he says. We have stopped using thumbscrews on accused people not merely because we have become too civilized for such acts, but also because we have come to realize that torture can elicit lies as easily as it can elicit the truth. Barbaric methods, apart from being barbaric, don't work. People in pain — physical or psychological — will say whatever is necessary to stop the pain. What they say may be self-incriminating, but there is absolutely no assurance that it will be the truth.

Werynski and his wife both testified that he had been very sick, and that he had told the two arresting officers that he was sick and did not want to speak to them. However, the first police officer on the witness stand denied this. His recollection was that the defendant did not complain of any sickness when arrested in his home, and that he talked to the police voluntarily. The officer was absolutely positive about it. He was also quite convincing, and would not yield an inch on cross-examination.

I felt equally positive in my own mind that he might be lying, so when the second police officer came into court to take the witness stand, I pulled out one of the simplest questions from the cross-examiner's bag of tricks:

"Just to assist us with the timing, officer, can you recall whether Mr. Werynski first complained to you about being sick inside the house or on the porch?"

This witness, of course, had not heard the evidence of his fellow officer; until called to the stand he had been excluded from the courtroom. He had no way of knowing if the first officer had not, after all, admitted the truth. He wasn't going to stick his neck out at this point, so he answered:

"I think it was outside the house."

Bingo. Werynski's inadmissible statement was, of course, excluded by the trial judge. As it happened, it did not benefit Werynski much in the long run. There was no question that he had assisted in the fraud — he admitted it himself on the witness stand — and his defence rested on the complex legal issue of duress. The police may have honestly believed in his guilt, but no police officer was qualified to say whether or not he was guilty *in law*. Nor was it any police officer's business: that's what judges get paid for. The police had only one obligation, and that was to tell the court the truth, the whole truth, and nothing but the truth — and that was what one officer chose not to do.

A reason would not excuse lying, but here there wasn't even a reason. No one accused the officer of having beaten a statement out of Werynski. In the circumstances, the admissibility of a statement was not central to the Crown's case. Yet an officer elected to take the risk. His crime of perjury could have drawn a far heavier sentence under the Criminal Code than Werynski's offence.

The risk of false police evidence is even graver where the truth might make the Crown's entire case go down the drain. The point is illustrated by two further episodes from my files. They didn't happen in some lawless region of the deep South, but in civilized Canada.

NOTES

p.117, l.9: In the context of the United States, see "The Rules of the Justice Game" in *The Best Defense* by the American lawyer and legal scholar Alan M. Dershowitz. Rule 4, according to Dershowitz, reads: "Almost all police lie about whether they violated the Constitution in order to convict guilty defendants." Rule 5 says: "All prosecutors, judges and defense attorneys are aware of Rule 4." Rule 8 is: "Most trial judges pretend to believe police officers who they know are lying." As for Rule 9: "All appellate judges are aware of Rule 8," etc.

p.117, l.21: The role of two senior Toronto police officers in the Lorenz-Allen murder case, discussed later in this book, is a further illustration of this point.

p.118, l.31: In dismissing Werynski's appeal against his sentence, Mr. Justice Schroeder was moved to remark in his judgment delivered for the Ontario Court of Appeal on January 27, 1972: "While a term of four years imprisonment is by no means a lenient sentence and may be greater than one or other of the members of this court might have imposed . . ." etc. Translated into plain language this means that, even while not wishing to disturb the sentence, the appellate judges wanted it to be known that it was rather stiff.

# 8. Hi Mom, Guess Who's in Jail

*1* On Saturday, May 24, 1980, a six-year-old girl named Lizzie Tomlinson, having received her allowance of seventy-five cents from her mother after lunch, went out with her sister to buy some candy. Lizzie was an affectionate little girl who, in the words of her aunt, liked to eat "any kind of candy she could get". Her nature was as sweet as her tastes; though shy with strangers, she was often hugging and kissing people she knew well. Blonde and pretty, Lizzie's skin was marred only by some flea-bites — from her cat, some people said, or from her sister's dog, according to others — which she was in the habit of scratching until they bled. There were quite a few such scabs on her arms and legs.

Lizzie and her sister bought candy and returned home; then, around 2 p.m. Mrs. Diane Tomlinson let Lizzie go out again, this time with a six-year-old cousin named Harold Spooner and his little sister Mary, aged two or three. The children were going to play in a tiny park nicknamed Stinky's, at Sumach and Shuter streets, a favourite spot for children in Toronto's Cabbagetown area. Despite its unappealing name, the park is well equipped with slides, swings, and sandboxes, and it has benches from which assorted mothers, baby-sitters, and other people can watch the children at play.

During the next two or three hours several adults and children saw Lizzie playing in the park. Some of them also saw her leave the playground with a man between 3:30 and 4:15 p.m., as they variously estimated the time. Others saw Lizzie walking along Shuter Street accompanied by this man shortly after 4 p.m. A taxi driver named Kenneth Stiff remembered picking up a man and a little girl matching Lizzie's description at the corner of Wascana and Sumach streets around that time, and driving them to a point a few hundred feet north of King Street on a nearby road known as the Bayview Extension. He let them out of his taxi at a spot where there was nothing but grass and railway tracks.

Lizzie was certainly gone from the park by 5 p.m., because that was when Mrs. Tomlinson, having started supper, sent Lizzie's eleven-year-old sister Ramona to bring her home. She couldn't find her. A short time later Ken Tomlinson, a self-employed carpenter, arrived home from work and he also went looking for Lizzie. As time passed, the Tomlinsons anxiously explored the whole neighbourhood in the family car. The police were called some time after 7 p.m.

The search for Lizzie was quickly announced by the news media in the Toronto area. Several neighbours and relatives, their cars equipped with CB radios, joined the searchers. Children who wander off in a city usually turn up within a day, but Sunday passed with no trace of Lizzie. Her body was eventually found by a Constable Baird some forty hours after her disappearance, around 11 a.m. on Monday, May 26, in a spot that had been searched by others before. It was an empty field underneath the elevated railroad tracks, frequented mainly by derelicts, not far from the place where Kenneth Stiff remembered letting a little girl and a man out of his taxi.

There were some bushes and a fair amount of debris around the site. Lizzie's body was hidden under a pile of old railway ties. Her jaw had been broken and there were many contusions and bruises on her body and face. Large stains of blood were visible on her T-shirt. The cause of death was asphyxiation, though the absence of fingernail marks on her neck indicated that it was not the result of manual choking. The little girl had been sexually assaulted by the vaginal insertion of a long, hollow stick, extending to the pleural cavity underneath her right shoulder. The pathologist Dr. Kent Mancer estimated that, though probably unconscious, Lizzie would have lived for another hour or two after the assault.

Among the searchers for Lizzie was a young man named Gregory Guerin. He was, in fact, related to Lizzie, his mother and Ken Tomlinson's mother being cousins. He lived with his family on the Tomlinsons' street only two doors away. When Ramona first started looking for her sister she bumped into Gregory, who told her that he had been with Lizzie in Stinky's park earlier. He saw her fight with little Harold over a pop bottle, he gave them twenty cents, and then they went to get a five-cent Mr. Freeze. Gregory added that when he left the park to go home and take a shower around 3 p.m., Lizzie was still playing on the swings with two black children.

In the course of the next thirty-six hours Gregory would tell exactly the same story to a number of people, including several police officers. For some reason it came to be interpreted, certainly by Gregory himself and perhaps also by the investigating detectives, that he had been "the last person to see Lizzie alive".

Though twenty-six by chronological age, Gregory had the mental age of a child of twelve or thirteen. He had an IQ of around seventy-five, two standard deviations below the mean, close to the bottom five per cent of all scores normally obtained on the Wechsler Adult Intelligence Scale. He also suffered from occasional seizures.

Gregory was not helpless; he could certainly tie his own shoelaces — he could even hold down simple jobs — but he had marked impairments of dexterity, vision, writing, speech, and judgment. During one psychological test at the age of twenty-six, when asked what he would do if he found a sealed, stamped, addressed envelope in the street, he replied that he would open it. When asked what action he would take if he were the first person to see smoke and fire in a theatre, he reported that he'd yell "Fire!" (For the benefit of law students, the correct answer to the first question is "Mail it." I'm not sure myself what the correct answer is to the second question.)

Gregory's limitations were evident to everyone. Not only the psychologists testing him, but his family, friends, and even strangers who had only fleeting contact with him, noted his lack of co-ordination, his immaturity, or the mild impropriety of his responses. The only exceptions were some police officers, who would later testify that to them Gregory seemed a perfectly normal, even bright and intelligent, young man. It is anybody's guess whether this spoke to the officers' intellectual standards, to their powers of observation, or to their capacity for truthfulness.

Gregory's problems were not the result of a birth defect. When he was five, in 1959, a fall from a height of forty-two feet had left him unconscious for a period of twenty-four days. He suffered brain damage and a loss of sight in his right eye. In 1960 he underwent a tantalum cranioplasty, the insertion of a metal plate into his skull. Two years later another accident — he ran in front of a streetcar — resulted in a further, though much briefer, period of unconsciousness.

Gregory, seven years old at the time of his second accident in 1962, spent many of his subsequent years in psychological treatment and assessment centres. His vision, perception, memory, and intellectual abilities did not improve much, and between the ages of eighteen and twenty he started developing seizures. Even as he grew older he continued to feel far more comfortable in the company of children than with adults of his own age. His few attempts at holding down undemanding jobs, such as being a "roadie" for a rock group or working as a security guard, did not last long. There was a small amount of money, some $25,000, held in trust for him as compensation for his childhood accident, and it was supposed to last him a lifetime.

Living with his family, Gregory developed into a kind of neighbourhood fixture, getting along with everyone, spending much of his time with the rest of the children in the area, being engaged in pursuits normal for his mental, if not his actual, age. He became as reliable a baby-sitter as any other thirteen-year-old. Most adults felt well disposed to him, or maybe a little protective; he was never so incapacitated as to become a burden, a nuisance, or a figure of fun.

Gregory was aware that his accident made him different somehow from other people. He was quite sensitive to it: he suffered from periodic depressions, and twice attempted to commit suicide. He never showed any sign of malice or violence to others, however. He liked people and he wanted them to like him. Later extensive interviews with parents, or with his friends, the neighbourhood children, revealed no episode of a sexual nature. Some children hugged and kissed Gregory, as they did other adults, simply because they liked him. Lizzie Tomlinson had hugged and kissed him. This fact would later acquire considerable significance.

I did not begin learning any of these facts until June 4, 1980. On that day the police charged Gregory Guerin with first-degree murder and his parents retained me to defend him.

During the nine days between the discovery of Lizzie's body and Gregory's arrest, the search for the little girl's killer had aroused immense public and media interest. The police investigation was often headline news in the *Toronto Sun*, a popular tabloid, but it was also a front-page feature in the *Toronto Star* and the national morning newspaper, the *Globe and Mail*. Other stories were backgrounders about Lizzie, the neighbourhood, or the grief-stricken Ken and Diane Tomlinson and their surviving daughters, Ramona, Tina, and Tammy.

Lizzie's funeral, at which Gregory had been one of the pallbearers, received wide coverage. Gregory's own picture, in group shots but photographed from a close and prominent angle, appeared in several newspapers, although (a fact that later turned out to be significant) none of the captions identified him by name at that time. The *Star*, for instance, described him only as "a gentle hand guiding Diane Tomlinson as she leaves funeral chapel".

The main stories focused on the stranger who led little Lizzie from the playground to her death: a man described by eyewitnesses in almost unanimous detail. It was this strange man who exercised the imagination of the reporters, and of the experts and prominent personalities they interviewed. Metro Chairman and Police Commission member Paul Godfrey promised a "massive manhunt" for him. Godfrey was quoted as saying that when he heard about the discovery of Lizzie's body, "nothing seemed important for the rest of the day." Indeed, playgrounds became deserted in the city; teachers were put on alert; stories with such titles as "How To Safeguard Your Children" appeared everywhere. One *Star* reporter, dressed in casual clothes, tried loitering around schoolyards to see if children would talk to strangers (out of thirty, only one child refused). Dr. Ruth Bray, a forensic psychologist, speculated that the stranger who killed Lizzie would now be very frightened, and would be holed up in a room or an apartment somewhere in the city.

Initially there was no doubt in the eyewitnesses' minds — and consequently in the minds of the police — about what the stranger looked like. They all described him as a man of average height and build — around 170 pounds and five foot eight or five foot ten — wearing blue jeans, probably a brown tank top, and brown (or maybe white) North Star running shoes. The man also wore sunglasses. He had dark, long, wavy hair; he had a moustache; and he had a full beard.

*A man with a beard*. This was the man the witnesses saw with a little girl they all identified as Lizzie. They saw them either in the park itself or in its immediate vicinity at exactly the relevant time. They told the police about what they had seen before the man's description appeared in the papers.

What the papers reported was, in fact, the description given by Rose Ann Neil, who had been with her own three children in the park (black children, incidentally, as Gregory mentioned to Ramona) and saw the bearded man sitting there with Lizzie. Or the description of Susan Jeschkeit, who actually knew Lizzie and watched her with the bearded man in the park for a period of an hour or more. Or the description of Sunny Conacher, who, while waiting at a stoplight in her car, saw the bearded man crossing River Street at Shuter with Lizzie shortly after 4 p.m. Or the statement of Pamela Heneault, who, though eventually saying that to her the man's beard seemed to be "close" or "new" rather than full, nevertheless agreed that it was a man with a beard that she saw walking with Lizzie along the Bayview Extension, around 4:15 p.m., next to the railway tracks on the grass.

There was one exception. Two children, Laurie and Glenda, also reported seeing Lizzie walk with a man on Shuter Street. Their description of the man's build and clothes matched the recollection of the adult witnesses, and Glenda thought that the man did have a beard. Laurie, however, didn't. Laurie, about eleven, claimed to have recognized the man as "one who lives somewhere around Lizzie's house" and "one who knows Ramona", and when she later saw Guerin in the back seat of a police car she also pointed him out as "That's him!" However, the taxi driver, Mr. Stiff, was "one hundred per cent sure" that the man who rode with Lizzie in his taxi to the Bayview Extension on May 24 was fully bearded.

In light of these statements it was not surprising that the police looked for a bearded man for the entire week before Gregory's arrest. A composite picture of a heavily bearded man circulated by the police appeared in all the papers. A special hot-line for sightings of bearded men — 368-7324 — was set up at 51 Division headquarters. Reportedly the police were pulling in men with beards at the rate of twenty a day for questioning — not counting those men investigated on the basis of tips that they had recently shaved off their beards. "The public response is unbelievable — I've never seen a case like this," Homicide Inspector James Crawford was quoted as saying. For a few days it was virtually unsafe in Toronto to be a bearded person.

This was natural enough. The bearded man seen with Lizzie in Stinky's park on May 24, the man taking her in a taxi to within a few hundred yards of the spot where her body would eventually be found, was clearly the most logical suspect. This man was very likely to be Lizzie's killer. If eyewitnesses described him in a certain way — as a fully bearded man — the police had no choice but to look for a man of this description.

There was only one problem. Gregory Guerin was clean-shaven. He had a thin moustache but at no time did anyone see him with a beard.

*The newspapers first reported that Greenspan had been retained to defend the man charged in the murder of Lizzie Tomlinson on June 6, 1980, a Friday. The next day Eddie's mother made her regular Saturday-morning telephone call to her son and grandchildren from her home in Niagara Falls.*

*The elder Mrs. Greenspan, usually a cheerful person, seemed very subdued on the phone this time. "Ma, is there anything the matter?" Eddie asked her. She replied that it was nothing, without changing her tone. "Come on, Ma, what's wrong?" Eddie kept urging her, knowing from her voice that something was wrong, though Mrs. Greenspan continued denying it. It was only at the end of the conversation that she said:*

*"So, you had to take that case?"*

*Greenspan played for time. "What case, Ma?" he asked, surprised at the speed with which news seemed to be reaching Niagara Falls these days.*

*"That case, you know, that case," replied Mrs. Greenspan, from whom wild horses wouldn't drag the word "murder", let alone "sex-murder".*

*"Ma, I'm a criminal lawyer!" yelled Eddie in exasperation.*

*"So, couldn't you give it to someone else at the office?" his mother asked, hanging up the phone.*

*Mrs. Greenspan wasn't alone at that point in not being impressed with what her son did for a living. In the public school attended by Greenspan's daughter Julianna, then eight years old, the murder of Lizzie Tomlinson had been a matter of much discussion in the days before Gregory Guerin's arrest. The tragic death of the pretty little girl shocked and upset everyone, including children and teachers. There was also a legitimate reason to believe that a maniac might be on the loose in Toronto.*

*As usual in the wake of such cases, for a short time "streetproofing" children became the thing to do. Such warnings are necessary, of course, but some teachers are better at it than others, and children also react to tales of danger in highly individual ways. In some schools there was an ambiance of needless anxiety, even hysteria. Children were having nightmares and showing a sudden, morbid fear of all adults.*

*This was followed by a feeling of relief after Guerin's arrest had been reported. See, the bad man had been caught. In Julianna's school the children were being reassured that there's never any reason to worry because the police solve every crime and never make a mistake. Julianna was more than a little disturbed, therefore, when some kids at school told her that her father was defending the bad man the police had caught. On the weekend she confronted Greenspan:*

*"Dad, why are you defending the man who killed Lizzie?"*

*Greenspan hesitated. Explaining the adversary system and the presumption of innocence to an eight-year-old is not easy; even some mature people have had trouble with the proposition. He could say to her that all people make mistakes, even if they wear uniforms, and that the police are only people in uniforms. In the end, though, he said something else:*

*"I'm not defending the man who killed Lizzie. Do you understand, Julie? I'm defending the man who didn't kill her."*

*Evidently Julianna understood, because she dropped the matter. There was still a question of not talking to strangers, however, which some kids were taking quite literally. Said Greenspan the Quipper: "Well, you don't have to worry. The man the police arrested wasn't a stranger, he was family. I guess this means you can talk to anybody now except your uncle Brian."*

While looking for the bearded man, the police were naturally gathering other evidence. These wasn't much to go on. Objects in the area where Lizzie's body was found appeared to yield no recognizable fingerprints. There was a lot of debris — candy-wrappers, empty cans, wine bottles, glue containers, plastic bags, cigarette packages, crumpled bits of paper — but there was no way of telling how long they had been there. Most if not all of the junk at the site must have pre-dated the murder.

In the end, the police settled on a few cigarette butts near the body as having been dropped by the killer — maybe, possibly. In fact, nothing could be established about them except that they were probably less than a month old. They were of a popular brand known as Player's Light. Two of them, in the opinion of Michael Philp, a forensic biologist, had been smoked by a "group O secretor". (Group O is a blood group, while a secretor is a person whose blood-grouping can be determined from body fluids, such as saliva or semen. Thirty-seven per cent of the population are O secretors.)

No semen was detected in Lizzie's body. Her own blood type was A, also a secretor. This was pretty much all the physical evidence there was.

In the early hours of an investigation everybody is a suspect, and quite properly so. The investigators evidently viewed Gregory in this light. The police always say that they keep an open mind, which in a limited sense is true: their mind *is* open until, at one point, it closes. That point comes when the decision is made to charge a person with a crime — sometimes on the basis of sound and sufficient evidence, sometimes not.

That's the point where the collective mind of the police snaps shut with an audible click. That's where impartial investigation stops, and is replaced by an attempt to secure the conviction of the person charged. To talk about an "open mind" from that point on is more than inaccurate. It is a joke.

Initially, before reaching that point, the police looked at Gregory along with everybody else. Three things made him, if not exactly a suspect, at least a person to be routinely investigated: the fact that he'd seen Lizzie in the park not long before the little girl's disappearance; the child Laurie's suggestion that he might have been the man walking with Lizzie; and his own insistence that he had been "the last person to see Lizzie alive", which he kept repeating to everyone. (It was impossible to reconstruct whether he came up with the phrase himself or had first heard it from a police officer.) A fourth factor could have been Gregory's entire being: the slight dent in his temple, the steel plate in his skull, and his vaguely inappropriate demeanour, which may well have seemed "strange" or "suspicious" to policemen who had no reference point as to what Gregory's "normal" demeanour was like.

Gregory told Lizzie's sister Ramona late on Saturday afternoon — approximately at 6:45 p.m., when the family was already looking for

Lizzie but the police had not yet been called — that he had seen his little cousin around 3 p.m. in Stinky's park, before going home to take a shower and watch *Bonanza* on television. Ramona recalled this conversation as being entirely normal.

Mrs. Tomlinson herself recalled seeing Ramona talk with Gregory outside the house. She did not remember whether this was before or after they had called the police — but she did remember that Gregory had no beard. Mrs. Tomlinson had never seen Gregory with a beard.

There was no dispute about what Gregory did next. A few minutes before 7 p.m. he went, as pre-arranged, to the home of a woman named Tracey Lee Chiang to baby-sit her son Cameron for the next couple of hours. Ms. Chiang recalled him as being "his usual happy-go-lucky self", well-mannered and, importantly, clean-shaven. He took Cameron to the park after Ms. Chiang left at 7 p.m. When Ms. Chiang returned around 9 p.m., she met Gregory and a friend named Basil just as they were coming back with her son. Gregory was carrying Cameron, who had cut his foot in the park and was still bleeding a little.

Having finished his baby-sitting chores, Gregory eventually returned to the Tomlinson house around 10 p.m. — by then, a place of great anxiety — and it was there that William Conroy, Lizzie's uncle, who had been out of town fishing, saw him at 1:45 a.m. They left the house together to continue the search for Lizzie. Gregory appeared as worried as everyone else, but otherwise Conroy noticed nothing unusual about him.

Lizzie's uncle specifically recalled that Gregory was clean-shaven, as always. In Conroy's view, Gregory was "a very clean person, always taking showers", and he had never seen him with long hair or a beard. (Kenneth Stiff, the taxi driver, who had seen Lizzie's abductor at closer quarters than any other witness, described the man not only as bearded but also as long-haired and "appearing dirty".)

Sunday morning Gregory accompanied Alton Cornell, a man whose Chevrolet was equipped with a CB radio, to continue the search for Lizzie. They went to their assigned area, Cherry Beach, but on the way back they also examined the bottom part of the Bayview Extension. This was Gregory's idea, according to Cornell, though Gregory only suggested the area as a whole without directing Cornell's attention to any particular spot. They saw other search parties already at work there, so they left.

Cornell would eventually say in court that he did recall seeing "a slight shadow" of a beard on Gregory's face that Sunday at 8 a.m. — not surprisingly, perhaps, if Gregory had been looking for Lizzie along with everyone else all night and didn't bother shaving in the morning. (Cornell also agreed that he might have been prompted in this recollection by the police just before being called to testify in November.)

Gregory was first questioned by the police on Sunday, May 25, as soon as he came back to the temporary headquarters set up by the searchers. Between noon and 5 p.m. he gave the police two statements in which he simply repeated everything he had told Ramona on Saturday after Lizzie's disappearance.

At one point Gregory yelled at Constable Juri Soorsk and Sergeant Gary Miller for insinuating that he would hurt Lizzie, but then he readily agreed to strip so that the officers could examine his body. Apart from noting some small scratches, and that his legs and feet were dirty (again, not surprising in view of the fact that he had just tramped through the fields searching for his cousin), the examination produced nothing remarkable. The event that impressed Sergeant Miller occurred shortly after 5 p.m. when he drove Gregory to Stinky's park, ostensibly for Gregory to point out the exact spot where he remembered seeing Lizzie for the last time.

At the intersection of Regent and Shuter streets, Miller's police car passed another police vehicle, one in which Sergeant Dave Kerr happened to be driving the little girl named Laurie to the police station. The meeting of the two police vehicles was completely accidental, but, according to Miller, as they passed he noted that Laurie was looking at Guerin with an expression of "shock and surprise" on her face. Sergeant Kerr stated that this was the moment when Laurie exclaimed "That's him!" — referring to Guerin as being the man she had seen walking with Lizzie from the park on Saturday.

Unlike this spontaneous moment, a deliberate attempt at identification Sergeant Miller had set up in Stinky's park a few minutes later produced the opposite results. While a constable stood with Gregory, the Sergeant walked a neighbour named William Noseworthy through the park twice, but Noseworthy could not recognize

Guerin as the man he had seen strolling by his house holding a little girl's hand the previous afternoon.

This happened on Sunday. Lizzie's body hadn't been found yet, the police hadn't yet closed their minds, and naturally Gregory was allowed to go home. Things took a far more ominous turn by Monday noon when Sergeant Kerr and his partner picked up Gregory again from his house. By that time a body had been found. Though it had not been positively identified, there seemed little doubt that it was Lizzie's body. The press were already swarming around the Tomlinson home two doors away.

To Sergeant Kerr, Gregory seemed "excited and happy" — which at the mental age of thirteen he might well have been, having not been told of Lizzie's death yet, and seeing himself involved with an important investigation. After all, he was receiving periodic assurances from the police that he was only "helping" them, or that it was all "routine" because he had been "the last person to see Lizzie alive". He became angry, depressed, and (as he himself put it) "frustrated" only when it appeared to him that he was being accused of having hurt Lizzie. For instance, after being driven home by the police on Sunday, and turning over in his mind some of the questions that he had been asked by Sergeant Miller and his partner, Gregory became upset enough to leave his house again and bang his fist into a mailbox — so hard as to require a trip to Wellesley Hospital, where they taped his hand and put his arm in a sling. Sergeant Kerr noticed the bandage when picking Gregory up the next day.

Still, he readily gave another statement to the police — saying exactly what he said before — then agreed to take part in a line-up (remarking to Kerr that he looked forward to the experience, having never been in a line-up before). He stood in the number 9 spot, clean-shaven among eleven men with beards and moustaches; not real suspects but "co-operating citizens". (One was a bearded employee of a newspaper — dragged from his delivery van by the police — who later wrote an article on his experience.)

The ten witnesses who viewed the line-up, including Kenneth Stiff, Rose Ann Neil, and Susan Jeschkeit, could make no identification, but one of the bearded citizens appeared to them to resemble the man they had seen leaving the park with Lizzie. None, however, picked Gregory Guerin.

Obviously the people who had actually seen Lizzie's abductor continued to be adamant about having seen a man with a beard.

With Homicide Sergeants Vaughan O'Toole and Kenneth Cenzura in charge of the investigation, the police were still diligently checking out bearded men at this point: at least one hundred men were investigated, though some reports put the number as high as four hundred. The problem was that there did not seem to be any solid suspects among them. As the days passed, the pressure on the police to solve the high-profile case became intense. Concerned citizens held a rally in front of Toronto's City Hall on Nathan Phillips Square, with toddlers holding up signs demanding the death penalty for "child sex slayers". A Cabbagetown mother started a petition for uniformed guards at playgrounds. The *Toronto Sun* began numbering its reports as Manhunt Day 4, 5, 6 — soon reaching Manhunt Day 9. "Our phones are still ringing off the hook," Inspector Crawford was quoted as saying.

A clean-shaven Guerin in the hand was beginning to look better than a hundred bearded suspects in the bush to the police at this stage. For what it was worth, he was a smoker of Player's Light cigarettes, and a saliva test showed him to be a group O secretor. He *had* been pointed out by one child (if by no one else) as the man walking with Lizzie. Coupled with Gregory's somewhat bizarre demeanour, and perhaps also a feeling that Lizzie, a shy girl, would be more likely to leave the playground with a cousin than with a total stranger, Guerin was shaping up as a respectable suspect — at least in the absence of a real suspect.

On Tuesday, June 3, eight days after the discovery of the little girl's body, Sergeant O'Toole went to Guerin's house and asked him to hand over the brown T-shirt he had been wearing on the day of Lizzie's death. Guerin picked it out of a drawer (obviously having made no attempt during the ten days since Lizzie's death to hide it or even to clean it). Then O'Toole and his partner drove him to the offices of the Homicide Bureau, where they warned him that they would be making notes which, in the case of a criminal charge being laid, could be used in a court of law.

"Are you guys trying to pin this on me?" asked Guerin, suspicion dawning.

"No, Greg, we're not trying to pin anything on anybody," replied O'Toole; "we're just trying to get to the bottom of this, okay?"

"Okay," Gregory replied, evidently reassured.

The conversation continued. "Do you have a girlfriend?" O'Toole asked.

"Off and on, girls, off and on," Gregory replied, flustered. "I don't fuss with them. I don't want any kids."

"When was the last time you went with a girl?"

"That's getting pretty personal," replied Gregory, quite accurately. Then O'Toole asked what was becoming the key question:

"When did you shave off your growth of beard?"

"I didn't," Gregory said, surprised. "I shave it off every day." (He had earlier told the police that he had shaved off his thin moustache — as had some other men questioned by the police, including William Conroy, Lizzie's uncle — because of the stigma attached to any facial hair in Cabbagetown since Lizzie's abduction. He had only shaved it off *after* being teased about it by the police, not before — and had told everyone, including Lizzie's mother, that he had done it, and why.)

"Greg, would you consent to taking a polygraph test?"

"What's that?"

"A lie-detector."

"What for? You guys are trying to pin this on me, aren't you?"

"No, Greg, we're not," answered Sergeant O'Toole, himself not being required to undergo a lie-detector test at that point. "When you finish the test you can go home."

Polygraph tests are always doubtful, and therefore most courts in Canada and the United States do not let test results be put in as evidence. Putting a brain-damaged person, a man on constant medication for epileptic seizures, on a polygraph is so doubtful as to be meaningless. (What is more meaningful, perhaps, is whether or not he is *willing* to take the test, which Guerin was. People with something to hide are less likely to agree.)

The police know all this; they know that test results cannot be used in court, and they ask suspects to take a lie-detector test for a different reason. If people refuse, it suggests to the police that they may be on the right track. (Said the polygraph operator, Sergeant Thomas, to Guerin: "If you are involved [in Lizzie's murder], it would probably be better for you not to take the test." Replied Guerin: "I'm innocent and you're trying to make me feel guilty. Let's get the test started.") If subjects agree to take the test and fail — or the police tell them that they've failed — some of them may confess.

Guerin took the test, and was told by the police that he had failed. He continued maintaining his innocence, and was allowed to go home with his sister. By the next day, the forensic biologist discovered a small, very faint blood smear on the back of Gregory's T-shirt, classified as type-A blood, the group to which Lizzie belonged. On the basis of this, and despite all the eyewitness descriptions, the decision was made to arrest Guerin for first-degree murder.

Sergeants O'Toole and Cenzura went to Guerin's home on July 4, a Wednesday. He appeared to be asleep in his room. When neither the policemen nor his mother could rouse him, an ambulance was called and Gregory was taken to St. Michael's Hospital. There the doctors discovered that he had taken rat poison in an attempt to kill himself.

I was sitting in my office with a client when Guy Kay, my articling student at the time, took a phone call from Gregory's frantic mother. In her excitement and desperation all she could say was: "My son is being arrested for the murder of that little girl!" It was enough for Kay to guess that, whoever her son was, she must be talking about the murder of Lizzie Tomlinson. In Toronto in June 1980, the phrase "that little girl" could refer to no other case. I knew nothing about Gregory then and had no idea whether or not I wished to act for him, but I told Kay to go to St. Michael's Hospital immediately. A man was being arrested and he was asking for a lawyer.

*As Guy Kay remembers it, Lizzie's murder was the only case during his articling year in Greenspan's office in which his law principal appeared to exhibit initial reservations about acting for an accused. Normally Greenspan's motto was: "A lawyer can't turn away a client just because he's charged with an odious crime any more than a doctor can refuse to treat a patient just because he suffers from an odious illness." This time, however, he seemed to temporize.*

*"Why don't we just wait and see," he mused over a Harvey's hamburger with some people from his office. "We have no idea, eh, what this case is about. A not-guilty plea in this murder trial is a year's work on Legal Aid. Do we need that?" The lawyers at the table smiled. The majority of murder cases are, in fact, Legal Aid, and Greenspan had not been known to refuse one yet for that reason.*

"Why don't you just admit that you don't want to defend a man accused of strangling a little girl?" someone asked. "A client charged with a really odious crime? Did you know that there was a mob of about a hundred people waiting for him outside the police station, ready to lynch him?"

Greenspan blushed. "What do you want from me?" he asked. "I've got two little daughters and a mother in Niagara Falls."

A practical friend finally said: "Listen, there are two alternatives. The papers say the man is brain-damaged. He has a steel plate in his head. Either he didn't kill the girl, in which case he ought to be defended, or he did, in which case he's probably insane. How can you lose?"

"Trust me," said Greenspan gloomily. "I can lose."

As Kay recalls it, the interview that may have convinced Greenspan to take the case occurred later that night. That was when Guerin's parents — "salt-of-the-earth people" as Greenspan put it — came to see him in his office. Guerin's mother was highly distraught, which under the circumstances was to be expected, but she also conveyed such a firm belief in her son's innocence that Greenspan, though as a rule he deliberately tried to avoid having his judgment affected by such factors, was in this instance obviously moved. Ashamed of his sentiment, however, he attempted to hide it by snarling, "I'm a sucker for mothers; my own or anybody else's!" before settling back into unaccustomed gloom.

Greenspan was seldom gloomy; as a lawyer he liked to look at the bright side of things. In his office, gloom, or at least grave sobriety, was usually represented by the two superb lawyers he had chosen as his partners, Marc Rosenberg and Chris Buhr. Their cool, realistic analysis of a case, their tendency to err on the side of pessimism, would counteract any tendency Greenspan may have had to err on the optimistic side.

At that point the possibility of Guerin's having no legal defence certainly existed. If he did in fact kill Lizzie, and the evidence showed him to be a child-molester who strangled his little cousin to stop her from telling her mother about whatever he did to her, he could be convicted of first-degree murder no matter how many steel plates he had in his head. The Crown would anticipate an insanity defence, a consideration that led Greenspan to send Guy Kay to St. Michael's Hospital on his way to the office early the next morning to make sure that Gregory exercised his legal right of refusal to talk to anyone — including the Crown's medical experts at this early stage in the proceedings, before the defence even knew how the case might shape up.

*Kay's assignment led him to an encounter with the formidable Dr. Andrew I. Malcolm, one of the foremost forensic psychiatrists in Canada, who had, in fact, been sent to the hospital first thing in the morning by Crown Attorney John Kerr. Dr. Malcolm is a rather stern man of tremendous reputation; what Kay did not know was that he also has a dry sense of humour. A young student, Kay was somewhat tense as he was telling the great psychiatrist that Guerin, as was his right, would refuse to talk to him.*

*The two men were standing somewhere in the labyrinthine corridors of St. Michael's Hospital at this point. "I want to ask you only one question," Dr. Malcolm said to Kay, "which you can answer without the slightest danger to the interest of your client."*

*"Yes?" Kay replied, guardedly.*

*"Where are the elevators in this place?" asked Dr. Malcolm. "I don't know how the hell to get out of here."*

Guerin's stomach was pumped at the hospital and he was arraigned on a charge of first-degree murder. As I began familiarizing myself with the case — the preliminary hearing was scheduled to begin at the end of July — I gradually came to the conclusion that Gregory had no need to rely on insanity for his defence. At that point I still knew little, but the evidence, as it would unfold later at the preliminary inquiry, indicated that Gregory simply wasn't the little girl's killer. I had absolutely no hesitation in defending him on this basis. Lizzie's murder was horrible; it was a grievous wrong against the laws of nature and man, but sending an innocent person to jail for it could hardly put it right.

I was sure that the child Laurie had made a mistake. Her evidence made it clear that she had absolutely no sense of time, and she had just confused seeing Gregory in the park earlier that day with the relevant time that everybody was asking her about — and maybe also with seeing him walk with Lizzie in the street on some entirely different occasion. She was too young to be sworn in as a witness, and I felt a court would see the error in her unsworn evidence for what it was.

The Crown's physical evidence, I thought, was negligible. At worst it did not exonerate Gregory, but it did nothing to implicate him either. We could show through expert witnesses, such as the marketing-research manager of Imperial Tobacco Limited, that, considering the distribution of Player's Light smokers in the total population on one hand and group O secretors on the other, the cigarette butts found in the vicinity of Lizzie's body could have been smoked by any one of twenty thousand men from the Toronto area alone. (In certain areas, such as Cabbagetown, Player's Light appears to be an especially favoured brand.) This was, of course, assuming that the cigarette butts had anything to do with the killer, which in itself was pure speculation.

No one could say which piece of junk found at the site, in addition to the cigarette butts, was or was not connected with the murder. Constable Fairly found a stained white Kleenex and a number of empty pop cans; Constable Ward, a grease-covered blue sleeve, a piece of cellophane, and a man's ripped and stained blue-and-white boxer shorts. Another policeman also named Ward found a page of the *Toronto Sun* dated May 25, 1980, indicating some human presence at the spot after the murder but before the discovery of the body — perhaps the killer returning, perhaps an innocent newspaper reader smoking Player's Light cigarettes — unless, of course, the page was simply blown there by the wind. A crumpled piece of paper may or may not have been thrown from a passing train. Constables Crawford, Sweet, and Finn found assorted candy-wrappers near the scene, and Constable Bancroft located two wine bottles. Sergeant Miller came up with two adult magazines, a racing form, and a copy of the magazine *Chatelaine*. Any of these items — or none of them — could have been dropped by the killer.

The place was a dump. Some items could even have been missed by the police — such as a crumpled, empty package of Export cigarettes, a brand that Guerin didn't smoke, found by my photographer at the scene a short time after Gregory's arrest. Singling out the Player's Light butts as "evidence" was close to being a misuse of the term.

A small type-A blood smear on Gregory's T-shirt was similarly meaningless — in fact, it pointed to his innocence. That shirt had not been cleaned for a month. Guerin could easily have come into contact with one of the 1,000,000 type-A secretors in Canada while wearing it. Considering the amount of blood on Lizzie's own clothes, if

Guerin's shirt had been the shirt worn by the killer it would have had far more blood on it than one faint smear. It was more likely that, if the blood was Lizzie's, it came from one of the flea-bites on her arms and legs that she had been in the habit of scratching until they bled. It was the evidence of Mrs. Pamela Conroy, Lizzie's aunt, that she had noticed scabs on her arms and legs the night before she died. She could have greeted Gregory with a hug or a kiss in the park, or on some previous occasion, which would account for one faint smear far better than the copious bleeding from a broken jaw and the twenty-seven external marks of violence counted by the pathologist Dr. Mancer on her body.

One piece of forensic evidence pointed to Gregory's innocence in a positive way. If Lizzie did not die for close to two hours after the sexual attack, and was buried under the railway ties only after she had died — this was a probability in Dr. Mancer's opinion — Gregory could not have been her killer. The timing alone would exonerate him. On the eyewitnesses' evidence, Lizzie's abductor would not have reached the Bayview site with her before 4:30 p.m., and Gregory was already seen by Ramona and Mrs. Tomlinson, looking neat and natural, at 6:45 p.m.

At that point the police knew as well as anyone that their physical evidence was next to non-existent. They knew that they had only two choices if they wanted to bring Gregory to trial for murder. One, they could try to discredit five independent, adult witnesses — the Crown's own witnesses — by suggesting that they had somehow *imagined* seeing a bearded man take Lizzie from the park.

But this was a tough choice. While witnesses are notoriously unreliable when it comes to identification — five people could, for instance, easily mistake one bearded man for another — it was hard to envisage several witnesses projecting a beard upon a clean-shaven man, especially when their description of his height, build, clothes, sunglasses — and of his route around the block — made it evident that they were all talking about the same person.

This left one other choice. For the prosecution to succeed, Gregory Guerin ought to have had a beard. So, the police could put a beard on Gregory Guerin. They could suggest that the witnesses couldn't recognize a clean-shaven Gregory — in court, or from his pictures, or at the police line-up — because when they had seen him with the little girl Gregory did, in fact, have a beard.

What other police theory would implicate the man they had accused? None, I suppose — unless they theorized that while a bearded stranger *took* the little girl from the park and drove her in a taxi to the Bayview site, he then handed her over to the clean-shaven Gregory to kill. (There wouldn't be a shred of evidence for this — and it would make the case the oddest sex-slaying in the annals of crime — but at least it wouldn't fly in the face of what evidence there was: a number of independent eyewitnesses seeing a bearded man. The idea must have crossed the police's mind, because they kept telling the media for some days after Gregory's arrest that they still wanted to talk to "a bearded man" who might be an "important witness".)

Having chosen a hypothesis, the police had to see it through by constructing a story as false as the beard they tried to stick on Gregory Guerin. They soon discovered, as have other prevaricating witnesses before them, that the problem with telling a lie is that it has to be supported by many other lies. One of these almost invariably proves to be a weak link, causing the whole chain to come apart.

2 A preliminary hearing is not a trial. The Crown presents its evidence; witnesses are called and they are cross-examined, but the judge does not have to concern himself with their credibility. He simply has to find that there is *some* evidence on which a trial judge in a higher court, or a properly instructed jury, could find the accused guilty. If he finds that there is such evidence, his duty is to commit the defendant to stand trial.

Normally, the defence does not stage a major contest with the Crown at a preliminary hearing. It may probe and retreat, but it seldom gives battle. The normal strategy is to treat the preliminary as a process of discovery, an opportunity to find out about the Crown's case that the defendant will have to meet and answer. The preliminary is often the defence's first and only chance.

No matter how "winnable" a case may be for the defence at trial, it can rarely be won at the preliminary inquiry. In order to throw the case out of court at that stage a judge must be impelled, in effect, to say to the Crown: "Look, why did you bring this defendant before me? There isn't any evidence against him." Few cases are weak enough for that.

The case against Guerin was one of these rare instances. In a sense it was something even rarer. Guerin's case, I felt, could be won at a preliminary — but it might be lost at an actual trial. Human prejudice against a bizarrely brain-damaged man, charged with the horrible sex slaying of a little girl, could make a jury forget that they swore an oath to try the defendant on the evidence alone. Some jurors might conclude — and convince the rest — that it would be safer to put such a man away for life. Whether the evidence proved him guilty beyond a reasonable doubt or not. Indeed, even if it showed him to be innocent. (Juries have at times a desire to "end" matters, as do the police: to assuage the community's anxiety by putting someone, anyone, behind bars.)

Prejudice was partially responsible for Guerin's being charged in the first place. If it continued to operate at his trial, his peers on the jury could give Gregory the barb of a suspicion instead of the benefit of a doubt. It was a risk. After reviewing the evidence with my associate Chris Buhr, we made the strategic decision to treat the preliminary inquiry as if it were the trial itself.

A bail application would have been futile under the circumstances, and it would have brought more damaging publicity, so we made none for Guerin. While I was preparing for his preliminary hearing, Gregory, twenty-six, was writing a thirteen-year-old's first letters from jail:

> "Hi everyone! Its now Saturday June 21, Wow Wee the first day of Summer. And guess whos in Jail. . . ." "Hello! Well its Tuesday! And every things just Gr-ate the only problem is sleeping at night. You know that I'm not a kid killer it hurts me deep inside of me to even say such a thing But i said it. . . ." "Hi! Well Jail is not a very nice place to be. It sure is an experience. . . . Well Mom and Dad it's time to say Goodnight and God Bless."

We appeared at the old City Hall in courtroom 33 before His Honour Judge W. Camblin on July 28, 1980. The problem that a person like Guerin could have before a jury was demonstrated at the outset. I had told Gregory that he must not interrupt anyone in court. However, as Lizzie's mother, the Crown's first witness, began testifying that all the kids, including Lizzie, had got along well with Gregory, the judge stopped her and turned to me:

"Excuse me, Mr. Greenspan, your client is making gestures toward the witness. Would you advise him not to."

Judge Camblin was absolutely right, but I wasn't sure what I could do. Gregory saw someone he knew — Lizzie's mother — so he was waving a cheerful hello to her. "I would hope there would be some latitude toward this particular accused," I said to his Honour. "I'm not looking for any special favours. It's simply that there is a serious and permanent problem that he has. He is childlike and . . ."

"The Court will take that into consideration," said the judge.

"I have told him to remain silent," I added, "but there is a spontaneity about him, a childlike sponteity that is very difficult to control."

The usual order prohibiting the publication of evidence was already in effect — a jury could later be gravely prejudiced by newspaper reports. The media often respond to this prohibition by writing "human interest" stories about the accused or the witnesses, since they can't report their actual testimony. Judge Camblin, very fairly, gave a specific order to the press not to report on Gregory's appearance or demeanour either. As a result, no one could write about an extremely telling incident that occurred in court a few days later.

On the whole, Gregory was behaving himself and sat quietly listening to the witnesses. However, when Tracey Lee Chiang described seeing Gregory carry her son Cameron, whose foot was bleeding a little, back from the park around 9 p.m. on Saturday, Guerin evidently believed that he was being accused of having done something wrong and he started crying.

"It was only a little piece of glass," Gregory bawled. "Hey, it was only a little piece of glass. It wasn't . . . it wasn't cut bad. It was only a little piece of glass and I took it out."

Even the Crown Attorney, John Kerr, Q.C., appeared moved. "We'll just pause for a moment, now," he said. Here was a twenty-six-year-old man charged with first-degree murder trying to make sure everyone understood that he was a good baby-sitter. "Only a little piece of glass and I didn't put it in the little boy's foot, but I seen him crying and I took the glass out," Gregory continued to whimper, desperately looking from one person to the other in the austere courtroom.

Judge Camblin ordered a short recess. No one will ever know how the incident affected him. It had no legal significance. But the judge and the lawyers on both sides avoided looking at each other, possibly because we were all close to tears. This childlike outburst was perhaps the most obvious sign of Gregory's utter innocence.

The eyewitnesses gave the defence no trouble. On the contrary. Kenneth Stiff, the taxi driver, a man suffering from cancer, had been so deeply affected by having inadvertently delivered a little girl to her death that he had to be hospitalized for several days. He was certain that Gregory was not the man with Lizzie, and said so in court. Only one witness, Pamela Heneault, thought that she could not eliminate Gregory as the man — but her evidence was somewhat undermined by the fact that she could hardly eliminate anyone in court, except Sergeant Cenzura, Crown Attorney Kerr, and, to my intense relief, me. In fact, when first asked to point to the one person who most closely resembled the man she had seen — the informal seating made it hard for her to tell who was the accused — Henault pointed to a bearded spectator, a university student, who became paralysed with terror. (Later he kindly consented to have his picture taken and filed as an exhibit.)

"I think your law student's in a lot of trouble, Mr. Kerr," said I as Ms. Henault kept pointing to various people.

"What about your student? We were just coming to him," Kerr replied, quite correctly, as Guy Kay's successor joined the ranks of those Pamela Henault couldn't eliminate. In the end they would probably have included most men in Metropolitan Toronto.

The two eyewitnesses who had seen the bearded man with Lizzie for the longest period of time in the park had no such problem. "There is no question in your mind," I asked Rose Ann Neil, "that Gregory Guerin is not that person?"

"The guy right there? No way," she replied.

"He's not the person you saw?"

"No way."

"With Lizzie Tomlinson?"

"No way."

If it was possible to be more emphatic than that, Susan Jeschkeit was. She had known Lizzie. She had seen the bearded man with her in the park for a period of an hour or more. There was virtually no need for me to cross-examine her, because she made no secret about her feelings. "The officers, they can tell you," she told Crown Attorney Kerr in direct examination. "I've called on the phone and I even told them that they don't have the right man, and that man that's in court right now is not the man that killed little Lizzie Tomlinson."

In spite of this, the real hurdle was going to be the police officers. The judge would not have to believe their evidence beyond a reasonable doubt; if he thought that their testimony about seeing Gregory with a beard amounted to *some* evidence, his duty at this preliminary stage was to resolve any doubt in favour of committing Gregory to trial.

My duty was to show the judge that what the police were saying was no evidence at all but, as I believed it to be, a total fabrication.

The first week of the preliminary was taken up with the identification witnesses; then court adjourned to resume in September. The police had to know, of course, that the identification evidence had been a fiasco: without a counter-offensive their case would be hard to salvage.

So, in September, a thirty-year veteran of the force named Sergeant Donald Bell took the stand. He was to be the first policeman to say that he had seen Gregory with a three- to four-day growth of beard Sunday morning at 5:30 a.m. at the Tomlinsons' house.

The police had brought Sergeant Bell's statement to the Crown's office only the day before; the Crown Attorney knew none of the details. John Kerr, as a careful lawyer and an officer of the court, was not going to be a party to any manipulation. As an experienced advocate he also knew that he had better plug any holes in the evidence of his own witness in direct examination, before a cross-examiner could put his fist through them. Therefore, the Sergeant's troubles in court started well before my cross-examination.

Bell said he was at the Tomlinson house at 5:30 a.m. He saw Gregory; then he went to the search-control area, then to 51 station after 6 a.m. and filed an "occurrence report". Kerr showed him a copy; Bell looked at it. Yes, that was his report. He typed it between 6 and 6:40 a.m.

Yes, but then why was the time noted on it as 5:30?

Oops. "It should be 6:30," said the Sergeant.

"Why does it say 5:30?" asked Kerr. "Can you explain why it has 5:30 on it?"

"No, I can't explain that. In fact, this is a very small typewriter and —"

"What's that got to do with it?"

A good question. Soon Sergeant Bell concluded that, while he did type out an occurrence, this seemed not to be the copy of the occurrence he had typed out. He had no answer as to why anybody else would type out another copy of his occurrence.

But this was only the beginning. The crux of Sergeant Bell's evidence was that when he saw a newspaper picture of the clean-shaven Gregory at Lizzie's funeral he was struck by the great discrepancy between the man in the picture and the bearded man at the Tomlinson house on Sunday. In fact, he wouldn't have recognized him, had he not seen his name in the caption. A bearded man turning into a clean-shaven pallbearer: supposedly this was what had really aroused Sergeant Bell's suspicion.

"Is that the picture you're talking about?" asked Kerr, showing him a photograph in the *Toronto Star*.

"That's the picture I'm talking about."

John Kerr seemed puzzled. "Does his name appear in it?"

Oops again. "No," the Sergeant replied. He started saying something about telling his partner that this was the man when Judge Camblin interrupted him:

"Excuse me, my notes must be incorrect. I have your evidence stating that you didn't recognize the person in the newspaper until you read his name."

"I thought . . ." the Sergeant paused. "For some reason, I thought his name was on . . . in the paper that day and that's why my attention was drawn to him and I could recognize him."

"But you said you didn't recognize him," Kerr said. I had to intervene at this point; the Crown was beginning to cross-examine its own witness. Kerr apologized. "Well, your Honour can perhaps appreciate the difficulty I'm having," he said.

"I can certainly appreciate it, Mr. Kerr," Judge Camblin replied.

No doubt the judge could appreciate it even more as Bell stuck stubbornly, pitifully, to his story under cross-examination, even when it was made clear that at that point Gregory's name had not appeared in *any* of the newspapers. All four copies of Bell's original report had been "lost", and he could offer no explanation as to why someone would retype his report changing only the time of day. Remarkably, four copies of a supplementary report Bell claimed to have written on Tuesday, May 27, had also mysteriously disappeared. He was supposed to have written this second report after telephoning an officer at 51 Division to tell him that Gregory used to have a beard and ought to be investigated. When his own notes for that day were found to contain no reference to such a phone call or report, Bell concluded that maybe he had written the report on Wednesday, May 28, after all. Interestingly, the police officer who supposedly took Bell's call, whether on Tuesday or Wednesday, could never be found.

Exit Bell.

Sergeant Folley, Bell's partner, also claimed to have seen Gregory with a beard — but his own notes said nothing about it or about any suspicion. In fact, he said, he and Bell never discussed the problem, except when he showed a newspaper picture to Bell (Bell said *he* showed it to Folley), and that he never discussed the question of being called as a witness (Bell said they had discussed it about six times).

Before Folley took the stand, Bell had said that in August he and Folley bumped into Sergeants O'Toole and Cenzura, and, knowing that the two homicide officers were in charge of the Guerin case, Bell asked them if he and Folley would be called as witnesses — though in re-examination Bell changed this to *not* having known that O'Toole and Cenzura were in charge and having been approached by them first. Now Folley recalled the same event as being approached by O'Toole to ask about Guerin's appearance. After this meeting Folley and Bell completed a joint statement. Their statement said that they had seen Guerin at the funeral, which in fact the officers hadn't attended. Folley had no explanation as to why he had signed the statement without correcting it first.

Exit Folley.

Sergeant Miller had originally appeared in court on August 1. At that time he testified that Guerin as he sat in court, clean-shaven, looked essentially the same as he had looked on that Sunday in May when Miller took a statement from him. However, when court reconvened on November 12, the Sergeant returned with a new story. This time he said that on Sunday, May 25, Guerin had a two-days growth of beard which he could recollect by the little hairs on his face. He had made notes of that day on foolscap and copied them into his notebook — but when it was pointed out to him that his notebook contained nothing about Guerin's facial features, Miller said that he only noted those on the foolscap without bothering to copy them. The foolscap, alas, was no longer available.

Why did he not mention Guerin's beard to any of the homicide officers? Why did he not mention it in his earlier testimony in court? Well, Miller said, he did not know it was going to be an issue. He didn't even recall the beard until Sergeants O'Toole and Cenzura had mentioned something to him about it.

Constable Bancroft had also seen Guerin on Sunday, May 25. He did make notes about his glasses and moustache; they were in his notebook. However, he now told the court that he could also remember Guerin having a growth of beard about a quarter of an inch long — very much like the composite picture of the killer.

He did not jot this down in his notes, no. But he could remember it.

Could he also remember what Guerin happened to be wearing? He couldn't, because he didn't write it down. Of all the things he did not write down, Constable Bancroft could remember only the beard.

Why did he not report it to senior officers earlier? Bancroft said he didn't think of volunteering any information. Why did he volunteer it now? Sergeant Miller had asked him to come to court. Come to court why? The Sergeant didn't say — but Bancroft gathered it had to do with Gregory's appearance.

Exit Miller. Exit Bancroft.

I thought it was quite instructive to watch the attempt by some police officers to turn Guerin into the bearded man; instructive, if not very impressive. Why not impressive? Because to have appeared as the policemen described him, Gregory would have had to achieve the following feat:

First, he would have had to have at least a three- to four-days growth of beard for the eyewitnesses to see him as "a bearded man" on Saturday as he walked with Lizzie from the park and hailed a taxi. Then, he would have had to shave it off to appear clean-shaven by seven o'clock the same afternoon to Lizzie's mother, to Tracey Lee Chiang, for whom he baby-sat until 9 p.m., and to Lizzie's uncle, William Conroy, who saw him around 2 a.m. Sunday morning. Then — and this was the real trick — he would have had to grow it all back by 5:30 a.m. on Sunday to achieve the desired effect of a three- to four-days growth for Sergeants Bell, Folley, and Miller, and Constable Bancroft.

Did the officers fabricate their stories with the criminal intent of misleading the court and interfering with the administration of justice? I would not go this far, until someone showed me evidence of their intent. Policemen, too, are entitled to the benefit of a reasonable doubt. They may have honestly remembered seeing what they deeply wished to have seen.

The Crown to its credit — though strenuously arguing in its memorandum of December 15, 1980, that Guerin should be committed to stand trial — did not rely on the police witnesses' vision of a bearded Gregory at all. John Kerr's only additional argument to Judge Camblin was based on the suggestion that Gregory's attempt at suicide could indicate a consciousness of guilt, as could one of Gregory's dreams in which he thought that he was choking Lizzie. (He related such a dream to Bill Conroy, Lizzie's uncle, just before trying to poison himself.)

I thought that it was rather scraping the bottom of the barrel for the Crown to rely on a dream — especially as, while talking about his dream, Gregory also reiterated to Conroy that he did not, in fact, kill Lizzie. (As an interesting sidelight, in describing his dream to Conroy, Gregory demonstrated manually choking Lizzie, which according to the pathologist, Dr. Mancer, was precisely *not* the way in which Lizzie came to be asphyxiated.) To me both the dream and the suicide attempt were equally consistent with the despair of a simpleminded man who was being wrongly accused of the year's most horrible crime. In our law, as I argued in my submission to Judge Camblin, even evidence equally consistent with guilt and innocence would amount to no evidence of guilt at all.

Judge Camblin agreed. In a terse judgment on December 23, 1980, he discharged Gregory Guerin, finding that there was no evidence against him from which a jury could conclude that he had killed Lizzie Tomlinson. It was the right decision. On the facts, it was the only decision. Given the climate surrounding the case, however, it was also a courageous decision. I think any judge would have been wrong to take the easy way out and pass the case on to a higher court, but some judges might have done precisely that.

I believe Judge Camblin would have made the same decision even if some police officers had not attempted to put a beard on Gregory. Still, whenever this kind of evidence is exposed, it cannot but weaken the case it was designed to bolster. Trying to achieve victory by unfair methods can result in losing a battle which, if fought fairly, might have been won.

If it had not been for their attempt to put a beard on Gregory, the police might have had a second kick at the cat. The Attorney General is entitled to send an accused person to trial on a so-called "preferred indictment", even if a judge has discharged him after a preliminary inquiry. Late in December there were indications that the Crown might be thinking of exercising this prerogative.

On the last day of the year 1980 I wrote a letter to Attorney General R. Roy McMurtry. While I had no standing before him in this matter under the Criminal Code, I submitted that he ought to wait for the transcripts of the preliminary hearing and study them carefully before making up his mind about a preferred indictment. I pointed out that the testimony of the police officers was "to say the least, questionable". I made mention of the missing reports and the conflicting evidence. "In this particular area I would like to ask you," I wrote to McMurtry, "to review carefully the evidence of the police officers as to whether or not there was an attempt to 'shore-up' a very weak case."

It was a hardball — thrown softly. I did not want to make an outright accusation of wrongdoing. Had I made one, it would have left the Attorney General with only two choices — first, laying charges against some policemen, or second, pressing for a preferred indictment against Guerin to take the heat off the police — and I couldn't be sure that he would make the right choice.

Hardball? Maybe. I had an innocent client who had already spent seven months in jail. I wanted people in authority to know that if they took Gregory Guerin to court again, if they exposed him to the risk of a miscarriage of justice, to the risk of being innocently convicted of a heinous offence, the consequences of which he might not survive — people jailed for the sex-killing of a child are frequently murdered by other inmates — the conduct of the police would have to come under very close scrutiny.

There should have been no preferred indictment on the merits of the case anyway. In the event, there was none. Gregory wrote his last letter from prison — "Hi Mom! I did not forget you Dad. Keep good care of your leg. I love you and Mom. Jailbird, Gregory" — and by January 1981 he was living at home again. The community had no difficulty accepting the fact of his innocence.

Lizzie's murderer was never found. It is doubtful if anyone ever looked for him after Gregory's release. New investigations are uncommon. Once a charge is laid, whatever the courts say about it makes little difference. The authorities seldom admit mistakes. The files are closed and the case appears in statistics as a crime "solved" by the police.

## NOTES

p.121, 1.2: Elizabeth Jane Tomlinson; her nickname has been variously spelled "Lizzie" or "Lizzy" in the press.

p.134, 1.22: Experts who champion lie-detectors regard them as 75 per cent accurate. If so, this itself makes them fall short of proof beyond a reasonable doubt. If they were allowed in court, they could result in the conviction of one innocent person out of every four accused (or the acquittal of three guilty persons out of twelve, for that matter).

p.134, 1.37: A number of subjects even confess falsely, which is an additional danger of lie-detectors or other high-pressure techniques. When repeatedly told that they are guilty, whether by a person in authority or by an impressive "scientific" machine, some people of feeble intellect or personality may confess, because they actually become convinced that they are guilty. The classic British example is Timothy Evans, a semi-retarded young man — in many ways not unlike Guerin — who confessed to homicides committed by the famous serial murderer John Reginald Christie. Evans did receive a free pardon eventually, but as it came after he had been hanged it may have been of scant consolation to him.

p.135, 1.35: As it turned out, Greenspan very nearly had to do the case for no fee at all. Legal Aid at first demanded that Guerin surrender the small settlement he received after his accident, kept for him in a trust fund, in exchange for his legal fees. Greenspan put his foot down. "This man gave up his IQ for that money," he said to the legal bureaucracy. "There's no way you or I are going to touch a penny of it." Eventually Legal Aid relented and paid Guerin's fees.

p.137, 1.34: Laurie actually told Crown Attorney John Kerr in court — possibly just because she was nervous — that she did not know the difference between the truth and a lie.

The Canada Evidence Act allows a young child who does not understand the meaning of an oath to testify without being sworn, provided the child is of sufficient intelligence, and understands the duty to tell the truth in court. However, an accused cannot be convicted on that evidence alone. The child's evidence must be corroborated by some other material evidence. If the Crown's case, even at a preliminary inquiry, rests solely on the unsworn evidence of a child, then the case must be dismissed. (Re *Stillo and The Queen*, 1981.)

p.148, l.24: The burden is on the Crown to prove guilt. If guilt and innocence are equally consistent with the facts, then the evidence has simply not reached the threshold of being evidence upon which a jury could, in law, convict. It is only if the accused's guilt is *more* probable than his innocence that there is even some evidence legally available upon which a jury can convict. Some authors have argued that even this should not be sufficient to let the case go to trial (see M. J. Fish, "Committal for Trial: 'Some' Evidence is Not 'Sufficient' " [1979], quoted by Lamer, J. [dissenting] in *Mezzo v. The Queen*, 1986).

# 9. A Large Blue Suitcase

The Crown's synopsis made it appear a simple matter.

On Thursday, February 28, 1980, members of the Metropolitan Toronto Police Force Intelligence Bureau were keeping a GMC pickup truck under surveillance. They followed it from Eastern Avenue to a public parking lot on Temperance Street, just east of Bay Street, in the heart of downtown Toronto. The pickup was being used, in the Crown's words, "by known members of the outlawed motorcycle gang, Para-Dice Riders".

The time was shortly after 8 p.m. The undercover policemen observed what seemed to them two males getting out of the truck, walking to Bay Street, and returning a few minutes later. They got back into the truck and moved it to another part of the parking lot, next to a 1978 model Ford Zephyr passenger car. Then they got out again and went to the trunk of the Zephyr, where they were met by a third person.

According to the undercover officers, this third man opened the trunk. He took out a large blue suitcase and a large garbage bag. He opened them. Then all three men looked inside the suitcase and the bag.

After a brief conversation the men put the suitcase and the garbage bag back into the trunk of the Zephyr. The two males in the truck drove off, and the third man walked off to Bay Street. After about half an hour, at around 8:55 p.m., he came back, got into the car, and drove off.

The undercover officers followed the Zephyr in three separate vehicles for a while. Eventually they called for the assistance of uniformed policemen, and had the Zephyr stopped on Bloor Street just west of Euclid Avenue. When stopped by the police (ostensibly for "speeding") and asked for his ownership papers, the driver told the officers that the car belonged to "a friend of a friend".

A search of the trunk revealed a large blue suitcase as well as several garbage bags, together containing about sixty-six pounds of marijuana. The Crown estimated the value of the illicit drug to be around sixty to seventy thousand dollars.

The man driving the Zephyr was charged with possession of marijuana for the purpose of trafficking. His name was Richard Goldman, and he was a lawyer by profession. A few days later he retained me to defend him.

If the events had occurred as the Crown's brief described them, there was a grave risk of a court's finding Goldman guilty of the offence. The substance in the trunk of the car he drove was unquestionably cannabis. The Zephyr did not belong to him, but since he had been observed taking a suitcase and a bag from the trunk and looking at their contents in the parking lot, it could be inferred that he saw the marijuana. If so, even if he did not know about it before, by the time he was stopped he could be held to be knowingly in possession of marijuana — and a court would be entitled to further infer that he possessed it for the purpose of trafficking from its quantity alone. People tend not to possess sixty-six pounds of the stuff for their own use.

However, my client told me that he was innocent — and I believed him.

As a defence lawyer, of course, a personal belief in Goldman's innocence would have been quite unnecessary for me to act for him as a client. Passing judgment on a defendant's version of the truth is the business of the courts; his lawyer's business is to present the client's version on his behalf. Any defence lawyer who tries to decide "the truth" in his own mind — while his client is maintaining his innocence — is simply in the wrong business. He should set up as a mind-reader.

Goldman told me that he had no inkling of what was in the trunk of the car that he drove. Ordinarily, this would have been enough, no matter what personal views I may have had about the credibility of his story. My own beliefs had no legal significance whatever. If this was my client's story, this was going to be our defence.

In this instance, however, I did not simply take the man's word. I actually, personally, believed him. My reason for believing him, moreover, had nothing to do with my professional evaluation of the evidence — at least initially. In the beginning it was as private a reason as I have ever had for making any judgment in my life.

The accused man happened to be an old friend. We had been at law school together. We were called to the bar in the same year. I *knew* him. Ricky Goldman was simply not a drug-trafficker. (Frankly, had he told me that he was guilty, I would have had a great deal of difficulty believing that. I would probably have assumed that he was trying to protect someone else.)

I had no difficulty whatever believing him when he said that he was innocent.

The strength of my personal feelings, in fact, worried me quite a bit. I was afraid that they might interfere with my ability to handle the case. Acting for a friend is almost like acting for oneself: not a good idea, generally speaking. Nor is it a good idea — contrary to what some trendy TV shows may suggest — to act for any client in whose innocence one has a passionate, personal belief. It is unavoidable sometimes, but it can cloud one's judgment. The ideal thing is to act in accordance with one's role as a defence lawyer in the adversary process, without addressing the question in personal terms at all.

The ideal option was not available in this case. Ricky *was* a friend and I personally believed him. With this handicap — as I considered it to be — I tried looking realistically at the facts.

Goldman was thirty-seven at the time, a practising criminal lawyer with an office on Bay Street. He was a fine lawyer and a fine human being, though possibly not the keenest administrator or businessman. He wasn't a buttoned-down, three-piece-suited person. In fact, one of the things I liked about him was that he was a pretty free spirit, without a touch of stuffiness or pomposity.

On February 28, having had a tiff with his wife, Goldman was without the family car and without a lift. After finishing his business in court early that day, he didn't feel like going home. He took the subway to Lawrence and Yonge, where he had lunch with a friend named Ulrich, then together they drove in Ulrich's car to another friend's home, where they had arranged to play a game of cards.

The friend's name was Stephen Cohen. Cohen had a visitor in his place when Goldman and Ulrich arrived, a man named Raymond Leach, someone Goldman had seen once or twice before but barely knew. Leach left a short time later, and Goldman, Ulrich, and Cohen, along with a fourth friend who arrived soon afterwards, started playing cards. Cohen was not feeling well and eventually retired to his bedroom, but the others continued playing until about 7:30 p.m.

Goldman had to be back at his office by 8 p.m. because he was meeting a client, a man named William "Woody" Theakston, who had phoned him earlier asking for an appointment. Not having a car, Goldman asked Ulrich for a lift. Ulrich, however, had to go home and couldn't drop Goldman at his downtown office. So Ricky asked his host, Stephen Cohen — who was running a fever and was not going to leave his home that evening anyway — if he could borrow his car. Cohen replied that he had already lent his own sports car to Raymond Leach — but since Leach had left *his* vehicle, a 1978 Zephyr, in Cohen's garage, Goldman was welcome to take that car for the evening if he wanted it.

Goldman took the Zephyr and drove downtown to meet his client, Theakston.

"Woody" Theakston, the man whose GMC pickup truck the undercover police officers followed from Eastern Avenue to the Temperance Street parking lot that evening, was a member of the Para-Dice Riders motorcycle club. Goldman had acted for him on various criminal matters over the years; currently he was acting for him on a charge of rape. What complicated matters on February 28 was that Goldman had in his office a valise containing a change of clothes for Theakston – used at a bail hearing on an earlier occasion — which Goldman wanted to return to his client. The valise had been sitting in his office for some months by then, taking up space.

Since Theakston had a habit of talking at great length about his personal problems — I know from experience that such clients are not uncommon — and since Goldman did not want to stay for hours in his office that night, he thought it might be prudent to put the valise containing Theakston's clothes in the trunk of the Zephyr before Theakston arrived. This way Goldman could discuss whatever legal issues there were to be discussed with Theakston in the office, then take him down to the parking lot and have him pick up his clothes.

Accordingly, having arrived at his Bay Street office before Theakston, Goldman picked up the valise, took it down to the parking lot on Temperance Street, and put it into the trunk of the Zephyr. Then he went to get himself a hamburger.

Goldman did recall seeing some garbage bags and another suitcase in the trunk at that time, but it did not even cross his mind to pay any attention to them. It was a borrowed car; there could be anything in its trunk. Whatever was there was none of his business.

When Goldman returned to his office a few minutes after 8 p.m., Theakston was already waiting for him in the hallway, accompanied by another person. (Who this other person was became important and we'll talk about it in a minute.)

After discussing his client's legal problems, Goldman went with Theakston and his companion to the parking lot, opened the trunk of the Zephyr, and gave Theakston his valise of clothes. Then client and companion drove off in the GMC truck, and Goldman went back to his office. He attended to legal business for another ten minutes or so, then returned to the parking lot, got into his borrowed car, and drove off.

About fifteen minutes later, he found himself under arrest.

This was all Ricky could tell me, and this made him guilty of absolutely nothing. If you borrow someone's car — or his jacket, apartment, or houseboat — the law does not oblige you to search it in case it contains illegal drugs. Not only is there no legal duty on anyone to do so, even ordinary prudence doesn't call for it.

I considered Goldman blameless not only in law, but also in the everyday sense of the word. He was a victim of circumstances that no one could have expected or guarded himself against. You can't run a check on everyone with whom you decide to play gin rummy, let alone on their friends.

This boiled the case down to one vital question at the outset. Assuming that the innocent circumstances under which Goldman came to drive the Zephyr could be established — as could the existence of Theakston's clothes in a valise, explaining why he would open the trunk in the parking lot — it would still not answer why Goldman would take out another "large blue suitcase" and a garbage bag, open them, and look at the contents with Theakston and his companion.

Goldman's answer was simple: he didn't. He took from the trunk nothing except the valise containing Theakston's clothes. He opened nothing and he looked at nothing.

But two undercover intelligence officers, Constable Michael Young and Constable Hugh Blake, were ready to testify under oath that they saw him opening the suitcase and the bag.

There was no question in my mind that the officers were either mistaken or lying. If Goldman was telling the truth, they had to be. A jury, however, not knowing whom to believe, might well choose to believe the officers. Twelve honest, ordinary citizens might pose themselves the old, standard question we've already considered in this chapter: why should policemen lie?

I could think of an excellent reason, speculative as it was. The two constables, along with a third one named Avery (who later died of an illness before the commencement of the trial), had been watching a biker — Theakston — suspected of having some connection with drugs. They saw him meet someone in a parking lot. This man opened, then closed, the trunk of a car. He was someone the officers didn't know and, for all they could tell at that point, might be Mr. Big himself. They had to make a quick decision about whom to investigate. Avery, knowing that they could always find Theakston later, not unreasonably made the decision for all of them to follow the new "suspect". They had him stopped and, to their considerable delight, discovered a whole quantity of drugs.

There they were, one happy lot of officers on Bloor Street, actually whooping, laughing, and hollering as they were looking at the open trunk of the Zephyr. One of them said "Holy shit!" a couple of times. They were good, eager undercover policemen, playing their parts with the enthusiasm of actors in a Hollywood movie, complete with full beards, old clothes — one even wearing a large Stetson hat with a feathered band. Their hunch had paid off. Their long vigil on the coldest evening of the year — it was 15 degrees Celsius below zero — had not been in vain. "You're fucking under arrest," one of them said to Goldman.

The fact that the man they had caught red-handed, as they believed, was not just anyone but a criminal lawyer only seemed to increase the officers' delight. This was not necessarily an expression of malice against lawyers, only of the fact that a bigger fish is always a better catch.

By the time of the bail hearing the next day, however, the officers had discovered the incontestable fact that Goldman did not own the car, and had in fact only borrowed it an hour or so before they had first seen him standing beside it on the Temperance Street parking lot. They knew quite well that the law, very wisely, makes no assumptions about anybody's knowledge of what's in a vehicle, unless he is the owner or the regular driver. It is not up to him to prove that he did not know what was inside the trunk. It's up to the prosecution to prove that he did know it. You don't "possess" drugs unless you know you have them.

But what if they had actually *seen* Goldman looking at the contents of the blue suitcase and the garbage bag? Then it would be a different story. Then Goldman would have to know. Then they'd get credit for "the collar", and a great night of solid police work would not end in disappointment for Constables Young, Blake, and Avery.

We had reasons for such speculation long before I had the chance to cross-examine the policemen in court. The officers presented themselves as keen observers. One claimed to have been looking through his binoculars, supposedly bringing the scene to within twenty feet of his eyes, as Goldman took the blue suitcase and the bag from the trunk, and opened both. The other constable confirmed this — though without the aid of binoculars (and, as it turned out later, contradicting the first officer in some vital details). But both keen observers said that Theakston's companion, the third person present, was a male. One officer even saw that he had a beard.

This was a little boo-boo. In fact, Theakston's companion on the parking lot that night was not anything like a male. Her name was Arlene Wallin, and she could not easily be mistaken for a male from twenty or a hundred feet away. Whatever she did have, the jury could see in court that it was not anything remotely resembling a beard.

But that was not all. Soon we had reason for believing that, while the policemen could distinctly "see" what would help the case for the prosecution, they couldn't "see" what would detract from it. At Goldman's bail hearing the morning after his arrest, the Crown Attorney on duty, a young woman named Donna McGillis — having been briefed by the police concerning details of Goldman's case, about which, naturally, she had not known anything before — told the judge that Goldman had been seen "passing a package" to two males in the parking lot.

This was very interesting. It was contrary to the Crown's eventual synopsis, but it described precisely what Goldman did do: he opened the trunk and gave Theakston his clothes. Except, by the time of the preliminary hearing, neither Constable Young nor Constable Blake could remember having seen that. As far as they were concerned, it never happened. For some reason they only wrote up their notes the morning after the arrest — in consultation with one another, at the end of the bail hearing — and their notes contained no mention of Goldman handing Theakston a "package". No police officer ever admitted telling any such thing to a Crown Attorney.

In that case, I thought, Ms. McGillis must be a remarkable woman. Either she could somehow divine things that no one ever told her about — or else she would just make up wild stories about people taking "packages" out of trunks to liven up the monotony of bail hearings. Frankly, I considered a third possibility, which was that the policemen were lying through their teeth.

In my opinion, what the officers did see was Ricky handing a "package" to Theakston — which was what he did do. Not yet realizing that this would hurt the Crown's case, Blake or Young mentioned it to the duty officer who briefed Donna McGillis the next morning. Once they realized how much it would hurt the prosecution, of course, the officers could no longer remember it.

However much this may have clinched matters in my own mind, the judge later at Ricky Goldman's trial accepted the Crown's argument that Ms. McGillis's statement at the bail hearing was double hearsay and inadmissible as evidence. Though an accused person does not have to prove his innocence — it is up to the prosecution to prove him guilty — it became of some importance for us to find out the real story behind the drug-laden Zephyr. My office began to investigate. By the time the trial commenced in the winter of 1981 before His Honour Judge Hoilett and a jury, we felt sure that we knew what happened.

The facts came out in the evidence of a witness named Ronald James Schott. This man testified under the protection of the Canada Evidence Act (which meant that whatever he said could not be used against him). He was a bright, well-educated man, with a young family and good prospects. He had been very reluctant to come to court because, though no longer involved in drugs since his wife's pregnancy, he used to be a dealer. Schott knew to whom the marijuana in the Zephyr's trunk belonged, because it was he who had arranged for its importation from Buffalo about eight days before Goldman's arrest.

It was Schott's evidence that Stephen Cohen, whom he knew, had asked him around February 20 to meet a friend who needed some help. The friend turned out to be Raymond Leach, and the help Leach needed was for Schott to arrange for the importation of one hundred pounds of marijuana from the United States. Schott made the arrangements, and the drug was duly delivered a couple of days later. It came in the wheel wells of a station wagon, and was unloaded by Schott and the courier who had brought it at a location near Terra Cotta, Ontario. It was packed, as Schott had seen while helping to unload it, in garbage bags.

Schott met Leach and explained to him exactly where outside Terra Cotta he could pick up the drug in some building, and where to return the key. He later checked and found the key; the "product" was gone.

On the day of Goldman's arrest, Leach called on Schott again, this time to ask Schott if he could store the marijuana for him for a while. Schott couldn't promise it, but told Leach to meet him the following day. That day would have been February 29, the day after Goldman's arrest. Of course, Leach never showed up for that appointment.

Leach, as seemed evident, had been stuck with most of the marijuana. He couldn't unload it, or he couldn't unload it fast enough. His additional difficulty was that the drug was sitting in the Zephyr's trunk — but the Zephyr did not belong to Leach. He had borrowed the car a few days earlier from a completely unsuspecting acquaintance, who (as he testified in court) kept demanding it back.

Leach couldn't very well return the car without disposing of the marijuana first — nor did he want to drive around town with the drug in the trunk. His solution was to borrow Cohen's sports car, leaving the Zephyr in Cohen's garage. In all likelihood Cohen had no idea what was in the trunk; otherwise he would not have allowed Leach to leave it in his garage, let alone offered the car to Goldman for an evening.

Not surprisingly, Leach denied everything on the witness stand, even claiming that he had borrowed Cohen's sports car only because Goldman had borrowed his Zephyr first. (The probability that Goldman would borrow the car of a man he barely knew was small. But if he did, why would he then ask Ulrich, with whom he had been playing cards in the apartment, for a lift — as Ulrich testified that he did — hours after he had supposedly borrowed the Zephyr? The probability of this was no longer small: it was non-existent. In court I could safely call it, along with the rest of Leach's evidence, an obvious lie. But Leach's "credibility" on this or any other issue was not the main problem for the defence.)

The Crown Attorney at Goldman's trial was Ted Ormston: a good lawyer and a dispassionate prosecutor; also, I've always felt, a very decent human being in personal terms. It was my feeling, however, that in this particular case he got carried away at the outset. He was not the first prosecutor (or defence lawyer, for that matter) to be so affected by the dynamics of a given trial.

Ormston began by suggesting that whatever Leach did, Goldman must have been in on the deal with him. However, since the prosecution couldn't offer one scintilla of evidence for this outrageous proposition — which was totally contradicted by Schott's emphatic evidence that Ricky's name never came up during his conversations with Leach — the Crown had a fallback position. It was that even if Goldman had been unaware of the marijuana initially, he was in possession, and therefore guilty, once he saw the drug in the parking lot.

This was the Crown's theory, and it took us straight back to police Constables Blake and Young. What did the two officers see on the evening of February 28?

Different things, as it turned out. In fact, just about the only thing they agreed on was Goldman's looking at the marijuana. Otherwise, they might as well have been watching different parking lots.

Blake started out by saying that he positioned himself on the first floor of the Simpsons department store garage, ten or twelve feet up, overlooking the public parking lot on Temperance Street. He said that he had a very clear vision.

We knew, however, that on the first floor a screen would have obscured what Blake could see. When I put this to him in cross-examination, Blake suddenly remembered that he was on the second floor — he always called the second floor the first floor — and there was no screen there. Anyway, he saw the GMC truck park in the second row on the lot, as he was watching the scene from the north.

Young, who was watching the scene from the south — from two hundred feet away but, as he said, through binoculars — saw the truck park in the third row, not the second. The officers also had the bag and the suitcase come out and go back into the trunk in different sequences. One had Goldman squatting down to look into the bag and the other didn't. However, the main point was this:

Young, watching from the south, swore the truck parked *north of the Zephyr*. (He had to say this. Had the truck parked south of the Zephyr, it would have been between him and the car, obscuring his line of vision to the area behind the car's trunk. He couldn't have seen a thing.)

Blake, watching from the north, swore the truck parked *south of the Zephyr*. (He had to say this. Had the truck parked north of the Zephyr, it would have obscured *his* line of vision and he couldn't have seen a thing.)

Where was Officer Blake, then: on the first floor or on the second? Was Goldman squatting or standing up? Was his car parked in the second row or the third? And, especially, did the GMC truck park north or south of the car? If south, how did Young see what happened at the truck area? If north, how did Blake?

The plain fact was, as cross-examination revealed, that both officers could not have seen what each of them swore he saw from where he was conducting the surveillance. It was a physical impossibility. "If Blake is telling the truth, Young is lying," I later submitted to the jury. "But if Young is telling the truth, Blake is a liar."

The third officer, the late Constable Avery, whose testimony was read into the record at trial, had not been an eyewitness. He had stayed in his car all along as the mobile unit of the surveillance team, directing the other two officers through his radio. However, his notes also contained a reference to Goldman handing a package to one of the "males" in the truck. Avery must have heard this from Blake or Young. Like Crown Attorney Donna McGillis, he couldn't simply divine it.

Goldman was obviously telling the truth about what he had done on the parking lot.

At the time of Goldman's trial, a charge of possession for the purpose of trafficking consisted of a two-phase procedure. In the first phase, to convict someone of possession, a judge (or jury) had to be convinced beyond a reasonable doubt that the defendant knowingly had the illicit drug in his possession. If so, the second phase began. To convict someone of having had the purpose of trafficking in a drug, the judge (or jury) had to be convinced on the balance of probabilities that he didn't possess it simply for his private use.

Goldman, for instance, could be found guilty of possession if the jury believed that, though he only discovered the marijuana on the parking lot, he then decided to keep it for himself. However, this would not make him guilty of possession for the purpose of trafficking. (If he had found it, then simply taken it back to his acquaintances, saying, "Here's your silly pot," it might or might not have made him guilty of possession for the purpose of trafficking. This wasn't what happened — but it would have raised an interesting legal question in court.)

After prosecution and defence completed their cases — Goldman took the witness stand himself, though of course no defendant is obliged to do so — both sides addressed the jury. I felt that the prosecutor chose to speak in a highly inflammatory fashion. Judge Hoilett warned him about it, but the damage was probably done. The jury, after deliberating for a full day, came back to say that they had found Ricky guilty of possession. The Crown had won the first phase.

I need not elaborate on how Goldman must have felt, but to say that I was dismayed doesn't begin to express my feelings. I was shocked and horrified. The jury convicted an innocent man — and knowing that this can happen sometimes, has happened before, and no doubt will happen again, does not make it any easier when it happens to your client.

Ricky was actually more philosophical about the matter than I was, and he ended up trying to console me. Much as I appreciated the gesture, it did not make me feel any better. In fact, it made me feel worse.

Nor was it any consolation that, at this point, the conviction was for only a relatively minor offence — simple possession — for which in 1981 the ordinary penalty was a fine, or possibly even a conditional discharge (though in this case the quantity involved — sixty-six pounds — made a discharge very unlikely). Still, because the penal consequences were not great, this would have ended the matter for most people, except for the humiliation involved in any criminal prosecution and, for an innocent person, the indignity of being wrongfully convicted.

But Ricky Goldman was a lawyer. For him to be convicted even of the simple possession of sixty-six pounds of marijuana could mean disbarment. At the age of thirty-seven he would be in danger of seeing his entire professional life go down the drain. No one — no businessman, teacher, plumber, journalist, musician, accountant, or doctor, perhaps not even a politician — would face such grave consequences for an offence of this kind.

Should he be convicted in the second phase of the far more serious offence of trafficking, there would also be the near-certainty of a jail sentence. The stakes were extremely high. Still, we decided to lead no evidence in the second phase because there was nothing for us to lead.

Though juries can't be asked why they convicted someone, I felt quite certain — and said so in my second-phase jury address — that it was because they thought Goldman had discovered the marijuana in the parking lot and was about to drive it back to his friends. There was absolutely no evidence for any other type of involvement on his part — but two policemen said that they saw him look into the large blue suitcase, and policemen are supposed to have no reason to lie. Still, this should not make him guilty of possession for the purpose of trafficking, and in a brief address I urged the jury to acquit him on this more serious charge.

Then Crown Attorney Ormston rose to speak again. He was brief enough, too. When he sat down, I didn't know whether to scream at him in fury — or embrace him warmly and kiss him on both cheeks. He had been so unfair that I was certain he had just given us a mistrial.

If Ormston's jury address was sufficiently inflammatory after the first phase of the trial for the judge to deliver a warning to him, this time he went off the deep end. He was not only inflammatory in the ordinary way of many over-zealous prosecutors, but he actually breached Section 4(5) of the Canada Evidence Act. He asked the jury to draw an adverse inference from the fact that, in the second phase of the trial, Goldman did not testify.

I couldn't believe my ears when Ormston said that. Goldman didn't even have to testify in the first phase. The law does not allow the Crown or the judge ever to make it a subject of comment if a defendant, as is his right, chooses to stand mute. And Goldman hadn't; he took the witness stand. What could he possibly have said in the second phase? Should he have denied that he possessed for the purpose of trafficking something that he had earlier denied possessing at all?

It was crazy. It was also clear grounds for a mistrial. The Crown handed it to us on a platter. I must have been slightly incoherent in my excitement, because his Honour pointedly suggested that we break for lunch before I could finish my motion.

After lunch, Judge Hoilett declared a mistrial. He ruled that the Crown was "in clear breach" of the Canada Evidence Act; that parts of his address "might be considered inflammatory"; and that, in his view, those parts were "all inappropriate". In conclusion, his Honour noted that "I was brought up in the tradition where the Crown neither won nor lost. . . . In my view, the Office of the Crown Attorney, and the individuals who represent that office, enjoy a certain aura and with that aura should go a corresponding meticulous attention to proprieties."

I must pause here for as second. Having related the events as they occurred, I must add something to put them into perspective.

The adversary process, in my opinion, is the fairest and most effective method of arriving at the truth. I know of no better way to seperate the guilty from the innocent. I consider it the best safeguard yet devised against a miscarriage of justice.

However, the adversary process is a battle. It is a battle by its very nature. It is a contest of one side against the other.

As in all battles, the adversary process is intense. The finest, most prudent advocates can at times be carried away by it. The fairest, most meticulous lawyers have caused mistrials by the odd intemperate remark, made in the heat of battle. This has happened on the Crown's as well as on the defence's side of the bar.

The late County Court judge John Greenwood, who prosecuted Peter Demeter when he was a Crown attorney, had always believed in his own mind that he had nearly caused a mistrial close to the end of Demeter's trial for murder by letting a remark slip in front of the jury. What he said was: "I'm not interested in the defence, I'm interested in the truth." In the context of the moment, it was not a trivial remark.

I argued at the time that a mistrial should be declared. I was not successful, but when Greenwood became a judge he said that, had he been a judge then, he would have granted my motion. Maybe Greenwood was being too hard on himself in retrospect. Mr. Justice Campbell Grant, a meticulous trial judge, did not take nearly as stern a view of the Crown's gaffe. Yet the fact is that Greenwood — a fair prosecutor, and later a very fair judge — did let the remark slip.

I argued against him, as I argued against Ted Ormston, but I certainly did not consider what they had done a grave reflection on either. In the course of the adversary process, such things can't always be avoided.

Ricky Goldman won the right to a new trial, and it commenced nearly a year later, in September 1982, before His Honour County Court Judge H. O'Connell, sitting alone. Everybody testified again. The truthful witnesses repeated the truth; the lying witnesses repeated their lies — changing them just enough to detract from their credibility even further. They were duly examined and cross-examined. On September 29, Judge O'Connell delivered his judgment.

Concerning the marijuana dealer Raymond Leach, his Honour found that "I cannot attach to his evidence any credibility" and concluded simply that the Zephyr lent to Goldman was supposed to have been returned to its rightful owners by Leach on the day in question. As to the various police officers, Judge O'Connell came almost word for word to the same conclusion I had invited the first trial jury to draw in my initial address:

"If the evidence of Young is to be believed," his Honour said, "then the evidence of Blake is not to be believed. If the evidence of Avery is to be believed, then the evidence of Young and Blake is not to be believed.

"I conclude that those discrepancies in the evidence lead and flow from the fact that when [the officers] met the day following and realized that the car was a borrowed car . . . they then realized the position they were in and proceeded to make notes unrelated to the events as to chronology, but with the express purpose of making it appear . . . that Goldman knew what was in the trunk of the car."

It could not be clearer. The court found that the officers of the surveillance unit made up their evidence in order to secure the conviction of someone they had arrested on a hunch.

The possibility cannot be excluded that, in their own minds, the officers honestly believed Goldman to have known what was in the trunk of the car. It is possible that they would not have tried to make up stories about a person that they, even in their own minds, believed to be innocent. But this is immaterial. It only underlines the importance of trying defendants on the evidence, and not on what policemen or anybody else may believe, however honestly.

Richard Goldman was, of course, acquitted. His ordeal had lasted for over two and a half years, from February 29, 1980, to September 29, 1982. Had a lawyer charged him a minimum standard fee for the preliminary hearing and the two trials (for personal reasons I submitted no account in this case), the policemen's false evidence — the fact that they swore to what they, at best, believed rather than to what they saw — would have cost Goldman about $35,000–$50,000, which he could probably never have recovered. Certainly not without putting a like amount at risk in a civil suit.

What the preliminary and the two trials cost the taxpayer is anybody's guess. On a hunch, I'd say at least a quarter of a million dollars.

The preceding chapters may create the impression that police officers are worse than most of us. I would certainly not subscribe to such a view. On the whole, police officers are not worse than most of us; they may even be somewhat better. The problem is that this is not enough. In the nature of things, the police have much more power than ordinary citizens. Each and every officer has much more power; each and every officer has greater opportunities to do harm. Is each and every officer a significantly better person than human beings generally are? We cannot count on it. This is why we must continue to surround police powers with stringent safeguards.

It is equally instructive, however, to look at the other side.

Being human, the police can victimize — but for the same reason they can also become victims. If officers can lie, they can also be lied about; if they can be unfair, they can also suffer unfairness. This will be the subject of some of the cases that follow.

## NOTES

p.162, l.37: The Charter of Rights has now resulted in the abolition of the two-stage trial. The Supreme Court of Canada has held in *Regina v. Oakes* (1986) that placing the burden on the accused to prove his innocence at stage two offends the Charter guarantee in Section 11(d) to the presumption of innocence. As a result, there is no two-stage trial any more — all the issues, possession *and* purpose, go to the jury at the end of the trial.

Ironically, this has disadvantaged some defendants. For example, where the Crown's case on possession was thin, the accused could reserve his defence, hoping the Crown would not succeed in stage 1. If the case did get beyond stage 1, the accused could then testify and explain his purpose. Now such an accused only gets one chance. He must decide whether he wishes to advance his defence or to take his chances on an acquittal based on the weakness of the Crown's case.

p.165,l.8: The full phrase is usually rendered: "The Crown does not win or lose as long as Justice triumphs." It is to suggest that the prosecution ought to concern itself with a just result rather than merely with a courtroom victory.

# DO IT FOR THE QUIPPER

*On Sunday, May 28, 1978, Greenspan decided to take instructions from his friend George Jonas in the operation of a 750-cc Yamaha motorcycle. Eddie bicycled from his house in Moore Park to the nearby grounds of his daughter's school, where he was to meet Jonas, who was waiting for him in the deserted schoolyard with the big machine.*

*Explaining the controls to Greenspan took about fifteen minutes. The ride that followed lasted about fifteen seconds. At the end of it, the 520-pound motorcycle lay crumpled up in some rose bushes with its front end demolished, while not too far away Greenspan was lying on the grass with his front end in only slightly better shape. The brick wall which he had hit head-on remained undamaged.*

*Greenspan asked Jonas for a cigarette, and then the two friends chatted, waiting for the ambulance to arrive. Both of Eddie's hands were broken, while his shinbone stuck out in plain view underneath a gash in his right leg. Within minutes a small crowd had gathered around him.*

*Eddie appeared to be in good spirits, even euphoric, as people often are when suffering from the after-effects of shock. He was cracking one joke after another. He was unaware of making a particular remark — and Jonas did not hear it either — but Gary Dunford quoted it next day in his* Toronto Sun *column. "To think that Peter Demeter could have saved himself all that trouble by buying his wife a motorbike!" Eddie was reported as saying.*

*Demeter, of course, was the protagonist in one of Canada's most notorious murder cases. He was the well-to-do Toronto developer who had been convicted in 1974 of having hired some person or persons unknown to kill his wife Christine, a beautiful Austrian model. At the time, Eddie had been junior counsel to Joseph B. Pomerant, the senior lawyer at Demeter's trial.*

*Demeter was not amused by Eddie's quip when he read it in the newspaper the next day. He was still maintaining his innocence while serving a life sentence in penitentiary for his wife's murder. It was* common knowledge that he was not happy with Greenspan for associating with Jonas, who with the journalist Barbara Amiel had written a book about the Demeter affair.

Greenspan did not remember making the quip; if he did make it, he had been barely conscious in the most immediate sense of the word. Still, it had only been the extreme end of a normal variation. When it comes to making quips, Greenspan has existed in a state of marginal consciousness all his life.

There are compulsive quippers; there are obsessive quippers; but Eddie has always been a quipper in a class beyond mere compulsion or obsession. To make a quip, most people require the engagement of some voluntary part of the central nervous system. Greenspan, somewhat like Pavlov's dog salivating at the sight of food, has always quipped reflexively, with no apparent reference to the higher regions of the brain.

A man of great tact, consideration, and judgment, a man of intellectual seriousness, a man who (outside the arena of the courtroom) would never consciously hurt another person, Greenspan has often been helpless when facing the slightest stimulus to his funnybone. His quips have been as involuntary as a hiccup or a sneeze.

Eddie could never repress a pun or a joke, whether directed against himself or against others. For instance in 1980, while battling his constant weight problem and still tipping the scales at around three hundred pounds, he was retained to defend Gregory Guerin, the man charged with the murder of little Lizzie Tomlinson. At a press conference he was asked about the evidence against his client. "I wish," replied Greenspan, "that I were as thin as the evidence in this case."

His family and his friends have also been fair game. Talking of his wife, who comes from Morocco, Greenspan once remarked: "When I was growing up in Niagara Falls I always thought a JAP meant a Jewish American Princess. After I met Suzy, though, I realized it really meant a Jewish African Princess."

It is somewhat pointless to speculate whether Greenspan's sense of humour — like the cutting and even acerbic humour of some other criminal lawyers, war correspondents, or pathologists — may or may not be a sensitive person's defensive reaction against the depressing side of the human condition that is an inevitable part of his daily existence. (Greenspan himself would shrug off the suggestion, or make a crack about it.) In any case, it has never created a problem for his wife or his children, who share and often exhibit the same sense of humour them-

*selves. (Once a journalist proposed, while interviewing Suzy and Eddie together, that on the general subject of sex-life he would direct his questions to Suzy. "Whose sex-life," queried Suzy innocently, "mine or Eddie's?")*

While rarely hurtful and never unfunny, Greenspan's quips have often been sharp. After a visit to Asia, a group of trendy lawyers were extolling the virtues of conducting court proceedings out of doors, suggesting that it should also be tried in this country. Commented Greenspan: "The only judicial proceeding I know that works outdoors is a lynching." It put an end to any further discussion of the subject.

For Greenspan's friends, far from being a problem, quips have only been an endless source of competition. The regulars who sit with him at the Courtyard Café, at Stubby's, at the Coffee Mill, or at the Cakemaster fire quips at each other non-stop, disputing the original authorship of some of Greenspan's remarks while he is disputing theirs. The usual gambit is a wounded Greenspan stopping someone in mid-sentence: "But how can you say that that's your line!" The standing joke is, "You will, Oscar, you will!" — referring to Frank Harris's famous retort to Oscar Wilde when the latter said that he wished he had uttered one of James McNeill Whistler's quips.

Like other people who can't resist a crack and hold that anything funny is inoffensive by definition, Greenspan has had his quips land him in trouble with earnest people who don't share his sense of humour or who regard certain things as not being proper subjects for jokes. This is not uncommon for reflexive quippers, but Eddie has carried his compulsion a step further. He can spend hours building up a case for something — then, reflexively, undermine his own argument with a quip if the opportunity presents itself.

During one of the public debates on capital punishment in the spring of 1987, Greenspan, who is a fervent opponent of the ultimate penalty, expended great efforts on a somewhat hostile audience to convert them to his own abolitionalist views. Then a member of the audience asked him why politicians who betray a public trust shouldn't be hanged. "Because," replied Greenspan promptly, "we do not have enough rope."

In 1982, when he was acting for the Hold-Up Squad of the Toronto police, the popular film of the day was a movie in which Neanderthal characters were talking in the unintelligible gibberish of a supposedly Stone Age language. When asked what he thought of his new clients, Eddie was said to have replied: "Well, they are the only people in Toronto who can understand the dialogue in Quest for Fire."

*With one exception, Greenspan has never felt apologetic about his
sense of humour: he was not running for office, and if some people
didn't like it they could lump it. The one exception was a remark he
made to Barbara Amiel when she asked him what the defence was going
to be in a case where a juvenile offender was charged with raping an
eighty-year-old woman. "Our position is that she lied about her age,"
quipped Greenspan — in a private conversation, as he thought, and off
the record. Amiel's rule as a journalist, however, has always been that
she is forever on duty and nothing is off the record. When she put
Greenspan's reply in a magazine story, Eddie felt very guilty. The quip
just slipped out; he really didn't mean it. The investigating officer, a
Sergeant Fantino, was so offended that he wouldn't speak to Greenspan
afterwards for months.*

As I began practising law in Canada nearly a hundred years after
the last war between Indians and settlers, there was only one
occasion in my career when I had reason to fear that I might be
scalped for making an argument in court. I nearly *was* scalped, as it
turned out, though not by the Indians. The people who were after
my head were the French.

I was retained by a women's group to argue in the Supreme Court
of Canada that a native Indian woman should not lose her status for
marrying a non-Indian. The proposition made sense to me; the
Indian status carried certain benefits, and no Indian man jeopar-
dized *his* status by marrying a non-Indian woman. (The reverse
would have seemed more natural to someone of my Jewish heritage
in any event: the laws of my tribe always regarded descent as
matrilineal.)

The proposition, however, seemed quite unnatural to a large
number of Indian chiefs. They surrounded the Supreme Court building in Ottawa while the arguments were being heard. At night, they
sat by their bonfires complete with full head-dress and war-paint.
They looked to me as if they meant business, and a brief address by
the Liberal cabinet minister Jean Chrétien seemed to do little to
improve their temper.

The name of the case was *Laval-Bedard*, and it was being widely covered by the media. The papers reported that I appeared to be lost for words when Mr. Justice Spence pointed out that the French version of the applicable statute did not contain the key word "discrimination".

In fact I wasn't lost for words at all. It was simply that, looking for a minute or so at the section handed to me by the clerk without understanding any of it, even after attempting to turn it upside down, I suddenly remembered that I can't read French. I wouldn't dream of disputing the French fact in Canada, but Niagara Falls where I come from happens to be a town of the English fact. Perhaps it was to make up for this that I married a girl whose native language is French, thereby becoming a member of a truly bilingual family.

The line was out before I could stop myself. "Perhaps, my Lord, I could show the section to my wife tonight," I murmured, getting a laugh from Chief Justice Bora Laskin and some of the other justices who knew Suzy. What I also got the next day was an editorial in a French-language newspaper, holding me up as a particularly offensive example of English lawyers being disrespectful to the French language.

What I did not get was the slightest sympathy from Suzy. She wouldn't even translate the section. "Think of another funny line in court tomorrow, why don't you?" she said. "It's your sense of humour that makes everyone like you so much."

PART FOUR

# THE POLICEMAN'S LOT

# 10. Torpedoing the Dry Submarine

It was a tragic year. Between August 1978 and August 1979 eight men were shot to death by the police in Toronto.

One of them, Paul Reid, a sixteen-year-old escapee from a training centre, had been holding a young girl at knifepoint. He appeared to be about to cut her throat when he was shot by hostage-negotiator Superintendent Frank Barbetta. This was an example of a policeman using his gun only as a last resort. The other seven men, however, were killed under far more dubious circumstances, capable of raising disturbing questions about the police's use of lethal, unlawful, or unnecessary force.

To begin with, six of the seven victims appeared to be misfits rather than criminals. They were reportedly pugnacious, drunk, or somewhat unbalanced at the time of their deaths, but without necessarily posing an immediate threat to members of the public (or to their own families). While, at the ultimate moment, the policemen shooting them may have acted in unavoidable self-defence, some people argued that the officers were not blameless in the development of the initial conflict. The policemen's confrontational approach — at least as it appeared in hindsight — may have aggravated situations that might have been defused by cooler or wiser tactics, and in this sense the act of policing itself could have led to the needless tragedies.

Five of the seven victims were shot inside their own homes. Three of them were alone at the time, and for this reason not posing an acute threat to anyone. Of the remaining two cases, the shooting of a black Jamaican immigrant named Albert Johnson seemed in particular to arise from a confrontation provoked by the police. Two officers entered Johnson's home to prevent, as they claimed to have believed, some act of domestic violence. This impression, honest as it may have been, turned out to be totally mistaken. After the death of Johnson there was a great public outcry, followed by manslaughter charges against the two constables (named Inglis and Cargnelli, both ultimately acquitted by a jury). It was the only case in the twenty-four-year history of the Metropolitan Toronto Police force in which police officers had been charged with manslaughter as a result of a shooting while on duty.

The 1978-79 incidents in Toronto were only the tip of the iceberg. Altogether, between 1970 and 1978, eighty-eight persons were shot to death in Canada by the police. The number of people wounded by police bullets was two to three times higher. True, these shocking figures were put in some perspective by the fact that in the United States during a given ten-year period (1966-76) more than 6000 people met their deaths by the police's use of firearms. But, while in Canada the situation was relatively less alarming, in absolute terms eighty-eight deaths were alarming enough.

In addition to these figures, there were also recurring allegations of police brutality. Reasonable people could agree that there was a problem to look into — though just from the figures one could not conclude that it was a problem of police misconduct alone. The statistics were probably influenced by other factors creating a potential for social tensions and consequent violence. To name only a few, the sixties and seventies brought shifting patterns of age distribution within the population; changes in the treatment and supervision of the mentally ill; a sudden influx of large immigrant groups from widely divergent cultures; and a new style of political "activism", including confrontational tactics. One type of conflict was created by a growing public acceptance of personal conduct that was nevertheless still regarded as criminal by the law (such as certain drug or sexual offences); while a converse type of conflict resulted from legal sanctions being attached to other kinds of personal conduct the public had never traditionally regarded as proper areas for police interference (such as some new regulatory, economic, social, or domestic offences). While not directly responsible for all of the lethal incidents, these factors were likely to have played a part in straining the social fabric and creating a sense of alienation between several segments of the population and the constabulary.

Having to enforce outmoded, unpopular, or superfluous laws often gives rise to the most volatile situations. There is less personal hostility between a policeman and the average non-violent criminal than between a policeman and a normally peaceful citizen when the latter feels frustrated by a law he considers antiquated, or needlessly intrusive, and views the action of the officer who is obliged to enforce it as harassment. Experienced officers expect more resentment and abuse, even danger, when interfering in a domestic argument than when arresting a safecracker or a burglar. The most confrontational assignments can include quieting down a noisy party, stopping a motorist for not wearing his seat-belt, or enforcing some law concerning "public decency" — not to mention municipal prohibitions against the raising of chickens in people's backyards. An over-regulated society, in which too many types of conduct become matters for the police, will inevitably experience an increase in violence against (and by) the police as well. A society both over- *and* under-regulated — one that insists on an open-door policy in mental hospitals, but sends the police after citizens who cut down trees on their own properties or kick their cats — cannot be altogether surprised at a rising incidence of tragic confrontations.

Still, by the early 1980s, set against a background of seven (arguably) needless police killings in one twelve-month period, the time was ripe in Toronto for raising some legitimate questions both about the conduct of the police, and about the way citizens' complaints arising out of such conduct were being handled by the authorities. "Overall, it can be seen that the Albert Johnson shooting and its aftermath constituted a very important point in the emergence of the issue of police reform," was the conclusion of a 1984 study by the Centre of Criminology at the University of Toronto.

Legitimate questions were, in fact, raised by many people in various legitimate ways. The provincial government of Ontario had introduced legislation in the spring of 1981 to establish the new Office of the Public Complaints Commissioner. The Commissioner was to be Sidney Linden, Q.C., a respected lawyer and civil-libertarian, who was take up his duties in December 1981, when the new act came into force.

Other people, however, preferred raising questions about possible police misconduct in ways that were, in my opinion, illegitimate. It was as a result of this that I came to act for the Hold-Up Squad of the Toronto police.

In 1981 the Hold-Up Squad consisted of eighteen officers. They were highly experienced policemen, with an average of almost nineteen years' service on the police force, and an average of about four years' service on the Hold-Up Squad itself. In the normal course of their duties, like all such squads on any metropolitan police force, they were called upon to deal with armed robbers, the most danger-ous and desperate criminals.

People who use guns to hold up banks, armoured cars, supermar-kets, or jewellery stores are not Robin Hoods. They rarely rob the rich to give to the poor. Though killing people is only incidental to their crimes, armed robbers are among the most ruthless killers. In 1980-81, robbery-related homicides were responsible for the violent deaths of twenty persons in Toronto.

These desperadoes, then, were the Hold-Up Squad's "clients". Not unnaturally, in view of the type of criminals they had to deal with, the Hold-Up Squad was made up of eighteen correspondingly tough police officers. They were selected for their own courage, experience, and street-smarts. Probably any one of them could have lifted one and a half times his own weight over his head (and for some this would have meant lifting a considerable amount of weight). There was nothing surprising about this, considering that part of the Hold-Up Squad's job was to capture criminals who had deadly weapons and tempers. Probably few of the eighteen officers could be characterized as gentle and contemplative, but no society turns to lyric poets for protection against armed robbers.

On October 22, 1981, at a meeting of the Metropolitan Board of Commissioners of Police, letters were tabled from seven Toronto criminal lawyers. Each of the letter-writers alleged that one or more of his or her clients had been tortured by officers from the Hold-Up Squad of the Toronto police.

Some of the seven letters described briefly the nature of the alleged tortures; the rest gave no information whatever. None of the letters contained the names of the alleged victims or the names of the individual police officers accused by them, nor were the dates of the alleged incidents given. There was, in fact, nothing before the Commission but seven letters, containing pretty sensational charges and calling for a public inquiry.

The charges, predictably, were picked up by the media. "POLICE TORTURING PRISONERS LAWYERS GROUP CHARGES" was one *Toronto Star* headline on October 23, 1981. "COPS ACCUSED OF 'GESTAPO TACTICS' LAWYERS WANT INQUIRY" wrote the *Toronto Sun* on November 5, 1981. The newspaper stories gave some details of the alleged tortures, which centred around suffocation by towels, T-shirts, or garbage bags — a technique supposedly known as "dry submarining". According to the allegations, suspects were being deprived of oxygen through the use of this method by some officers of the Hold-Up Squad, who then told the suspects to "stomp their feet" when they were ready to confess.

The only thing not mentioned was *who* had been so tortured, *when*, and by *whom*. The seven lawyers stated that they could not advise the complainants to identify either themselves or the officers they accused, or to provide any further details, until the authorities had acceeded to their request for a public inquiry. "[U]ntil a Public Inquiry is convened I cannot at this time reveal my clients' names," wrote Dianne L. Martin, a Toronto lawyer and the organizer of what became known in the press as the "Martin-group" of lawyers, in her initial (October 14, 1981) letter to Police Commission Chairman Phil Givens.

The reason given by the Martin-group for this secrecy was that their clients feared repercussions on the part of the authorities. If, for instance, the policemen accused were found to be innocent by a departmental inquiry or by the courts, their accusers could face a charge of public mischief. They could also be subject to civil suits. In addition, some people claiming to have been tortured by the Hold-Up Squad were currently facing criminal charges for various offences, and for them to bring such allegations against the police at this point could have an adverse influence on their cases in court. For these reasons, the seven lawyers said, they would advise their clients to speak out only under the immunities provided by a public inquiry.

A public inquiry, of course, would have provided the accusers with splendid immunities, without giving any protection whatever to the people accused by them. This was the problem. The terms of reference and the evidentiary rules of public inquiries may allow wild and unsubstantiated allegations to be brought against any person, doing irreparable harm to the reputation and career of an individual regardless of what the ultimate findings of the inquiry may be many months or years down the road. They can also undermine public confidence in organizations and institutions — often undeservedly, and in a manner very much against the public interest. The big headlines will be made by the accusations, while the answers, no matter how convincing, will usually be printed on the back pages of the newspapers much later.

Public inquiries or royal commissions are rarely held to investigate allegations of individual wrongdoing, or even institutional wrongdoing in the abstract. The process ought to be quite the reverse. First, a wrong, or a series of wrongs, should be established to the satisfaction of the courts (or other competent bodies). Then a public inquiry may be held to determine how such a wrong, or series of wrongs, could have come about, and how best to avoid them in the future.

As the Martin-group knew, or ought to have known, this is the proper function of public inquiries. You don't convene them on the basis of people dropping anonymous postcards in the mail. If held in advance of the facts to be established, public inquiries become kangaroo courts — or, as Police Commissioner Phil Givens put it, "public circuses". Among the many voices in the press, it was the *Hamilton Spectator* that saw the matter most clearly. As it said in its editorial on October 31, 1981:

> A fishing expedition in the form of a public inquiry or royal commission . . . is putting the cart before the horse.
>
> At this point . . . all we have is a number of accusations by anonymous people against unnamed policemen — hardly a compelling reason to mount an expensive and time-consuming inquiry which could well end up unjustly slurring all members of a police department without putting any real burden of proof on the complainants. . . .
>
> To argue that neither our police nor the courts are "impartial" enough to deal with serious accusations of brutality by individuals is to argue that *our laws and institutions sworn to uphold those laws are no longer valid or working.* [Emphasis added.]

The *Spectator* was more accurate than it perhaps realized. Some of the people accusing the Hold-Up Squad did have precisely this aim. The very impression they wanted to create in the public mind was that our laws and institutions were neither valid nor working, and should be replaced by some other social system of the accusers' own preference. I believe that in the eyes of these activists the charges against the eighteen officers of the Hold-Up Squad were purely incidental to this larger political goal. For a time, and to a limited extent, they succeeded in carrying with them other people and groups that had no such aims at all, such as some civil-libertarians and part of the membership of the Criminal Lawyers Association.

I did not know about any of this in the beginning. The understanding came only when, having been retained by the Hold-Up Squad to represent them, I started looking into the political background of the controversy.

About half a year earlier, on May 15, 1981, the provincial government had introduced Bill 68 to establish the office of a Public Complaints Commissioner. This bill, following closely the recommendations of three earlier reports on methods of investigating alleged police misconduct, seemed insufficient to some special-interest groups comprising, among other alliances, the Working Group on Minority-Police Relations. It is doubtful if anything would have satisfied these radical activists, short of being put in charge of the police themselves. At least, the language of their recommendations — or "demands", to use the word they preferred — led to no other conclusion.

"The only effective longterm solution," wrote the Working Group on Minority-Police Relations in a letter to the Police Commission on February 11, 1981, ". . . is to have [Attorney General] Roy McMurtry and the Progressive Conservative Government *surrender* [emphasis added] control of your Commission to the local municipality. . . ." The local municipality, of course, would in turn be heavily influenced , if not actually controlled, by such aldermen as David White, who became one of the leaders of the "police reform" movement. "It would probably be useful for [City] Council to once again *demand* [emphasis added] that control of the local police be given to the local community," wrote Aldermen White and Pat Sheppard in their *Report on Police Raids on Gay Steambaths* submitted to City Council on February 26, 1981. Implicit in the report was the hope that control of the "local community" would be in the hands of Aldermen White, Sheppard, and others sharing their social and political views.

The government's Bill 68 threatened to take the wind out of the sails of those radicals who were using the issue of police misconduct as another platform from which to mount their general attack on the "system". The bill was therefore immediately opposed by a coalition of approximately forty groups, led by the Urban Alliance on Race Relations. By the summer of 1981 this opposition led to the formation of a new group known as Citizens' Independent Review of Police Activities (CIRPA). This organization consisted, among others, of such groups as Religious Leaders Concerned About Racism and Human Rights, Dignity Toronto, Gays and Lesbians Against the Right Everywhere (*sic*), South Asian Origins Liaison Committee, the Rape Crisis Centre, etc. Though fond of using such words as "community" and expressing a desire to "open locked doors", CIRPA was, in fact, a pressure group of like-minded individuals, who had no patience with the views or interests of the larger public.

David White was involved with CIRPA from the beginning, as was an ex-alderman named Allan Sparrow. Sparrow, having earlier lost a civil case against the police, claimed to be unable to pay his court costs. It was Sparrow who became the procedures chairman of CIRPA. On July 8, 1981, CIRPA adopted, as one of its first positions, an exclusionary policy on who could or couldn't join the organization or attend its ostensibly public meetings. For a group bent on "opening locked doors" it was a curious stance to take. "From the outset," note the authors of the University of Toronto study quoted above, "[CIRPA] began to take on at least one of the characteristics [of the institutions they opposed,] namely secrecy."

CIRPA's position was, of course, surprising only for those who took its slogans at face value. In fact, CIRPA was a pressure group of the far left. Like some of its right-wing counterparts, it was not interested in justice, only in having its own way. Its own way included a rejection of civil-libertarians like Commissioner Sidney Linden. What CIRPA wanted (in the words of its July 13, 1981, press statement) was "a real alternative complaint review process to the farce that has been proposed at Queen's Park. . . ." The "farce" was, of course, Bill 68, creating the office of the Public Complaints Commissioner.

What the "real alternative" would have been was then demonstrated by the anonymous accusations against the officers of the Hold-Up Squad tabled with the Police Commissioners on October 22 by the Martin-group. Though Dianne Martin stressed that her group was only a few "concerned individuals", independent of CIRPA or other organizations, the charges brought by her group were carefully co-ordinated with similar charges brought by CIRPA at the same time. "I understand," Martin wrote to the Commissioners on October 21, 1981, "that a signed complaint making similar allegations has been given to CIRPA and is also before you." In a letter to members of the criminal bar in Ontario, Martin solicited lawyers who might have received complaints of a like nature from clients to give them to "Alderman David White's office no later than Tuesday, October 20 for presentation to the Police Commission." The players were all assembled, and they were resolved to play to the gallery.

They had, in fact, no other forum to play to, since it was the basis of their contention that none of the institutions within our system were capable of investigating a complaint against the police. It was the view of CIRPA and the Martin-group that the internal procedures of the police, the new Public Complaints Commissioner, and the law courts of Canada were all unable, and perhaps unwilling, to investigate an alleged wrong and put it right. Our system was a fundamental failure. Only CIRPA and its allies could and would bring justice to it; and justice could only be done through the methods they demanded. Until those methods were adopted, CIRPA *et al.* would continue hurling public charges but would co-operate with no one else's attempt to get at the truth.

An attempt to get at the truth was made by the Police Commission right away. In spite of the highly questionable manner in which the Martin-group brought its charges, the allegations contained in them were extremely serious. Police Chief Jack Ackroyd very properly decided not to disregard them. The next day, October 23, 1981, he appointed a team of three senior police officers under Staff Superintendent Jack Reid to start an immediate investigation. Though Public Complaints Commissioner Sidney Linden would not take up his office until late December under the terms of the new act, he met with Staff Superintendent Reid on October 26 and agreed to monitor the process.

For a day or so the Martin-group seemed to waver. "I'm satisfied that our concerns were taken seriously," Dianne Martin was quoted as saying in the *Toronto Star*. (Indeed, an immediate investigation, monitored by a civilian from the outset — especially a civilian like Linden, former General Counsel to the Civil Liberties Association and Vice-President of the Criminal Lawyers Association — ought to have answered, at least as a preliminary step, most of the reformers' ostensible concerns for a civilian review of the police.) But CIRPA chairman Mark Wainberg struck an immediate dissenting note. Wainberg apparently wanted to see the senior officers of the Hold-Up Squad transferred, starting with the officer in charge (at that time Staff Inspector Bernard Nadeau). However, as Wainberg complained to the *Star*, the Police Commission "didn't promise to take any action." Clearly, CIRPA's fair-minded reformers expected penalties to be assessed on their say-so before, and perhaps without, any investigation of their charges.

By October 29 this also became Dianne Martin's posture. Her group would not co-operate with the police probe or with Sidney Linden. They would not give the investigators any names or details. Martin was quoted in the Toronto *Globe and Mail* as saying that her "satisfaction with Chief Ackroyd's receptive attitude . . . has been misinterpreted." The "concerned individuals" were obviously synchronizing their positions.

There was to be no help given to the internal police investigation monitored by Sidney Linden. However, the media publicity about the anonymous allegations, along with the pressure for a public inquiry, was to escalate. In November, Ronald G. Thomas, Q.C., the President of the Ontario Criminal Lawyers Association, wrote to the Attorney General asking for a probe of the charges against the Hold-Up Squad under the *Public Inquiries Act*. Then, in the same month, a group of seventy-one criminal lawyers were persuaded to sign a petition to Amnesty International requesting it to investigate the allegations against the Hold-Up Squad.

These were the same allegations about which no Canadian authority could be trusted with any details: no Crown Attorney, no court of law, and not even a former counsel to the Canadian Civil Liberties Association. Tortured citizens in Canada had no reliable allies except CIRPA and Amnesty International. By signing the petition, seventy-one criminal lawyers joined the implication of radical activists that Canada, as a country, belonged in the ranks of General Pinochet's Chile or the Gulag Archipelago.

Creating this impression was, no doubt, the conscious aim of only a few of the signatories. It may not even have been the conscious aim of some of the organizers. Lawyers are often too busy mapping out their next court case to think about the fine print of socio-political issues. When they see the motherhood-name of Amnesty International on a piece of paper, they may sign it without even bothering to read the text, thinking that they are protesting about police brutality in Cambodia. Manipulative political activists count on this fact.

(A good example of how activists try to hijack legitimate organizations, or try to make it appear that they speak for them, occurred in May 1982, some months after I had been retained to act for the Hold-Up Squad. By that time Dianne L. Martin had abandoned all pretence of "independence". In a letter to members of the Criminal Lawyers Association she actively solicited support for CIRPA, saying that "Counsel can assist this organization by providing details of complaints, on a strictly confidential basis, by referring cases for direct assistance, or by becoming more actively involved. . . . CIRPA is supported by a broad range of community groups and should be considered seriously by all defence counsel."

This would have been fine, Martin being free to solicit support for whomever she wished — except that her letter exhibited the letterhead of the Criminal Lawyers Association and it began with the phrase: "The efforts of our association and its members . . ."

I was more amused than upset, and wrote to the Association's president, Ronald G. Thomas, Q.C., asking: (a) if Martin's letter was authorized by the Association's directors, and (b) if so, whether I might have authorization to use our Association's letterhead whenever I write letters on behalf of the Hold-Up Squad.

Thomas replied that the use of the Association's letterhead had not been authorized and it "occurred by inadvertence in our association office." Dianne Martin was assistant secretary of the Criminal Lawyers Association at the time. Thomas was obliged, of course, to send a letter of explanation to the Association's membership about the "inadvertence".)

In view of these tactics, it was not surprising that a number of lawyers were lulled or hoodwinked into signing the Amnesty petition. As it happened, my own brother, Brian Greenspan, signed it in an absent-minded fashion (then publicly disavowed it later). I believe that many of the signatories would not have signed if they had bothered thinking about the implications for even a minute.

In what may have been a similarly unthinking gut-reaction, Secretary General Thomas Hammarberg of Amnesty International wrote back to Attorney General Roy McMurtry in January, echoing CIRPA's request for a public inquiry. Eighteen Toronto police officers of long service and unblemished record were acquiring, in the public eye, the reputation of the Gestapo — without even learning who was accusing them. On the basis of seven anonymous complaints, no less a moral authority than Amnesty International was calling for a public investigation into their conduct.

I could only trust that Amnesty International was giving more careful consideration to some of its other interventions before going on the record with them.

*The petition to Amnesty International escalated the conflict, as it was probably designed to do. Many police officers were outraged by what they regarded as a cheap shot and a provocation. Some of them got sufficiently hot under the collar to respond by an open declaration of war on the lawyers who had signed the CIRPA document.*

*In the Metropolitan Toronto Police Force publication* News and Views *an article appeared under the signature of editor Paul Walter. It listed the names of the seventy-one signatories, calling on police officers "to be guided accordingly when having contact with these individuals".*

*In practice this probably meant a "work to rule" approach in dealing with these particular lawyers, devoid of the usual minor courtesies extended in the course of official contact. Such courtesies can make a significant difference in humanizing and expediting bureaucratic procedures. They rarely have an effect on the legal disposition of a case, but their absence can cause lawyers and their clients much inconvenience, along with some expense and humiliation.*

*Greenspan was very unhappy when he heard about this. He discussed the matter with George Jonas, who found the police's move equally ill-advised. It was, in fact, likely to play into the hands of the opposition. Greenspan did not feel that it would be proper for him to interfere, but Jonas, as a private citizen and journalist, was labouring under no such constraints. He asked a high-ranking police officer, with whom he happened to be on personally friendly terms, to a breakfast meeting at the Windsor Arms Hotel.*

*"Don't do it, fellows," said Jonas to his friend over coffee. "You'll be punishing the clients. Clients have no idea what their lawyers signed or didn't sign."*

"Isn't that too bad," replied the police officer. He was visibly angry. He was one of the toughest but also one of the most respected and influential officers on the force, with some of his cases and exploits having become legendary over the years. Now he felt betrayed by the citizens he had more than once risked his life to serve and protect. "Let your liberal friends sign petitions," he said to Jonas, "and we'll do what we'll have to do."

Jonas, who had few friends among the supporters of CIRPA, persisted. "Don't go down to their level. If those lawyers who called in Amnesty don't care about the interests of their clients, you should. Deal with everybody the same way, as before."

"I promise you nothing," said the officer. "Understand? Nothing."

That's how the matter was left. In fact, as it turned out, the officer took the position with his fellow officers that the police should continue dealing with everybody the same way. The others may have listened to him, as there were no reported incidents of police mistreatment of any of the lawyers whose names had appeared on the list.

Defending the Hold-Up Squad was a novel experience for me in many ways. By 1981 I was used to some people getting upset by the fact that I was defending accused criminals. (I'm not quite sure who else they would have expected a criminal lawyer to defend.) Now, however, an equal number of people seemed to be upset that I was defending accused policemen.

Of course, I've never defended either criminals or policemen as such. Like other lawyers, I've only defended the rule of law: the right to a fair trial, the presumption of innocence. That was all I was defending in this case as well. Yet, as the columnist Barbara Amiel pointed out:

At the moment, Greenspan is in the eye of a controversy. It illustrates, exquisitely if tragically, what happened to real liberalism in our society.

It is ironic that Eddie Greenspan could and did defend — without anyone questioning his liberalism — all elements of society from alleged pornographers to alleged murderers. But when he defends the police against unspecified, sweeping accusations, precisely in the name of liberalism which others profess but he alone seems to uphold, his motives are for the first time questioned.

Amiel was right: my standing as a good liberal had never been questioned for defending criminals (though my standing as an upright citizen had been, by some people). That never changed. However, by 1981 some categories of crime (or defendants) seemed to have become untouchable. Acting for them could put one's liberal credentials into question in the eyes of the very people who liked to think of themselves as liberals. Just representing "privileged" or "wealthy" defendants could do it. Some liberal lawyers, so called, did not even feel safe defending a male — any male — against a sex-related charge brought against him by a female.

Defending the police would certainly head the list of tasks a liberal lawyer should not undertake in this novel view — which, of course, had about as much to do with real liberalism as the ideas of the Ku Klux Klan.

The police were stymied when they came to me, and, in a sense, so was I. Of course, I was ready to defend the Hold-Up Squad in the same way as I would defend any other group or person — but defend them against what? They were supposed to be the Gestapo, with Amnesty International after them — but what exactly had they done, and to whom? When did they do it? And, whatever it was, which one of them did it?

I can't stand it when people say confidently: "We know what the truth is," and when you ask: "Well, how do you know?" all they can answer is: "We know!" In my view, this is the most insidious and unfair position to take. Yet this was the position of the accusers of the Hold-Up Squad.

I had absolutely no doubt (and I have none today) that some police officers may be sadistic or brutal. I had equally little doubt that some armed robbers or robbery suspects were capable of lying, and lying was not nearly the worst thing of which they were capable. As generalities, both propositions were equally true, but both were equally immaterial. Cases can't be decided on the basis of generalizations, guesses, or sympathies. What and where was the evidence?

I started shaking the bushes, looking at whatever files became available to me. Did any officers seem to have more problems than others? Were any of the allegations ever accepted by any court? Eventually I concluded that there was nothing. There was absolutely no evidence against any member of the Hold-Up Squad.

On the contrary. I discovered, for instance, that one of the allegations related to a certain armed robber, who had attempted to make the same allegations twice before, at his preliminary hearing and at his trial, to keep the jury from hearing a statement he had made to the police by having it characterized as "involuntary". In both instances, after lengthy *voir dires* involving fifteen witnesses, two separate judges rejected the man's claims as fabrications, and eventually sentenced him to a term of fourteen years for a string of offences. Far from being "dry-submarined" by garbage bags, the only garbage bag in this man's case turned out to be the one in which he kept the rifle and balaclava used in his robberies.

By February 17, 1982, Staff Superintendent Reid's investigative team, monitored by Sidney Linden, had come to the same conclusion. On the basis of what was contained in the Martin-group's letters, plus whatever the police could discover on its own, there was simply no case to answer. Staff Superintendent Reid put the facts before a Crown Attorney, who concluded, in the eventual words of Commissioner Linden's report, that "there was no evidence to justify laying either criminal charges or *Police Act* discipline charges against any police officer."

That was that, then — yet, in another sense, it wasn't. The opposing side was not concerned with actual evidence. They were not waging their war in court: they were waging it in the media. This was a new arena for me: I had never tried a case in the press before. This time I felt that I had no choice. The press was where the case of the Hold-Up Squad was being tried.

On February 17, the same day Staff Superintendent Reid informed the media of the conclusion reached by his investigation, I issued a statement to the press myself on behalf of the Hold-Up Squad:

> When I was first approached by the Hold-Up Squad to act on their behalf, I was taken aback because as a defence counsel for 12 years I have never acted for police officers. . . . But I quickly realized the members of the Hold-Up Squad are truly the maligned underdogs in this case.

Last October, a group called CIRPA [and] a group of criminal lawyers made allegations against officers of the Metropolitan Toronto Police Force [relating] to treatment of persons arrested by the Hold-Up Squad. . . . They talked of widespread torture. Yet when this group of criminal lawyers and CIRPA were asked to give the specifics of their allegations so they could be properly investigated, they refused to do so.

CIRPA and this group of criminal lawyers would not cooperate with the Chief of Police. . . . They would not cooperate with the Attorney General of this province. They would not cooperate with the Public Complaints Commissioner. They would not charge any of the members of the Hold-Up Squad in our courts of law.

They don't trust the Chief of Police. They don't trust the Attorney General. They don't trust the courts. They don't trust the legislators of this province, who created the office of the Public Complaints Commissioner. They don't trust the *law* of our land. They don't trust anybody. . . . But they say: "Trust us, even though we don't trust you, and hold a Royal Commission because we say so."

For lawyers to say that they will not give up their sources, that they will not name the officers, and then to continue making these allegations, is pure, raw McCarthyism. . . . The press reported that the Criminal Lawyers Association called for a [public] inquiry. However, [it did not report] that no vote of the membership was taken, and that there are many members of the Criminal Lawyers Association who do not support the request of its present president. . . .

The greatest affront to the citizens of this city was a request to Amnesty International to investigate the Hold-Up Squad. It is impossible to think of any single act more calculated to insult or offend normal law-abiding citizens of this country.

Amnesty International is an organization whose primary purpose is to examine merciless, powerful tyrannies, where people are thrown into prison, tortured or killed because of their political or religious beliefs. . . . That organization was established for noble reasons. Any right-minded individual should support its fight against fascism and communism; against the Soviets, Cambodians and the like. But to forward unnamed, unsubstantiated allegations — that in some instances had been rejected by the duly constituted courts of this land — is to suggest that these so-called responsible lawyers have no respect whatsoever for the legal institutions of

Canada. Attempting to equate these specious, unsupported allegations to the Gulag Archipelago is hysterical rhetoric.

The Hold-Up Squad is a proud Squad and has remained silent too long. Its 18 members have served for a combined total of 340 years in the police department and a combined total of 70 years on the Hold-Up Squad. In 1980-81 the Squad processed 1190 charges of robbery and related matters. Its record is the envy of all law enforcement agencies in North America. Every member of the Squad is married, with children, and their children have suffered greatly by these unsubstantiated, unwarranted and reckless allegations made by a group of people who don't seem to mind slinging mud for the sake of hurting innocent people.

(I may have been mistaken in this last remark. The Martin-group and CIRPA were not slinging mud for the sake of hurting these eighteen policemen in particular; they probably couldn't have cared less about them one way or the other. They were just slinging mud to accomplish a political purpose — and tough luck to those who got in the way.)

I ended the press conference by informing the reporters that the Hold-Up Squad had asked me to invite Public Complaints Commissioner Sidney Linden to recommend to the Attorney General the establishment of a committee. The committee would consist of Linden himself, Professor Anthony Doob, Director of the Centre of Criminology, University of Toronto, and me. Our job would be to create and recommend new procedures for the interrogation of all accused persons arrested by the Hold-Up Squad. The Squad, in turn, would abide by our recommendations.

The Hold-Up Squad's press conference proved to be a fatal blow to the momentum of CIRPA and the Martin-group. It took the fight into the arena that, until that moment, they had considered to be their private preserve: the media. It showed them, in effect, that the time had come to put up or shut up.

Five days later, on February 23, having requested a meeting with Sidney Linden, the Martin-group issued a press release of their own. Somewhat grudgingly they told the press that they had decided, after all, to provide the Public Complaints Commissioner with the details of nineteen allegations. "Mr. Linden's office is not an entirely satisfactory alternative," their statement read, "but it is presently the best available."

Not an entirely satisfactory alternative to what, I wondered when I looked at the statement. To a smear campaign?

The Martin-group's press release also contained an excerpt from Amnesty International's request to Roy McMurtry for an independent public inquiry. "Mr. McMurtry has written a reply to Amnesty International," the release continued. "We do not know its contents."

*At this point in recounting the story, Greenspan stopped, as he did not know the contents of McMurtry's reply either. His collaborator Jonas became curious. He had some private hopes that McMurtry might have told Amnesty International to go fly a kite, or at least that its Nobel Prize-winning moral authority would be better employed investigating political prisons in Mozambique or re-education camps in Red China.*

*A little research revealed that, while McMurtry had couched his reply in polite language, he did tell Amnesty to back off. "I must say that I am troubled," McMurtry wrote to Amnesty's Secretary General Thomas Hammarberg, "that Amnesty International which has an admirable record in promoting human rights and highlighting abuses, would, as you did in your letter, categorize these allegations as serious and warranting an expeditious independent inquiry, before even taking the trouble to check them out. Surely you can see this basic element of fairness is lacking in your rush to judgement that they warrant an inquiry. The police who are the subject of the allegations have rights, too."*

*Quite so. Both Greenspan and Jonas felt that, since Amnesty International's request is part of the public record, so should be the Attorney General's response.*

Approximately two years later, in March 1984, the Public Complaints Commissioner issued an exhaustive report on the Martin-group–CIRPA allegations. Sidney Linden and his staff had ended up investigating 23 complaints, all but one concerning the Hold-Up

Squad. Eighteen of the 23 complainants had been convicted of robbery charges (11 of them following a guilty plea, and 7 after a trial). The cases of two other complainants were still under appeal.

Linden found that in 12 of the 23 cases he could draw no conclusions at all because the complainants had either withdrawn their complaints, refused to co-operate with the investigation, or could not be located.

In 5 of the remaining 11 cases Linden came to the conclusion that the allegations were not substantiated by the evidence.

This left 6 cases in which, in the Commissioner's words, "[M]y investigation left me with questions that were not answered to my satisfaction. . . ." He added, however, that "In no one individual case was the evidence conclusive, nor was it particularly strong."

Still, Linden felt that those 6 cases should be referred to the Attorney General to determine if there was enough evidence for the laying of criminal charges against the police officers involved. These 6 cases, then, were closely examined by a group of senior Crown attorneys over a period of time. Their view was that there was "insufficient evidence of a trustworthy nature on which to base the laying of criminal charges".

That was it. That was the sum total of the case against Toronto's "Gestapo" which would have warranted, in some people's opinion, the intervention of Amnesty International. Those were the real merits of the Martin-group's allegations: not one case worth even *trying* in court.

Very properly, however, in accordance with the mandate of his office, Sidney Linden made a series of recommendations designed to both "protect suspects from abuse and police officers from unfounded allegations of abuse". One recommendation, perhaps the key one, concerned the use of video cameras to record the questioning of suspects at police stations. This recommendation had frequently been made by many significant authorities, here as well as in Britain and in the United States. It had been a suggestion of the Martin-group of lawyers as well.

I don't think much of the idea myself. To me it seems to stem from a rather faddish infatuation with modern technology. If adopted, it will at best fail to solve the problems it is designed to solve. At worst, it will create many additional problems.

Cameras are only as truthful as the cameramen behind them.

Video equipment has no integrity other than the integrity of the people operating it. In a police station the operators are the police. If their integrity is high, the equipment is unnecessary; if their integrity is low or absent, the equipment won't change that.

On the contrary: video pictures may give judges and juries a false assurance that they are witnessing the truth, when in fact they are only witnessing a technological boost to deception. In my view, lies are pretty powerful on their own. It's unnecessary to give them electronic wings.

Nothing's easier than to intimidate a suspect off camera first, then record his "voluntary" confession in living Technicolor. You could point a shotgun at a suspect's head, out of camera range, while he is being questioned. If we believe that some officers "dry-submarine" suspects, why would we put such a deception beyond them? We would only make it easier for dishonest officers to prove a lie.

Nor would such methods protect the police. How would a court distinguish, for instance, between bruises sustained by a subject while resisting arrest, and bruises sustained through torture? The camera can't tell the difference. We would still have to rely on someone's word as to how the physical injuries had been inflicted.

There is, in my opinion, a simpler, safer, and more radical way to ensure the integrity of evidence in court. This, too, has been recommended by a number of authorities. It is to exclude as evidence everything a suspect tells the police — everything — unless he tells it to them in the presence of his lawyer.

Some authorities, such as Professor Edward Ratushny, have gone even further. They have made good arguments for excluding all utterances made to the police by an accused person, whether his lawyer had been present or not. A confession is not a key element in any but the weakest cases. It should be possible to obtain a conviction by evidence other than the defendant's own words.

Even if we don't go as far as this, what objection can there be to excluding defendants' statements other than those made in the presence of counsel? One lawyer at the police station is worth a thousand pictures. This method may not win police officers any Oscars, but it will ensure that all statements received in court will be truly admissible evidence.

NOTES

p.176, 1.25: The men shot in their own homes were Hans Nattinen, Steven Kalemis, Aquilino Torcato, Albert Johnson, and Michael Wawryniuk. Torcato, Nattinen, and Wawryniuk were alone at the time (though, when initially called, the police could not be certain about this).

p.177, 1.5: See "Police Use of Lethal Force: A Toronto Perspective" by John D. Abraham, John C. Field, Professor Richard W. Harding, and Steven Skurka in *Osgoode Hall Law Journal*, Volume 19, No. 2, p. 226.

p.177, 1.12: Ibid., pp. 200-1.

p.178, 1.26: *Policing Reform: A Study of the Reform Process and Police Institution in Toronto* by Maeve W. McMahon and Richard V. Ericson.

p.182, 1.15: The Maloney Report (1975); the Morand Report (1976); and the Pitman Report (1977).

p.190, 1.9: A *voir dire* (from the old French expression "speak the truth") is a hearing in the absence of the jury, usually held to determine if some evidence is admissible or not, but particularly to determine the admissibility of confessions to the police. In cases heard by a judge alone, the judge must disabuse his own mind (in so far as that is humanly possible) of all the evidence he had heard but ruled inadmissible at a *voir dire*.

p.192, 1.18: People may ask what this political purpose was. It was never spelled out, and it probably varied from participant to participant. On the whole, based on the general rhetoric employed by CIRPA and allied groups, it appeared to be the replacement of liberal parliamentary democracy with what its supporters may have described as "participatory" democracy, and what others might describe as some confused populist system of the New Left, combining elements (or at least buzz-words) culled from Maoism, Trotskyism, the theories of such writers as Marcuse and Fannon, and enveloped by what the American journalist Tom Wolfe once called "pseudo-Marxist fog".

CIRPA and its supporters were, of course, as entitled to their sociopolitical views as anyone else. They were entitled to regard the Hold-Up Squad or the Police Commission as "red-necks" or "Neanderthals", just as some officers may have regarded *them* as "pinkos" or "commies". Such things are a matter of opinion. What CIRPA was not entitled to was to publicly accuse a group of policemen of criminal acts (and the justice system of covering up criminal acts) without disclosing their evidence.

# BREAKFAST OF CHAMPIONS

Greenspan's taste in restaurants has always been eclectic. One man's eclectic, of course, is another man's idiosyncratic. Some of Eddie's favourite haunts require no explanation: they are simply among the best restaurants in the world. Who, for instance, would not enjoy the Caviar Kaspia in Paris? (Who could afford it is a different question, because at places like the Caviar Kaspia, lunch for two might run to $200.)

Most people could afford Greenspan's favourite restaurants of another type. The trouble is, they might consider them beyond the pale from a gourmet's (or a nutritionist's) point of view.

The fact is, Eddie likes junk food. American junk, European junk, or Far Eastern junk. A nice, sizzling double hamburger with things dripping from all sides. A Transylvanian Fatányéros, with its huge assortment of breaded meats and innards, consumed in the peculiar ambiance of one of Toronto's ethnic eateries on Bloor Street. A big bowl of hot Korean Mandoo Kuk. Once, when the writer Norman Snider was doing a magazine profile on Greenspan, Eddie dragged him for a 2 a.m. crawl of hamburger joints and doughnut shops in Toronto, populated at that time mainly by tired hookers and their pimps. It was a memorable night, with Greenspan saying such things as: "Isn't this great?" or "Aren't you having the time of your life?" to the puzzled journalist.

Then, there is Stubby's, the scene of the great breakfast caper.

Sam "Stubby" Steinbaum's establishment is not easy to categorize. It is definitely not a greasy spoon. It doesn't serve junk food. It features a tasty home-cooked soup; delicious, lightly breaded whitefish; onions-and-eggs; or fresh sliced tomatoes in sour cream, all meticulously prepared by Stubby himself. Still, decent food is not enough to put a place at the top end of the scale. No one, not even Stubby himself, would regard Stubby's as one of the great restaurants of the world. Tourists are not likely to hear about it, and it would not appear on Yuppie lists of the Toronto scene. Yet for some reason the little lunch-room on Bathurst Street draws much the same crowd, especially on Saturday mornings, *whose members might otherwise be seen at their regular tables at Winston's, Il Posto, Le Bistingo, or any of the top Toronto restaurants of the eighties.*

*In a sense, Stubby's is a monument to reverse snobbery. Far from having armies of waiters, busboys, and maître d's to hover over them, patrons don't even look for the one waiter, Jimmy, who is (sometimes) in evidence. Regular guests will simply grab their own Diet Cokes from the fridge or go behind the counter to get their cutlery, pour their own coffee, butter their kaisers, and, if they feel really established and privileged, cook their own onions-and-eggs. The dress code — there is a dress code, unspoken as it may be — is also reversed. It's not that you wouldn't be served if you wore a three-piece suit to Stubby's (nobody is served anyway), it's that you would feel sadly out of place.*

*There's no use asking for the bill, either. Stubby is busy behind the counter, and he will not discuss money in any event. If you really insist on paying, and if you can find Stubby's daughter or son somewhere, you may tell them what you recollect about your breakfast, and they may suggest an amount in response. The price for the same order will vary from time to time, but it will always be less than any other place would charge for food of similar quality, or for the opportunity of rubbing elbows with some of the biggest movers and shakers in the city.*

*Developers A. I. Diamond and Harold Green, real estate wizard Eddie Cogan, North York mayor Mel Lastman, Toronto Sun publisher (and former Metro Toronto Chairman) Paul Godfrey, media personalities Arthur Vaile, Michael Cohl, Gary Dunford, and Michael McGee, ex- or current cabinet ministers Mitchell Sharp, Robert Kaplan, David Crombie, and Roy McMurtry, lawyers like Goodman & Goodman partner Herb Solway or Minden, Gross litigation chief Peter Israel, power-consultants Jim Coutts, Sam Wakim, and Dusty Cohl (who prefers to be known as an "accomplice") have all been regular or occasional guests at Stubby's, along with dozens of other financial or political power-houses of their ilk. The reason, without doubt, has been "Stubby" Steinbaum himself, the one-time concentration-camp inmate, liberated from Dachau with the number B5258 tattooed on his arm. Somehow, the ambiance Stubby creates — and "creates" may be the wrong word, since he makes no conscious effort to create anything except the perfect onions-and-eggs — is a cathartic, humbling purification of the soul: a reminder to the high and mighty of their common origin and destination. Everyone gets the same nod from Stubby (unless he's too busy to* nod) or, as a mark of special favour and recognition, maybe a good-natured insult. Then the big shots can find a spot at one of the cafeteria-style tables, pull up a chair, and fend for themselves.

No wonder Stubby is a Tolstoyan (though he doesn't talk about that, either). If there were an inscription on the wall, it would probably read: "From dust to dust — but meanwhile relax, and have some whitefish."

In 1981 Greenspan, a semi-regular at Stubby's Saturday breakfasts, gave Steinbaum some legal advice. (This was unusual in itself because Stubby's concerns were not in the area of criminal law, and Greenspan generally refrains from advising people on civil matters. "If you want me as a lawyer, get yourself arrested for murder" is Eddie's customary reply to all civil-law queries.) However, in Stubby's case he made an exception. When the matter was settled, Steinbaum dropped Greenspan a note asking what he owed him for the consultation.

Greenspan replied that, as a high-priced lawyer, his advice did not come cheap. Stubby owed him a hundred breakfasts.

Stubby immediately replied that he found the legal fee quite reasonable, but he was not in the habit of paying his bills on the instalment plan. Greenspan could have his fee any time he cared to come with a friend to eat his hundred breakfasts at one sitting.

Greenspan phoned George Jonas. "That's a challenge," he said. "What am I going to do about it?"

"Can you eat one breakfast?" Jonas asked.

"Yes," Eddie replied with great conviction. He didn't even have to think about it.

"Well, then it's just a matter of coming up with a friend who can eat ninety-nine," said Jonas. He did have one particular person in mind. About a year earlier he had produced a television show for CBC in which a retired wrestler named "Big" Lou Pitoscia had played a small role. In the same scene there was also a walk-on for a donkey. The donkey, displaying a well-known character trait of its breed, refused to walk — walk on or off, period. Perhaps it wanted a bigger role or its own dressing-room. Coaxing and carrots had no effect, but "Big" Lou knew how to persuade donkeys. He simply picked up the reluctant animal and deposited it in the required spot. (At 60 inches, "Big" Lou's chest was a couple of inches deeper than the donkey's, though their neck sizes, at 19$^1$/$_2$ inches, were just about the same.)

Jonas telephoned Pitoscia. "Lou," he asked, "can you eat a hundred breakfasts?"

"A hundred? No way," replied Lou.

"On television?"

"Sure I can eat a hundred breakfasts," said Lou, who liked show business. "There's nothing to it."

That settled the matter. On May 2, 1981, with the news photographers' lights flashing and the TV cameras rolling, Stubby deposited the first dozen orders of sizzling eggs, onions, whitefish, sliced tomatoes, and buttered toast in front of his guests. Greenspan had his one order served on a plate; Lou his eleven in a big iron pan.

Dusty Cohl was holding the bets.

Eddie was cracking jokes, but Lou tucked in with an expression suitable for going ten rounds with Whipper Billy Watson in the ring. This was serious business; possibly even a matter of gladiatorial honour for Lou. He looked formidable and Stubby was clearly worried. Still, poker-faced, he kept heaping more eggs, onions, and whitefish onto the hot grid behind the counter.

In a few minutes Eddie finished his helping, and lit a cigarette. Lou was going strong, stalking the whitefish in the iron pan with the calm, co-ordinated movements of a seasoned pro. The odds edged up slightly in the breakfasters' favour. "Big" Lou looked as though he might go the distance.

Stubby, sensing that he was in trouble, kept putting new orders into Lou's iron pan. There was the champ, chomping away, yet the pile would never diminish. On the contrary: imperceptibly at first, but steadily, it started to grow. Soon it was growing in an obvious and threatening manner. With twenty orders finished, there was more whitefish and eggs-and-onions in front of Lou than ever before.

Especially more onions. Lots and lots of onions.

The wrestler was eating much more slowly now, but his expression made it clear that he would never give up. Eddie, and some of the others, were beginning to cast anxious glances at each other. As splendid a specimen of physical culture as Lou was, he was no longer in his first youth. He had already tucked away 60 eggs and 60 pieces of whitefish, with another 240 eggs and whitefish to go. The joke was getting a little out of hand — but there seemed to be no way to stop Lou. He was obviously not going to say "Uncle!" Stubby stopped putting more eggs on the grid, but Lou glanced at him threateningly. "Let's go eat," he growled. "I'm hungry."

"You're his partner," Dusty Cohl whispered to Eddie. Greenspan nodded, and looked around for a dishcloth. Grabbing it, he threw it on the floor. "We're throwing in the towel," he announced.

At this "Big" Lou stopped eating. He stood up, testing his limbs carefully. He shook hands with Stubby, then slowly walked out of the restaurant. He never conceded defeat, but, once out of camera range, he did agree that it had been one of the tougher challenges of his career. It wasn't the whitefish and it wasn't the eggs. "It was the onions, see," said Lou. "If he hadn'ta put in the onions, it woulda been a breeze."

# PART FIVE

# JUSTICE IN HIGH HEELS

# 11. The Sting

In the early months of 1986 Canadian feminists declared an open season on Greenspan. For a few weeks he became the subject of scathing press comments by various women's-movement spokespersons as well as by the resident feminist columnists of several major newspapers. One representative contribution was a "vinegar valentine" penned by Marylin Linton of the Toronto Sun:

> Oh, Greenspan with worries so big,
> Are you not a male chauvinist pig?
> Those feminists, you pout,
> Influence courts with their clout.
> Well, Eddie, we don't give a fig!

The reason for the furore was a speech Greenspan gave to the Ontario Psychiatric Association in January 1986, in which he warned that on several issues, ranging from pornography to sexual assault, feminist pressure has influenced substantive as well as procedural law in Canada. Acknowledging that some of this influence has produced just reforms, Greenspan called attention to those areas of the law where it did, or threatened to do, harm. He also pointed out that, in some instances, feminist influence has amounted to intimidation, posing a potential danger to the independence of the judiciary. He specifically deplored attempts to use the Judicial Council as an agency of the women's movement through the filing of complaints against judges whose decisions or passing remarks do not accord with the feminist world-view.

As if determined to prove Greenspan right, several feminist critics responded with abuse and fury. When, in the course of researching material for this chapter, George Jonas looked at their statements in the press, they struck him as textbook displays of the incapacity of modern pressure groups to accord legitimacy to any interest but their own. Greenspan's opponents, whether or not they couched their disregard for *the concerns or values of others in slightly more sophisticated terms than Marylin Linton, truly didn't "give a fig". For them, outside the enchanted circle of their pet peeves and ambitions, the world appeared to consist only of rooting, grunting chauvinist pigs.*

*The tone of Greenspan's critics was illustrated by the opening paragraphs of Doris Anderson's column in the* Toronto Star:

> *The way top Toronto criminal lawyer Edward Greenspan tells it, Canada's legal system is tottering on the brink of capitulation before hordes of women intent on "feminizing" the courts.*
>
> *"Make no mistake about it, that this [feminist] viewpoint is beginning to carry the day in the courtrooms of our land," Greenspan,* who earns about \$250 an hour, *warned the 66th annual meeting of the Ontario Psychiatric Association recently. [Emphasis added.]*

*Anderson (who earns about \$100 an hour, unless she writes more slowly than most columnists) then went on to make two points. The first was that "The idea of judges cowering on the bench" in fear of feminists would probably make "any female practicing in Ontario's courts double over in helpless laughter." Her second point was that "perhaps it's just as well that [some judges] are beginning to cower a little and the more inhibited they feel . . . the better."*

*This, in turn, had the effect of making Jonas (whatever he earns an hour) double over in helpless laughter. Anderson and her friends evidently couldn't make up their minds whether to characterize what Greenspan was saying about feminist influence as untrue, or true but highly desirable. Eventually they took the position that (a) it was false, and (b) it was a good thing. The fact that the two statements were mutually exclusive could always be minimized by pointing out that Greenspan was a \$250-an-hour male chauvinist pig.*

*In fairness, these were not the only feminist voices in the press. For instance in a* Toronto Star *interview, Laura Sabia, first chairman of the Ontario Council on the Status of Women, said: "[Greenspan will] get a lot of reaction from very, very militant feminists. But if he has the guts to say it, I have the guts to agree with him." It was an interesting confirmation, from one of Canada's lifelong leaders of the women's movement, that by 1986 views such as Greenspan's took "guts" to express or even agree with.*

*That, in a nutshell, was Greenspan's point as well. That was what he meant when he talked about the intimidation of the judicial system.*

By the mid-eighties the extremists had moved from the fringes to the centre of the women's movement. Sabia's "very, very militant feminists" aimed at entrenching their ideology in Canada's institutions, and putting all contrary views beyond the pale. "We have a long way to go before the legal system in this country is non-sexist," Marjorie Cohen, vice-president of the National Action Committee on the Status of Women, was quoted as saying. "I hope what [Greenspan] says about the judiciary in 10 years time is true, because we would have a much fairer judiciary." (Greenspan had predicted a "judicial embracing of the feminist perspective in ten years' time".) In any case, as Bonnie Diamond of the Canadian Coalition against Media Pornography reassured the press, "only a few judges are intimidated by feminists."

A non-sexist judiciary as envisaged by the Action Committee on the Status of Women reminded Jonas of democracy as envisaged by Turkey's ruling junta, which in the early 1960s passed a law decreeing that anyone who publicly stated that Turkey was not a democracy would go to prison for two years. That would probably be the fate of anyone in Canada who pointed out that a feminist judiciary could hardly be anything but "sexist" by definition. The truth was that Jonas could not repress a certain amount of schadenfreude — the German word meaning delight in someone else's misfortune — over the feminist attacks on Greenspan. For many years Greenspan had looked on feminism with considerable sympathy, and regarded Jonas's dire warnings about a repressive and authoritarian strain in the women's movement as highly exaggerated. Eddie certainly did not believe that feminists might threaten some of the fundamental safeguards and presumptions of the legal system; that they might endanger procedural fairness, or attempt to bring pressure on judges to influence their decisions or reasoning in given cases.

Greenspan's views began to change only after a careful observation of what feminist influence was gradually doing to the law. Eventually he did become concerned (perhaps more concerned than Jonas, who by then had only become amused, muttering gleefully, "I told you so, I told you so").

Among the cases illustrating Greenspan's concerns were the rape trials of a Windsor policeman named Wayne St. Louis, and the charges laid against a Toronto nightclub owner — in this account we will call him Jeno Kujon. (We have christened his nightclub, for the purposes of this story, The Floating Gypsy, changing no other essential facts.)

*There have been worse and more extreme cases in recent years — but*
*Greenspan wanted to select two that had happy endings.*


The incident that required Jeno Kujon, part-owner of a Toronto
nightclub and a businessman of unblemished reputation, to retain
me as his counsel occurred on a Thursday afternoon in 1984.

A woman (I will call her May in this account) had called Kujon a
few days earlier for an appointment. She said that she was an artist
and wanted to show Kujon something that "he would have to see to
believe," adding that she had been trying to get through to him for
three months. Kujon found this unusual, as he always takes (or
returns) his phone calls himself — about thirty calls every day — and
he couldn't remember having had any messages from this lady. Still,
he agreed to see her at 3 p.m. in his office, which is on the first floor
of The Floating Gypsy nightclub in suburban Toronto.

May arrived at the appointed time. She turned out to be a woman
of around fifty. She came accompanied by a short, stocky, well-
turned-out man who looked about her age or perhaps a few years
younger. When Susan Roka, Kujon's long-time secretary, returned
from lunch, she found May and her friend waiting for Kujon, who
still had another visitor in his office. May was drinking a cup of
coffee a waiter had served her, and she told Susan that Kujon was "a
difficult man to get hold of". The secretary was also mildly surprised
by this remark: she couldn't recall May's having phoned for any
appointments before. At that point, however, Kujon appeared in the
doorway of his inner office, saying good-bye to his earlier visitor. On
noticing May and her friend in the reception area, Jeno asked both of
them to enter.

The man declined, but May, wearing a long white skirt and a
bandanna in her hair, followed Kujon into his office. The door
between the office and the reception area was left open.

The door, in fact, stayed open most of the time during the next ten
to fifteen minutes. At one point a waiter named Istvan took in a cup
of coffee and a glass of wine, and when he left he closed the door after
himself. (The club was not serving customers yet, but some employees had already started their shifts.) Within a minute or two, Susan
herself entered the office to take in some notes. Kujon was talking on

the telephone and May stood looking at one of the pictures on the wall. She asked Susan if she knew who painted it. The secretary replied that she had no idea. She didn't feel like chatting with the woman, who seemed a trifle too loud and eccentric to her. Just as Susan was coming out of the office, the stocky man who had accompanied May stuck his head in to tell his friend that "he couldn't wait for her any longer."

As Susan recalled, the stocky man closed the door again as he left.

Phone calls kept coming in for Kujon during this time, which Susan put through as usual, with Kujon taking them all. There must have been two or three calls while May was in the office. After a few minutes Susan went into the office again to bring in a box that had just been delivered for her boss. At that point Kujon was sitting behind his desk, while May was sitting in a chair on the other side. Jeno asked his secretary to open the box, which contained a wildly coloured tie with an invitation to the opening of a new restaurant.

Susan left the office, leaving the door open once more, and a few minutes later May herself emerged. She came out of Kujon's office in a totally unremarkable manner. She appeared calm and unhurried. She said good-bye to Susan, and Susan said good-bye to her. Everything seemed completely normal to the secretary — as it did to Jeno Kujon, who came out of his office about twenty minutes later to dictate a business letter to Susan.

There was no reason for things not to appear normal to Kujon: nothing had happened in his office that would have caused him to take the slightest notice. On entering, May had declined his offer for more coffee, but when Kujon buzzed for some coffee for himself she asked if she could have a glass of wine. Istvan, the waiter, brought both, and she drank her wine while Kujon was taking a phone call. After some desultory conversation in which she described herself as an artist and mentioned the names of some people that Kujon knew, May pulled out a photograph of what appeared to be a large decorative rabbit made of majolica. This, apparently, was May's creation, and she wanted Kujon to buy it. Jeno said he wasn't interested. She then asked if he might be interested in a smaller, four-foot version; he replied that he wouldn't be, but she could send him a photograph of it if she liked. They chatted for a few more minutes between Kujon's telephone calls — Jeno remembered her mentioning that she was divorced and had a sixteen-year-old son, a talented artist, though a difficult boy — and then she left. In fact, Kujon recalled being on the telephone as she stood up and walked out — perhaps a bit abruptly, not that Jeno gave the matter much thought. He felt under no duty to be an attentive host to strangers trying to sell him large rabbits.

For another couple of hours nothing happened. Kujon attended to business matters until around 5:15 in the afternoon, at which time he retired to his office for his customary siesta. It has long been Jeno's habit to hold all his calls, lock the door of his office, and take a nap for about forty-five minutes in preparation for the long night's work ahead.

At a few minutes after 6 p.m. May burst into the nightclub accompanied by two men. One was the same stocky, well-dressed man who had accompanied her earlier, while the other one was younger and rather shabby. They brushed aside Mokus, the maître d', and banged on the door of Kujon's office.

Jeno had already got up after his siesta; in fact he was just in the process of putting on his pants. Thinking that the manager of one of his suppliers, whom he expected, had arrived, he opened his door. May barged in, with the two men in tow. "What's the problem?" Jeno asked as the woman yelled at him and attempted to strike his face. Her answer was a string of abuse and the accusation that "you touched my breast!"

"You're a liar," said Kujon, taken aback.

The woman continued yelling that she'd "go to the lie detectors, the newspapers, just to get you." Meanwhile the two men grabbed Kujon's pants and jacket and threw them in a corner.

"Don't be stupid," said Kujon, taking another pair of pants from the closet at the back of the office. He told the maître d' to get a couple of the bartenders from downstairs and call the police. The bartenders came promptly and stood between the two men and Kujon, while May went to get a glass of water.

Within minutes two police officers arrived. They talked with May; they talked with the two men; then they asked Kujon a couple of questions. They asked if the woman had been in his office earlier, and they asked if Jeno had had some garlic for lunch. Kujon's answer was yes to the first question and no to the second.

Then the officers gave Kujon an appearance notice. He was to appear in court on a charge of sexual assault.

According to May's statement to the police, she had never been to the nightclub before but thought that Mr. Kujon might be interested in her large rabbit creation "as he has very influencial [*sic*] clients." She stated that as soon as she entered the office and went to shake hands with Kujon, "he kissed me square on the lips." Apparently this did not disturb May because "I thought, well being Hungarian, this was his way of greeting."

This ethnographic notion must have persisted in her mind because — on her story — she went on discussing her artwork with Kujon even though after a few minutes of conversation Kujon tried to kiss her *again*.

"At this point [the police statement read] the Victim was asked:

"*Q*: Why didn't you leave at this point?

"The victim replied:

"*A*: Only because my sister married a Hungarian, *I knew what they were like*, so I didn't want to over react [*sic*] and I continued the conversation." (Emphasis added.)

May stated that Kujon did not persist, and they kept talking. She got up to leave when, she alleged, Kujon went over to her, saying, "I had a nice smile and touched my left breast with his hand." At that point, May said, she left the office, remarking to Kujon that "I didn't need this."

May stated that at no time was there any "yelling" or argument. Kujon did not insist on his advances and made no attempt to stop her from walking out.

After leaving Kujon's office, May continued, she dropped in at her bank, then went downtown to shop at the Eaton Centre for a purse. She was scheduled to meet her "real-estate agent" (the well-dressed man who had initially accompanied her to Kujon's office) and another "friend" (the younger man wearing shabby clothes) at the Park Plaza Hotel about an hour later. When she did meet the men, "I explained to them what happened and [they] said that something should be dealt with. [*Sic*.] We returned to tell [Kujon] off. We knocked on the door and Mr. Kujon let us in, and once inside I hit him across the face.

"Mr. Kujon called the police."

This was May's statement. Kujon called it an outright lie — which later proved to be precisely what it was. However, as a lawyer, I had a more fundamental problem with May's story.

What if the lie had been the truth? How would Kujon's actions have added up to sexual assault, if what May said *had* been an accurate description of what transpired in the office?

Assuming for a moment that May's statement was factual, it described a woman being kissed by a man upon entering his office. All right. In Canada every day a thousand men kiss, touch, or put their arms around a woman (or vice versa), and not one of them commits a crime. Touching, kissing, or putting one's arms around a person is not a crime, whether it is done at the first encounter or after the thousandth (provided the person is not underage or feeble-minded). When done with sexual undertones, such acts have always been regarded as a "pass", which could be welcomed or rebuffed by the recipient.

Only if someone persisted after a rejection did a pass run the risk of becoming a sexual assault.

In this instance, on May's own story, after the initial kiss the "passee" sat down in the "passer's" office and asked him for a glass of wine. She gave him no indication of a rejection whatsoever. When the second pass was made, she still said nothing to him and continued sitting in his office. At the third pass she finally rebuffed him — and that was it. The man did not persist.

In this series of actions, as described by the complainant, what would have constituted an "assault"? It wasn't a question of whether such acts were "nice" or "tasteful" or not, but what could possibly make them a matter for the police? Which element in the complainant's story would have required the intervention of the criminal law?

By cultural tradition, possibly by nature, in our species it is usually the male who initiates sexual moves. This has been so in virtually every society throughout human history. True, the male ordinarily makes his move after he has received some sign of sexual receptiveness from the female. These signs may range from the very subtle to the all-too-blatant, and the male generally interprets them correctly. Sometimes, however, he doesn't. In such a case the woman will pull away, or say: "Kindly keep your hideous fingers to yourself."

After she pulls away or says that, any woman's person becomes inviolate. The law has no sympathy for men who press on regardless (and neither have I).

However, the law does not require people to be romantic experts. Misinterpreting signals is not an offence. Being rejected is not a crime. If it were, then whenever a man tried to kiss a woman he'd have to keep his hideous fingers crossed for an enthusiastic response, because if the woman as much as turned her head away he'd be guilty of sexual assault. It would make every young boy's unsophisticated or inexpert move on his first date a potential police matter. Even if he did nothing to persist.

The law protects a woman's right to refuse a pass — refuse it even from her *husband*, let alone from a social or business acquaintance — but the law doesn't and can't guarantee that only those men whose passes a woman might welcome will try to make passes at her. Nor does the law require a man to be a mind-reader. If a woman consents to his pass, he is not under a duty to divine whether she actually enjoyed it or consented merely not to hurt his feelings. Or in the hope that he might buy a large rabbit from her.

A woman has every right to consent to a dozen passes, yet still refuse a further one. What she can't do is to make her refusal retrospective. She can't say: "Well, I really didn't enjoy the first dozen, I only tolerated them, so looking back I think they were sexual assaults." That's not what an assault is. A sexual assault is insisting on the one pass that is not being tolerated.

Needless to say, even an intial "pass" can be so brutal as to amount to an assault. A man obviously can't tear off someone's blouse or jump at a woman from the bushes, then say: "Gee, I was just making a pass." But on May's story, no one jumped and no one tore off anything. It was a tolerated kiss, followed by a touch.

I felt that no interpretation of May's story — if her story were true in the first place — would make Kujon guilty of any offence under the Criminal Code. At worst it could render him liable to some action under the "sexual harassment" provisions of the Human Rights Act — and that only if his position as a potential buyer could establish him as being in some position of economic power over the complainant. (If the Act could be so interpreted, incidentally, it should make any male think twice before having a private meeting with a female salesperson.)

When, after being retained by Kujon, I raised some of these points with the Crown Attorney, he only shrugged. I think that as a fair-minded and skilled lawyer he did not feel like arguing the matter.

His shrug confirmed to me what I knew anyway. In the current climate, if a woman laid a complaint of a sexual nature against a man — almost any complaint, on almost any set of facts — the police and the Crown would feel obliged to run with it. It was too "political", the authorities seemed to say. Let the courts sort it out.

It infuriated me. It still does. Policy has a legitimate role in the administration of justice. But policy — as the old legal maxim has it — is an unruly horse. You can't just decide, as a matter of policy, to treat a pass as if it were an "assault". Not if you want to preserve the rule of law. If, under feminist pressure, the lawmakers of Canada want to turn a man's making a pass into a crime, at least they should have the honesty and courage to put it on the books.

I must confess that I almost wished that May's story had been true. It would have made the case far more interesting for me as a lawyer. As it was, all I ended up having to do was to investigate and prove it a lie, which required some legwork but little legal finesse. This is the kind of "lawyering" Perry Mason does on television. It may be great showbusiness, but it's far removed from what criminal lawyers normally do. At any rate, it does not come up in my practice too often.

Jeno Kujon told me that the woman was lying. It was his view (supported, interestingly enough, by the privately expressed opinion of one of the policemen at the scene) that May and her friends probably wanted to try their hands at a little extortion. (A Freudian psychiatrist would have found it interesting that May, after being "assaulted", immediately bought herself a *purse*.) She and her friends might have expected Kujon, as a prominent businessman anxious to avoid a scandal, to offer them a deal. What foiled their attempt was the fact that, instead, Jeno had immediately called the police. Since the officers arrived within minutes, the trio had no chance to make any monetary demands: they were still at the "outraged" stage of this type of scam. (Perhaps it would have been better for Jeno to play with them a little before calling the law — but as an innocent man taken in his office by surprise, he naturally wasted no time in turning to the police for protection.)

I agreed with Kujon's assessment — people who burst into someone's office instead of laying a complaint are likely to have ulterior motives — but my agreement didn't amount to proof of anything. The woman would hardly admit to an attempted shake-down on the witness stand. I was certainly not going to let matters become a credibility contest between my client and a lying witness if I could help it. Not in any climate, but especially not in today's.

I couldn't count on the police. The police may investigate a murder or a narcotics case very thoroughly, but would not waste wiretaps or undercover agents on a minor sexual assault. A case of this sort is generally of no importance to anyone but the defendant, whose reputation and business are at stake.

Luckily there are a number of ex-policemen and former security agents who specialize in private investigations. I imported two of the best from out of town. One was to pose as an international investor, and the other as his realty lawyer. (This second operative was, in fact, a lawyer.) I could give them one lead only, which was that the well-dressed, stocky man who accompanied May to Kujon's office was supposed to be a real-estate agent.

It proved to be enough. Within twenty-four hours of arriving in Toronto, my operative reported that he was negotiating for the purchase of May's house, which was up for sale. He was in contact with the stocky real-estate agent who had come with her to Kujon's office — we'll call him Harper. While they were looking over the property, Harper described May, the owner, to my private investigator as a woman he had known for some time on a "personal basis". She was, Harper said, "a little crazy" but a nice person, interested in exporting her artwork abroad.

My operative said that this was an amazing coincidence, as he had a keen interest in the importation of artwork.

A dinner was arranged for May to meet my investigator, now the art collector. In the meantime the private detective discovered that the shabbily dressed younger man — we'll call him Costin — had a criminal record for assault, and was currently in the nightclub business himself.

In the dining-room of the Park Plaza Hotel, while my operative held forth rather expansively on his business of purchasing real estate, artwork, and nightclubs, Harper suddenly turned to him and asked if he had ever heard of a man named Jeno Kujon and a nightclub called The Floating Gypsy.

"No," replied the detective, reminding May and her friend that he was from out of town — which, at least, was true.

Harper looked at May. "Tell him, tell him," she said. "I think we can trust him."

Harper then proceeded to tell my operative who Kujon was, and that he had been charged with sexually assaulting May. Then a discussion ensued on the business opportunities that this would provide for anyone who wanted to take over The Floating Gypsy nightclub. It was to be a venture, Harper suggested, in which my operative might be interested.

May then gave the investigator her story in a significantly different version from her statement to the police. In this story she was still being greeted by an embrace and a kiss by Jeno Kujon, as well as an embrace upon leaving, in the course of which Kujon had "accidentally touched" her breast. However, none of this bothered her, May said, since she knew that "all Hungarians are like that." It was only when she related the events to her friends Harper and Costin later that afternoon that young Costin insisted that they should go back and create a confrontation. "You don't understand," May quoted Costin as saying, "we must go back and make a scene. This is what it's all about. We can own the nightclub."

Apparently, in Costin's opinion, Kujon's reputation made him extremely vulnerable to charges of this kind. He would be forced to sell his place at a distress price.

May was intrigued by this, because in addition to her artwork, as she told my operative, she had always been interested in becoming a singer and a piano-player in a nightclub.

"You see," Harper interjected at this point, "the three of us are a team, and Costin should run The Floating Gypsy. The owner of The Floating Gypsy is old and Costin is thirty-three, and he'd make a perfect owner."

The conversation continued in this vein for a while, with May speculating that the case would never come to court, since Kujon's lawyer "is trying to bribe some judges to get him off the hook," but that if she did have to go to court, she'd just take a trip and disappear. Harper said that he could not afford to appear in court either, because he was a married man and his wife might "misunderstand" what he was doing with May in the nightclub.

The sexual-assault charge against Kujon had been reported in a local newspaper (without mentioning the name of the complainant, of course). "How," asked my investigator, "did the paper find out about it?" Harper assured him that his friend Costin was well connected and that he "leaked the story" to the press. The implication was that this would add to the pressure on Kujon making the acquisition of The Floating Gypsy possible.

After several hours the dinner ended. Harper picked up the check. A further dinner was going to be set up at which my man and the second operative posing as his "realty lawyer" would meet with May and her friends, so that my investigator's involvement in the purchase of The Floating Gypsy could be discussed.

I read the summary of the dinner conversation's transcript with interest. The plan of buying The Floating Gypsy seemed far-fetched, and I couldn't tell whether or not this was a fallback position for the trio since their original simple shakedown did not materialize. It also seemed that, even while May and Co. were being subjected to a "sting", they were trying just as hard to con my detective into laying out money for their scam. This was amusing, but not quite satisfactory. I certainly didn't think that it would be necessary to buy May's house to gather enough evidence for what we needed, but I felt that one more dinner between the conning parties, captured this time on video tape as well as on sound-track, might be a worthwhile investment. There was, according to my investigator, a lot of body language involved in the conversation, which I thought might entertain a judge in court.

I'll let George Jonas tell this part of the story. As a producer, he knows more than I do about showbusiness.

*In fact, Jonas's involvement in the case was minimal: he simply put Greenspan in touch with another private investigator, who until his retirement from one of the western security services specialized in wiring sensitive installations for picture and sound. The "installation" in this case was far from being sensitive, since it was only a room in a mid-town Toronto hotel, the Four Seasons. That was where May and her friends were going to dine with Greenspan's investigators.*

*The electronic-surveillance operative, who for literary purposes likes to go by the name of Sullivan, used to be one of the top men in the service of his government. The assignment ought to have been a piece of cake for him. However, one of Greenspan's conditions landed him in unexpected difficulties.*

*While intercepting communications without lawful authority is a* criminal offence, it is quite legal to make an audio-visual record of any encounter or conversation between two parties with the knowledge and consent of one. In this instance, the consenting parties would be Greenspan's two out-of-town investigators. This meant that at least one of the two operatives had to be present at all times, because leaving the subjects alone, even to go to the bathroom, could render the entire operation illegal — unless Sullivan immediately terminated the electronic surveillance. It wasn't a problem, only a new "wrinkle", as Sullivan thought of it. Such considerations never arise in working for the government.

The operatives' hotel room would constitute, in Sullivan's language, "the target premises". After wiring the room, he would monitor the happenings from "the allied premises", or in plain English the room next door.

Considering that in Sullivan's normal line of work the "target premises" are often separated from the "allied premises" by several well-guarded embassy blocks or large empty fields surrounded by electrified fences — and the "wiring" may involve crawling through sewers or digging 100-foot tunnels — Greenspan's assignment sounded like a real retirement project to him. The only thing that Sullivan left out of his calculations was a condition conveyed to him in the last minute by Greenspan, namely that he could only employ equipment that was — horrors! — commercially available.

Governments do not operate under such constraints either. Even private employers do not specify it, as a rule. They generally want to get the job done, and that's all. We live in a result-oriented society. By specifying commercial equipment, Greenspan, as a cautious lawyer, was going the extra mile to make certain that even the subtlest detail should not render the evidence inadmissible in court.

Judging by Sullivan's expression when he heard the news, Jonas doubted that he had ever worked with equipment that one could buy in a store. There is, of course, a wide variety of security cameras and omni-directional microphones available anywhere — but they are about five times as bulky as and ten times less sensitive than the usual hardware used by Sullivan and his colleagues in government work.

The phone rang in Jonas's apartment in the wee hours of one night in August 1984. It was Sullivan. "Do you happen to have," he asked Jonas in a plaintive tone of voice, "a pair of black pantyhose?"

Rendering Jonas's reply verbatim might offend some readers. Suffice *it to say that the required item was eventually secured. What the problem had been was made clear in Sullivan's final report of the operation. "Due to the configuration of the equipment," he wrote, "some difficulty was experienced both in terminating the audio/video output cabling and in secreting the camera. Eventually, the camera . . . was positioned within the airconditioning vent overlooking the meeting area of the target premises. [It was] enclosed in pair of black panty hose and mounted so as to escape detection."*

*A far cry from the pinpoint lens on the head of a nail that James Bond sticks into a wall.*

*Still, the operation was satisfactory enough. As Sullivan wrote in his report afterwards: "[The tape] does illustrate the female participant's state of mind and current feelings for what allegedly took place in the nightclub office."*

The recording certainly did illustrate the state of mind of May and her friend Harper. They were having a great time describing to my investigators, amid much laughter and merriment, how they tried to make sure that Kujon would be in the most awkward position by taking away his pants when they burst into his office. They discussed at length the idea of my operative purchasing The Floating Gypsy for them to run. Although by that time (as it turned out) May and her friends had been warned by their own lawyer to be cautious of new acquaintances because they might be trapped into some admissions, Harper and May could not quite resist the lure of a "rich German investor" and his lawyer, which my operatives represented themselves to be. Even though the careful Costin did not show up at the Four Seasons dinner, the conversation (along with one further encounter, at which Harper explained to my investigator that there was "a lot at stake" for everyone and that my investigator should buy May's house to establish his "credibility" with May and Costin before proceeding with their plans) added up to sufficient evidence of an attempted shakedown in my mind. It enabled me to go to the Crown and show him something of the defence's hand — just enough to encourage a serious second look at the charges against Kujon.

Some time passed. In the spring of 1985 the Crown told a judge in Provincial Court that after a "thorough investigation", the "alleged victim" felt that she did not wish to proceed with the case. The authorities were satisfied, the Crown added carefully, that she was "not intimidated or coerced" in coming to this decision. The Crown now believed that "it would be in the best interest of justice that the charges against Jeno Kujon be dropped."

I agreed, but not quite. In the best interest of justice the charge should never have been laid by the police. At least, it should have been laid only *after* a "thorough investigation", not before — which amounts to the same thing, since after a thorough investigation it would not have been laid at all. Only in the current climate, in my view, could this even have gone as far as it did.

May and her friends, far from being intimidated or coerced, tried to salvage their scam by getting my investigator to put money into it as a "gesture of good faith" — in addition to an attempt to unload May's property on him. They did it with an audacity I almost admired. Jeno Kujon, rather magnanimously in my view, agreed not to sue or prosecute them, which is why I'm not mentioning their real names. Naturally, since my client is the victim, I've decided to protect his identity as well.

# 12. Out of the Mouths of Babes

Mohawk Racetrack is about an hour's drive west of Toronto. It serves some of the best hamburgers in the country — or at least it did in 1981, when I still had an interest in such things. (These days I eat mainly sashimi and salad, as a result of which I've lost about 100 pounds, along with some of my joy of living.)

In any event, in the late summer of 1981 George Jonas and I drove to Mohawk Racetrack: he primarily for horseflesh and I mainly for ground beef. It was during that drive that we came up with an idea and a format for a broadcast series, *The Scales of Justice*. (Apparently Jonas had told one of the great movers and shakers of Canadian showbusiness, Susan Rubes, then of CBC Radio Drama, that he'd have a program proposal for her by Monday, and it was already Friday afternoon.) So we decided to recreate true events in Canadian crime, in a dramatized form but with documentary accuracy. Both Jonas and I felt that while stories about cops, robbers, and the criminal-justice system make up more than 75 per cent of radio and TV entertainment, the shows themselves bear less than a 25-percent resemblance to real life. We thought that we could do better.

The program went on the air, initially on CBC Stereo, in the fall of 1982. Jonas and my one-time articling student Guy Gavriel Kay wrote, researched, and produced; dozens of the finest Canadian actors and actresses performed; and I took the part of narrator and host. The audience liked the show (which by now has aired fifty-six episodes). Some of the scripts have been published in two books which, along with tape-cassettes, are being used as teaching aids in high schools (and some law schools) across Canada. The program has also, I'm very proud to say, won a string of national and international awards, including the inaugural "Scales of Justice Award" created by the Law Reform Commission and the Canadian Bar Association for the best treatment of a legal subject in the media. Even such a notorious scoffer as Guy Kay seemed suitably subdued when he took the award from the hand of Canada's Chief Justice, Brian Dickson.

I myself was nominated for an award one year as the best host. I didn't win, but I understand that Barbara Frum and Peter Gzowski spent sleepless nights, as well they might, until the results were announced.

Less happily, *The Scales of Justice* gave me my first personal taste of the kind of intimidation and censorship some feminists try to exercise over all institutions in Canada, from the criminal-justice system to the media.

Our program deals with criminal cases. We look at crimes of every description, from homicide to narcotics offences; from criminal negligence to sexual assault. We base our programs on the actual trial records. Our show, though dramatized, is a documentary; it has no "sympathy" for either side in the legal contest. We reserve all our sympathy for the law itself. We do our best to outline the case for both the prosecution and the defence in a straightforward, unbiased fashion, and try to show how the legal system works in this country.

One case we examined in our first season was the British Columbia rape trial of a man named Pappajohn. It was a case that attracted widespread attention in the late 1970s when it occurred, both in legal and in media circles. The case eventually wound up in the Supreme Court of Canada. In a majority decision — with Mr. Justice (as he then was) Dickson dissenting — the court upheld Pappajohn's conviction for rape.

In recreating the case on *The Scales of Justice* we gave full value, as we always do, to the theories of both the prosecution and the defence. In Pappajohn's case the defence was that the complainant had consented to sexual intercourse, and in any case the accused had an honest belief in her consent, whether in fact she consented or not. There was some evidence to support these propositions.

Shortly after the broadcast we received a letter of complaint from a feminist about the program. The gist of her complaint was "that it is not only incorrect but unwise to base a dramatization of a 'true story' on the potential of a woman to lie about sexual assault."

The letter-writer had, of course, every right to express her opinion; that wasn't the point. The point was that she sent copies of her complaint to the CBC's top brass as well as to several of the regulatory agencies in the country which Canada's taxpayers in their wisdom have seen fit to fund. It was clear that not only did she want to express her views: she expected the "authorities" to enforce them.

Indeed, the CBC's head office in Ottawa kept pressuring Jonas, as the producer of the program, to answer the complaint. Jonas would have done that in any event, but he couldn't recall a single other instance in two decades of producing programs when his CBC Ottawa superiors would have pressed him for an answer to a piece of audience mail (unless it raised some legal issue, such as libel or infringement of copyright). Clearly, the top brass was running scared.

Needless to say, talking about "the potential" of a woman to lie about being raped, far from being "unwise" or "incorrect", is fundamental to any analysis of the law on sexual assault. Pappajohn's case, like many contested rape cases, rested on it. The fact is that a charge of sexual assault generally gives rise to one of three defences: (a) that the assailant was someone other than the accused; (b) that no sexual contact took place at all; or (c) that all sexual contact took place with the consent of the complainant (or that the accused had an honest belief in such consent).

If these defences were not available, there would be no need for a trial. It would be enough to follow the British writer Auberon Waugh's tongue-in-cheek suggestion concerning male victims of rape, which is to make "one postcard or telephone call to a police station sufficient to put the guilty woman behind bars."

While the first of these defences rests on the complainant's mistake as to *identity*, the other two obviously rest on the complainant's mistake as to the *truth*. It's possible to make an honest mistake about identity; it's much harder to make an honest mistake about whether or not one engaged in, or consented to, a sexual act. In such cases trials are held precisely to determine who is lying, the complainant or the accused. The acquittal of an accused is by no means proof that the complainant is a liar, of course, only that a court has been left in a state of reasonable doubt about whether she is or not.

This is the law, and (short of Auberon Waugh's suggestion) it would be hard to envisage it's being anything else. As Jonas wrote in his reply to our critic:

> In a court of law all issues are specific, not statistical. It may be rare
> for a woman to bring a false charge of rape, [but] the rarest thing may

be true in a particular instance, and our courts try individual human beings, not statistical units. In a consent-defence it is irrelevant whether men *generally* rape or whether woman *generally* lie about being raped. The obvious answer is that they generally do neither, but since some can and do, *did* they in this particular case? That's what trials are all about.

In the closing paragraph of your letter you express the hope that "In the future . . . [we] will be more accurate and sensitive in [our] portrayal of such issues." I can make no such promise. We produced a drama-documentary based meticulously on the record, presenting objectively both sides of the issue on which the case in question was actually tried, and on which the probable majority of rape cases are tried in this country. If the "potential of a woman to lie about sexual assault" were, as you suggest, a "myth", a significant number of rape cases in Canadian courts would be tried on the basis of a myth. You are entitled, of course, to have such a contemptous view of our legal system, but perhaps you need not accuse others of inaccuracy for not sharing your contempt.

I suggest that critics like you are not interested in accuracy and responsibility, even though you call for them on the part of others. Your interest seems to be solely in propaganda: programs that look at events and issues from the exclusive perspective of a particular ideology.

In my experience it is precisely programs that are objective, accurate and responsible that are anathema to the ideologically committed critic. He or she wishes all public utterances to reflect his or her myths, his or her ideas, his or her point of view. As it happens, I consider it a duty of responsible journalists trying to work in the best traditions of their craft to resist pressures such as yours, which would spell the end of objective inquiry into the law, social issues, or human nature.

I fully endorsed Jonas's reply, which of course was addressed to the CBC's bosses and the various regulatory bodies as much as to the writer of the original complaint. The problem was that by 1983, when this exchange took place, some newspapers, many government agencies, and even the judicial system were no longer working "in the best traditions of their craft" when it came to feminist issues.

The worst surrender, in my view, was making dangerous changes in the law with respect to those sections of the Criminal Code that deal with various forms of sexual assault. Most of these changes were procedural; they had to do with the abrogation of certain traditional rules.

For instance, in common law the "recent complaint" rule used to permit complainants to bolster their own testimony by leading evidence that they *had* complained about being sexually assaulted at the first reasonable opportunity. This was simply to show consistency on their part — something that no other type of witness would be allowed to show (unless the other side challenged them by suggesting that their evidence was a recent fabrication). The rule *favoured* complainants. The downside of the rule was that, in the words of one judgment, "the jury must . . . be instructed that the absence of a recent complaint gives rise to an inference that tells against the truthfulness of a complainant's evidence." This rule was abolished. Curiously, while abrogating the rule made it easier to bring sexual-assault charges about which the complainant said nothing to anyone — whether at the first reasonable opportunity or ever — it *took away* a complainant's chance to show the consistency of her allegation by a recent complaint.

The problem here was simple. Our knowledge of human nature has always suggested that, on the whole, a real victim of sexual assault (or any other type of crime) *would* complain of it at the first reasonable opportunity. However, the new rules, while making life potentially easier for a lying complainant, made it harder for those truthful victims who did complain. Hindering witnesses who are somewhat more likely to tell the truth in order to help those who are somewhat more likely to lie did nothing, in my view, to assist the courts in their primary purpose, which is to arrive at a just result.

Corroboration requirements were also abrogated, giving rise to a similar dichotomy. Judges used to be required to warn juries that, while it was open to them to convict on the uncorroborated evidence of a complainant, it was dangerous to do so, unless some other evidence connected her story to the alleged offence in some material particular. The abolition of this rule was actually welcomed by many defence lawyers, since in practice it often had the effect during the judge's charge of focusing the jury's attention on dozens of insignificant or dubious details in the Crown's case as "corroborating" the complainant's story. (For instance, the grass's being flattened on a piece of ground could be held to "corroborate" a complainant's story that she was raped at that spot — even though the fact in itself was just as consistent with the defendant's claim that he had *consensual* intercourse with the complainant: the grass would be flattened in either case.) Still, while some reforms were needed, the total abrogation of corroboration rules tended to turn sexual-assault trials into a "her word against his" type of contest in which neither the truthful complainant nor the truthful accused could expect any help from the rules of evidence.

But all this was dwarfed by the real problem, which was to severely curtail the defendant's ability to test the complainant's evidence against him through cross-examination. In some respects, complainants ceased to be compellable witnesses altogether. A complainant could no longer be asked many types of questions about her conduct — not even in a closed *voir dire* hearing to help a judge determine whether or not he should allow those questions to be asked in front of a jury.

The reasons for curtailing cross-examination were to save complainants from embarrassment, to protect their privacy, and to encourage them to come forward with complaints. However, whatever their merits, these reasons were not sufficient to deny natural justice to a man presumed to be innocent by preventing him from confronting his accuser, or to stop a judge from even *considering* whether an accused, by not being able to ask these questions in a given case, would be denied natural justice or not.

It was becoming increasingly difficult for anyone accused of sexual assault to exercise a citizen's fundamental right to make full answer and defence to a criminal charge. Some courts finally put their foot down: in 1985 the Supreme Court of the Northwest Territories (*R. v. Oquataq*), the Newfoundland Supreme Court (*R. v. Coombs*), and the Ontario Supreme Court (*Re Gayme and The Queen*); and in 1986 the Court of Queen's Bench in New Brunswick (*R. v. Brun*) held that the new rules limiting cross-examination, specifically those contained in sections 246.6 and 246.7 of the Criminal Code, violated the Canadian Charter of Rights.

Evidently many Canadian judges had not yet resigned themselves to asking participants to submit to a test of fire, as courts did in the Middle Ages, to see who was telling the truth. They wanted to preserve cross-examination — the finest instrument the law has for separating fact from fancy.

Some of the new laws were downright silly. For instance, a kiss could be defined as a sexual assault if the recipient did not consent to it, and a charge of sexual assault could be brought against spouses actually living with each other. In theory, this made it possible for a husband to be found guilty of sexual assault on the following fact situation:

HUSBAND (to his wife after a disagreement): Oh, let's kiss and make up.

WIFE: No.

HUSBAND: Aw, come on. (He kisses her. Enter police. Arrest, trial, conviction.)

The media — usually the keenest watchdog against any unfairness or injustice in society — often seemed to lose all sense of fairness when it came to feminist issues. Journalists would wax indignant over a judge's sentencing a rapist to "only" four years in prison "in spite of the Crown's demand for a sentence of ten years". I could hardly believe my eyes seeing such examples. What did the Crown's "demand" have to do with whether or not the sentence was appropriate? In the same courthouse on the same day, as the reporter ought to have known, judges were sentencing to four years all kinds of non-sexual offenders for whom Crown attorneys were also "demanding" ten-year sentences. It is a normal part of the adversary process for the Crown and the defence to make widely disparate sentence submissions, and for the judge to decide what is right. The press might have just as easily reported that despite a defence lawyer's submission for an eighteen-month sentence in reformatory, the judge gave the accused four years in a penitentiary.

But some feminists wanted to "re-educate" judges — that is, to bully and coerce them to look at everything from their point of view — and latched upon the idea of using the media for the purpose. Perhaps this was made possible by the fact that reporters assigned to cover the courts (with some honourable exceptions) know surprisingly little about the law. Unlike journalists assigned to cover science, politics, or entertainment, court reporters and their editors often do not have even a well-educated layman's understanding of the legal process about which they are expected to inform the public. (This is not just my opinion, incidentally; it was a frequently expressed complaint of Canada's late Chief Justice, Bora Laskin.)

Nothing illustrates this better than two recent examples in which judges were vociferously castigated in the press for remarks made in the course of sexual-assault trials.

In one case a judge, while sentencing a man to a prison term for raping an exotic dancer, made some remark about a stripper being in a business designed "to inspire lust". Immediately a cry arose in the media demanding that the judge be censured.

There would have been excellent reasons for censure, of course, had the judge held that raping exotic dancers is not a crime — but he did nothing of the sort. He *convicted* the man. There might have been reason for censure if the judge had given the rapist an inappropriate sentence — but, having regard to all the circumstances, no one suggested that the sentence was inappropriate. The judge was being raked over the coals solely for making a remark: a remark that was both accurate — a stripper's business *is* closely connected with lust — and not at all irrelevant to the judge's business. If the victim had been a nun or a young girl of previously chaste character the judge would have been expected to regard it as an aggravating factor. No one would have dreamt of censuring a judge for saying to the rapist of some Mother Superior: "Considering your victim, I find your act especially repugnant."

Clearly, the obverse was also true — as long as it was followed, as it was in this case, by an appropriate disposition. (Even if it hadn't been, a public censure would have been unnecessary: a higher court could have adjusted the sentence following an appeal by the Crown. That's what higher courts are for.)

Calling for censure in such a case, in my opinion, was nothing but an attempt to intimidate the judiciary. In so far as it was also made by some lawyers, it may have amounted to contempt of court. In the past, lawyers criticizing judges in this fashion had often been requested to apologize to the judges involved. In the case of feminist objections — as I put it in a speech to the Ontario Psychiatric Association in 1986 — it was some of the judges who ended up apologizing to their critics.

The press was even wider off the mark in another case. That was a case in which an Ontario judge was being crucified in the media for rating a rape — again, after convicting the accused — as "a 2 on a scale of 1 to 10".

Nothing, except politics and ignorance, could explain the editorial furore over that remark. Implicitly at least, the law itself rates rape, along with the overwhelming majority of all other crimes, on a scale of 1 to 10. When a judge has the discretion, as he has in most instances, to fix a penalty for a crime for which the maximum sentence is, say, ten years in prison and the minimum sentence is an absolute discharge, what else *can* he do but rate the given example of that crime on a scale of 1 to 10? He doesn't have to say so — perhaps he shouldn't say so — but he must do it. It is his job.

No one objected when a judge in Nova Scotia called a homicide victim "a man on the outer fringes of humanity". That was a case in which a woman was convicted of manslaughter for shooting her abusive husband in his sleep, and received a sentence of six months' imprisonment for a crime that, at the upper end of the scale, is punishable by imprisonment for life. There was nothing objectionable about the sentence, of course — it was, in the circumstances, perfectly appropriate — but it could have caused the sentencing judge to say that this particular homicide, on a scale of 1 to 10, rated a near zero. He almost said so by describing the victim as he did.

Whether or not it would have been prudent for the Nova Scotia judge to use the metaphor of a sliding scale instead, it would not have been inaccurate. A judge can describe a homicide victim as a man on the outer fringes of humanity, just as he can describe a rape victim as someone in the lust-business, without implying that homicide or rape are frivolous offences.

It is the common experience of mankind that crimes can be committed under varying circumstances and to varying degrees of blameworthiness. Stealing is stealing — but the difference between a hungry man stealing a loaf of bread and a strapping youth stealing money from a blind beggar's cup is self-evident. The same is true of sexual assault. A woman, for instance, has every right to refuse a second act of sexual intercourse even though she freely consented to the first act with the same person five minutes earlier. (After all, she might have had enough, or doing it again might make her miss the last subway.) If her assailant forced her to submit, as a judge I'd convict him — but I might also call his sexual assault a 0.5 on a scale of 1 to 10.

"There occurs at times," wrote A. Bartlett Giametti, former president of Yale University, "a tyranny of group self-righteousness, manifesting itself in a rage to ideological or dogmatic purity." In the last number of years this has characterized some elements of the women's movement. While continually charging others with "insensitivity" to their concerns, these feminists have demonstrated an astounding insensitivity to just about any human concern from justice to common sense. Indeed, they seem unable to conceive of such concepts outside their own terms of reference. Their influence on the law — unlike the initially valid and fair influence of the women's movement — has by now become baneful.

One recent illustration from my own files is the case of a former Windsor, Ontario, policeman named Wayne St. Louis. I still find it difficult to distance myself from the case. Fearing that I might not be sufficiently detached, I asked George Jonas, who had initially researched the story for *Toronto Life* magazine, to tell it from an outsider's point of view.

*Who knows what most people would say if, out of the blue, two policemen came to the door and told them that they were under arrest for rape. Many people might say what Wayne St. Louis said. He said only one word, and it was: "What?" He uttered it in a tone of astonished disbelief.*

*In January 1983, Wayne St. Louis was a first-class constable employed by the Windsor police. He was twenty-nine years old, divorced, with one child from a previous marriage. He had never been charged with, let alone convicted of, any criminal offence. It is unlikely that he could have been a policeman if he had been.*

*No one can blame the police for not wanting criminals in their ranks. The police represent the law. It is their duty to enforce it upon others, and it's natural that they wish police officers to be untainted of even a suspicion of being lawbreakers themselves. But, as we shall see later, natural as this desire may be, it can give rise to a special kind of unfairness.*

*After uttering the word "What?" St. Louis got dressed and accompanied fellow officers Constable William Delaney and Staff Sergeant Ian Chippett to police headquarters. There, a routine ensued with which St. Louis was not unfamiliar. The routine is standard police practice, especially when there's little or no evidence against a suspect. It often* works. An inspector took St. Louis to an interview room, and told him, "We know you did this, we're ashamed of you. . . . Think about it, admit it." There was a hint that if he did confess, he might be allowed to resign quietly, though the final decision about this would be "up to the Chief".

Constable St. Louis didn't take the bait. As he was to put it later, "I knew enough not to make a statement." He had a minor and a major reason. The minor reason was that hints or half-promises of leniency in exchange for a confession are usually worthless. The major reason was that he knew he hadn't raped anybody.

The girl whom we will call Sarah went to the police in November 1982, about two months before Wayne St. Louis was arrested. She was fifteen years old at the time. The story she told the police was this:

After the divorce of her parents she lived with her mother, but in 1980, when she was thirteen, she moved to the home of her father — we'll call him Paul — a small-businessman in Windsor, Ontario. At that time her father was living with his common-law wife, a lady named Gisele. Nine-year-old Joyce (not her real name), Gisele's daughter from a previous marriage, was also living with them.

Sarah liked Joyce, and the two girls became friends. However, about six months after Sarah moved into her father's house, Gisele and Paul broke up. By the fall of 1980, Gisele and her daughter, Joyce, had moved to a place of their own in another part of town.

Sarah seemed to attribute the break-up of her father and Gisele to a friendship that had developed between Gisele and a neighbour — the neighbour being Wayne St. Louis. During the summer of 1980, according to Sarah, while she and Gisele roller-skated on their quiet street of townhouses, she noticed that neighbour St. Louis "was getting very friendly with Gisele." She also told the police that on one occasion during that summer, while she was roller-skating alone, St. Louis made what she interpreted as a physical pass at her. "He grabbed my hips from behind and pulled me back towards him . . . gave me a hug and said good-bye and shoved me away."

Then, Sarah's story went, in the early part of 1981 Gisele and Wayne St. Louis moved in together into a townhouse at Polonia Park. Since Joyce was "like a sister" to her, she'd continue to visit occasionally. "A lot of times when I visited there," Sarah said to the police, "Wayne would compliment me on my legs, my bum, and my face, and he would *say I was a really pretty girl." She also described to the police one occasion when St. Louis "pulled me down on his lap and gave me a bear hug and said I was really cute and cuddly."*

*Once during that summer — Sarah continued in her November 1982 statement — she went bicycling with St. Louis to the Pumping Station Park on Riverside Drive. "I wanted to talk with Wayne about why Gisele left my father." On that occasion, as they were sitting in the grass talking, St. Louis touched her breasts and private parts, and when Sarah yelled, "Wayne!" he stopped and apologized.*

*The rape, Sarah alleged, happened a short time later, on September 1, 1981. It happened in the townhouse at Polonia Park. Once again she went there to visit Joyce, but as the girl and Gisele were out, she accepted Wayne's invitation to sit in the living-room and wait for them. This was when the rape occurred.*

*Sarah gave a detailed description of the rape in her statement, including a physical description of the Polonia Park townhouse, the curtains, the furniture. She fixed the date by remembering that "it was just before school started."*

*As to why she had waited for more than a year to report the rape, Sarah's answer was that, during the assault, St. Louis had said, "I took Gisele away from you and I could easily take your father." At that time she saw a hand-gun visible on the bedroom dresser. She had been afraid.*

*The reason she decided to go to the police in the end was as follows. While she did continue visiting Joyce, "Wayne never bothered me for about a year after this." However, in the couple of months preceding her complaint to the police, Sarah claimed that St. Louis started bothering her again. Not by making passes at her when she was visiting Joyce and Gisele in his home, but by hang-up calls (including one in which he identified himself as "Wayne") and by following her as she was walking or bicycling. In one specific incident, which Sarah could date as October 14 at 7:45 p.m. by a TV program she was going to watch at her boyfriend's house, St. Louis followed her in a police car.*

*Finally, on November 9, around 11:50 p.m., as Sarah was baby-sitting at an acquaintance's home, Wayne St. Louis rapped at the window, smiled and waved at Sarah, then disappeared in the dark. The following day Sarah went to the police.*

*There it was, Sarah's story, for the police to make what they would of it. Like any complaint, it might have been true. Only God can see into human hearts and minds; the Windsor city police can't. All they can do is check and investigate, then lay a charge if they feel that the evidence they assembled might be sufficient to prove an accused person guilty beyond a reasonable doubt.*

For more than two months following Sarah's complaint the police laid no charges. It is not difficult to guess at the reason. Though opinions vary on what constitutes sufficient evidence for the laying of a criminal charge — in Canada, as in other countries, charges are sometimes laid on the basis of evidence the courts are later moved to describe as frivolous — it must have been obvious to the police that Sarah's story, standing by itself, was hardly enough to bring St. Louis to trial, let alone convict him. All other considerations apart, the police don't like to waste the courts' time, or their own, by starting a prosecution that cannot succeed.

Sarah's story must have appeared at best marginally sufficient — taking a charitable view — to prove someone guilty, even if the accused stood mute and presented absolutely no evidence in his defence. The onus is on the Crown to prove its case beyond a reasonable doubt, and this onus is hardly discharged by a totally uncorroborated complaint made fourteen months after the alleged incident. Especially when, on the complainant's own story, she continued her occasional visits to the townhouse where the alleged sexual assault occurred for another year; and when a degree of personal enmity may be inferred by the complainant's resentment of the accused, whom she views in her statement as the probable cause of the disruption of her father's common-law marriage: "I also noticed he was getting very friendly with Gisele."

All this must have been obvious to the police at the outset. Getting some corroboration for Sarah's story — not an easy task after a lapse of fourteen months — must have appeared vital to proceed on the complaint. Whatever method of investigation the Windsor police might have employed in a pre-electronic age for finding facts that might have proved or disproved Sarah's tale, this was the year 1982. As in most forces, the thoughts of the Windsor police naturally turned to recording conversations on tape.

The law makes duly authorized wiretaps available to the police in Canada under a variety of circumstances. They may well be a useful aid in many types of investigations. The trouble is, police forces have increasingly been using wiretaps, body-packs, and other electronic/aural/optical devices of surveillance as a panacea — worse, as a substitute for other investigative methods. This creates more than problems of potential injury to privacy and civil liberties. Helpful as wiretaps may be as a support for traditional detective work, they are a very poor substitute for it. As old-time detectives know, a single phone call made by an investigator may be worth a month of listening to phone calls made by others.

Since Sarah talked about threatening and hang-up calls in her statement, the police put recorders on her father's phone as well as on the phone of the lady for whom Sarah was baby-sitting and in whose home she also claimed to have received threatening calls from St. Louis. The police instructed Sarah's father and the lady in the use of the recording-devices. Then they waited for two months. No hang-up or threatening call was ever recorded.

It was at this point that the police decided to confront St. Louis with the charges, receiving only the answer "What?" Clearly, as corroboration was forthcoming neither from the tape recordings nor from the accused's own lips, the investigation was back where it had been two months earlier. The police had nothing but Sarah's unsubstantiated complaint made more than a year after the fact. Having alerted St. Louis, further surreptitious inquiries would be difficult. They could drop the matter or proceed.

The police chose to proceed. After the confrontation, the inspector told Constable St. Louis to go to work at a desk job and surrender his service revolver. Two days later, a formal charge of rape was brought against him, and he was suspended with pay.

Finding the truth is never an easy task. It's possible that if instead of — or in addition to — tape recordings the Windsor police had engaged in more old-fashioned legwork, they might have discovered a few important facts. They might have found out, for instance, that certain parts of Sarah's story couldn't possibly be true. Whatever Sarah (or her father) may have believed, Gisele did not leave her common-law marriage in 1980 because of Wayne St. Louis. When she moved out with her daughter, St. Louis didn't even know where they had moved to. For another year he was still living at home with his own wife. He did not start seeing Gisele until the spring of 1981, after a chance encounter.

Sarah couldn't possibly have paid occasional visits to Joyce at Gisele and Wayne's place at Polonia Park in the summer of 1981. At that time they did not live together, nor did Gisele and Joyce live at Polonia Park.

*They lived at an entirely different address, and though by the late summer Wayne St. Louis would be a frequent visitor there, he did not share that home with Gisele and Joyce as Sarah seemed to believe.*

*Sarah said she visited Polonia Park during the summer of 1981, and claimed that she was raped there by St. Louis on September 1, just before school started. She described the bedroom, the curtains, the furniture accurately enough. There was only one problem with the particulars of her statement.*

*Wayne St. Louis didn't move out of his own house until October 1981. He did not lease, or have access to, the place at Polonia Park until the last days of October. And he did not move there with Gisele, Joyce, and the furniture until November 7. He couldn't have raped anybody there under any circumstances until the end of October. Under the circumstances described by Sarah, having regard to the furniture and the rest, he couldn't have committed rape there until after the first week of November.*

*Much of this the police could have discovered simply by consulting their own records: St. Louis had been dutifully reporting his changes of address and phone number at the appropriate dates. For another thing, also by consulting their own records, the police would have discovered that on October 14, 1982, at 7:45 p.m., Wayne St. Louis did not have access to a police car. He could not have followed Sarah in one, as she alleged, unless he had stolen it, and no police cars were reported stolen that day.*

It has been argued that when the police believe that someone may have committed a crime, it is their duty to lay a charge, even if the evidence against the accused is marginal. At the same time efficiency and common sense suggest that the police should exercise the discretion available to them and not waste the courts' time and the taxpayers' money with cases in which a conviction is all but impossible. Expediency and cost-effectiveness are not the only reasons. Some police officers honestly believe that harassing an accused for no reason or exposing him to the chance, however remote, of a perverse conviction is simply unfair.

The exceptions to this rule are high-profile crimes (such as, say, murder) or high-profile suspects (for instance, members of "organized crime" or very wealthy or famous persons). In such cases the police have been known to lay charges on very little evidence. Other exceptions include crimes that attract a lot of social pressure to prosecute no matter what, such as rape has become in recent years. Or any crime in which the suspect is a policeman.

There is a common belief that "the police protect their own." It is not entirely baseless. When an accusation or a complaint against a police officer arises out of police matters, when it has to do with over-zealousness — with running a red light, so to speak, in the course of an investigation — the police have in some cases protected their own. At times even against such serious charges as assault, perjury, or homi-cide. However, when the complaint has nothing to do with police work, when it arises out of an officer's private conduct, far from "protecting their own", the authorities in Canada generally come down on them like the proverbial ton of bricks. They may prosecute them mercilessly, even on very dubious evidence. The presumption of innocence, to which every citizen is entitled, may go flying out the window.

As for rape, it has always been regarded as a very serious crime. Historically, except for murder, it was the only other crime for which the death penalty remained available in some jurisdictions. However, pre-cisely because it was taken seriously, the courts were especially careful to have it proved beyond a reasonable doubt against an accused. Judges recognized that, while it exposed the accused to grave penal conse-quences and much social opprobrium, rape was a charge very easily brought against a person. Unlike other legal systems, English law never subscribed to the maxim of testis unus testis nullus, which prohibits conviction on the evidence of a single witness.

For this reason, much latitude used to be given to the defendants' lawyers in the cross-examination of complainants. Sometimes — depending on the trial judge, who could always limit such questioning to relevant issues — this gave rise to an atmosphere in which rape trials were harder on the complainant than on the accused. It was said, with some justification, that the courts "put the victim on trial." At times complaints of sexual assault were heard in court in a climate of intrinsic disbelief.

It might have been possible to remedy all this intelligently, but — in the opinion of many lawyers — it wasn't. In recent years it was remedied by simply reversing the unfairness. From intrinsic disbelief (which was unfair, of course), the climate changed to one that seemed to echo the rhetorical question "Why would a woman lie about being raped?"

But this is a silly question. As silly as asking, "Why would a man

rape?" Generally, of course, men don't rape and women don't lie —
about being raped or anything else. Most people tend to observe the
biblical injunction against bearing false witness against fellow human
beings most of the time. However, some people do lie sometimes, and it
is the task of the criminal-justice system to separate, beyond a reasonable doubt, the minority who do from the majority who don't. This
cannot be accomplished by presumptions either way, only by a meticulous, case-by-case examination of the facts. In the words of the English
jurist Sir James Stephen, "the power of lying is unlimited, the causes of
lying and delusion are numerous. . . ." It is not the courts' business to
say why a woman would lie about being raped, only to make sure no
innocent person is convicted in the rare instance when she does.

Self-evident as all this may be, it can be put aside by the politics of
the day. The day Wayne St. Louis walked into the Windsor courtroom
was in October 1983. On that day he had two strikes against him. One,
he was a policeman charged with a crime arising out of his private
conduct. Two, the charge he was facing happened to be rape.

It is possible that Wayne St. Louis's first lawyer, Michael Stoyka, took
the somewhat unusual step of waiving a preliminary hearing and going
directly to trial because he felt that the minute he revealed, through St.
Louis's testimony and documentary evidence, that St. Louis didn't even
move to the townhouse where the offence was supposed to have taken
place until two months after the date alleged by Sarah, the case would
be immediately thrown out of court.

It didn't happen that way.

The trial began before Mr. Justice John O'Driscoll, sitting without a
jury. (Electing to go to trial before a judge sitting alone is not unusual,
and lawyers often choose it when they feel that they have a strong legal
defence, while the purely emotional component of the case — such as the
testimony of an innocent-sounding teenage girl — might favour the
prosecution.) Sarah gave evidence, confirming that the rape occurred on
or about September 1, 1981, at Polonia Park, and even committing
herself to such details as having gone there wearing only jeans and a T-
shirt: appropriate dress for a late-summer day.

Sarah also confirmed other details in her initial statement, such as
St. Louis following her in a police car on the evening of October 14,
1982, and added new ones, such as St. Louis wearing civilian garb
when he appeared at the window of the house where Sarah was baby-

*sitting on November 9, 1982. It was this last incident that was supposed to have impelled Sarah to go to the police fourteen months after the rape.*

Having no other evidence, the prosecution rested its case. Sarah stayed in the courtroom listening to the evidence by the defence. She had already heard Staff Sergeant Andrew Warner — called initially by the Crown — reveal in cross-examination that on the evening of October 14, 1982, St. Louis could not have had access to a police car in which to follow her. (Amazingly, the police had no idea about this until, at the request of defence lawyer Stoyka, Staff Sergeant Warner checked the records.) Now Sarah also heard that Wayne St. Louis, Gisele, and Joyce did not move to Polonia Park until late October/early November. She could not have visited them there in the summer of 1981. She could not have been raped there on or about September 1.

The court recessed for lunch. After lunch, Sarah told Crown Attorney Brian McIntyre that she had made an error about the date of the offence. The Crown moved to reopen the prosecution's case. Mr. Justice O'Driscoll granted the motion — over the defence's strenuous objection, of course.

Sarah took the stand again. Now she testified that she could no longer remember the exact date of the rape, but that it must have been somewhere between the middle of October and the end of November in 1981. It must have been an unusually warm day because she did remember wearing her jeans and T-shirt and nothing else. It must have been a school holiday for both Joyce and herself, otherwise she wouldn't have gone to visit at Polonia Park around noon. Her earlier visits, which she had said took place at Polonia Park and during which she had said she was complimented and hugged by St. Louis, must have occurred at Gisele and Joyce's previous residence.

As for St. Louis's following her in a police car a year later, Sarah now said: "It has been my past experience that when something happens to me I tend to dream about it, and the only thing I can say is that I think that I dreamt about this . . . and in the dream it was a police car, and that is what I see, like, in the back of my head."

The judge permitted the prosecution to amend the indictment. Suddenly, in the middle of his trial, St. Louis had to answer the new charge that he had raped Sarah some time between October 15 and November 30, 1981. He denied the new charge as he had denied the old one, along with the rest of Sarah's allegations of hugging and fondling, but Mr.

*Justice O'Driscoll preferred Sarah's story. He convicted Wayne St. Louis and sentenced him to nine years in prison.*

*It was at this point that Greenspan entered the case. As the lawyer for St. Louis's appeal, Eddie advanced several grounds why the Ontario Court of Appeal should set aside the conviction and acquit Wayne St. Louis or, alternatively, order a new trial for him.*

When a jury returns an unreasonable verdict, lawyers often call it "perverse". When a judge, sitting alone, renders a perverse verdict, lawyers usually call it "unreasonable". In his first ground of appeal, Greenspan contended that Mr. Justice O'Driscoll's verdict was unreasonable. "The totally uncorroborated evidence of the complainant, given in the context of the circumstances which occurred during the trial, was incapable of being believed beyond a reasonable doubt," Greenspan said.

This was being very polite to the trial judge. Quite apart from calling Sarah, a girl who offered her dream as evidence and changed her story in vital particulars, a "credible witness" who "tells it like it is" (sic) Mr. Justice O'Driscoll's reasoning was demonstrated by the following:

St. Louis had testified to an incident where Sarah showed up on his doorstep in the late fall of 1982 — that is, not only more than a year after the alleged rape but about a month after she had finally complained about it to the police. Crying, she asked him to give her a ride to the Family Planning Clinic because she was worried that she might be pregnant by her boyfriend, and her father didn't leave her any money for the bus. St. Louis testified that, though he was rather angry with the girl for getting into this kind of trouble, he did give her a lift to the clinic. (At that point he didn't know, of course, about the allegations Sarah had made against him to the police.)

Sarah flatly denied that she ever asked St. Louis for a ride on this or any other occasion.

St. Louis gave no other details about the drive to the clinic in direct examination. Only when, on cross-examination, Crown Attorney McIntyre asked him how, if Sarah was broke, she was going to get back home from the clinic did St. Louis explain that on the way he stopped at Sarah's bank so that she could get some money from her account. He identified the bank.

The police checked — and found that on December 3 Sarah visited the Family Clinic and on the same day she took out $100 from her bank.

*This, of course, supported St. Louis's evidence; and it was elicited by the Crown itself on cross-examination. St. Louis didn't even bring it up until asked by McIntyre.*

*Mr. Justice O'Driscoll dealt with it in his judgment by saying that it was "cute". He said: "[St. Louis] is a cunning prevaricator who set a 'plant' and knew full well that it would be followed up. . . . I find that the accused staged the whole scenario."*

*At least to this reporter, this was not a reasonable inference that could be drawn from the evidence. How could it be postulated that St. Louis "staged" something that he did not even mention in court until the Crown asked him in cross-examination? If anything, the evidence supported the opposite inference: namely, that St. Louis was telling the truth about this episode and Sarah was lying.*

*Greenspan further submitted to the Court of Appeal that the trial judge should not have allowed the Crown to reopen its case under the circumstances in the middle of the trial, and that he erred in letting in certain evidence against St. Louis, which had nothing to do with the case and should not have been admitted. In a brief judgment the Court of Appeal agreed with some of Greenspan's grounds, and ordered a new trial for Wayne St. Louis.*

*By the time the new trial started in 1985, St. Louis had spent more than a year in custody. He could not get bail pending the outcome of his appeal, though he did get bail once a new trial was ordered. Still, since the Windsor police were going to suspend him without pay right after his conviction, he had no choice but to resign. Getting back some of his pension contributions was the only way he could foot his legal bills.*

*Being incarcerated for a sexual offence is very dangerous. Convicts do not have a higher opinion of sexual offenders than the rest of society, and tend to express their disapproval in far more tangible ways. Being incarcerated for any offence is very dangerous for an ex-policeman. For an ex-policeman to be jailed for sexual assault on a minor — which Sarah was at the time of the alleged rape — can be the equivalent of a death sentence. Lloyds of London might have charged a fair premium against the odds of Wayne St. Louis's emerging from his nine-year sentence in penitentiary alive.*

*Perhaps the only bright moment in St. Louis's existence at that time was when Gisele married him after his conviction.*

*Having won the appeal, Greenspan defended St. Louis at his new trial before a Toronto jury. (A change of venue was important, of course, because of the media coverage of St. Louis's first trial.) By cross-referencing his client's shifts with school holidays for both Sarah and Joyce, Greenspan found that the only two days on which the alleged rape could possibly have been committed according to Sarah's new story were November 4 or November 11. On the first of these dates the furniture would not have been arranged as Sarah described it. On either of the dates the temperature would not have permitted anyone to wear only a T-shirt and jeans.*

*As for St. Louis's appearing in civilian clothes at the window of the house where Sarah was baby-sitting on November 9, 1982, Greenspan called evidence to show that St. Louis was on duty and in uniform that night. He did briefly leave the station to get coffee around the relevant time, but if he had somehow used the opportunity to go and smirk at Sarah, he would have had to do so dressed as a policeman. He could not possibly have had time to change.*

*The rest of the evidence was a frail as it had originally been. It took the jury next to no time to acquit.*

If Sarah concocted her story of rape, why did she do it? After the original trial, before sentencing, Gisele told the judge that Paul, Sarah's father, had at one time threatened to use his daughter to frame St. Louis on a sexual-assault charge if Gisele did not return to him. Who knows if he really did? Even if he had said so, it could have been an empty threat. If Sarah had gone through her ordeal — it must have been an ordeal — just for her father, she was clearly as much a victim as Wayne.

All this is less important than the fact that the Court of Appeal — while agreeing that "the preferable course for the trial judge would have been to declare a mistrial" after Sarah had changed her story, and that the judge should not have admitted certain "highly prejudicial" evidence — rejected Greenspan's first ground that the verdict was unreasonable. "We consider that there was evidence to support the verdict, and it cannot be said to be unreasonable," wrote the Chief Justice.

This indicates that, in law, it is possible to be convicted of sexual assault on an uncorroborated complaint, first made more than a year after the fact, shown to be inconsistent in vital details, altered in mid-trial to suit facts learned during the defendant's testimony, and presented by a girl who, in her own words, tends "to dream about" essential parts of her evidence. It is possible to find a man of unblemished reputation guilty beyond a reasonable doubt on this kind of evidence alone. It is not unreasonable.

*What, then, is unreasonable? Is it surprising that rape has been traditionally regarded as a charge very easy to bring and very hard to deny? Has it been wrong for the law in the past to surround defendants with certain safeguards? Or has it been a mistake for the law to remove them?*

I must add one thing to Wayne St. Louis's story that never became part of the trial record. While investigating the case, my office came upon a Windsor-area man who gave us the following statement:

I, [name, age], do hereby state: I reside in the village of Riverside and have done so for the past five years. Directly behind my house Wayne St. Louis once lived on Gateside. At my house I have a pool and a lot of the neighbourhood 12-16 year olds would come over and ask to go swimming in the summer of 1982. [Sarah] was a part of this group.

One night in September a number of girls came by very late and I refused to let them swim. They got very upset. The next day a plainclothes police officer came by and told me I had been charged with molestation, showing dirty movies to the girls on my VCR and raping two of them in and around the pool between August 15th and 25th. This was all completely false. I don't even have a VCR. I retained a lawyer, but a couple of days later the officer returned and told me the case was being dropped because the girls' story had changed too much. These charges were laid and then dropped at the same time as the trial of Wayne St. Louis began. I believe the reason the girls did this to me was to get back at me for forbidding them to use the pool. I have read the above statement over, find it true, and sign it by my hand this 18th day of January, 1984.

The police records confirmed the witness's statement (which I'm giving here in a condensed version). I didn't call him to testify at St. Louis's new trial — I didn't think it was necessary, and it would have required establishing a complex evidentiary link between Sarah and the girls in her neighbourhood who falsely accused this man of rape. My instinct was to keep St. Louis's trial as simple as possible; but I'm mentioning this witness here for the following reason:

If, as a matter of social policy, we go on "sensitizing" girls and women to the "coercive sexuality" of men; if we keep giving seminars and showing propaganda films on the subject in schools; if we keep suggesting to young people that they ought to be alert to "sexual harassment" and "bad touching" and invite them to view any gesture in the light of this possibility; if we positively urge people — as we are beginning to do — to have no tolerance of any "uninvited" sexual expression, not even "ogling" or "lewd remarks", and to resolve any doubt they may have in this regard by reporting the matter to the authorities — if we do this, we will inevitably end up with accusations like the ones levelled against the Windsor swimming-pool owner or Wayne St. Louis.

If, in addition, we keep diluting our evidentiary rules; if we threaten our police, Crown attorneys, and judges with censure for applying the *same* common sense, or the *same* discretion, in cases of alleged sexual assault as they do in all other criminal investigations and trials, we will inevitably end up with innocent people convicted and ruined.

This is not just a possibility or a likelihood: it is a statistical certainty. In any population group there will be a few spiteful or evil-minded liars. There will be a few wicked or impressionable children, and a few malicious or fanatical adults to manipulate them. Their numbers will undoubtedly be small, but one in a thousand is enough. In the old days of witchcraft trials it was impressionable, wicked, or manipulated children who most often testified about seeing accused witches flying around on broomsticks. If, as an experiment, all schools started showing films requesting children to be on the alert for their parents or neighbours turning into little green men from Mars, it is a statistical certainty that some reports of such sightings would be received by the police.

My sympathy for rapists and molesters is nil — either as a citizen or, for that matter, as a father of two young girls. Though I'm a firm opponent of the death penalty, if it were to be imposed for any crime, I'd sooner see it imposed on the sex-killers of women and children than on murderers of any other kind, including the murderers of jail guards or policemen. Police officers and jail guards take voluntary risks; women and children can't help being what they are, and must have society's full protection. This is not remotely in dispute. But there is a world of difference between protecting women and children, and inviting malicious, confused, or ideologically motivated individuals to use sex as a weapon against others.

As a criminal lawyer I have seen nothing to persuade me that we cannot achieve the first aim without "taking a chance" on the second. True, any system of justice entails the *incidental* risk of injustice, but justice is never achieved by wilfully creating a climate in which it becomes easier to prosecute or convict the innocent.

One final point. At times lawyers are accused of having an economic interest in the social measures that they advocate. Frankly, as a criminal defence counsel, my economic interest is in seeing the greatest possible number of middle-class people being hauled into court on criminal charges of all kinds. If, for instance, in child-custody battles every second wife were to charge her ex-husband with having molested the children — an increasing number are doing it already — I could soon keep a yacht in the Mediterranean. (I don't know what I would do with it since I hate boats, but I could keep it there — at a safe distance from me.)

No: I suggest the *economic* interests go precisely the other way. I suggest that we should take a second look at our feminist-inspired social policies before some people's vested interest in their perpetuation becomes overwhelming. As it is, an entire industry has sprung up around the educational, legislative, administrative, and enforcement aspects of feminist ideology. Pretty soon pulling back would entail having to add hundreds of bureaucrats, consultants, academics, educational-film makers, social workers, newspaper columnists, and other experts — along with their secretaries, researchers, and assorted support personnel — to the welfare rolls.

That is without mentioning the new censors, the behaviour-modification therapists, the anti-violence-and-pornography crowd that has become a contemporary meeting-ground between feminism and the Moral Majority. My 1986 speech to the Ontario Psychiatric Association centred mainly on them. I said at that time:

> These social scientists are the people who believe that behaviour is motivated only by external stimuli, dismissing individual judgement, values and morality. . . . But because their experimental work supports the assumptions that are congenial to the feminist viewpoint, they are being relied on by *all* the people who want to burn, ban or pulp books, film and art, and want to remake society in their own image.

These censors, who form the great bridge in our days between Right and Left, between arch-conservatives and "progressives", who forge ahead like the Light Brigade, deserve a chapter in themselves. A chapter like that would involve a discussion of art, literature, psychology, and philosophy. Since I don't want to step outside my own area, the criminal law, it will have to be written by someone else.

## NOTES

p.221, 1.6: The awards *The Scales of Justice* did win, in addition to "The Scales of Justice Award", were ACTRA's "Nelly" for the Best Radio Program in Canada (twice); a "Nelly" for Best Writer (it went to playwright John Douglas for one episode of the show); a "Gabriel" for the Best Radio Entertainment Program in North America; and the Gold Medal at the New York International Radio Festival.

p.222 1.33: It is important to reiterate that we are talking about *contested* cases. Many criminal charges, whether of sexual assault or anything else, are not contested. The accused pleads guilty, and none of these questions arise.

Also, in those (very rare) sexual-assault cases where the issue is honest belief, neither the accused nor the complainant need to be liars. A complainant may have honestly believed that she had withheld her consent, while the accused may have honestly believed that she had given it. It is uncommon, but possible, for people to profoundly misread each other's sexual signals. One complicating factor has been the criminal law's entry into areas for which it has been regarded as too blunt an instrument in the past. For instance, until recently, a charge of "rape" or "aggravated sexual assault" would not have been supported by a fact situation in which a non-consensual act of intercourse was preceded by a consensual act of intercourse within a reasonable time frame. If the complainant had been threatened or beaten in such a case, it would have been treated as an ordinary assault. For a victim to say: "We had lovely sex at 5, but at 5:20 he raped me," would have been regarded as lacking in common sense.

p.224, 1.16: *R. v. Kistendey* (1975), 29 C.C.C. (2d) 382 (Ont. C.A.).

p.226, 1.29: It is true that any offence may catch the media's imagination. When it does, it becomes fashionable for journalists to write almost daily about the insufficiently (or overly) harsh manner in which the justice system deals with such offences. In this sense feminist issues are not unique; drugs, the environment, drunk driving, etc., have all come in for their share of trendy treatment in the press. Sometimes the tide rises in favour of the "offenders", sometimes it rises in favour of the "victims". (Nor are the media invariably wrong, of course. Trends, like all other things, must be examined on their merits.)

p.226, l.40: See also *Trials and Tribulations*, an examination of news coverage given three prominent Canadian trials, a monograph by Peter Calamai and Nicholas Russel (The School of Journalism and Communications, University of Regina, Saskatchewan).

p.236, l.12: In the latest edition of *Wigmore, Evidence* (Chadbourn Revision), the leading American text, the learned author has this to say, in part:

> Modern psychiatrists have amply studied the behaviour of errant young girls and women coming before the courts in all sorts of cases. Their psychic complexes are multifarious, distorted partly by inherent defects, partly by diseased derangements or abnormal instincts, partly by bad social environment, partly by temporary physiological or emotional conditions. One form taken by these complexes is that of contriving false charges of sexual offenses by men. . . . On the surface the narration is straightforward and convincing. The real victim, however, too often in such cases is the innocent man; for the respect and sympathy naturally felt by any tribunal for a wronged female helps to give easy credit to such a plausible tale.
>
> [But] the lamentable thing is that the orthodox rules of evidence in most instances prevent adequate probing of the testimonial mentality of a woman witness, so as to reveal the possible falsity of such charges. Judging merely from the reports of cases in the appellate courts, one must infer that many innocent men have gone to prison because of tales whose falsity could not be exposed. . . . [I]n some states the so-called age of consent has been raised to 16 or 18 years . . . and in a few states even life imprisonment may be imposed; so that a plausible tale by an attractive, innocent-looking girl may lead to a life sentence for the accused, because the rules of evidence (and the judge's unacquaintance with modern psychiatry) permit no adequate probing of the witness veracity.
>
> The facts are that there exist occasionally female types of excessive or perverted sexuality, just as there are such male types; and that these are often accompanied by a testimonial plausibility which

should not be taken at its face value. [*Wigmore, Evidence:* Testimonial Impeachment, §924a., pp. 736-7. Little, Brown and Co. (Inc.). Reprinted by permission.]

These are current views held by the text. The late Dean Wigmore's opinion was that no judge should let a sex-offence charge go to the jury without a psychiatric examination of the complainant. Wigmore, one of the greatest legal scholars on evidence, felt that the courts' proper concern was not so much why, or how frequently, women lie about being raped (important as those questions may be for a psychologist or a sociologist), but that no innocent man should be sent to prison.

p.236, l.14: The following may be a typical example of how some progressive intellectuals view this question. At a private gathering, Greenspan outlined examples of "reverse unfairness" to former Ontario NDP leader Stephen Lewis (Canada's current ambassador to the United Nations) and his wife, the journalist Michele Landsberg. Greenspan assumed that, while Lewis and Landsberg might not have addressed their minds to this problem, once it was called to their attention they would find it, like any other type of unfairness, a matter of concern. To Greenspan's amazement, both Lewis and his wife expressed the opinion that while the current practices of the legal system may be unfair, this may be the only way to balance the unfairness of the past.

To hold this logically, one would have to be prepared to hold that the acquittal of a guilty person yesterday is redressed by the conviction of an innocent person today. The argument shows that, whatever sense affirmative action may make in other areas of social policy, it is incapable of making any sense in criminal law.

*Like other men of action, Greenspan is generally too impatient to write. At times he is too impatient even to speak into a Dictaphone. In his line of work this could be a problem because, both as a practising lawyer and as a legal scholar, he must deal with masses of written material.*

*To mention only a few examples, there are lengthy documents that must be prepared for the appellate courts, setting out both the facts and the legal arguments for a given case. There are jury addresses, some of which take days to deliver and may be as thick as a book. There are head-notes and commentaries for* Martin's Annual Criminal Code, *which Greenspan edits, as well as for the weekly* Canadian Criminal Cases *and* Dominion Law Reports, *for which he acts as editor and associate editor respectively. In addition, there are his innumerable public speeches, university lectures, and radio and television debates, all requiring written preparation, because Greenspan is not an off-the-cuff speaker by preference. There are his articles and forewords, in anthologies, in learned journals, and in the popular press. There is narration and commentary to be written for Greenspan's award-winning dramatized re-creation of noted criminal cases,* The Scales of Justice, *fifty-six episodes of which have been aired since 1982.*

*This is a lot of scribbling for someone who hates to write; it would be quite a bit even for someone who likes it. Greenspan has solved the problem (somewhat in the manner of Alexandre Dumas the Elder, the great French author of* The Three Musketeers*) by selecting some of his close associates for their writing skills as much as for their other qualities. In his office, both Marc Rosenberg and Chris Buhr, in addition to being first-rate lawyers in their own right, are skilled writers of legal material. George Jonas and Guy Kay act as producer and associate producer for* The Scales of Justice. *Like a latter-day Dumas* père, *Greenspan wanders about his little writing-factory, dispensing notions, ideas, and direction.*

*Many people who claim to be too "impatient" or too "busy" to write could not, in fact, write a decent line to save their lives. There are, however, exceptions. Alexandre Dumas was certainly one, and so in his own way is Greenspan. When, however rarely, he actually decides to shut his door and put pen to paper, the results can be impressive. What Greenspan excels in is the epistolary arts.*

*Some of his letters have been published in the press, but his epistolic best, having been written for private purposes, have had only a private circulation. Some people's favourite is a letter of recommendation he wrote for the Toronto lawyer Phil Epstein.*

*Epstein, a noted barrister specializing in family law, is one of Greenspan's oldest friends. The offices of their two law firms share the top floor of Toronto's Simpsons Tower. In 1983 Epstein was up for election to the coveted legal honour of Bencher of the Law Society of Upper Canada.*

*Election to the Benchers is a complex procedure, and Greenspan, who has a tendency to view such honours wryly, could never quite figure out what the requirements are and what a recommendation should contain. In the end he wrote the following letter:*

Phil Epstein turned forty years old this year. The first sign of his mid-life crisis is his desire to be a Bencher. I can see no other way for him to get through this crisis, other than to have us actually elect him.

If Phil loses this election, you won't have to deal with his disappointment, but I will. That is why I am making this plea on his behalf. The plea is not so much for him but for me!

I could lie to you and say that he has all the qualities necessary to be a great Bencher, but the fact of the matter is, I have no idea what qualities are necessary to be a great Bencher.

I could tell you the absolute truth about him, but then you might not vote for him. Instead, I would like to give you a number of reasons to vote for him.

1. PROTECTION OF THE PUBLIC. As a Bencher, Phil will be kept away from his practice and will have to turn away cases, thereby protecting the public.

2. MOTHER. His election would make his mother, Esther, very very happy. If he is not elected, Esther will be very unhappy and I cannot think of a good reason why you would want to make her unhappy. (This may be the best reason I can think of to vote for Phil!)

3. *ISSUES. I have canvassed the issues and I am satisfied that they are too complex for Phil to ever understand, which will make him one of the least dangerous Benchers.*

4. *LEGAL AID. I particularly like Phil's view of Legal Aid. It is a radical view, but one with which I agree. Phil feels that Legal Aid should be given to people who cannot afford to privately retain their own lawyer.*

*A vote for Phil may not make you feel better but it will make me feel better. It will make Esther deliriously happy and curiously enough, it will do wonders for Convocation.*

*P.S. Phil's contribution to the profession is widely known. He is truly worthy of your support.*

Other people maintain that the year 1985 produced an even better Greenspan letter. This note was addressed to Milton A. Davis, of the firm of Bresver Grossman Scheininger and Davis. The occasion that gave rise to it was as follows: One of Eddie's law students, instead of picking up Greenspan's ailing Cadillac from the underground parking garage as instructed and delivering it to Addison Cadillac on Bay Street to be repaired, picked up instead a Cadillac belonging to the lawyer Stanley Z. Grossman of the aforementioned firm. Though Grossman's Cadillac needed no repairs, Addison fixed it just the same.

As it happened, the incident occurred in April, shortly after a threat had been received from a group purporting to be Armenian terrorists, saying that they would bomb the Toronto subway system. As a result, a number of people were afraid to take the subway for a few days. (This "threat" was only a hoax, and even as a hoax it might not have come from Armenian sources. There was some evidence that it may have been perpetrated by Turkish intelligence to arouse popular feelings against the Armenian community in Canada.) Grossman also happened to be in the process of selling his Cadillac, and had a prospective buyer lined up to look at it the very afternoon on which Eddie's student picked it up from the garage by mistake.

Davis wrote to Eddie saying, inter alia, that "As a result of this unfortunate confusion, Mr. Grossman has sustained severe and irreparable harm including pre- and post-traumatic neuroses, clinical depression, blockage of the synapses, hives, nose bleeding, hiccups, delirium tremens and other related diseases. He has also become an alcoholic and a drug addict." Davis added that he had retained Phil Epstein,

Q.C., to act for Grossman in the matter, who, in case Eddie didn't know, was an expert "in the area of the Charter of Rights and its effect on the ownership of Motor Vehicles".

Replied Eddie:

Dear Milton,

Please tell your neurotic, depressed, nose-bleeding, hive-infested hiccuping pothead drunken client that he has nothing to fear. Fortunately, I act for the Armenian community and I immediately imposed a moratorium on all Toronto Transit Commission bombings until this matter is cleared up.

As to the sale of the car, your client should take comfort from the fact his trunk now stays open, his hood stays open and his glove compartment is fixed. As well, his front door lock cylinders have been repaired and lubricated, and his air conditioning is also fixed. In short, his car today is worth $72.12 more than it was worth yesterday.

I am enclosing a bottle of champagne without prejudice in the hope that your client will find it in his heart to forgive me. If that is not enough, I am prepared to cut off the right hand of my dumb student or fire him outright or give him to you.

P.S. I find your choice of counsel laughable.

There are regular correspondents who exchange bantering letters with Greenspan several times every year. They include such close friends as the head of the Canada's Association for Civil Liberties, Alan Borovoy; Judge Rosalie Abella; lawyer and showbiz maven Dusty Cohl; and Greenspan's namesake, the well-known lawyer and political pundit David B. Greenspan, Q.C.

In 1986, after reading an article by David B. Greenspan in the Toronto Globe and Mail, in which David touched on a number of subjects with approval (e.g. the Liberal Party) and on some subjects with disapproval (e.g. street crime), Eddie wrote David the following letter:

Dear David:

As counsel for the "Creeps in the Streets", I am writing to complain about the unfair way you treated this very fine group of individuals in your op-ed article in the recent Globe and Mail.

Considering the events of the last few years, I would have thought *that the "creeps in the streets" have given a better account of themselves than the Liberal Party of Canada.*

*The Liberal Party has never put food on my table. The "creeps in the streets" have always looked after my family's fortune. People know where they stand with the "creeps in the streets". No one knows where they stand with the Liberal Party of Canada. The "creeps in the streets" have a firm appreciation of their role in society and never deviate from that role. In that sense, they are a much more reliable group than the Federal Liberal Party. The "creeps in the streets" believe that if you can't do the time, don't do the crime. The Liberal Party never believed that.*

*If you would only take the time to get to know the "creeps in the streets", I am confident that you would find that they are, on the whole, a much better group than the Liberal Party.*

Another exchange between Eddie Greenspan and David Greenspan occurred in 1987, when David wrote Eddie a note soliciting funds for municipal politician June Rowlands' aldermanic campaign, saying as a joke that if Eddie hurried up he might still get in on a $500 slot reserved for him. As David knew, Eddie likes June Rowland in personal terms, but has more than once locked horns with her over public issues. (Rowland's first concern tends to be social policy, while Greenspan is far more likely to be worried about civil liberties.) Replied Eddie:

*Dear David:*

*I am enclosing my cheque in the amount of $500 for June's campaign.*

*This cheque is given on the condition that June takes the following public positions:*

*1. Smoking be permitted in all public buildings, in all restaurants, and all elevators and everywhere else;*

*2. All forms of pornography be made available in all public school and high school libraries and that she publicly states that pornography is a good thing.*

*If June rejects these conditions then she can still keep the $500. She will need it because I propose to give $100,000 to her opposition.*

It happened only once that Eddie wrote a letter of this type to someone who was not a close personal friend. In fact, Greenspan had only met the lawyer Joseph Potts a few times before the latter's appointment to the Supreme Court of Ontario in 1981. From their few meetings, however, it seemed to Eddie not only that Potts had an excellent sense of humour, but that it was the same kind of humour as Eddie's. Greenspan hesitated for a day or two — what if he was mistaken, or what if his Lordship would take it the wrong way? — but finally he couldn't resist. He wrote:

Dear Joe:

I read with sadness of your appointment to the Ontario Supreme Court.

To think that you will spend the rest of your life dealing with rapists, murderers, child molesters, Mafia thugs, welfare fraud artists and dope pushers in such exotic places as Fort Frances, Timmins, Cornwall, Chatham and Welland, makes me wonder what you could possibly have done for providence to deal you such a cruel blow.

I wish you every success as a Jurist. I hope you will not consider me disrespectful in pointing out to you two principles of law that you are undoubtedly unfamiliar with and probably fundamentally opposed to. But they may come in handy every now and then in your new role.

The first principle is that in this country an accused person is presumed to be innocent. The second principle, as strange as it may sound, is that in this country the Crown must prove its case beyond a reasonable doubt.

I know these principles will make you laugh but I can assure you they are the law of the land. Some day you may thank me for reminding you of these principles.

There is also a rule of practice in criminal law that you should know. It has become the custom not to sentence an offender until after he has been convicted.

If you remember the legal nuggets in this letter, the Court of Appeal can never really hurt you.

Replied the Honourable Mr. Justice Joseph Potts to Greenspan:

Dear Ed:

Many thanks for your kind note of condolences and sympathy prompted by my recent appointment.

*You have obviously and understandably failed to detect the funda-mental trait which has characterized my career to date, i.e. my life has always been a constant sacrifice. I have often repeated that to my children and I now draw it to your attention and commend it to your future endeavours.*

*I am deeply grateful to you for drawing to my attention the two principles of law which had previously escaped me. You suggested that someday I might thank you for reminding me of these principles. I am delighted that I do not have to wait for someday to thank you as I do here and now express my heartfelt thanks. You have clearly saved me from some very embarrassing situations which I might otherwise have en-countered in the future.*

*Kind personal regards,*

*Joe.*

# PART SIX

# OF COUNSEL

# 13. Playing God

I can't say that all people applaud what I do for a living. My own mother is ambivalent about it. Ambivalent may not be the right word. At times I think that Al Capone's mother probably had a more tolerant understanding of her son's profession than my mother has of mine. But while some people may not like my occupation, I can't say that they are not interested in it. In addition to hostile questions (such as the classic: "How can you defend those people?") I'm often asked questions of genuine curiosity about being a defence lawyer. What is a criminal lawyer's role? Why did I choose to become one?

I will try to answer by telling a story.

As undergraduate students in our university residence, my friend Peter Williams and I designated a drawer in his room as our petty-cash box. Petty cash was the only kind of cash either of us had in those days. Peter and I viewed a dollar bill as a large-denomination banknote, but we got into the habit of shoving our loose change into the drawer against a rainy day.

One Friday afternoon — it was actually a sunny day, as I remember — I emptied the drawer of coins and took the resulting pennies, nickels, and dimes across the street to the student council's snack-bar. Peter had gone out of town for the weekend; I was strapped, and decided to turn our kitty into dollar bills for myself. Life in the big city — Toronto — was pretty expensive for a student in 1965. I can't remember how much I got at the snack-bar for my rolls of pennies, nickels, and dimes, but it was probably around five dollars. The crisp bills in my pocket gave me the smug feeling of being in funds. I would not suffer from hamburger deprivation this weekend.

Later in the afternoon there was a loud knock on my door. When I opened it, I found myself face to face with two large plainclothes policemen.

"Where did you get those coins you cashed in at the students' snack-bar?" one of them asked, after identifying himself.

The other detective answered him before I could. "We know where he got them from, don't we. He got them from robbing that coffee truck."

I guess my jaw fell. The detectives — after glancing at each other with knowing looks — enlightened me. Apparently, just around the time I strolled into the snack-bar with my rolls of coins, a lunch truck had been held up not far from my residence on St. George Street. The heist netted the masked bandit a small bagful of nickels and dimes. Cashing in *my* nickels and dimes within a few minutes just around the corner from the robbery made me a natural suspect.

I protested my innocence but, as it seemed to me, to no avail. I explained to the policemen about our petty cash. I offered to take them across the hall to Peter Williams' room where the drawer was, but even as I made the suggestion I realized that an empty drawer would prove nothing. My friend was out of town. There was no one to back up my story. I began to sweat, and I felt myself becoming incoherent. I probably looked scared, but my impression was that I was looking guilty. For some inexplicable reason, I was *feeling* guilty. As an innocent man I ought to have been indignant for being suspected, and maybe I was indignant — but when I tried to act indignant it seemed like a pretence.

The detectives looked at me with narrow eyes. "All right, you'll hear from us," one of them said. As they were leaving, he turned back from the doorway. "You'd better not leave town," he added.

I spent the weekend in a daze. There was no one I could talk to. Talking to people was the last thing I wanted to do anyway; I couldn't very well call my mother in Niagara Falls and tell her that I was now a robbery suspect. As it was, I felt that everyone who looked at me in the street could see a suspected criminal. It was all I could do to resist the impulse to buttonhole perfect strangers and tell them that I was innocent.

I especially tried to steer clear of fellow students at my residence. Unlike strangers in the street, they probably *did* know that something was up. They must have seen the detectives stomping through the house; maybe somebody even had to show them where my room was. The people at the snack-bar had to know about it, too; after all, they were the ones who sent the police after me. And, as I suddenly realized, the police couldn't come on campus to investigate anything without permission from the university's president and the college principal — which meant that University of Toronto President Claude Bissell and Douglas LePan, the gentle poet and scholar whom I admired, had to know about the police suspecting me as well. Both of them knew me because I was president of the University College student council that year.

This was more than embarrassing. This was awful. I began to rue the day Peter and I decided to hoard our petty cash. Our petty cash was turning into a nightmare.

Reassuring myself that it was all a misunderstanding didn't help: *I* knew that it was a misunderstanding, but how could anyone else know it? The police suspected me and, as people are always quick to say, there's no smoke without fire. Maybe from now on, no matter what happened, everybody would describe me as "Oh, you know, the guy who was involved with that stick-up".

By Sunday night I was becoming frantic. I hadn't shaved since Friday; I huddled in my room, keeping close to the telephone. My mind started playing tricks on me; I wanted the police to call me, or failing that to come and arrest me, just to get it over with. Let them try me, convict me, throw me into jail, if that's what it took to put everything behind me. Maybe I was really guilty: maybe I did hold up that truck while suffering from a black-out and now I couldn't remember. The police knew about these things better than I did: if they thought that it was me, then maybe it was. Perhaps I ought to do the right thing and confess.

By Monday morning I couldn't stand it any more. I called the police station.

It took me a long time to make the desk sergeant connect me with one of the detectives. Finally he came on the line: "Oh yeah," he said. "You're the fellow we talked to about that truck on St. George, eh? Well, that's okay now; we got the two kids who did it."

"When?" I nearly screamed into the phone.

"We arrested them on Saturday."

Saturday! I had huddled in my room, an entire weekend of going through hell for nothing.

"Why didn't anybody tell me?" I demanded. "I was requested not to leave town. All weekend I was sitting here thinking I was being suspected of a crime . . . " I took a deep breath. "Okay, now I want you to call everybody and tell them it wasn't me. Do you understand? I want you to call the president of the university, I want you to call the principal, and the students' snack-bar, and . . . "

"Yeah, well, we're a little too busy here to be making phone calls for people," said the detective and hung up.

I could say that it was this incident that made me decide to become a criminal lawyer, except it wouldn't be true. I had wanted to be a criminal lawyer since the age of nine or ten. But being a robbery suspect, even if only for a day or two, illustrated something to me that I could never forget.

Sitting in my room, waiting for the phone to ring, my rational thought was that this was just a simple mistake. Obviously I had done nothing wrong. The police had to investigate a robbery — it was their job to follow up all leads — the whole thing would be cleared up pretty quickly. However, one irrational thought kept intruding. Maybe, I thought, it wasn't so easy to clear up such matters.

I was an undergraduate student in a strange city. No one knew me in Toronto; no one knew my family. I had no reputation of any kind. I had been alone in my room before going to the snack-bar; I had no alibi. I certainly *needed* the money; on my own story, I was cashing in pennies to get me through the weekend.

What if the police had no alternative suspects? What if the masked hold-up man had a similar build to mine? What if the victim, even if he couldn't make a positive identification, would look at me, shrug, and say: "Well, he had a mask on — but yeah, that could be the guy."

Wouldn't that be enough for a charge to be laid? And, once a charge was laid, would it not mean that the police thought it was me? And if the police thought so, why should anyone think otherwise? After all, no one would know anything about the case. No one would know anything about me. Why shouldn't people just go with what the police thought?

Would there be one person — outside my immediate family or closest friends — whose automatic first thought might be the opposite? One who might *start* with the assumption that the police must have made a mistake?

After my scare was over, I dismissed my thoughts as irrational: the police couldn't make such an obvious error. But today, after nearly two decades of practice as a criminal lawyer, I would not call such thoughts irrational any more. The error was obvious to me, but it need not have seemed so obvious to the police — or to anyone else.

Whenever a crime is committed (or whenever some people in the community suspect that an act may amount to a crime), a large, impersonal machinery goes into motion. Its initial purpose is to determine if some act or event was, in fact, a crime — and if it concludes that it was, to find the individual (or group of individuals) responsible for it.

Once this appears to be accomplished, the machinery shifts into second gear. It tries to establish the accused individual's *degree* of responsibility. Then, in third gear, his or her appropriate punishment. Sometimes there is a fourth gear: the machinery may turn its attention to some social or legal condition in the hope of making it easier to define, prevent, or detect such crimes in the future.

This process can involve dozens and dozens of people in its various stages. Ideally — and often in actual fact — they are highly trained, intelligent, dedicated, and hard-working human beings: people of great personal integrity. They are police officers, forensic experts, medical doctors, prosecuting attorneys, court officials, judges, jurors, parole officials, prison administrators, and lawmakers. Except for the jurors, they are all professionals. Many of them have the authority to knock on anybody's door and ask for information and assistance. Even when they cannot compel people's co-operation by law, they can expect people to co-operate with them as a civic or moral duty. They also have at their disposal support personnel and sophisticated, expensive equipment, the best society can provide, to help them in their work.

There is nothing wrong with any of this, of course. Crime cannot go undetected, undefined, or unpunished. No community could function without protecting itself from crime.

However, this great, impersonal, awesome machinery has one built-in bias. It is an unconscious, functional bias, somewhat like an aircraft's bias for leaving the ground as soon as it has attained a certain speed. The bias of the justice system is to find guilt. That is, first, to define any human act that comes to its attention as a crime; then, to define any suspect as a person who has probably committed such an act; and finally, to define any human being who has committed such an act as a criminal. That's the way the justice system flies.

Everyone knows that in a given individual case none of this may be true — yet the great machine of the criminal-justice system may thunder down the runway and take off regardless.

Once an act is initially defined as a crime and a person is accused of having committed it, every official in society becomes his adversary or, at best, his judge. One set of skilled and dedicated professionals (the police and the prosecutors) set out to convince another set of skilled and dedicated professionals (the judiciary) that the act *was* a crime, that the accused person *did* do it, and that he should be punished for it as severely as possible. Either before or after deciding on his punishment, a third set of professionals may be consulted about the best methods of "curing" or "rehabilitating" such a person, or about the best methods of protecting society against him. (This may happen sometimes even before he has been convicted of any crime, for instance at a bail hearing.)

An accused or convicted person has no friends in society. He may still have *personal* friends, of course; he may still have his family; he may even have the detached benevolence of some psychiatrists, case-workers, or priests, who look at him as a "patient" or as a "lost sheep". However, from the public representatives of his community all he can expect is, at best, an open mind (judge, jury, parole officials) or an open enmity (prosecutor, police). No official of his country will be on his side.

None of this is my discovery, by the way. Others may not have used these particular words to describe what happens to a person accused or convicted of a crime, but society has always been aware that any encounter between one individual and the entire judicial system is a collision of epic disproportion. Even in the absence of any other factor, such as malice, error, or negligence, this disparity alone creates a potential for injustice. Even a wealthy, powerful person can be swept away by it like a piece of fluff — prominent people, as discussed elsewhere in this book, may in some respects have a special disadvantage — to say nothing of an average, anonymous citizen.

Our justice system has tried to counteract this potential by two remedies.

First, on an abstract level, the remedy is the law's presumption that every person is innocent until proven guilty on relevant evidence beyond a reasonable doubt.

By saying "on an abstract level" I don't mean to imply that this presumption is unimportant. On the contrary, it is vital and fundamental. Everything else flows from the presumption of innocence.

However, without a second remedy on a concrete level, it could remain as ineffectual as a sheathed sword. Or, to use a more up-to-date metaphor, as an engine without a driver.

This second, concrete remedy is the lawyer for the defence. He drives the abstract engine of the presumption of innocence. He is the one person in the entire world, apart from the accused person's mother, who *starts* with the assumption that the authorities must be mistaken.

To balance the awe-inspiring machinery of the criminal-justice system, the law permits one individual to be the accused person's friend. He is, as the legal expression goes, to be "of counsel" to him. Simply put, his job is to "believe" the accused — or at least not to disbelieve him. His job is to look at every circumstance surrounding the allegations against a defendant with the assumption that they prove, or are consistent with, his innocence.

The defence lawyer is to balance the dozens of powerful professionals whose task is to investigate and prosecute an accused person. We give the defence lawyer this task in the knowledge that a defendant may *be* innocent. Innocent, not just as an abstract legal idea (because in that sense he is innocent anyway until found guilty), but as a matter of plain, actual fact. What he is accused of may not amount to a crime, or he may not have committed it. If it is a crime and he did commit it, it may not be as serious a crime as his adversary, the prosecutor, suggests. And even if it is as serious, there may be something about the circumstances, or about the defendant as a human being, that makes him something else than a criminal deserving the worst punishment.

Since this may be so, our system has decided that there must be one person in the defendant's community who acts as if it were so. One man or woman who is not the defendant's inquisitor, accuser, or judge. One who doesn't merely keep an open mind about him. One person who is the defendant's advocate.

Society assigns this role to the defence lawyer. He is the one person whose duty is to assume the best about a defendant at every step of the way. The defence lawyer alone, among all the defendant's fellow citizens and neighbours, must act on the assumption that whatever the defendant says is true. He must act on the assumption that the defendant's accusers are mistaken. Mistaken — or possibly malicious. They may have their own axe to grind. The defence lawyer must put everything they say about the defendant to the strictest test of proof. In so far as the law permits, he must put the accusers on trial.

This is the defence lawyer's duty. It's a duty not just to his client, but to his society. It is not something the defence lawyer decides in his own mind: it is an obligation the community places on him. The defence lawyer chooses his occupation voluntarily, but he does not choose his role: his society defines his role for him. The moral essence of this role has been distilled by the common experience of our legal tradition over the centuries. It is that a community can retain justice and freedom only as long as it gives standing to one person to take, within the limits of the law, the defendant's side in court.

It is important to remember this: the *defendant's* side, not the side of abstract justice, or efficiency, or society's interest, or objective truth. Those are all vital concerns, needless to say, but not the defence lawyer's concerns. The entire justice system is concerned with those values, and rightly so, but the defence lawyer is concerned only with the defendant. He serves society — and abstract justice and objective truth — simply by serving his client.

Is this a roundabout route to justice? Other systems have attempted more direct routes — and invariably failed. (The best inquisitorial systems of continental Europe proved capable of adaptation by tyrannies, but the adversary system, never.) In communist Bulgaria an attorney once said to the court in a treason trial: "In a socialist state there is no division of duty between the judge, prosecutor, and defence counsel. . . . The defence must assist the prosecution to find the objective truth in a case." Then the attorney went on to explain why society must take the gravest view of the defendant's crimes, and why it was regrettable but necessary that he should be subjected to exemplary punishment. The court accepted the defence's submission, and the client was duly convicted and executed. Some time later the state had second thoughts about the objective truth. The court decided that the verdict was a mistake, entitling the defendant to "rehabilitation". There was a ceremony of sorts with red flags and speeches, and they moved the client's remains to a different grave.

The example may be extreme, but it illustrates the principle. In the type of "trial" where the defence joins hands with the prosecution to look for "the objective truth", the verdict is a foregone conclusion. In a real trial, where finding the truth *is* the actual aim of the court, a defence lawyer would be of no assistance unless he took the opposite side from the prosecutor. Nothing can be found if you look for it in only one direction — not even a lost object, let alone something as elusive as the truth.

Some people, agreeing with this, might conclude that the defence lawyer is a kind of necessary evil in a ritual, something like a devil's advocate. But that's missing the point. The defence lawyer is an innocent person's advocate, not the devil's, and not by his own assumption, but by the law's. Once society has decided that every person is innocent until proven guilty, it can't then turn around and decide that every accused is the devil with a slick lawyer as his advocate. The second assumption would make a mockery of the first. This is why there is no conflict between the professional obligations of a defence lawyer and ordinary human (or social) values. How can there be a conflict between human and social values and defending innocent people?

The defence lawyer, as many people have pointed out, only defends a client (or a client's act) and not a crime. Central to any defence, other than a submission in mitigation of sentence, is the position that the client *didn't* do something. Or that whatever he did was not wrong in law, or at least not as wrong as the prosecution contends. If a lawyer suggested that yes, my client did shoot this man deliberately and in cold blood, but the victim was a nasty fellow who deserved to be shot, *then* he would be defending a crime — but no lawyer does that. (The only exceptions in our times have been some "activist" lawyers who attempted to gain the acquittal of murderers on the basis of some "higher" political or social motive.)

But these are only aberrations — albeit dangerous ones — and we need not concern ourselves with them here. Like most criminal lawyers, I defend clients, not crimes. Which is why I find questions like : "How can you defend those people?" or "Is there any kind of crime at which you'd draw a line?" meaningless.

I haven't the slightest moral conflict defending people accused of homicide, sexual assault, business fraud, environmental offences, or even crimes against humanity. I don't "draw the line" at anything. If I defended *crimes*, maybe I would — but I don't defend crimes. I only defend innocent people. Until they are found guilty there are no other kinds of people for me to defend, and what difference does it make what an innocent person is accused of?

And if my clients are convicted, I still continue to defend *them*, not their crimes. The prosecutor asks the court to focus on the one moment in their lives when they did something wrong, when they succumbed to greed or lust or passion. I ask the court to also look at thousands of other moments in their lives. I don't defend the crime of embezzling or drunk driving, only remind the court that it can't send the embezzler or drunk driver to jail without also jailing the human being that goes with him. A crime may not be the whole story of any human life. Which one of us would like to be defined solely by the worst thing we have ever done?

My conscience would bother me only if I took it upon myself to act as judge and jury; if I convicted a person in my own mind by refusing to defend him before he had had his day in court. That is the type of arrogance that would make me ashamed of myself, or make me feel that I had shirked a social and legal duty. In that case I would be exactly like the Bulgarian lawyer, prattling about "objective truth" while my innocent client went to the gallows.

I would not cherish such a role. Far from sitting in judgment over people who come into my office, I try to see them as if I were seeing myself huddled in a room twenty-three years ago, waiting for the police to phone me back. That's why every client is my kind of client, and every crime is my kind of crime.

As are other criminal defence lawyers, I'm called upon to make some fundamental decisions affecting people's lives. It is very much like playing God, and it may tempt the best person to put too much reliance on his own idealism and conscience. That, I think, is a dangerous mistake. Why unbounded idealism and conscience may be a mistake has been best expressed, not by a lawyer but by a playwright. Robert Bolt, in his play *A Man for All Seasons*, which is about the Lord Chancellor of England, Thomas More, has the following exchange between More and his idealistic son-in-law named Roper:

More: I know what's legal, not what's right. And I'll stick to what's legal.
Roper: Then you set Man's law above God's.

More: No far below; but let me draw your attention to a fact. I am not
  God.

Far from being God, I'm not even sure what God's law is. I suspect
He has many laws, but they didn't teach most of them at Osgoode
Hall when I went to law school. They taught me mainly Canadian
law, and I tried to learn as much of it as I could. So, while I may not
know what's "right" any more than Thomas More did, I know
reasonably well what's legal.

For instance, I couldn't tell if someone was guilty or innocent as a
matter of conscience. However, if I know a set of facts, I can tell the
likely legal consequences that will flow from them in a court of law. I
can't tell whether someone did something or not, but I can tell if
there is enough admissible evidence from which a court may conclude one way or the other. And while I often can't tell whether what
someone did was "right" or "wrong", I can generally tell whether a
court might come to the conclusion that it was lawful or unlawful.

Which is what I try to keep in mind when the time comes to
advise a client about the most important decision *he* has to make
about his case.

Essentially, a client makes only two decisions. The first is
whether or not to hire (or fire) me. In that decision he is on his own.
The second is whether to plead guilty or not guilty. That, too, is his
decision, not mine, but I act as his adviser. I try my best to push him
in the direction in which I believe he ought to go, up to a point. But —
and this is the key — *not* on the basis of what I believe to be right or
wrong. I try not to advise him according to my moral sense. I try to
advise him according to my legal judgment.

If a man tells me he is guilty, I can't tell him to say he's innocent.
If a man tells me he's innocent, I can't tell him to say he's guilty. But
in either case I can tell him what, on the basis of the evidence, the
law is likely to think of his act, and what I think of his chances in
court. He must decide how to plead according to his own lights and
conscience, but, as his lawyer, I must make sure that he will make
an informed decision and not one based on either false hopes or
needless despair.

Once, within a fairly short space of time, I had three clients who
had been charged with murder (arising out of three different incidents). I will call them Larry, Hank, and Gilbert, which are not their

real names. Their cases were similar in that all three said that they had to kill another man to save their own lives. If they were telling the truth, all three were completely innocent — and I certainly believed that they were telling the truth.

Larry was a young man, married, with no criminal affiliations or record of any kind. In fact, he was a tradesman, making a good living. His only "crime" was that he hadn't been getting along with his in-laws too well, so while he and his wife were visiting them one weekend he made up his mind to sleep in his car on the beach.

Unfortunately, a gang of young punks decided to party on the same beach and they got into a fight with Larry. There was ample evidence that they *were* punks, and there was ample evidence that they had initiated the fight. Larry defended himself, and the leader of the punks died of a knife wound.

Hank was also a young man, but of a less clean-cut lifestyle than Larry. While not a criminal himself, he hung around with some "street-people" who were engaged in drug-dealing and petty crimes. Hank was a kind of errand boy for them, and his misfortune was that one of the gang, a short-tempered, assaultive, and brutish fellow, took a great dislike to him. One day, possibly high on drugs, he threatened Hank. My client locked himself in the washroom, and the brutish man followed him there, threatening his life with a knife. Hank fled to the bedroom, where he picked up a sawed-off shotgun and shot the other man dead.

Gilbert was much older, a man in his late thirties. He was very big and strong, but not quite as big and strong as his oldest, lifelong friend. They had been in business together, and one night his friend got angry with Gilbert over something. He (and his wife) came to the house where Gilbert was living with his wife. A furious argument ensued, in the course of which his friend punched Gilbert a few times and threatened him with more physical violence. He was in an excellent position to carry out the threat, weighing about 250 pounds of solid muscle. He also had about thirteen ounces of alcohol in his system. Gilbert said he'd call the police, but before he could do so his friend picked up the phone himself and told the police to "send a few guys", because he was going to make mincemeat of Gilbert. My client, wisely, retreated. He went upstairs to his own bedroom. His huge and angry friend followed him. Gilbert was in the process of trying to unlatch the window to escape to the roof and wait there for the police when his friend burst into the bedroom. There was nowhere to retreat. Gilbert picked up a small-calibre hand-gun lying on the television table. (The gun was lying there only because my client had acquired it on a trip from which he and his wife had just returned, and while he had already unpacked his suitcases, he hadn't yet got around to putting his things away.)

In any case, as his friend advanced upon him and punched him again, Gilbert shot him through the heart. It was a measure of the victim's strength that he turned around, walked out of the house, and, carrying a bullet lodged in his heart for about sixty to seventy yards to a parking lot, actually got back into his car before he slumped over the seat and died.

All three clients would have had to stand trial on charges of either first- or second-degree murder, but on the facts it was open to all three of them to plead guilty to the lesser and included offence of manslaughter. Because of the circumstances, their likely sentence on a manslaughter plea would probably not have exceeded four years, and it might have been even less. I could feel pretty confident that none of them would have to spend much more than a year in jail before getting paroled.

Going to trial *could* mean exoneration and freedom; on the other hand, it could also mean a conviction for murder. The latter would entail a mandatory life sentence, with no chance of parole for either ten or twenty-five years, depending on whether the conviction was for second- or first-degree murder. (Even being convicted only of manslaughter after a trial would probably mean a longer sentence than I could negotiate in a plea agreement with the Crown beforehand.)

These, then, were the stakes. No matter how good the case (or the lawyer) is, going into court is like throwing dice. If there is evidence on which a jury *could* convict, convict it might. Knowing this makes most lawyers, including me, favour a deal. But can any lawyer advise a man who believes himself to be innocent to plead guilty just because it is safer? Is it right to advise a client to do such a thing? On the other hand, is it right not to advise him clearly and emphatically about the risk, or even twist his arm — and thereby expose him to a long term in prison?

Okay, *advise* him, most lawyers would say, but don't push him. You're not God, and it's his decision. Oh yes, but aren't you playing

God just as much by not pushing a client when you ought to? By stepping back and assuming a lofty distance?

There is a famous anecdote involving Arthur Martin and Charles Dubin, now both Ontario Court of Appeal justices, but at the time distinguished criminal lawyers. The story goes that a lawyer of no particular renown consulted Martin about a murder case. Martin looked at the facts, then told the lawyer to advise his client to plead guilty to manslaughter. Dissatisfied, the lawyer went away and consulted Dubin; same result. The lawyer was unhappy with the advice of his seniors, and he pleaded his client not guilty. They went to trial, and the jury acquitted. "Have you seen this case in the paper?" Dubin asked Martin when they bumped into each other the next day. "Yes," Martin replied. "That client was really lucky that he didn't go to a good lawyer."

None of my three clients wanted to plead guilty. The question was: was I a "good" lawyer? Should I force them? Should I play God with their lives?

"Force" is really the wrong word: you can't "force" a client to do anything, but you can try to persuade him. You can twist his arm. You can tell him that you won't act for him unless he takes your advice. This isn't true in every case; for instance, if a client makes an outright denial of an act, no lawyer can advise him to falsely admit to it. You can't tell someone who claims not to have pulled the trigger to say "Okay, I pulled it" or you won't act for him. But if the act itself is not in dispute, a lawyer can certainly urge his own opinion on a client as to how that act is likely to appear to a judge or a jury. A lawyer can advise a client about the probable view that the law is going to take of his action. That's one of the things for which a client consults a lawyer in the first place.

In Larry's case, there was a deadly surprise witness for the Crown. At the preliminary hearing I found that demolishing all the other witnesses for the prosecution — the punks who were involved in the fight — would be like shooting fish in a barrel, but then the Crown put this young man on the stand. He told a story about observing the fight from a nearby house and jotting down the details. On his evidence the fight was already over, the punks were already walking away, when Larry went back to his car, got a knife, ran after them, and stabbed their leader. On the story of this witness, Larry did not act purely in self-defence, and was guilty at least of manslaughter.

This witness was not one of the punks. He was just a kid. In fact, he was a policeman's son. He saw everything and took *notes*, the way he'd seen his father do it. While cross-examining him at the preliminary hearing, I threw at him everything short of a hand-grenade — and I couldn't shake him. I couldn't beat that kid.

Larry denied his guilt, and I believed him. I believed him unequivocally. But I also knew that walking into court on a murder charge with such a witness against you was suicidal. Larry, an intelligent young man, could see it too, but insisted that he wouldn't plead because he was innocent.

Had I speculated, I would have said that maybe Larry wanted to be punished for murder. He wanted to plead "not guilty" precisely in order to be found guilty of the greater crime. And, from some abstract moral view, pretending to see into souls when I knew that I couldn't, I might have said: so be it. He did kill a man — let him choose the worst punishment for himself if he likes. Maybe it's the right thing.

But, like Thomas More, I don't know what is right. I only know what is legal, and I stick to it.

From the only point of view that I could consider, the legal view, I couldn't see Larry's case surviving that young witness in court. Maybe a *bad* lawyer could have seen it — and maybe a bad lawyer would have been right, as in Martin's and Dubin's story — but I couldn't. So I got the Crown to agree to an eighteen-month sentence on a manslaughter plea — in practice maybe three to six months in jail before parole — and then I advised my client that the rest was up to him. I twisted his arm.

Larry pleaded guilty to manslaughter. However he may have continued to define "guilt" in a moral sense in his mind, he admitted that his act was unlawful.

I also wanted to twist Hank's arm, but he wouldn't let me. In his case, it wasn't the question of any one witness as much as the entire mood surrounding the events and the people that made me very dubious about the outcome. They were all petty hoods and their girlfriends, with my client as a sort of hanger-on. There was some evidence for the Crown's theory that Hank shot the big, brutal bully in revenge for having been beaten up by him before. I believed that Hank was innocent, but I didn't think much of his chances, and the charge against him was first-degree murder: twenty-five years, rain or shine. Maybe, since he adamantly refused my advice to plead guilty to manslaughter, I would have stopped acting for him, but the trial was coming up and there just wasn't enough time. You can't force a client to look for a lawyer at the last minute, or go into court on a murder charge unprepared. So, since walking out on him would have been unconscionable, I defended him on a "not guilty" plea against my better judgment.

Hank was acquitted.

Naturally, once the decision was made to fight, all my misgivings were put to one side and I fought for Hank the only way any lawyer can fight for a client, which is like hell. One problem for the defence was that the knife with which Hank said the deceased had threatened him in the washroom was never found. We believed that a friend of the dead man, a witness for the Crown, had hidden it before the police had arrived at the scene, but whatever happened to the knife it had disappeared. I wanted the members of the jury to have a knife in front of their eyes, so I went out and bought one of the same description — explaining to the judge and the jury, of course, what I had done. Then I showed the knife to various witnesses in court to ask them if it was the *type* of knife that the deceased had owned. It was a vicious-looking weapon, and I would have loved the jury to take it with them into the jury-room during their deliberations. Of course, there was no way I could introduce it as an *exhibit* — it was just a knife I had bought myself — and no matter how I racked my brains I couldn't think of any arguments that might have made it admissible evidence.

Help came from an unexpected quarter. Halfway through my cross-examination of a witness, the prosecutor suddenly rose to his feet. "If my friend," he said to the trial judge, "keeps waving that knife around, perhaps he should introduce it as an exhibit."

"Mr. Greenspan?" the judge looked at me.

I couldn't believe what was happening. "I have no objection, my Lord," I replied, trying to keep the excitement out of my voice. The knife went into the jury-room, at the Crown's request, as if it had been the deceased's own knife with which he had threatened my client! It couldn't help but play a part in Hank's acquittal. To this day I keep it in my office for good luck.

Gilbert didn't want to plead guilty to manslaughter either, and even though I couldn't be sure that he was right, I decided not to twist his arm too hard. The charge against him was second-degree murder, but it was hard to see a jury convicting him of anything but manslaughter at worst. A person is unlikely to kill someone, except in self-defence, *when he knows* that the police are already on their way: people tend not to commit murder under these circumstances. The evidence was undisputed that Gilbert had retreated as far as he could go — to his own bedroom — and there was evidence that he tried to retreat even further by attempting to climb out on the roof. What more can a man do to avoid the threat of grievous bodily harm by an infuriated 250-pounder who is adamantly going after him? Under the circumstances, an acquittal was a reasonable expectation, and manslaughter a worst-case scenario. Much as I prefer a negotiated deal to a trial as a rule, when my client felt himself to be innocent, when he *was* innocent in law as far as I could see, I wasn't going to play God by threatening to withdraw from his case unless he pleaded to the lesser offence.

Gilbert was convicted of second-degree murder. He was sentenced to life imprisonment with no parole eligibility for ten years.

Should I have twisted Gilbert's arm harder? I don't know, but I doubt it. Had I pushed him the way I had pushed Larry, he would have been walking the street for a long time now. This way, Gilbert is still in jail. The case still haunts me. But if I had succeeded in twisting my other client Hank's arm — as I certainly tried — Hank would have spent a year or two in prison. As it was, by taking his own counsel rather than mine, he walked out of court exonerated and free.

What do these cases tell about defence lawyers? Only that we can propose but cannot dispose. What do they tell about trials? Only that not all trials are fairy-tales with happy endings. Which is the reason I push clients — but only up to a point. It is the reason I allow a defendant to make his own decision, as I must — but without allowing myself to keep at a lofty distance from it. This way God can go about his business of being God, while I go about my business of being a lawyer.

# 14. Twelve Good Men and True

I will continue discussing the "Gilbert" case, as I call it in this book, because it illustrates another point.

Naturally every accused person prefers to be tried fairly rather than unfairly. However, if you ever get convicted of a crime you did not commit, pray to God that you get convicted in an *unfair* trial. If your trial has been fair, the higher courts can't help you much. If you had a fair hearing but a jury (or a judge, sitting alone) happened to come to the wrong conclusion, you're pretty much out of luck. Courts of Appeal rectify errors of law, but they seldom change findings of fact.

I don't know why the jury convicted Gilbert. (It is no longer lawful for a jury in Canada — as it once used to be, and as it still is in the United States — to reveal anything about their deliberations.) I think it was an unreasonable verdict, perhaps just short of being perverse. In my view, there was more than enough evidence to raise a reasonable doubt about whether or not Gilbert had acted in self-defence when he shot his drunken, 250-pound friend who had forced his way into his bedroom, and he was entitled to the benefit of that doubt. However, since all this was set out to the jury with sufficient clarity, when the jurors convicted Gilbert they convicted him in a *fair* trial.

The Crown Attorney was very fair. The trial judge (though he had made a couple of errors in his charge to the jury, which formed the basis of the appeal) was also generally fair to the accused. In Gilbert's case the verdict was a thunderbolt out of the blue. The trial as a whole had seemed to be going for the defence. The facts, just barely supporting a murder charge, did not make a murder conviction likely at the outset, and the way the evidence unfolded during the trial did little to bolster the prosecution's theory. Some key Crown witnesses faltered, while the defence witnesses were unshaken under cross-examination. The attending journalists (some of whom always gamble on the outcome of any interesting trial) were giving four-to-one odds in favour of an acquittal. Before the jury returned with the verdict, the Crown Attorney very graciously came over to the defence table to congratulate my associate Chris Buhr and me on what he himself expected to be a defence victory.

I couldn't bring myself to reciprocate *after* the verdict. I was too crushed. How my client must have felt, anyone can imagine.

I asked my brother, Brian, to handle Gilbert's appeal with my partner Marc Rosenberg. I don't think I'm biased in saying that Brian and Marc make one of the strongest defence teams in any appeal court in Canada. Marc is a legal scholar as well as a leading legal practitioner: if I were a defendant I would hire him without a moment's hesitation to take my case to a higher court. As for my brother Brian, much as it pains me to admit it, he has few equals and no superiors in the practice of criminal law, either as a trial or as an appellate counsel. He prepares meticulously (preparation is ninety per cent of any defence lawyer's work) and he also happens to be a stubborn fighter. If it weren't for the fact that sibling rivalry would make us kill each other within a month, there's no criminal lawyer with whom I'd sooner share a practice other than Brian.

Brian needs no goading, but just to be safe I told him that he would never speak to his nieces again if he lost Gilbert's appeal. In truth, I was worried that the appeal just couldn't be won. As a rule, higher courts will not interfere with a jury's verdict for anything except major errors in law — such as important evidence wrongly admitted or excluded, or a judge misdirecting a jury on some vital point in his charge — or for some new, relevant, and credible fact that, having emerged only after the trial, would not have been available to the original jury. Other than these two reasons, a verdict would have to be "perverse" — that is, simply incapable of being supported by the evidence — before an appeal court would interfere with it.

It is next to impossible to charge a jury after a complex trial without making some trivial mistakes in law, so when lawyers go over a judge's charge with a fine-tooth comb they can nearly always find one or two small errors. As cases would have to be sent back for new trials forever on this basis, higher courts look at the judge's charge as a whole to see if a jury might have been misdirected by it. In Gilbert's case, I wasn't sure if the few errors turned up by Brian and Marc's fine-tooth comb were sufficient to impugn a charge to the jury that, on the whole, was quite fair to the defence. Nor was there any wrongly admitted or excluded evidence. This left nothing for us to submit but that the jury's verdict was unreasonable, which was the last and, to my mind, the strongest point of our appeal.

It wasn't, however, strong enough. This was the eventual finding of the Ontario Court of Appeal. Much as I regretted it, I could not totally disagree. There was *some* evidence that my client committed murder, and the Crown simply had to satisfy a jury after a fair trial that it was *enough* evidence: satisfy it beyond a reasonable doubt, to the point of moral certainty. This jury was evidently satisfied, and that was pretty much the end of the matter in law.

Perhaps no other jury would have found it proven beyond a reasonable doubt that Gilbert, punched and pursued to his very bedroom by his huge, drunken assailant, did not act in self-defence when he shot him — but this jury did. Perhaps no other jury would have been morally certain that Gilbert wasn't even provoked sufficiently to reduce his act to manslaughter — but this jury was. On the evidence, it was just barely open to these twelve good men and women to reject Gilbert's defence — but they rejected it. They sent a man to jail for life whom, I firmly believe, virtually any other group of twelve good men and women would have found to be totally innocent — but they were not another twelve good men and women.

I've lost jury trials before. Like all lawyers, I've been very dismayed over losing, but I've seldom been puzzled. The twelve jurors in Gilbert's case were the first whose verdict genuinely surprised me. Still, their verdict did nothing to make me question my faith in the jury system.

I think that, on the whole, twelve ordinary men and women are far more likely to arrive at a just result than any one individual would, no matter how learned and clever. Nor can I envisage any panel of "experts" or scholars bringing a greater sense of responsibility and fair play to their task, or making a more inspired guess at whether witnesses tell the truth or not, than twelve honest people picked almost at random from the community. No group of judges, lawyers, or social scientists would be less influenced by pet ideas and prejudices than a group of average citizens drawn from all walks of life.

While this may sound as if I have just discovered something that

Anglo-Saxon jurisprudence has known all along, the fact is that there have been so many attacks on the jury system, especially in recent years, that it is necessary to reiterate the point. Juries, perhaps more than any other institution, reaffirm one's faith in the democratic ideal that in those things that really matter all human beings are equal.

Perhaps this is why juries humble anyone who tries to second-guess them. They generally reach the right conclusion, but at times they may reach it in rather peculiar ways. When, much less often, they make a mistake, they'll make it in an equally unfathomable manner. I found out how some juries' minds work about fifteen years ago when it was still lawful in Canada for jurors to discuss what went on in the jury-room during deliberations.

As a very young lawyer I acted for a man named Giguere. It was a rather sordid case of manslaughter in a Toronto flophouse — in the office we called it the "vat-murder" (a vat, as in a brewery). After an alcoholic argument a man killed another man with an iron bar, and my client was accused of aiding the killer by handing the iron bar to him. The evidence against my client was considerable: he was seen by a university student who lived across the street, and he also admitted handing the bar to the killer in a statement to the police. The statement was ruled admissible in spite of my client's contention that he was intimidated by the police into signing it. Obviously, I had no choice but to put Giguere on the witness stand to explain his position to the jury. It was elementary: if my client hadn't testified, his own statement to the police — along with the student's testimony — would have been uncontradicted evidence against him. His only chance was that the jury might believe *him*, rather than his earlier statement or the eyewitness from across the street.

However, the jury convicted Giguere of manslaughter. On the evidence it was a fair and totally unsurprising result.

Still, I'm always depressed when I lose a case. To cheer me up, my wife suggested that we go to a movie together that night. It turned out to have been a terrible idea. We were standing in line at the International Cinema on Yonge Street when the man in front of us looked back. He was the foreman of the jury.

"You know," he said to me casually, "if your guy hadn't testified, we would have acquitted him."

I thought I was going to be sick. "But how can you say that?" I asked. "There was a witness across the road, a student, who *saw* him hand the iron bar to the killer."

"Aw," replied the foreman, "we paid no attention to that fellow. It was too dark for him to see properly."

"But what about Giguere's own statement?" I asked desperately. "His statement to the police in which he admitted everything?"

The foreman chuckled. "How naive do you think we are?" he asked. "We knew the cops just beat that statement out of him. We wouldn't have believed a word of it."

"So why did you convict him? What made you think he did it?"

"Well, when he denied it on the witness stand," said the jury foreman, "we didn't believe *him* either."

The currently fashionable idea that by selecting juries "scientifically" — that is, by determining their individual prejudices ahead of time — one can determine the outcome of a trial is, I think, a pipe-dream. Luckily for justice, I might add. I utterly reject the cynical notion, held by some lawyers, that trials are won or lost by selecting juries for their prejudices. Lawyers who think so overestimate both the power of prejudice (most jurors take their oath seriously and try to rise above their bias) and, especially, their own power to accurately predict other people's prejudices.

There are, in fact, two issues here. Less importantly, can we reliably assemble a jury biased in favour of our side? More importantly, is it right for us to even try?

To deal with the less important point first, it seems to me that social scientists have done a bit of a con job by invading the criminal process in jury selection. The climate for this was probably prepared by the unparalleled success of the natural sciences in this century, making some people believe that so-called scientific methods can be transferred holus-bolus into other fields.

This type of "scientism" — the word used by some writers to describe the phenomenon — resulted in lawyers' accepting two kinds of recommendations from psychologists, sociologists, and assorted pollsters. The first kind was "scientific", all right, in the sense that it was based on abstract theories about how human beings function that would not have occurred to anyone with an ounce of common sense. It was pure, highfalutin science — and it was not only unreliable but generally wrong. Even if it had some statistical validity for big populations of ten thousand or more, as a basis for selecting a population of twelve, which is what a jury is, it was meaningless. Tossing a coin would have been better.

The second kind of recommendation was reliable enough — except it had nothing to do with science. It had to do only with common sense. It consisted of ideas that have been used by many good lawyers or policemen all along, minus the sociological mumbo-jumbo.

Let me give some examples. The "scientific" jury-selection process had its beginning in the anti-war years in the United States, and it was based on the idea that people are decisively influenced in all their views by their own backgrounds, social positions, and personal circumstances. (As an idea this was probably derived from the quasi-Marxist theory that people's opinions on everything are determined by their "class".) Coupled with this was another notion that, given this "class" position, a person's judgments would proceed from it in some straight, unbroken, predictable line.

If the first notion was merely exaggerated, the second one was wild. In this view a rich man ought to always acquit a rich man, a black ought to acquit another black, and so forth. Of course it was never put in such plain terms (because then it would have been immediately revealed for the nonsense that it was) but this was the essential theory.

So, at the famous Harrisburg Eight (Father Berrigan) trial in Pennsylvania, where Father Philip Berrigan was charged with conspiracy to raid draft boards and destroy records, the experts came up with what they thought was the perfect jury profile. The defence lawyers selected a jury on this basis. It included a woman who had four sons who were conscientious objectors on religious grounds. She seemed an ideal juror from the defence experts' point of view. So was a male juror for some similar reason.

But Father Berrigan was convicted of one count anyway. Since in the United States it is lawful for jurors to talk about their deliberations, we learned that two jurors had held out for conviction. One was the perfect woman juror. As for one male juror, he actually threatened to jump out of the courthouse window unless Father Berrigan was convicted.

In another famous case, President Nixon's one-time Attorney General, John Mitchell, and Maurice Stans were tried in New York City for having allegedly conspired to impede a Securities and

Exchange Commission investigation of the financier Robert Vesco in return for a $200,000 contribution to Nixon's re-election fund. Once again the social scientists came up with the "perfect" jury profile. It was to include, for some reason best known to them, only low-income jurors with no more than a high-school education. (They evidently figured that those were Nixon's crowd, revealing perhaps more about their own prejudices than about any juror's.) In any case, when Mitchell and Stans were acquitted it looked as if the social scientists had scored another triumph — until it turned out that at the beginning of the jury deliberations all the "ideal" jurors were voting for conviction, until one alternate juror — who got into the game only because a regular juror took ill — talked them into changing their minds. This key juror turned out to be the only one who *didn't* fit the scientists' profile: he was a highly educated man, thoroughly familiar with the world of finance.

When the social scientists did succeed in selecting a jury favourable to their side — such as the trial of the black radical Angela Davis, where the jury foreman actually gave a clenched-fist salute after the acquittal — it soon turned out that the reason wasn't the painstaking psychological analysis and interpretation of the prospective jurors' mannerisms, social background, or handwriting. The fact was that in California it was possible to go to prospective jurors' houses and look at their driveways, and in that state many people wear their politics on their bumpers. Since the "scientists" could read, they had no trouble deciphering the political views of some prospective jurors from their bumper stickers. This was how they came up with the clenched-fist lady, a fifty-one-year-old militant feminist named Mary Timothy, who signed the verdict "Ms. Timothy, Foreperson". Reading bumper stickers may have been a sound idea, but it hardly required a Ph.D. in psychology. It required some street-smarts and a private investigator with a high-school diploma.

In an example closer to home, there was much fanfare about social scientists' being involved in the jury-selection process at the trial of the abortionist Dr. Henry Morgentaler. Indeed, the doctor was acquitted in what could clearly be seen as a jury's defiance of the existing law on abortion. It was obviously a well-selected jury from the defence point of view, but how much *science* went into its selection? The key question was asking potential female jurors if they preferred calling themselves Miss, Mrs., or Ms. It was a very smart question, but even in charity one could not call it scientific. In fact it was the defence counsel, Morris Manning, who came up with it, not the social scientists.

A far more important point, however, is this: the courts in Canada frown on the type of "scientific" survey that aims at selecting jurors *for* their prejudices rather than simply weeding out prejudiced jurors. I think our courts are right, because there is a world of difference between the two practices. A defendant is obviously entitled to an unbiased hearing, but I'm not so sure that he is entitled to a hearing biased in his favour. As the great American lawyer Edward Bennett Williams put it: "All you're entitled to is a clean test tube." Also, should selecting *for* bias become an accepted practice, I'd be very anxious about the Crown's acquiring a similar right. Then jury trials would soon degenerate into senseless battles in which, instead of being concerned with the merits of a case, the Crown would be preoccupied with standing aside everyone who calls herself Ms. while the defence would go crazy challenging all the Misses and Missuses (or vice versa). This has little to do with law — and, incidentally, the defence would probably lose more often than win in this type of contest. The Crown has four peremptory challenges, plus forty-eight "stand asides", as opposed to the twelve peremptory challenges of the defence. In any case, replacing a quest for justice with a quest for prejudice would spell the end of the jury system.

For this reason I prefer the jury-selection process in Canada to the same process in the United States. Here, while lawyers can ask some common-sense questions of prospective jurors — if your client is accused of robbing a bank teller, it probably *is* wiser not to have too many bank tellers on the jury — sending a team of researchers to prospective jurors' houses to find out about their politics, dreams, hobbies, or investments (as one enterprising lawyer did once in British Columbia) would result in a wrathful judge's dismissing the entire jury panel, and probably holding the lawyer in contempt of court.

Though they are less costly and probably quite harmless, I don't think much of the quirky ways in which some lawyers select juries, either. This is the step-on-a-crack-break-your-mother's-back school of jury selection, and it makes no more sense than any except perhaps the "scientific" method. There are lawyers who will avoid left-handed jurors — I'm not kidding — or women in rape cases, or Central Europeans (or who will select *only* left-handed jurors, *only* women in rape cases, etc.). Once I took a psychiatrist along while we were choosing a jury because he claimed to be able to assess people just by looking at them — on the basis of his experience, he said, in doing mental-status examinations all the time. So a juror would come up who looked just fine and the psychiatrist would whisper: "Don't take him, he's a schizophrenic." After this happened the third time, I concluded, just from the probable distribution of schizophrenics in the population, that the only schizophrenic in the room was sitting next to me.

Judge David Humphrey — who used to be a great trial lawyer, one of the greatest in Canada — often argued that you could pick the first twelve people from a jury panel: it didn't matter. Although I do ask some basic questions of prospective jurors, I think that between those who are awed by the "scientific" process and Judge Humphrey, Humphrey is much closer to being right.

How does one select jurors? First of all, humbly. One selects them with the understanding that all human beings are feeling, thinking individuals whose behaviour cannot be predicted like a bunch of rats' just because they are in the same income or ethnic bracket. You try to eliminate plain, obvious prejudice in a given case. For the rest, you simply *look* at jurors. Not in the hope of diagnosing them as schizophrenics, but only to assess them on the basis of your general experience of human nature, as you do in all ordinary dealings in life.

I believe trials are won or lost primarily on the way the evidence unfolds in court. In other words, on their merits.

Secondarily, trials are won or lost on how well the opposing advocates do their homework. Jury (or venue) selection is certainly part of a lawyer's preparation for trial, but never the most important part. Remember, well-prepared lawyers are likely to win more *non-jury* trials as well as more jury trials. Though a judge sitting alone is every bit as "human" as an ordinary citizen, with just as many potential prejudices, you can't select him the way you select a juror.

Finally, like most human endeavours, trials can also be won or lost by luck. Professionals are generally loath to acknowledge the role that fortune plays in every campaign, be it marketing, legal, political, or military, but it is the truth nevertheless. Too many factors simply cannot be foreseen.

It happened during a very important and lengthy trial that I ran a motorbike into a wall and broke both my wrists. I had to address the jury some weeks later wearing casts up to my elbows. Naturally I apologized for looking like something out of Zombie's Return, explaining to the jurors what happened. They acquitted my client. I have no doubt that they reached their verdict primarily on the merits of the case, but there were, as I found out later, two motorcyclists on the jury. Bikers are said to be somewhat clannish. Finding in me a fellow biker might have "prejudiced" those jurors in my favour, yet who could have predicted — let alone done anything about — such a prejudice? Most lawyers, myself included, would consider running a motorcycle into a wall to impress a jury over and above the call of duty.

## NOTES

p.278, l.22: Social scientists might argue that they promise only a slight predictive edge, which in some cases could spell the difference between conviction and acquittal. The abstract notion isn't entirely baseless: if one could learn everything about a person — not just his background, but how he happens to relate to it, along with all other aspects of his personality, including his honesty, intellect, friendships, ambitions, etc. — one might indeed get a slight predictive edge about how he is likely to view a given issue. But no potential juror can be studied in such depth. In practice, "scientific" jury selection boils down to picking out a few gross features, and then acting on them as if they were the whole story. This is not only unhelpful, but generally misleading.

p.282, l.13: The trial was the "Hamilton Dredging" case, in which a number of businessmen were charged with conspiring to fix prices in connection with a tender to dredge Hamilton harbour, among others. It was an extremely complex proceeding, involving many defendants, and it lasted fourteen months. My client, Gérard Filion, a Quebec businessman and the former publisher and editor of *Le Devoir*, was acquitted, as were several other distinguished businessmen.

# 15. *Trial of Conscience*

Bear with me for a minute. This is a complex question but it is worth looking at in some detail. It has occupied many lawyers and law students for a long time. I do not necessarily have the answers, but I have some submissions.

I firmly believe that no defendant should have to pass a trial of conscience by his own lawyer in addition to his trial in court. One trial for one accusation is enough. I have no time for any legal practitioner who sets any "limits" (other than those set by his own skills) on the type of case that he will defend. You may decline a case involving, say, a ship lost at sea because you don't know enough about admiralty law. You may not be able to fit some cases into your court-calendar. You can certainly decide not to engage in the practice of criminal litigation at all. But a criminal lawyer who refuses to act for an alleged "organized" criminal, a corporate accused, a businessman, a Nazi, a communist, or for someone accused of crimes against women, children, or the environment — there are such lawyers — is like a medical doctor who refuses, as a matter of principle, to treat someone suffering from syphilis or AIDS.

I touched on this subject in earlier chapters. I'm raising it again here in order to take it one step further.

When the question is discussed in these terms, some people (even if they agree that no lawyer should refuse anyone) conclude from it that a good lawyer is a kind of legal automaton. Either he is so lofty as to be almost inhuman or, on the contrary, he not only lacks "conscience" in the everyday sense of the word, but is devoid of any social, political, or moral opinions. He's just a hired gun.

But this does not follow at all. To say that a lawyer must defend anybody is not to say that he must defend anybody on any basis. To say that an accused person, no matter what he is accused of, is entitled to his choice of defender is not to say that he is also entitled to his choice of defence. That is always his counsel's choice. In addition to his professional judgment — or limits set by law and legal ethics — it may well involve his counsel's conscience, in my opinion.

I am a Jew. During the Second World War the entire European branch of my family was murdered by the Nazis. My personal feelings about Nazism need not be enlarged upon. Knowing this, some people have asked me: "Would you have defended Zundel?" My answer is, "Yes."

I would have been ready to defend Canada's notorious neo-Nazi pamphleteer Ernst Zundel who, among other things, claimed in his publications that the Holocaust did not happen. (I did, in fact, appear on behalf of the Canadian Civil Liberties Association to seek intervenor status to support some aspects of Zundel's appeal before the Ontario Court of Appeal.) Had Zundel wanted to retain me, I would have acted for him at his original trial on the basis of a number of defences that were, in my opinion, available to him in law.

But I would not have acted for Zundel on the basis that he may be *right*. I would not have acted for him on the basis that an untruth may be the truth. Unlike the counsel he did retain, a lawyer named Douglas Christie, I would not have acted for him on the basis that there may be a Judeo-Bolshevik-plutocratic conspiracy in the world, or that the Holocaust might not have happened. That position may have been central to Zundel's hate propaganda, but it was by no means his best legal defence. I would have defended Zundel, but not by offering him a platform for his views. Christie did — which, presumably, is why Zundel retained Christie.

A lawyer like me, as I have pointed out before, only defends clients. Clients, and not crimes (or hate or lies). Lawyers like me go to court for one reason only, and that is to get the best result for a client. Ideally, an acquittal.

I do not look at the courtroom as a theatre for the display of ideas, not to mention an arena for indoctrination into a set of opinions. I'm not even sure that a court is a proper instrument for social change. I tend much more to the view of the eminent American jurist Oliver Wendell Holmes, who said: "While there is still doubt, while opposite convictions still keep a battlefront against each other, the time for law has not come." Or, as the great American advocate Clarence Darrow once said to a jury: "I shall not argue to you whether the defendants' ideas are right or wrong. I am not here to defend their opinions. I am here to defend their right to express their opinions."

Many lawyers share this credo. It's not only that we don't defend crimes, hate, or lies: on the whole we prefer not to defend causes. We defend clients.

So-called activist lawyers tend to make different distinctions. They may refuse to defend some people on principle, but when they accept them as clients they are ready to defend their opinions and sometimes even their crimes. They believe in making common cause with their clients, for better or for worse.

I always disapprove of defending crimes, and I generally find making common cause with clients unnecessary. I can't flatly say that I disapprove of making common cause with clients, because that obviously depends on the cause: one day I might make common cause with a client myself.

On that day, however, I will have to be very careful how I choose. On that day, in addition to my conscience as a lawyer, I will have to consult my moral, political, and social conscience.

A client need not pass a lawyer's trial of conscience before the lawyer will *defend* him, but he may well have to pass a lawyer's trial of conscience before the lawyer will make common cause with him. At least he has to pass the lawyer's test of political or social opinion. A client is entitled to a legal defence, but he is not entitled to his lawyer's turning a court into a guerilla theatre for his benefit. A lawyer may choose to do so, or even join his client on the stage, but lawyers who make common cause with their clients may then be legitimately judged by their clients' crimes. At any rate, they *can* be legitimately judged by their clients' philosophy.

As a lawyer, it is my duty to act for an accused political terrorist. It is not my duty to act for political terrorism. If I do so, it will be my choice. Like all choices, it may have consequences for me. It may diminish me in the eyes of those people who abhor political terror.

That's why, when law students ask me: "Would you ever refuse to defend someone on principle?" I can answer: "Never. But I may refuse, on principle, to advance certain arguments on his behalf." If a law student were to ask me the next, harder question: "But what if those very arguments that are against your principles were your client's best defence in law?" my answer would be this: "In any legal system in which my client's best defence would consist of arguments I could not advance on his behalf in good conscience, I could not practise as a lawyer." Luckily, the question rarely if ever arises in our system at present because the best *legal* defence of my clients almost invariably consists of arguments I can advance on their behalf in good conscience.

Just think about it: suggesting that the Holocaust didn't happen, or that illicit drugs are beneficial, or that people should be entitled to kidnap or blow up their political opponents, are not good legal defences in Canada. They are not likely to lead to an acquittal by a jury. The fact is that they're pretty hopeless defences in law, even though they have all been advanced by one "activist" lawyer or another.

What I would suggest to law students is this: If a client comes to a lawyer wishing to plead not guilty, the lawyer can't refuse to act for him if, on the facts, and in the lawyer's best professional opinion, it appears that the client has at least one of the following defences available to him:

1) that he did not commit the act that would make out the offence; or

2) that the act, whether or not he committed it, does not amount to the crime with which he is charged; or

3) that the law which defines the act as a crime is itself unconstitutional or is open to challenge on any other legal ground; or

4) that the evidence on which the state relies to prove the act is inadmissible or insufficient, thereby raising a reasonable doubt.

However, a lawyer need not act for a client who wishes to plead not guilty and who, in the lawyer's best professional opinion, has none of these defences available to him or does not wish to rely on them. He need not act for a client who desires to plead not guilty with the express purpose of raising political, philosophical, moral, or social grounds for his defence, unless the lawyer feels justified in his own conscience in advancing such grounds on his client's behalf.

In short, he need not act for a client who is looking for a stage rather than a courtroom — unless he likes his client's play and is willing to accept a role in it. In that case, of course, he will also have to learn to live with the reviews the next day.

A lawyer need not defend a cause or an opinion against his conscience. He need not carry a brief in a higher court or act as an intervenor for any socio-political idea or procedural proposition in which he does not believe. (Why? some people might ask. Isn't an intervening organization also a client? My answer is yes, but not an *accused* client. Not a client in jeopardy or facing opprobrium. An association that wishes to present a brief on behalf of some cause or idea wants to be an engine of social change or influence. While this is a perfectly legitimate desire, it obliges a lawyer to nothing. He can drive the engine if he chooses, or refuse to drive it if he prefers.)

On the other hand, I can't think of any reason for a lawyer to refuse a client who wishes to plead *guilty*. There is no human being for whom nothing could be said in a sentencing submission, and it is the defence lawyer's duty to focus on mitigating factors in any client's case.

Finally, and speaking purely personally, if that hypothetical law student asking tough questions ever took it right to the edge, to that highly unusual case in which a client's best legal defence was one that I could not advance without offending my conscience, I hope that I would have the strength to choose my client's best defence. I am a lawyer; my client *is* my conscience.

However, I can't pretend that I would have this strength in some cases. For instance, if Zundel's best defence were — as, I repeat, it is not — to try to prove that the Holocaust didn't happen, I could not cross-examine a survivor of a Nazi camp on whether or not he saw smoke coming out of the crematoria chimneys. I could not do it and I would not do it — but as a lawyer I would be wrong not to do it. I confess my inability because it is a fact, but not with pride. I regard it as a human weakness that prevents me from meeting the test of an ideal I believe to be right.

Does this mean that the ideal is only a myth? I don't think so. No more than any other human ideal which, in some extreme situation, an individual may not be able to meet. No one can honestly say what he will do if his ideals are put to some final, cataclysmic test, but it does not follow that there are no ideals or that no ideals have any validity. All standards could be abandoned on the basis that they cannot invariably be met. Would it be wise to abandon (or alter) all standards on this basis? My problem with the philosophy of legal activism is that it distrusts general standards, and looks to the triumph of preferred causes rather than to the triumph of justice as its ultimate aim.

In practice I've never had to face such dilemmas. For example, I've never had the slightest problem defending clients whom other people have regarded as "professional" or "organized" criminals. I've defended such clients (among many other things) on drug-related charges of various kinds. I might have had a big problem, though, had I ever been called upon to defend the *idea* of, say, trafficking in illicit drugs.

I not only know that the selling of LSD or marijuana or heroin is illegal, but I also happen to believe that it is wrong. Some people may have different views about this (certainly with regard to so-called "soft" drugs) and they are entitled to them, but they are not my views. I would not act for a drug-dealer who wished to be defended on the basis that "turning on" the world was a beneficial activity.

I would defend him, though, on the basis that in a given instance he did not sell, make, or import illicit drugs, or that the Crown could not prove that he did so beyond a reasonable doubt.

The same is true for other crimes. For instance, in a rather well-known trial in Vancouver, British Columbia, I defended Rocco ("Remo") Commisso and his brother Cosimo Commisso on charges related to the possession of counterfeit money. Much of the Crown's evidence consisted of wiretap tapes in which the defendants were discussing the selling and transportation of legitimate merchandise, such as ceramics or "American greens" — *ceramica* or *verdi americana* in Italian. The prosecutor contended, however, that the Commisso brothers were not talking about decorative figurines or Boston lettuce: they were talking about counterfeit American dollars.

That was, of course, purely the Crown's interpretation of those words: the everyday meaning of the words in no way supported it. On the same basis the prosecutor could have claimed that whenever the Commisso brothers said "good morning" on the telephone they really meant "let's kill so-and-so", and then charged them with conspiracy to commit murder. I thought that letting jurors make up their own minds about certain words was one thing, but putting expert witnesses on the stand to swear that *ceramica* "meant" counterfeit money was something different. It gave me an opportunity to tell one of my favourite stories of Second World War espionage to the jury.

Apparently at one point during the war Hitler took it into his head that it would be a good idea to assassinate the Allied leaders,

Churchill, Roosevelt, and Stalin, in one single coup. Obviously the three men had to be together in one place for this, so Hitler gave orders to his intelligence services to be on the lookout for the location of the next Allied summit meeting which all three leaders could be expected to attend.

The Germans were able to intercept Allied communications to a certain extent, and they were also able to break some of the Allied codes. However, someone in British intelligence hit upon the bright idea of sending all coded traffic in Portuguese. This meant that once the Germans had decoded a message, they had the additional task of translating the text from Portuguese into German. While this may have struck the German cipher analysts as bizarre, it seemed to make little difference: had the Allies used English or French they would have had to translate it into German anyway.

One day German intelligence reported to Hitler with great excitement that they had now discovered the location of the next Allied summit conference. Accordingly, a team of top-notch Nazi assassins was immediately dispatched to — Washington, D.C. Their orders were to wait for the three Allied leaders to turn up together at the White House.

Why the White House? Because the German analysts, having deciphered the Allied code, dutifully continued to translate the Portuguese text into German, including the word "Casablanca". *Casa blanca*, of course, translated all the way into German, did not mean a town in North Africa any more but "white house". So, while the assassins were being dropped off by German subs in the Gulf of St. Lawrence, the Allied leaders were on their way to their famous conference in Casablanca, Morocco.

The Vancouver jury may have liked the story, and in any case they acquitted Remo Commisso. (Cosimo, against whom the Crown had some circumstantial evidence in support of the wiretaps, was convicted.)

The case, incidentally, was a perfect illustration of how much today's reliance on wiretaps can dull the normal investigative techniques of the police. Acting on an undercover agent's tip, detectives followed a suspected courier from Vancouver to Toronto. Then, when he flew back to Vancouver carrying some counterfeit bills in a bag, they followed him back to Vancouver, where they arrested him. However, they did not bother keeping him under surveillance in

Toronto itself, figuring that the wiretaps would reveal anyway who in Toronto gave the man the counterfeit money. More precisely, since the police had already made up their minds "who" that person was going to be, they probably felt: why waste shoe leather? The wiretaps alone would be enough proof. This, of course, did not even take into account the possibility that the police's idea of who the culprit was might be mistaken. As it turned out, the wiretaps could prove nothing beyond a reasonable doubt.

"Okay, pigs, now listen and listen good. There is a bomb in the Army Math Research Center, the university, set to go off in five minutes. Clear the building. Get everyone out. Warn the hospital. This is no bullshit, man."

These were the words with which a caller warned the police in Madison, Wisconsin, on August 24, 1970, around 1:30 a.m., a few minutes before an explosion ripped through a University of Wisconsin building known as Sterling Hall. The blast killed Dr. Robert Fassnacht, a scientist, who was working late in his laboratory. One of the suspects, who allegedly placed the mixture of ammonium nitrate and fuel oil which exploded with the force of some 3400 sticks of dynamite on a ramp leading inside the building, later escaped to Canada. He was an anti-war activist by the name of Karleton Armstrong.

In 1972, after a court in Canada ruled that Armstrong should be extradited to the United States to face trial for murder, I became one of the lawyers involved with his appeal.

Like many young people of my generation, I had a dim view of the war in Vietnam. Politically, I had much sympathy for those who opposed the United States' military involvement in Southeast Asia on both moral and practical grounds. Had I been an American voter, there is little doubt that my vote would have gone to those candidates who, like Eugene McCarthy or George McGovern, represented the anti-war spirit in mainstream American politics.

However, then as today, I thought little of people who put bombs into buildings and blew up scientists working late in their laboratories on "army math" research or on anything else. This was independent of whether the bombers did so for political or any other motives, and of whether I had some sympathy for their politics or not. I considered political bombers in democratic countries — countries that deny no group of people the opportunity to shape their society through free speech, free association, and an open electoral process — nothing but terrorists. If they killed anyone in the process, intentionally or recklessly, I considered them murderers.

At the same time murderers, alleged or convicted, were hardly news to me. As a citizen I believed that they were entitled to a fair trial and to every safeguard available to them in law, and as a criminal lawyer I was ready to give effect to this belief by acting for them in court.

So, when I agreed to serve on Karleton Armstrong's defence team, my sympathy for the anti-war movement had as little to do with my decision to act for him as my abhorrence of terrorism would have had to make me decide otherwise. I would have acted for Armstrong just as readily had he *favoured* the war in Vietnam, but in neither case would I have considered the act of blowing up a scientist at the University of Wisconsin an act of legitimate political protest.

This was not the position of some "activist" lawyers on the Karleton Armstrong defence team. They were ready to oppose his extradition to the United States essentially on the basis that the act of which Armstrong was accused made him a "political" rather than a criminal fugitive, and thus not subject to extradition. While I had no problem whatever acting for Armstrong, I had a problem with this particular defence.

Two problems, in fact. One, that nobody would buy it. Two, that nobody should. I thought that it was a ludicrous defence in law, and that the courts would ultimately reject it as it deserved to be rejected.

The State of Wisconsin did not propose to extradite Armstrong on the allegation that Armstrong opposed the war in Vietnam, but on the allegation that Armstrong killed a human being. True, someone who allegedly kills a human being in the course of an insurrection or a civil war might possibly come under the "political character" exception of the Extradition Act, but I thought it inconceivable that a court in Canada would hold that anything like a state of civil war existed in the United States in 1970. It simply didn't: people opposed the war in Vietnam openly and publicly, without endorsing any violent action against the central government. Millions of Americans opposed the war, but not their own democratic institutions.

They did not oppose scientific research for national defence. Only a handful of extremists did that. Our courts would hardly issue an invitation to people to please commit the most hair-raising acts anywhere in the world, then come to Canada and escape the consequences, provided that they committed their acts in the belief that they might further their political aims, whatever they might be.

At the same time I believed that Armstrong, who by no means conceded his connection with the Wisconsin bombing, ought to be entitled to cross-examine the American authorities who were accusing him of murder. The right to cross-examine one's accusers is fundamental to our law. Even though the Extradition Act has no specific provisions for it, I felt that there was a chance that the Federal Court might give effect to this vital safeguard under the "Diefenbaker" Bill of Rights.

In 1972 any foreign country with which Canada had an extradition treaty could hire a Canadian lawyer and give him a bunch of affidavits setting out some allegations against a resident or citizen of Canada. If a court found that the material alleged in those documents made out a *prima facie* case against the defendant — and if the alleged offence was covered by the extradition treaty — a judge could order the fugitive to be surrendered to the requesting country to be tried there according to its laws. There were no provisions for the accused to cross-examine the witnesses making the allegations against him.

I was prepared to argue, then or today, in Armstrong's case or in any other, that this is wrong. It's easy to allege anything and write it down on a piece of paper. If an accused can't test it through cross-examination, he is deprived of a chance to prepare for his defence. The Canadian court is also deprived of a chance to see if, on the face of it, the accusers can make out a case against the accused. In effect, while a Canadian court would not let a Canadian Crown bring someone to trial if he couldn't make out a preliminary case against him, our courts must allow a foreign prosecutor to do so.

This was a point I was not only prepared to argue, but was looking forward to arguing, on behalf of the alleged bomber of Sterling Hall. I would have been ready to argue it on behalf of someone accused of being the Devil. On the other hand, I was more than happy to let my activist colleagues do the arguing that Armstrong was a "political" fugitive. (Would I have argued the point if it had been the only defence available to our client in law? Yes. I would have had no other choice. But, if I had no other defence, I would have reluctantly argued it at the extradition hearing of a member of the John Birch Society as well. I rather suspect my left-wing colleagues wouldn't have.)

In fairness to my confrères, their arguments were capable of being made under the wording of the Extradition Act, and the Federal Court gave them serious consideration. In the end Judges Thurlow, Cameron, and Sweet rejected their arguments — but they also rejected mine on the issue of cross-examination. The Supreme Court of Canada refused our request for leave to appeal the Federal Court's decision, and soon afterwards Karleton Armstrong was extradited to the United States, where he ultimately pleaded guilty.

The argument I lost under the Bill of Rights was raised eleven years later, in 1983, by my brother, Brian, acting for a Canadian woman named Cathy Smith, who was facing a murder charge in California in connection with the drug-overdose death of the comedian John Belushi. Brian raised the issue of the right to cross-examination under our new Charter of Rights and Freedoms in the Supreme Court of Canada — and he lost. Evidently our new constitution changed nothing in this regard: the law of 1972 was still the law in 1983, as it is in 1987. However, I predict that the issue will not go away. Denying accused people the right to test the accusations against them is dangerous and wrong, and it is not, in my view, a justifiable precedence of utility and policy over fundamental justice. I'm confident that our courts will examine the matter again.

In 1974, as (unpaid) counsel to the Canadian Civil Liberties Association, I carried an intervenor's brief in the matter of Dr. Henry Morgentaler before the Supreme Court of Canada. Dr. Morgentaler had been acquitted on abortion charges by a Quebec jury, but the Quebec Court of Appeal overturned the jury's verdict and substituted a conviction.

This was an anomaly of Canadian law at the time, and it was very wrong. A higher court in the United States, far from substituting a finding of guilt for a jury's acquittal, could not even send the case back for a new trial. The prosecution simply could not appeal an acquittal by a jury, period. The Americans have held that ordering a new trial after an acquittal would constitute double jeopardy for an accused.

Whether or not American law is carrying things too far, there was no reason why appellate judges in Canada shouldn't just order a new trial if they found legal errors in a proceeding or, on the evidence, regarded the jury's verdict as unreasonable. For a group of judges to substitute a finding of guilt for innocence — without even the benefit of looking at the witnesses or listening to their evidence in court — was in many people's view an arrogant, patronizing, and fundamental negation of the jury system. Claude Sheppard, acting for Dr. Morgentaler, carried the argument before the Supreme Court of Canada on this issue — and I thought that it was the very point on which the Civil Liberties Association ought to have intervened in support of Dr. Morgentaler's appeal. It was an excellent civil-liberties issue. Claude Sheppard, a first-rate advocate, might not have fared better even with our intervention, but in fact the appeal was lost. (A short time later, however, Parliament wisely amended the Criminal Code. No appeal court can substitute a finding of guilt for a jury acquittal in Canada any more.)

The issue on which we did choose to intervene illuminates a different point. I argued it in 1974, but I do not think that I would argue it today. My heart would not be in the argument at all.

My heart? Yes. As I have outlined earlier, I think when it comes to so-called *amicus curiae* or "friend of the court" briefs, a lawyer's conscience, and even his social or political opinion, can play a very legitimate role.

A defence lawyer is not a whore for defending every accused any more than a doctor is a whore for treating every patient. It is his duty to do so. However, no lawyer is obliged to argue an abstract political, social, or jurisprudential issue before the court unless he believes in it. I would never condemn a lawyer who chooses to take any brief on any side of any issue — it's his business — but I would fully sympathize with one who chooses not to do so. This *is* a matter for a lawyer's personal conscience.

The reason I agreed to carry the Canadian Civil Liberties Association's brief on behalf of Dr. Morgentaler's appeal was because at the time I believed that a woman's decision to procure an abortion for herself should be entirely her choice. This was not something I would have had to believe to support Claude Sheppard's argument that higher courts should not substitute convictions for jury acquittals: I could have supported that argument in any case. To argue, however, as the Civil Liberties Association's brief required me to do, that the law was unfair because of unequal access to abortion clinics, I had to base my argument at least implicitly on the assumption that nothing must interfere with a woman's choice in the matter, and that abortion was simply a "civil liberty". (Clearly, we were not arguing for fairness itself. We were not asking the court either to strike down the law and permit abortion on demand or, in the alternative, to toughen the law and permit no abortions at all because some women found it easier to get to therapeutic-abortion clinics than others. While this would have been an argument of mindless egalitarianism, at least it would have been more honest. It would have made fairness the central issue, rather than our support for abortion on demand under the guise of fairness.)

One incident at the appeal stands out in my mind; I mention it because it showed two lawyers at their best at a critical moment. It happened in a back room just before the hearing was to begin, and it was never reported in the press. I'm recounting it here according to my best recollection.

Some years earlier, Mr. Justice de Grandpré, one of the Supreme Court justices on the Morgentaler appeal, had been the president of the Canadian Bar Association. At that time he had been involved in a series of discussions on the abortion question. In the context of these discussions he allegedly made some remark to the effect that if he were given a rope, he'd hang Morgentaler himself. On the very morning of the appeal, just before the proceedings were to begin, Claude Sheppard raised the issue before Chief Justice Bora Laskin. Possibly he raised it at that late date because he had just then found out about it.

It was a moment of extreme tension; I don't think I've witnessed a moment as tense in a judge's chambers before or since. The late Chief Justice was silent for a few moments, then very calmly and politely said that judges could not be held accountable for what they said about issues before their appointment to the bench or in their role as law professors; that he himself couldn't sit as a judge on constitutional issues, and perhaps no constitutional scholar could, if that were the case. Then he suggested that we begin the hearing, with Mr. Justice de Grandpré sitting on the court, of course.

I was very impressed with both men. With Sheppard, because it took a lot of guts to raise the issue, especially at such a late moment, and with the Chief Justice because, without the benefit of prior notice, he handled a question relating to the integrity of his court in such a thoughtful and calm manner. The problem itself seemed to be quite complex to me; on the whole I think I agreed with Chief Justice Laskin. In the course of a legal career that must precede the elevation of any judge to the Supreme Court he would have to have been involved with many issues, taken many different sides, and expressed many opinions. If that precluded any judge's dealing with matters before the court in a fair manner, probably only a complete cipher could ever be appointed as a judge.

I met Dr. Morgentaler at the appeal, and I liked him very much. I found him a charming, decent, sensitive man with an absolutely honest belief in the cause for which he crusaded, and still does, at considerable risk and inconvenience to himself. I admired him for it then, and I admire him today — only, while in 1974 I thought that I believed in his cause, today I'm sure that I don't believe in it.

Of course a woman has a right to control her own body. That is not in dispute. The law intervenes only when she wants to have control over someone else's body, namely that of the embryo or the fetus. Even then the law acknowledges the primacy of the woman's interest, only asking to be satisfied that there is some physical or mental reason for her decision. It doesn't even have to be a compelling reason; it doesn't have to meet any objective test of a "reasonable woman"; it is just a subjective test pertaining to her, individually. The test simply requires her decision to go beyond a mere whim as a gesture to the sanctity of life. I now believe that abolishing this gesture would be dangerous. An embryo or a fetus is obviously a "life", because if we do nothing to it, it will go on living. We have to do something to it to stop it. It is a "human" life, since on emergence from the womb human embryos don't turn into cats. Since we must terminate it by taking some positive action, I think society has the same right to define the circumstances under which such positive action is justified as it has to define how any other form of human life may be terminated. We do permit killing under a variety of circumstances, but it is not unreasonable for society to define the circumstances under which it is permitted.

I find it ironic that some highly liberal people would abolish capital punishment for all crimes, except for the crime of inconveniencing a woman. That, they feel, should be a personal choice of the inconvenienced party.

I'm not urging my views concerning abortion on anybody, so I will say no more about the subject. I raised it simply to illustrate the area in which a lawyer can, in my opinion, make a legitimate decision of conscience. As a lawyer, I would unhesitatingly act for an abortionist on the basis of any number of defences that may be available to him in law, and I would present an intervenor's brief in support of his appeal on a whole variety of legal issues; I would simply not support the idea of abortion on demand. In the same way, though I am a firm opponent of capital punishment, I would act for anybody who, being a supporter of the death penalty, shot an accused or convicted murderer. I would defend such a client — but I would not present a brief on behalf of the Association of Police Chiefs (in the unlikely event that they ever asked me) to re-introduce capital punishment in Canada.

That's where I'd draw the line — which I believe lawyers are as entitled to do as anyone. They just have to make sure that they are, as lawyers, on the right side of the line that they have drawn.


NOTES

p.284, l.4: It was one of my relatives, or so my family believes (he spelled his name Grynszpan), who shot on November 7, 1938, Ernst von Rath, the third secretary of the German embassy in Paris. This became the pretext for the infamous "Crystal Night" in Germany, when Nazi mobs went on the rampage destroying thousands of Jewish homes and businesses as well as killing and injuring many Jews.

p.284, l.15: In the opinion, also, of the Supreme Court of Canada. As this is being written, Canada's highest court has refused to hear the Crown's appeal from a ruling by the Ontario Court of Appeal ordering a new trial for Zundel.

p.284, l.36: Oliver Wendell Holmes, "Law and the Court", Speeches (Little, Brown and Company, 1934).

p.288, l.19: See also Chapter 6, "Everybody Plays Hardball", for a more detailed discussion of the Commisso brothers.

p.289, l.28: The story is recounted in *Hitler's Plot to Kill the Big Three* by Laslo Havas (Cambridge, Mass.: Cowles, 1969).

p.293, l.20: Some legal scholars may argue that by having raised the matter too early under the "Diefenbaker" Bill of Rights, I created a precedent, a legal peg, on which the Supreme Court of Canada could hang its hat later and refuse to hear Brian's appeal. I find this view exaggerated. Legal precedents do influence the courts in our system, and rightly so, but the Supreme Court of Canada would not have been inhibited in any way from giving effect to the right to cross-examine under the Charter, if it so desired, only because this right was given no effect in extradition cases under our old Bill of Rights.

# INTERLUDE: THE CRUSADER

*Greenspan has always been an opponent of the death penalty. When, in the spring of 1987, the public debate on capital punishment erupted in Canada once again — the government having decided to put the matter to a free vote in Parliament — Greenspan put his legal practice on the back burner and went on the road. No politician running for office could have put more energy into his campaign for election than Eddie did into his personal crusade of saving the country from what he saw as a barbaric practice, needless and indefensible in civilized times and places.*

*The death penalty is, of course, a highly emotional issue. While both opponents and proponents of capital punishment seek to support their positions with rational arguments, their views are usually influenced by pre-rational impulses and are received by others in a sub-rational frame of mind. One could say (though Greenspan would adamantly disagree with this) that crusading either for or against the death penalty means preaching to the converted. No doubt some people keep a genuinely open mind on the subject, but most listen to the debaters in a state of righteous rigidity.*

*For this reason it is exceedingly difficult to gauge whether one's arguments are having an effect or not. Greenspan felt frustrated. After his countless radio and television debates, public appearances, and nearly two months spent on the road discussing the question from one end of the country to the other, he couldn't really tell whether he was "getting through" to the big jury of his peers in Canada or not. Letters appeared in the press regularly, of course, supporting or opposing his position, and his own stack of mail was piling up in the office. His correspondents were heaping praise or abuse on him, but those who liked what he was saying may have been people who simply considered their own initial stance on the subject reaffirmed by Greenspan's arguments. It was hard to tell.*

*Finally Greenspan received a letter that left him in no doubt about the question. The writer plainly stated that he had firmly supported capital punishment until the current debate. Now, said the writer, he had become an opponent of the death penalty. Greenspan's arguments had changed at least one man's mind.*

*Delighted with the contents of the letter, Eddie looked at the signature. Then he looked again, because he couldn't believe his eyes. He turned the letter over and checked the envelope to make sure that it wasn't a practical joke.*

*It wasn't a joke. His correspondent was Clifford Olson.*

---

NOTE

p.300, l.9: Identifying Clifford Olson is probably unnecessary for the contemporary Canadian reader. Others, however, may not be aware that Olson is possibly the most despised multiple murderer in this country's history. After his capture in the mid-seventies he received a highly controversial payment of $100,000 from the government in exchange for leading the authorities to the graves in which the bodies of his eleven young victims were buried. To a significant extent, it was his crimes that precipitated the capital-punishment debate in 1987.

However, Olson wasn't the only person to change his mind about the death penalty. Judging by the results of a public-opinion poll (published in May 1987) the anti-capital-punishment crusade, for which Greenspan was probably one of the most visible spokesmen, did have an effect on the public's perception of the issues. Before the debate in the spring of 1987, seventy-three per cent of all Canadians favoured the re-introduction of capital punishment; two months later sixty-one per cent did, according to the poll. On June 30, 1987, Parliament voted against the reinstatement of the death penalty. This result seems to support Greenspan's contention that offering rational arguments against the death penalty has an influence beyond preaching to the converted.

# PART SEVEN

# IT IS GOOD LAW

# 16. Murder or Nothing

Greenspan sighed, and put the photograph on the low coffee table in his office. He rose from the couch and walked back to his desk, then sat in his chair and leaned back as far as he could, with his hands clasped behind his head. It was a characteristic pose his visitor knew well.

"This is going to be very, very difficult," Greenspan said.

The visitor picked up the photograph. It showed the interior of a small, shabby variety store. There was a cash register on the counter, with a hand-lettered sign saying in ever smaller letters, as an inexpert hand appeared to be running out of space: SORRY NO personal cheQues. Thank. you. The face of the counter itself was dominated by a large poster showing a smiling woman with her hand on the shoulder of a young boy, sipping some drink through a straw. The sign on the poster read: "Caffeine. Your children don't need it any more than you do." The floor of the shop seemed wet, as though people had had to tramp through a lot of snow to get inside, where the slush would melt off their boots, leaving large puddles. Opposite the counter there was a medium-sized freezer. Next to the counter, and at a ninety-degree angle to it, there was a candy rack. The top four shelves were filled with Mars, Aero, Virginia, and Oh Henry! chocolate bars. On the bottom shelf there seemed to be nothing but empty boxes marked Virginia Donuts and General Bakeries Limited.

Flush with the candy rack, but again at a ninety-degree angle, there was a magazine display. It was facing the freezer, leaving some walking space in between. A soggy mat covered the wet floor in that spot, and another sign on the wooden post above the magazines read: For Rent Trailer Space, giving a phone number.

"Where is this place?" asked Greenspan's visitor.

"Orillia, Ontario," the lawyer replied. "It's called 'Gold Star Food Market'. It's a kind of convenience store for a place named the Gold Star Trailer Camp."

"So, who is charged?"

"The proprietor," said Greenspan. "A little Italian guy. I call him 'little' because he is, in fact, very short. He's married; I think he has two children. His name's Antonio Scopelliti."

"Why do you say it's a very difficult case?" the visitor asked.

Greenspan snorted, and threw up his hands. "Have you looked at that picture?" he asked. "That's the picture the jury is going to see."

Greenspan's friend picked up the photograph again. He had, of course, seen the two bodies lying on the wet floor, but now he looked more closely.

The body in the foreground was curled up on its side, facing the freezer and almost touching it. It was the body of a young man, dressed in blue jeans, brown winter boots, and what looked like a kind of padded plastic windbreaker or ski jacket. He wore his watch face down on his left wrist, showing off a racy imitation-leather strap. His features were nearly covered by the peak of a baseball-type cap that must have slid over his face as he fell. Only half of the triangular sign on the cap was visible. It read Young Pioneers of America.

The other young man was lying on his back, more or less, in the walking space between the freezer and the magazine rack. The first man appeared to be clean-shaven, but the second one had a short beard. There was a magazine in his outstretched left hand, showing the picture of a nearly nude woman under the title Curious. He was wearing a green parka, a zippered jacket over a padded vest, and construction boots. He had a metal bracelet on his right wrist. He must have suffered a facial or a head wound, because his moustache and one side of his beard were matted with blood.

"Hmm," said the visitor, putting down the picture. He paused for a moment to distance himself from what he had seen. "Let me guess," he said finally. "Two people tried to hold up a store, and the owner shot them. The police turned around and charged him with murder. I know a murder charge is always difficult, but when you say 'difficult' about this one, do you mean — as opposed to what? Other murder charges?"

"Yes," said Greenspan.

"Is it a difficulty one should be able to see just by looking at this photograph?" asked the visitor. "I'm not sure if I can."

"Look again," said Greenspan, grimly.

"Well . . ." The visitor hesitated. "The victims look pretty young . . ."

"Young?" Greenspan said. "Young? Let me tell you something about these two boys that my client shot. They were both seventeen years old."

*1* I could not see how it was possible for anybody not to be troubled by that photograph — I mean, more troubled than by photographs of most other homicides. I was more troubled, and by February 1979 I had seen many, many pictures of violent death. Those two young men lying on the floor of the dilapidated small-town supermarket were only boys: a couple of ordinary high-school boys, such as you might see walking out of any schoolyard in Canada. True, they were not *small* boys; one could see that they had been pretty muscular, well-built youngsters — rather good-looking youngsters, in fact — but they were still only kids. I found looking at them lying in a store like that, gunned down, profoundly disturbing.

So, I felt sure, would any jury.

Nor was this a case where I could say to the jurors: "Yes, this is terrible — but my client had nothing to do with it. It was somebody else who caused these deaths."

No. It was Antonio Scopelliti who shot these two boys on January 22, 1979, around 9:55 p.m. By about 9:59 p.m. he had told his brother-in-law what he had done. Within another five minutes or so he had also told the police officers who had arrived at the scene. Whatever else may have been in doubt about the case, this much was certain from the beginning.

The facts that emerged were as follows:

January 22, 1979, was a Monday. It was no colder and snowier than most January days are in Orillia, which meant that it was cold and snowy enough. A young man named Michael McRae, just two months shy of his eighteenth birthday and still living at his parents' home, got up as usual at 5:30 in the morning to get to his regular job at a place called Dimension Enterprises by 7 a.m. He was a strapping youth: six feet tall, weighing 190 pounds. Michael worked all day, then came home to have supper with his family. At 6 p.m. he received a phone call from a boy of about the same age named David Sutton. McRae and Sutton were close friends, and David would call Michael right after work almost every night.

Sutton was also a strapping young man; he, too, was six feet tall and weighed 190 pounds. His day had been different from McRae's, though. Sutton did not have a job. Though he borrowed his parents' truck around 11:30 a.m. saying that he was going to the Manpower office to check on job prospects, what he did was to go to the house of a friend named Shawn Langley where the two of them drank a case of beer. The boys had about twelve bottles of beer each, after which (as Langley was to put it in court later) they were "fairly drunk but not that impaired". In this condition Sutton drove his parents' truck back home at around 4:30 p.m., so that his mother could take the family vehicle and pick up Sutton's father from work.

By 6 p.m. Sutton was back at Langley's place, bringing with him another 24-pack of beer. That was when he phoned Michael McRae, who arrived at Langley's house by about 7 p.m. The boys continued drinking until about 9:30 that evening. As Langley was to estimate it later, Sutton had another eight bottles of beer, while McRae had about five or six. Then Sutton and McRae left Shawn Langley's place together, and Langley never saw them alive again.

Antonio Scopelliti, part-owner and manager of the Gold Star Trailer Camp in Orillia, had the same kind of day he had had for many years. He opened his variety store at 8:30 a.m., as he did every day of the week, including Sunday, and prepared to keep it open for the next fourteen hours. On this round-the-clock schedule the store cleared $10,000 for the Scopelliti family in its best year.

On that Monday, Antonio worked in the store until about 4 p.m., then he drove his nine-year-old daughter, Paola, to her skating lesson. Normally he would have driven back to the store and continued working until it was time to pick up the little girl again, but on January 22 the roads were bad. Scopelliti decided to wait at the skating rink until Paola's lesson was finished. Meanwhile, his wife Rosa and his ten-year-old son Domenic were looking after the shop.

Around 6 p.m. Scopelliti and Paola got back to the trailer camp. Antonio took over from Rosa, who started cooking dinner in the kitchen behind the variety store. The Scopelliti family had their meal together, after which Rosa washed the dishes and left for home with the two children. Scopelliti stayed behind alone. The store was not due to close until 10 p.m., another two and a half hours away. It was not likely to be a busy evening, but the Gold Star Food Market was the kind of operation in which every penny counted. The province had put in a new highway in 1976, which meant fewer and fewer customers were stopping by the store.

At 9:57 p.m. a telephone call was logged by a Bell Canada operator, Joanne Groves. For Groves, the call came at the tail end of an uneventful shift in the small Ontario town, frozen in midwinter. A caller, speaking in a heavily accented voice, requested her to send the police immediately to the trailer camp. The caller seemed extremely agitated. As soon as he had said this (in a voice so high-pitched that Joanne couldn't even be certain if it was a man's voice or a woman's), he hung up. A calm and experienced operator, Groves stayed on the line, certain that the caller would pick up the receiver again.

He did, a few seconds later. "Send ambulance . . ." he began. "Hello, you send ambulance. . . ."

"Stay on the line please, stay on the line, okay?" Groves replied. "You tell the police what you want. I'm connecting you to the police."

The police dispatcher on duty was a Constable Edgett. As it happened, Wayne Edgett immediately recognized the agitated, accented voice on the telephone as that of his neighbour, Antonio Scopelliti. The constable knew him simply as a mild-mannered small-shopkeeper in town.

Scopelliti did not recognize Edgett's voice. "Okay, police officer, come over here, Gold Star Trailer Camp," he said, breathing heavily. "I got two guys in the store. I think they take ambulance. . . ."

Constable Edgett confirmed the address and reached for the microphone to dispatch a cruiser. Scopelliti stayed on the line and tried dialling again. As he had not cleared the line by hanging up first, this was impossible. Telephone operator Groves offered to assist, and at Scopelliti's request connected him with the Orillia Curling Club. At the club Scopelliti spoke to his brother-in-law, Joe Zito, a man in his late thirties, who ran a barber-shop in Orillia. They spoke in Italian. As Zito was to testify later, what Tony said to him was: "You'd better come over here. I just shot two guys."

The two officers who arrived in their cruiser two minutes after Scopelliti's call to the police were Constables Jeffrey Lawrence and Scott James. They did not know Scopelliti. On entering the shop, Lawrence immediately saw the bodies of two young men. Scopelliti was standing beside the counter a short distance away. Lawrence could detect no pulse on the bodies, and told James to go out to the cruiser and radio for an ambulance. Then Lawrence asked Scopelliti to direct him to a telephone, and the shopkeeper pointed to the back room behind the counter.

While on the phone, speaking to the desk-sergeant at the police station, Constable Lawrence noticed a small semi-automatic pistol on the first shelf below the counter. It was lying next to some open cartons of Rothmans and DuMaurier cigarettes. Beside the gun's grip were a box of matches and a coin, while its barrel pointed at an empty box of Eat-More peanuts. Lawrence did not want to touch the weapon, but since Scopelliti was still standing in close proximity to it, after the officer got off the phone he asked his partner, Constable James, to walk the little shopkeeper to another part of the store.

"Could you, ah, step this way, sir?" asked Constable James, and Scopelliti meekly followed him closer to the window. There, standing beside the two officers, Scopelliti supposedly spoke a few words. Constable Lawrence jotted those words down on a piece of paper as he remembered them. Later, at Scopelliti's trial for murder, that piece of paper became Exhibit 44. The words noted on it by Lawrence were, in a sense, the heart of the Crown's case against Antonio Scopelliti.

According to Constable Lawrence, he asked Scopelliti: "Okay, what happened here?" The shopkeeper supposedly replied, speaking in a calm, flat voice: "I shoot them. *They gave me hard time.* . . . I go out now turn off my car? I lock car door."

Scopelliti had apparently been preparing to close up for the night when the two young men entered his store shortly before 10 p.m. He had gone out a few minutes earlier to warm up his car, as the evening was turning bitterly cold. Everything that happened in the store occurred in the next six to seven minutes between that moment and the arrival of the police. Outside, the car's motor was still running. Now Constable James took Scopelliti's keys, unlocked the car's door, and turned the engine off.

The shopkeeper was taken to the police station in a cruiser. Inside the office of Staff Sergeant Francis B. Smith, with Staff Sergeant Smith as well as Constable Lawrence present, another conversation occurred between Scopelliti and the investigating officer in charge of the case, a police sergeant by the name of Ralph Hough. According to Sergeant Hough's later testimony in court, Scopelliti, speaking in a heavy Italian accent, confirmed again that he had shot the boys, then telephoned the police. At this point Sergeant Hough said: "Well, you told Constable Lawrence what happened, so you can tell me."

"Five to ten, about, I go out to start the car to warm him up," Scopelliti replied, according to Hough (though in court the sergeant made no attempt to render, as I do here, Scopelliti's accent and syntax). "I close at ten. . . . Two guys come inside the store and tried to hit me, slap me, but I duck, he miss."

"Which one?"

"The tall one, one in blue," Scopelliti replied. (This was the teenager whose identity would be established as David Sutton, wearing the padded blue windbreaker and baseball-type hat.)

"And where was the other one?" Sergeant Hough asked.

"His foot, he had on chocolate-bar display. I say move, three time; he go get magazine." (The "other one" would later be identified as Michael McRae, who lived with his family almost directly opposite the trailer camp. He was still holding *Curious* magazine in his hand when he fell.) According to Sergeant Hough, Scopelliti said that when he told the boys he wanted them to leave, they replied: "We don't want to go, you'll have to make us."

"The tall skinny one [Sutton] he try to open the till," Scopelliti supposedly continued. "I said to him to get away and the other one say, 'You don't have to pay him. . . .' "

"Well, what did they buy?" asked Hough.

The answer was important, though it sounded innocuous enough. According to Hough, Scopelliti's reply was: "Some 25-cent chips and bubble gum."

"And what happened next?"

"I reach under the counter where was the gun," said Scopelliti.

"Was the gun loaded?"

"Yeah, loaded. . . ."

"Then what happened?" asked the sergeant.

"I shoot one in blue first . . ." Scopelliti replied, according to Sergeant Hough.

"And what did the other one say or do then?"

"He call me son of a bitch, bastard; I shoot him too."

"Did he try to get at you at all?" Sergeant Hough said he asked Scopelliti next. The shopkeeper's alleged answer to this question was: "No."

"Well, did they indicate to you as if they were going to rob you?" was the sergeant's final question. Scopelliti's reply to this contained a phrase that became significant: "Don't say, but I don't know if they rob me," the shopkeeper supposedly said, "or *they're just horsing around*."

Following this interview, Scopelliti was charged with murder in the first degree.

Even accepting the shopkeeper's conversation with Sergeant Hough at face value would hardly have supported a *first-degree* murder charge. First-degree murder must be planned and deliberate, or it must be murder committed in the course of certain specified offences, such as kidnapping. In this instance, Scopelliti's statement did not contain a shred of evidence of planning and deliberation, to say nothing of kidnapping or any other offence specified in the Criminal Code. The charge, as laid, was a perfect example of over-charging a defendant, whether for the purpose of plea bargaining or simply as a matter of routine.

From a bureaucratic point of view it is always safer to overcharge: no policeman or Crown Attorney has ever been called on the carpet for it. It is much easier to reduce a charge later than to increase it. In one sense, overcharging defendants is simply a way for officials to cover their posteriors.

However, on the face of it, Scopelliti's alleged statements to Constable Lawrence and Sergeant Hough might well have sup-ported a charge of culpable homicide against the little shopkeeper. Not murder in the first degree, but possibly second-degree murder or manslaughter.

In law, almost nothing justifies homicide except self-defence. The legal definition of self-defence is complex, but put in simple terms it means that you can justifiably kill a person to defend yourself or your family from death or grievous bodily harm. You may be justified in using force, even if the use of such force results in death, under some other (highly limited) circumstances as well. But you certainly cannot pull out a gun and start shooting people because they "gave you a hard time" or because they were "horsing around".

But did Antonio Scopelliti do that?

What kind of person would kill two teenagers just because they annoyed or irritated him? What kind of a shopkeeper would empty a gun into a couple of kids for not leaving the store when he wanted to close up, or for putting their feet on the candy display? And (what-ever Constable Lawrence or Sergeant Hough may have thought Scopelliti said to them right after the shooting) was there any evidence for Scopelliti's being that kind of person?

This was the first question to which I sought an answer when I was retained to defend Antonio Scopelliti in February 1979. Having been denied bail in the Supreme Court of Ontario on January 29, Scopelliti was still in custody awaiting his preliminary hearing. I wanted to bring an application for a review of Mr. Justice Eberle's denial of bail right away. The Scopellitis were not wealthy people; Mrs. Rosa Scopelliti, Antonio's wife, was also in poor health. With the shopkeeper in jail, there was no one to mind the store which provided for the Scopelliti children, ten-year-old Domenic and nine-year-old Paola.

The first information a court must have in weighing an application for judicial interim release — bail — relates to an accused person's previous character: his reputation, his roots in the community. This information helps a judge decide on the twin tests of a bail hearing: whether or not an accused, if released, is likely to turn up for his trial, and whether or not he will represent any danger to society in the meantime.

In Scopelliti's case, the information that emerged made the crime with which he was charged even more inexplicable. He appeared to have been a peaceful family man. However, this did not alter the fact that two seventeen-year-old boys had been shot to death or that the charge against the shopkeeper was first-degree murder. According to the police, Scopelliti shot two kids in his store because they had been "horsing around". Not surprisingly, this had a great effect on the judge at the bail hearing. It no doubt had a similar effect on Chief Justice Howland of the Ontario Supreme Court when he turned down my application for leave to appeal Mr. Justice Eberle's decision. Bail would continue to be denied to Antonio Scopelliti. The preliminary inquiry was set for April 30, 1979.

2   In 1979 my client was thirty-seven years old. He had been born in the small village of Fiumara, Italy. His parents were tenant famers, raising sheep. The family consisted of six children, Antonio being the third. After finishing Grade 5 in the local school, he had to drop out to help his father on the farm — though "drop out" may not be the right term. The elder Scopelliti was not in good health, and among poor families in a small Italian village it was not unusual for "older" children of ten or eleven to start helping out on the farm instead of staying in school until their late teens, as they tend to do in Canada.

In any case, Antonio worked on the farm until he was twenty years old. Then, like many young men from poorer regions of Europe, he went to a more industrialized country as a guest worker — in his case, to Switzerland. (By then his eldest brother had already emigrated to Australia with his family.) For the next six years Antonio lived in Switzerland alone, sending most of his salary home to his parents (and also visiting them once a year, during the Christmas holidays), while at night he attended a trade school to learn welding. Finally, in 1968, he decided to get married.

The girl of Antonio's choice was named Rosa Zito. She was twenty-five years old in 1968, about a year younger than Antonio. She, too, had been born in Fiumara. Rosa and Antonio grew up together as children in their native village, but while Antonio went to work in Switzerland, Rosa and two of her brothers, Joe (Giuseppe) and Rocco Zito, had settled as immigrants in Canada. In 1967 the Zito brothers opened a barber-shop in Orillia, which was why Antonio came to this small Ontario town a year later to claim Rosa as his bride.

Antonio and his brothers-in-law had known each other since they were children in Fiumara. They got on well together. After marrying Rosa, Antonio and his new wife stayed with Joe Zito and his family in their home for the next year and a half. Antonio — or Tony, as people started calling him in Canada — found a job as a welder within three weeks, and in June 1969 he bought a house together with his brother-in-law Joe Zito. It was a somewhat run-down, six-room, two-storey building, for which they paid $8000. Some people might not have regarded it as much of a house, but it was to this home that Tony moved with Rosa to start a family. Their two children, Domenic and Paola, were born in that house, and it was there that Tony supported them on his income of about $100 a week until 1974.

In that year Tony went into business for himself. The business was the Gold Star Trailer Camp, which he purchased in equal partnership with his brothers-in-law, Joe and Rocco Zito. The trailer camp consisted of two acres of land. It had a variety store with attached living quarters in the back, a couple of gasoline pumps, and rental space for fifteen mobile homes. Scopelliti and the Zito brothers bought the camp for $65,000, and Tony, who was to act as manager, moved his family into the back of the variety store.

From the first day of April 1974 until the night of January 22, 1979, Tony worked seven days a week, fourteen hours a day, running the Gold Star Trailer Camp. Once in a while Rosa helped in the store, but she also had two little children to look after. Tony would open the store at 8:30 in the morning and close it at 11 o'clock at night (until about three months before the shooting, when he decided to take it easy and started closing at 10 p.m.). After the summer of 1978, Scopelliti had bought a new house — again in partnership with his brothers-in-law — so that his wife and children would no longer have to live at the back of the store. In practical terms it may not have made life much easier, because Rosa would still have to cook the evening meal in the kitchen behind the store so that Tony and his family might at least dine together. But the Scopellitis of Fiumara were not complaining. They could put food on the table for everyone in the family, and there was enough money left for the mortgages.

Scopelliti had no criminal record. He had never been treated for a mental illness of any kind. He wasn't even known as a man with a short fuse. On the contrary, family members, friends, and neighbours who gave affidavits in support of his bail application, or who offered to stand surety on his behalf, used words like "gentle", "even-tempered", "considerate", and "humble" to describe him. They said that they had never seen him angry or violent. They all stressed that Tony was an unusually hard-working man, with no interests outside his wife, his children, and his business. These friends and neighbours would describe their own reactions as "shocked" and "stunned" on hearing about Tony's being charged with murder.

Yet, according to the authorities, this gentle, even-tempered, and considerate man had shot two boys to death just because he got angry at them.

By then I knew that Antonio Scopelliti had a completely different explanation of what really happened in his variety store on the night of January 22 — but even if I had not known his story, the police version of events would have sounded unrealistic to me. People do not act so much out of character without a reason. Even so-called crazy crimes make a crazy sort of sense, but the Crown's theory of this incident made no sense at all. More precisely, it would have made sense only if accompanied by some evidence of illness (even if short of legal insanity) such as some rare attack of diabetic or epileptic rage, supported by the appropriate medical findings.

But Scopelliti had no sickness of a mood-altering potential, nor did the Crown advance any theories of a medical nature.

This left one other theory for the Crown: personal enmity. In rare instances even the gentlest, most even-tempered people have been known to kill as an act of personal hatred or revenge — kill, say, a sexual rival, or maybe a person who had previously done them some grievous injury. My partner Chris Buhr, then my student-at-law, raised this possibility with me, as there was some evidence that Scopelliti was acquainted with the two boys (at least, he knew David Sutton by sight and Michael McRae also by name) and that he had had trouble with them on some previous occasions.

What kind of trouble? Well, apparently, a year or two earlier, when Sutton and McRae would have been fifteen or sixteen years old, Scopelliti had to call the police because the boys were spitting Coca-Cola in the shop all over the floor. Then the following Christmas the two boys threw snowballs, breaking a light over the entrance door, though Scopelliti did not report the incident to the police. Finally, in January 1978 Tony had observed David Sutton walking away from the gas pumps carrying a red container. On checking the pumps, Scopelliti found five gallons of gas missing. This time he did call the police, and an officer came out and followed footprints in the snow from the pumps to the McRae home across the road. However, since the policeman could find no young men at the McRaes', that was the end of the incident.

I listened to Chris Buhr's outline with some concern. Far-fetched as the theory seemed, the charge against Scopelliti was first-degree murder at that point: a charge involving planning and deliberation. Would the prosecution now contend that Scopelliti was lying in wait with a gun to avenge himself on two teenage boys? That a shop-keeper who worked seven days a week and fourteen hours a day to build a future for his family would then risk it all to get even for a broken light bulb, five gallons of gas, and a spilled bottle of Coke?

And if so, would the Crown contend that a man filled with so much hate as to gun down two boys for such ludicrous reasons would then immediately and hysterically call an ambulance for them?

"You'd have to be a prosecutor to believe that," I remember saying to Chris Buhr. Yet stranger contentions have been made in court, and there was some evidence that could be interpreted to lend support to the Crown if it wished to advance such a theory.

David Sutton was hit in the body by three bullets; Michael McRae was struck in the head by two. (Sutton was also creased by two further bullets which had then gone wild.) There was no question that the bullets hit McRae in the face and the temple, but the pathologist, Dr. George F. Buckley, raised a question about three of the bullets — including the fatal one — that struck Sutton. In his original report the pathologist stated that the fatal bullet entered Sutton's chest, pierced his heart, and exited through his back. Later, however, having thought about the matter, and after reading a report prepared by the Centre of Forensic Sciences in Toronto as well as some other relevant literature, Dr. Buckley revised his findings. Now his best opinion was that the fatal bullet (as well as one or both of the others) hit Sutton in the back.

Was it possible that, whatever the boys had done in the shop to begin with, they beat a retreat after Scopelliti had produced the gun? Had David Sutton already turned away when he was shot in the back?

There was more. Scopelliti's pistol was a semi-automatic .32-calibre Beretta. Such weapons eject a casing as they are fired. Four casings were found sitting on the counter (Scopelliti having picked them up, as he was to testify, from the floor behind the counter while he was waiting for the police to arrive). Another casing had rolled to the far corner of the store. But one casing was found on the rug just a few feet from the freezer where Sutton's body lay. Was Sutton actually lying on the floor, dead or injured, next to the freezer, when the shopkeeper walked over and fired another shot into his body?

Of course, neither the pathologist's opinion nor the casing on the rug *proved* any such theory — an ejected casing might roll anywhere — but if the prosecution wanted to speculate that this was what happened, the evidence would not be inconsistent with it.

Ironically, Scopelliti's case might have appeared in a worse light to the police, as well as to Crown Attorney John H. Madden, through the efforts of the very people who were trying to help Tony: his two brothers-in-law, Joe and Rocco Zito. When first interviewed by Sergeant Hough, they both said that they were shocked to hear about the shooting because they "never knew" that Tony had a hand-gun. They had never seen a hand-gun in Tony's house.

This was not true. As both Rocco and Joe Zito knew quite well, Scopelliti had purchased the .32 Beretta in Switzerland fifteen years earlier and brought it with him to Canada. It was an unregistered gun (and even unregisterable in this country because it lacked serial numbers). While this did not seem like a big deal to people from the village of Fiumara, where guns did not have to be registered and most men had firearms, the Zito brothers felt that possession of a gun "might hurt" their brother-in-law, so they denied that Tony possessed one.

The fact was that when he was alone in his shop Tony would keep the Beretta under the counter. When his wife or children were in the store with him, or after closing for the night, he would keep the gun locked up in a kitchen cupboard.

I could understand why Rocco and Joe would lie to the police about this, but it was still a grave error. The fact that the gun was unregistered had no significance. Murder is murder, whether committed with a properly registered firearm or not, and I doubted if a trial judge would allow the question of registration to be placed before a jury. It was irrelevant and highly prejudicial. However, by saying that they had never seen the gun before, the Zito brothers might have caused the prosecution to believe, and possibly to argue in court, that Scopelliti had recently bought the weapon for the purpose of killing Sutton and McRae. If the gun *had* been newly purchased, the Crown could have used it as some slight evidence for a planned and deliberate murder.

Having learned about this when I was retained in February, I advised Rocco and Joe Zito that they would have to tell the truth when the time came for them to testify in court. They'd have to tell the truth, of course, even if it hurt their brother-in-law — but, as it happened, telling the truth was the only way for them to help him. They had to admit to the jury that they had lied to the police.

This was not a matter for the preliminary hearing, however. I rather doubted if the Crown's wholly unreasonable charge of first-degree murder would survive a judge's scrutiny, regardless of any issue connected with the gun. There wasn't any evidence for "planning", while the evidence against it was overwhelming: Scopelliti was about to go home, with his car's engine already running, when the youngsters entered his store. He clearly wasn't "planning" to murder anyone.

On the other hand, unlike the Guerin or the Sayegh cases, this was not a case I could hope to win at the preliminary stage. The best the defence could expect was to discover as much as possible about the case of the prosecution. The result of the preliminary inquiry, I thought, would be a committal for Scopelliti to stand trial on a charge of second-degree murder.

Which turned out to be Provincial Court Judge L. T. Montgomery's decision. "I cannot find the planning that I feel is required [for first-degree murder] and, accordingly, I commit the accused for trial before a court of competent jurisdiction in respect to charges of second-degree murder," he ruled. The trial date was eventually set for the Assize Sittings of the Supreme Court of Ontario at Barrie, on Monday, March 24, 1980. That was almost a full year away. It was a year which, having been refused bail, Scopelliti would have to spend in jail.

3 What really happened in the Gold Star Food Market, according to Scopelliti?

David Sutton and Michael McRae entered just as the shopkeeper, having started his car, had walked back into the store. It was a few minutes before 10 p.m. Scopelliti recognized the boys as the two youngsters who had come into his shop many times before. They always came together, and frequently gave him trouble. He knew one of them, though only by his surname, as "McRae". The McRae family lived almost directly across the road, and the boy's father would also come into the store once in a while to buy gasoline for his lawn-mower.

On the night of January 22 young McRae walked up to the chocolate display and put his right foot on the lower rack. Scopelliti asked him to remove his foot. McRae said nothing but gave Scopelliti a look suggesting to the shopkeeper "that he did not like what I said to him."

At this point, Scopelliti said, he began feeling "nervous and frightened".

Meanwhile, David Sutton had picked up two packages of gum-balls from a rack on the other side of the counter behind which Scopelliti was standing. The packages cost five cents each, and Sutton threw a dime in the direction of Scopelliti. The coin landed on the floor. The shopkeeper picked it up and put it on the counter. He did not open the cash register because he was afraid.

While Scopelliti was bending down to retrieve the dime, Sutton opened the package and put the gumball into his mouth. He chewed it for a second, then took it from his mouth with his fingers and threw the wad into Scopelliti's face. "This gum is no good," he said.

The shopkeeper pushed the dime that was still on the counter in Sutton's direction. "This is no good, then take your dime and leave, please," he said. "I want to close'm up the store."

Sutton's response was to take a swing at him, according to Scopelliti. He stepped backwards when he saw the boy raise his hand, and the punch missed. "Go away, I'm going to call the police," the shopkeeper said. He now felt truly frightened. He was alone in a store late at night with two hostile young men, who each stood six feet tall to his height of five foot five, and weighed 190 pounds to his 160 pounds. He did not feel that he was any match for them.

Missing Tony's face seemed to make Sutton, in Scopelliti's words, "more nervous". He put his hand in his pocket and demanded the money in the cash register, saying that he would kill Scopelliti before he could call the police. Tony also remembered the words "bastard" and "son of a bitch", though he couldn't say which of the two boys uttered them. At the same time, with his other hand, Sutton was reaching for the cash register.

Scopelliti remembered being more scared than he had ever been before in his life. He felt convinced in his mind that the boys would rob the store, then kill him. They would have to: he knew both of them by sight, and he also knew the identity of one. Keeping his eye on Sutton's hand to see "what movement he would be doing", Tony reached under the counter for the gun. "The money is in there, take it if you want to," he said to Sutton. He believed that he was about to die.

Then his own hand found the gun on the shelf under the counter. Releasing the safety catch with his thumb, he hauled it out and started shooting. He did not take time to aim. He did not know how many times he pulled the trigger.

This was Antonio Scopelliti's story, as he would eventually tell it on the witness stand. Under most circumstances, since it came from a person of Scopelliti's previously unblemished reputation, I would have felt reasonably confident in submitting it to the judgment of a jury. In this instance there were several factors that made me feel less optimistic.

First, there were the ages of the two victims: seventeen years old. In my own mind I couldn't get away from this. They both looked like handsome, clean-cut youngsters, with open, even angelic, faces. The effect this would have on a jury was incalculable.

Second, there was the fact that the young men were essentially unarmed. McRae did have a small, sheathed knife on his belt and Sutton had a pocket-knife, but neither of them had guns. They had not covered their faces with nylon stockings or balaclavas. (While this may have made Tony all the more fearful that they would have to kill him after the robbery, it might make a jury doubt that the boys had intended to rob Scopelliti in the first place.)

Third, there was the pathologist's opinion that Sutton had been shot in the back.

Fourth, there was the fact that the two boys came from stable, decent family backgrounds. What is more, they came from middle-class WASP families in an essentially middle-class WASP town. Scopelliti was an Italian immigrant. I could not predict the degree to which this might prejudice a jury against him, but the potential was there. (I felt that, in light of the evidence, the very insistence of the authorities to proceed against Scopelliti on a charge of first-degree murder might have been an indication of some prejudice. I wondered if the same evidence would have resulted in a first-degree murder charge against a local WASP businessman.)

Fifth, there were Scopelliti's own alleged statements to Constable Lawrence and Sergeant Hough right after the shooting, including the sentence: "I don't know if they rob me, or they're just horsing around." The defence had a theory about these statements — supported by solid evidence — but a jury might still prefer the testimony of the police officers.

These five factors made me very uneasy. They made me so uneasy, in fact, that during the preliminary hearing I put a hypothetical question to Crown Attorney Madden.

Would he consider in a case of this kind, I asked, a plea to manslaughter with a ten-year sentence?

I had no idea whether my client would have consented to such a deal, but I wanted to find out the extent of the Crown's commitment to its own theory. Had Madden said yes, it would have been my duty to raise a manslaughter plea with Scopelliti for his consideration as an alternative to the awesome risk of a murder conviction with its mandatory sentence of imprisonment for life.

But the prosecutor said no. It was murder or nothing. He might have gone as far as second-degree murder — which would have meant a mandatory life sentence with eligibility for parole after ten years instead of twenty-five. This did not interest me. I had little doubt that, on the evidence, Judge Montgomery would only commit Scopelliti to trial on second-degree murder anyway. But whether first-degree or second-degree, Madden's answer made it clear that the authorities viewed what had happened in the Gold Star Food Market as a species of murder.

This left the defence with no choice. The question would have to be decided by a jury of Antonio Scopelliti's peers.

By the time the trial began before Mr. Justice Edward Saunders in the Supreme Court of Ontario, I had come to the conclusion that, as a matter of strategy, the defence would have to be conducted focusing on two themes. I felt that both were necessary for us to succeed.

First, I believed that we could establish, through a combination of cross-examination and defence evidence, that Scopelliti was in a state of emotional shock after the shooting. This, along with his marginal knowledge of English, resulted in his being able to understand only some of the police officers' questions, while they in turn could understand only some of Tony's answers. I felt the defence could show that whenever the police did not understand Scopelliti they "filled in" the blanks with what they believed his answers ought to be according to the police-theory of events.

In court, this led me straight to Exhibit 44 — the piece of paper on which Constable Lawrence had jotted down Tony's alleged answer to his first question on the night of January 22. The question was: "What happened here?" and the alleged answer: "I shoot them. They gave me a hard time. . . ."

I noticed, though, when I looked at the paper at the preliminary hearing, that the line "They gave me a hard time" looked significantly different from the rest of Constable Lawrence's notes. This remark was sort of tucked in between two other lines. "You obviously used another pen and wrote this in much smaller print at a later time, right?" I asked Constable Lawrence in cross-examination at trial.

"Right," the constable replied.

"And that is your recollection of what was said in the presence of Officer James, right?"

"That's what I heard the accused saying, yes," came the reply.

That was Constable Lawrence's evidence. When it was Constable James's turn to take the witness stand, I looked at *his* notes. There was the same question — "What happened here?" — but the reply was merely: "I shoot them. . . ."

Nothing about a "hard time".

Constable James had been standing right next to Constable Lawrence in the Gold Star Food Market when Scopelliti was being questioned. "If you had heard anything else, you would have written it down?" I asked Constable James in court.

"Yes," replied James.

So, of two policemen standing side by side, only one could hear the remark — and the one who claimed to have heard it remembered to jot it down only *later*, using a different pen. This, of course, had to raise an enormous doubt about the first of Tony's alleged statements. It seemed that Constable Lawrence "remembered" the key line in it (which his partner didn't hear at all) only after listening to Sergeant Hough's interview with Tony at the police station.

As Sergeant Hough would admit in cross-examination, during that interview Scopelliti appeared very calm and flat. He showed no animation. This was important, as there was little doubt in my mind that Scopelliti had been in a state of total emotional collapse. Virtually anybody, except a hardened killer, would be after shooting two human beings. Tony's entire behaviour — his hysterical phone calls, followed by an unnatural calm; a strange request he made at the police station, asking an officer to let him sign his lottery tickets as soon as he was taken to a cell after the shooting — indicated to me (whatever they may have indicated to the policemen) that Tony was suffering from an attack of acute psychological anxiety and panic. He had next to no idea what he was saying or doing. The defence would be calling an eminent forensic psychiatrist, Dr. R. L. Fleming, to testify that in a traumatic shock people can appear outwardly calm, while their minds are totally scattered and can't focus on questions and answers.

There was also physical evidence to support the shopkeeper's story. It corroborated the defence theory that when Scopelliti was interviewed by Sergeant Hough, neither of the two men had any real notion what the other one was talking about.

Sergeant Hough thought Scopelliti told him that Sutton and

McRae had bought "some 25-cent chips and bubble gum". Tony's evidence was that he told the sergeant no such thing. All right: if Hough did not misunderstand Scopelliti, *where was the bag of chips?* It should have been either on the floor, or on the counter, or on the person of one of the boys. In fact, it was nowhere.

What the police did find on the floor was a wad of chewed-up gum, which supported the evidence Scopelliti gave on the witness stand. Tony's testimony was that Sutton put the gum into his mouth, then spit it out and threw it in Tony's face.

As Scopelliti would testify, he couldn't remember saying to Sergeant Hough many of the things attributed to him by the officer. For instance, he couldn't remember saying that, after he had told McRae to take his foot off the candy, the boy went to get a magazine — in fact, Scopelliti had no idea at all what McRae did right after he had removed his foot from the candy rack. (I thought that this was a typical example of police conjecture. Since McRae was found with a magazine in his hand, the conjecture that the shopkeeper saw him go and "get a magazine" was put into Scopelliti's mouth.)

Nor could Scopelliti recall telling the sergeant that either of the boys had said, "You don't have to pay him" or "We don't want to go, you'll have to make us"; or that "the one in green" (McRae) called him "a bastard and I shoot him too"; or that he didn't know whether the boys wanted to rob him or were just horsing around. (In answer to my question on re-examination, Scopelliti said that he had never heard of the expression "horsing around" — which surprised no one who knew him. Tony's grasp of English idiom, to say nothing of slang, was minimal.)

Scopelliti's evidence was that Sergeant Hough would at times accompany his verbal questions with hand gestures. Tony might not understand the words, but would respond "yes" or "no" to what he thought the officer's gestures were meant to convey. This was why, for instance, he said "no" to Hough's query of whether or not the "one in green" tried to get him. "Being so frightened, sir," said Scopelliti, answering Crown Attorney Madden through an Italian interpreter on the witness stand, "I was not in a position to explain to [Sergeant Hough] what they had done to me."

This, too, was supported by Sergeant Hough's own evidence, as it emerged earlier during my cross-examination. At the police station the Sergeant had brought Scopelliti before a justice of the peace so that he could officially remand Tony into custody. After the justice of the peace left, Scopelliti asked Sergeant Hough if he was a *priest*. He clearly mistook the remand process for spiritual ministrations. This did not create the impression that Scopelliti could understand much of what he was being asked or told on the night of January 22.

The second defence theme, however, posed a major legal problem.

Our investigation indicated that Sutton and McRae, in spite of their youth and clean-cut appearance, had been rather aggressive youngsters. Few boys are hardened criminals at seventeen and there was no suggestion that Sutton and McRae were, but they did appear to have been mischievous and violent. In the past, they had on various occasions assaulted peaceable citizens with no provocation.

In November 1978, Sutton and McRae, driving a truck, pursued a commuter named Keith Henderson to the parking lot of Henderson's place of work. The boys accused Henderson of having "cut them off". They abused him verbally and punched him in the face three times. Henderson's employer laid charges against the two teenagers, which resulted in both Sutton and McRae being convicted and fined.

About a month after this incident, a young man named Brian Barnes was walking along the street with his girlfriend when Sutton and McRae jumped out of their car and pinned him against the wall. Barnes knew Sutton from school, but didn't know McRae at all. Saying, "I don't like the looks of you," Sutton struck Barnes four times on the face and arm, while McRae was standing by. According to Barnes, he had done nothing to provoke the assault, which he did not report to the police.

In April 1978, Braden Litster was driving with his fiancée, Carol, when a car with four youngsters in it began chasing them. Two of the boys were Sutton and McRae. Litster drove through town to escape them. When he stopped in front of a police station, the youths in the pursuing car jumped out and tried opening the doors of his vehicle. The couple drove to the back of the station, where the other car did not follow them. Braden and Carol reported the incident to the police. Later Litster swore out an information seeking a peace bond on David Sutton, but after speaking with Sutton's father he decided to let the matter drop.

These were senseless and fairly vicious attacks. I wanted the jury to know about them — but I had to overcome a major hurdle in law. Sutton and McRae were not on trial; they were the victims. Scopelliti had no personal knowledge of these violent incidents, so they could not have affected his state of mind. Ordinarily, evidence of a victim's propensity for assaultive behaviour is admissible only if the defendant knew about it, because only then could it have made him fear for his own safety. The courts have generally held that in all other instances such evidence is irrelevant and prejudicial. Irrelevant, because it could not have influenced the accused person's state of mind, and prejudicial because it could create a feeling in a jury that the victims "deserved" to be killed for their misdeeds in the past.

I agreed with the wisdom of this evidentiary rule — up to a point. Of course these two boys did not "deserve" to be shot because of what they might have done in the past: no one ever does. Of course violent acts that Scopelliti did not know about could not have caused him to be afraid of Sutton and McRae. But how could a jury decide whether or not Scopelliti was telling the truth about what happened in his variety store on the night of January 22 if they knew nothing about the youths who confronted him?

Should twelve citizens arrive at such a vital determination simply on the basis of how Scopelliti looked to them on the witness stand? Or how well a Grade 5 school dropout like Tony might stand up to a skilled prosecutor in cross-examination? Should they just base it on some gut-feeling or a hunch? Was it fair to deny the jury evidence that tended to corroborate Scopelliti's explanation?

It seemed common sense to me that knowing the truth about a victim, as long as it pertained to a relevant issue, could only help the jury in finding out the truth about an accused. Admitting such evidence would not lead to criminals willy-nilly accusing the people they've assaulted. On the contrary, only the gentlest, most peaceful defendant could ever avail himself of this strategy, because the minute he led evidence about his victim's predisposition for violence *it would be open for the Crown to lead evidence about violent episodes in his, the defendant's, past*. No vicious, violent criminal could take such a risk.

This, at least, was my view; the decision would be up to the trial judge, Mr. Justice Saunders. I knew only that if he did decide for the defence, it would be a ground-breaking decision. With the exception of one unreported case, the defence could refer him to no Canadian or English precedents.

Crown Attorney Madden and I made our submissions on the matter. Mr. Justice Saunders thought over our arguments, then made his ruling the following day. "The evidence was fully summarized by Mr. Greenspan," the trial judge said. "If accepted, it tends to show that both victims were predisposed to unprovoked violence. . . . In view of the extraordinary nature of the evidence I have decided that it should be admitted as corroborative of the explanation of the accused of the events of January 22.

"The jury will have to be charged as to the limited use they may make of the proposed evidence," the trial judge continued. "It is evidence only in support of the accused's explanation of events, but is not evidence that should be taken into account when they consider the accused's state of mind, nor should they feel that the victims deserved some sort of punishment as a result of their behaviour."

This critical ruling enabled the entire evidentiary basis for the defence to be placed before the jury. However, to my mind, it did not come close to settling the matter. John Madden was a skilled and combative prosecutor, not at all prone to taking things lying down. I was very apprehensive while he subjected the defence witnesses to gruelling cross-examinations. At one point Madden attempted to bring in through the back door the fact that Scopelliti's gun was unregistered, which was previously ruled inadmissible by the trial judge as irrelevant and prejudicial. The Crown tried to do it by asking Joe Zito (who admitted to the jury that he and his brother had lied to the police about the gun) when it was that he first mentioned the weapon to *me*.

This was the only point in the trial when I lost my temper. "My Lord, this is . . ." I started — then swallowed the unparliamentary remark I was about to make. "If I differ with [Mr. Zito] does this mean that I now have to go into the witness box and say exactly what and when he told me? There's a privilege. . . . My friend should know better than that."

The judge ruled, of course, that the prosecutor could not pursue this line of questioning. Later Madden tried asking Scopelliti why, if right after the shooting he had been too excited to explain matters properly to the police, he did not call Sergeant Hough in a couple of weeks' time when he was calmer? This, too, was an unfair question: a question that ignored a fundamental principle of our law. In our system the accused has an absolute right to remain silent. It is up to the authorities to prove a defendant guilty, not up to a defendant to explain himself to the authorities. Naturally his Lordship ruled that the Crown could not ask that question either.

When Scopelliti took the stand in his defence I decided to end my direct examination with the one question that was at the core of the trial. "Why did you shoot," I asked Scopelliti, "David Sutton and Michael McRae?"

"God has created humanity, the people to love each other and not to kill," replied Scopelliti. "Death is a horrible thing. But when afraid, every one of us forget, you go away from God's commandment, you defend from death."

Mr. Justice Saunders looked up. "I'm sorry, I didn't get that last phrase," he said.

I glanced at the Italian interpreter. "You defend from death, my Lord," she repeated, raising her voice.

The defence rested; the Crown called no witnesses in reply. In my jury address, after reviewing the evidence, I contented myself with saying to the jury: "We would suffer, all of us, if a man in his own place could not be allowed to defend his own life. It is good law and good sense that a man, when attacked, may defend himself. Antonio Scopelliti acted in self-defence to protect his life. I ask you to acquit him."

Crown Attorney Madden suggested in his jury address that Scopelliti acted in anger rather than in fear. The prosecution's position, as Mr. Justice Saunders summed it up later in his charge to the jury, was that "the action of the victims . . . so angered [Scopelliti] that he intentionally shot and killed them; that his action was unnecessary under the circumstances as the mere production of the gun would have been sufficient."

I found this interesting. It amounted, as far as I could see, to an admission by the prosecution that there was some "action" on the part of the victims that was at least serious enough to warrant the "production" of a gun on Scopelliti's part. In seven days of trial we had moved pretty far from the Crown's initial charge of first-degree murder.

The jury deliberated for five hours after Mr. Justice Saunders' meticulous and even-handed charge on the law. They were no doubt the longest five hours of Scopelliti's life.

It was 10:29 p.m. when the jury returned to the courtroom. The verdict was "Not guilty".

This, however, was not quite the last word. Tense months followed as the prosecution appealed. The Crown contended that the trial judge had made an error in law by letting the jury hear the evidence of the people assaulted by Sutton and McRae. In the end the Ontario Court of Appeal unanimously upheld the jury's acquittal — with consequences reaching far beyond Scopelliti's fate. Mr. Justice Saunders' ruling became the law in the province of Ontario, with a heavy influence on the law in the entire country and perhaps in other common-law jurisdictions as well.

Scopelliti's case has shaped our legal system in a way that some people may not consider beneficial. Some say that it has caused the "victims to be put on trial" rather than the accused. Though this has become a popular phrase, I think it expresses a simplistic view. Such a view puts the cart before the horse: it tries to assume a result before a trial. It attempts to argue backwards, which is misleading and dangerous. The fact is, we don't quite know who the "victim" is until we've weighed all the evidence.

The victim may not always be the party that is the most grievously hurt. Guilt or innocence do not depend on the severity of injuries and cannot be determined by medical reports alone. We cannot judge solely by the *outcome* of an incident who is to blame for it, or who is to blame for it more. Nor can we decide it on the basis of who complained first, who started crying "Thief!" or "Rape!", or who has been charged by the police. If we could, we wouldn't need courts and judges. These questions can only be answered by a judicial process in which all relevant evidence is placed before the triers of fact, according to law. Otherwise, all we would ever have to ask is who "won" a fight, and put that person in jail.

The greatest sympathy for victims cannot replace a quest for justice. In some cases, doing perfect justice is very hard. Nothing, for instance, could alleviate the tragedy of the Sutton and McRae families. David Sutton and Michael McRae, but for one disastrous moment in their lives, might well have grown up to be productive, decent citizens. As for Scopelliti, he was acquitted, but in the process he had lost nearly everything for which he had worked for seven days every week for fifteen years. He had spent over a year in jail, waiting for his trial. A year in prison would be less than justice for killing two human beings, but it is a grave injustice to a person found entirely innocent by his peers.

*The Scopelliti case was probably the only one of Greenspan's cases about which Greenspan and his friend Jonas did not see eye to eye. Eddie thought that it would be a very hard case to win; Jonas did not.*

*It was, of course, utterly irrelevant how Jonas saw the case. However, since his feelings generally coincided with Greenspan's, it became of some interest why the two friends' instincts should not mesh in this particular instance. Jonas became interested in reviewing the question because he felt that it might reveal something about Greenspan in human terms. (Greenspan agreed because, as he put it, he felt that it might reveal something about Jonas.)*

*Eddie looked at the case with unaccustomed pessimism all along. While there's no certainty about the outcome of any contested issue, it is often possible to guess at the percentages. In this case, Greenspan was reluctant to go as high as a twenty-five-per-cent chance for acquittal. His feeling was that Scopelliti might well go down for the count. Initially Greenspan was fearful that the shopkeeper would be convicted, at least of manslaughter, if the trial judge should rule against admitting evidence about the victims' past behaviour — but, even with that evidence admitted, he felt that the verdict could be touch and go.*

*Jonas had a different view. He agreed with the importance — the vital importance — of Greenspan's strategy leading to Judge Saunders' precedent-setting ruling about admitting Sutton's and McRae's unprovoked assaults on other people in the past. However, once that evidence was before the jury, he could see no more reason for pessimism about Scopelliti's acquittal. In fact, Jonas would have considered it perverse for the jury to go the other way.*

*Scopelliti did not have to prove that he acted in self-defence: it was up to the Crown to prove, beyond a reasonable doubt, that he did not. Scopelliti was a thirty-seven-year-old shopkeeper of unblemished reputation. He was a peaceful family man about to close his store for the night, with his car already idling outside. The evidence showed that the youngsters who came into his store at that moment were two boozed-up teenage bullies. If what a man like Scopelliti said on the witness stand about the actions of two such boys was not enough to raise a reasonable* doubt in a jury's mind, the jury would have to disregard the plain, everyday meaning of the term "reasonable doubt".

It is a common experience of mankind that sane, sober shopkeepers don't shoot their customers. They don't even shoot them when they are feeling cranky (or when their customers are feeling cranky). It wouldn't be good for business. A drunk or crazy shopkeeper may shoot a customer, but Scopelliti was neither. It would be entering the realm of fairy tales to suggest that a man of his type would shoot two boys for having spilled some Coke or broken a light bulb some time in the past. Scopelliti had to have another reason.

The reason he gave under oath was that the boys had tried to rob the store and threatened to kill him. Of course, no one could be sure any more whether Sutton and McRae had been planning to rob Scopelliti when they entered, formed an intention to rob him on the spur of the moment, or were just playing a cruel, bullying game with the little Italian. The boys were certainly not professional criminals; they had not been armed or masked. Had they been charged with attempted robbery — as they probably would have been if a policeman had entered the store at that moment and Scopelliti had told him the same story — they might have testified in their defence that they never really meant to rob the store and that, in their own minds, they were just "horsing around". (If so, as a juror, Jonas might have been prepared to give Sutton and McRae the benefit of a reasonable doubt as well.)

But this seemed totally immaterial to Scopelliti's defence. He was a small man, alone in an isolated shop late at night, confronted by two abusive youngsters twice his size, one of whom was making a grab for the cash register. (Whatever Sergeant Hough may have understood Scopelliti to say after the shooting, there was no dispute that the shopkeeper said this much right away.) Nor was there any dispute about Sutton's having consumed eighteen to twenty bottles of beer during that day, and even McRae's having consumed five or six bottles in the preceding two or three hours. The two boys were not falling-down drunks (perhaps it would have been better if they had been), but they were certainly full of booze, in addition to being full of piss and vinegar.

What was Scopelliti to do? He was not a mind-reader. He was not a karate expert. He was not a forensic psychiatrist, a policeman, or even a social worker trained in the management of aggressive, inebriated youths. He was a five-foot-five shopkeeper, trying to get home to his children in one piece, preferably with the day's receipts in his pocket. He could not hope to fight off Sutton and McRae, or to cool them out with the authority of his personality or his uniform. Scopelliti had no uniform and no authority. He did not even speak much English. He was, minimally, an ideal subject to bully for two youths who had an inclination for such activities and nothing better to do on a boring winter night, whether they actually meant to rob and kill Scopelliti or not.

Was it incumbent upon Scopelliti to find out exactly how far two such boys might go? How far they might go after throwing the gum in his face, after trying to punch him, and after grabbing for the till? How far they might go egging each other on, half-cut, attracted by their victim's fear and weakness? Was it Scopelliti's duty, at the risk of his own life, to find out whether they meant what Sutton said about robbing and killing him? Or to try explaining to these kids in one minute everything about civilized behaviour that their church or school had failed to teach them in seventeen years? Was the law putting any such new duties on shopkeepers?

Did the little Italian get scared faster than some bigger or stronger person might have? Maybe. Would a more self-confident man have waited longer before pulling the trigger? Yes, perhaps — but Sutton and McRae did not pick on a more self-confident man, they picked on Scopelliti. Did the shopkeeper refuse to take a chance that some other person might have been prepared to take? Possibly, but he wasn't some other person.

Was he wrong to refuse to take such a chance? Who could answer that question? Who would be rash enough to pass judgment in the safe, calm environment of a courtroom on a man who had to face two aggressive youths, alone, late at night? Who would dare to second-guess him now by putting him in prison for life for what he, under the circumstances, mistakenly or not, regarded as necessary for his defence? Who would do that, knowing that city morgues are filled with the bodies of store-owners or pawnshop employees who bravely took a chance on reaching for the telephone instead of a gun when some burly youths grabbed at their cash registers (or who, not having a weapon under the counter, didn't have a choice).

In any case, Scopelliti's peers had to answer only whether or not the evidence proved, beyond a reasonable doubt, that no ordinary person would have been afraid for his life under these circumstances, or that Scopelliti was not in fact afraid.

The evidence, Jonas felt, did not come close to proving any such thing *beyond a reasonable doubt. It did not even prove it on a balance of probabilities. If the jurors understood and obeyed the law, they would have to acquit Scopelliti.*

Greenspan, needless to say, fully agreed with much of this: it was he who argued it to the jury with great eloquence. This was the core of his defence on Scopelliti's behalf. But, even knowing and presenting some of these very arguments, and being convinced of their complete validity, he was still pessimistic. Why?

Greenspan's real concerns could not be ascribed to the weight of the Crown's evidence against Scopelliti — at least, not after what was left of it by the time the jury retired. In cross-examination Eddie proved, through the prosecution's own firearm expert, that a man scared enough to shoot without taking aim could fire the Beretta seven times in two and a half seconds. That's about as long as it'd take to say "one potato, two potatoes". Under these circumstances it was no longer decisive that some of the bullets hit Sutton in the back. Nor did Scopelliti's alleged statements to the police retain much weight after the defence had shown how little Scopelliti understood of what was being said that night. As soon as Greenspan brought out, in his cross-examination of Sergeant Hough, that Scopelliti thought that the justice of the peace was a priest, the rest of the alleged exchange between Tony and the police officers that night was not likely to carry a jury beyond a reasonable doubt.

Jonas could think of only three reasons for Eddie's pessimism, in ascending importance. First, Greenspan has always had a keen nose, maybe even an overly sensitive nose, for human prejudice. As a practising trial lawyer it has been his experience that cases are not always, or solely, decided on their merits. Eddie was worried that there might be some bias in the area against an immigrant killing two home-town boys. He was very fearful that some of this might filter into the jury room. (Eventually, to his relief, he found that this simply wasn't the case.)

Second, Greenspan has always had a prejudice of his own: a prejudice against firearms. Not just unregistered guns, or guns specifically in the hands of criminals, but any kind of gun in anybody's hands. He would look at the most properly registered side-arm carried by a trained policeman with barely less distaste than at a crazy kid waving a sawed-off shotgun. There have never been any weapons in Greenspan's background. His mother would not have approved of guns. In Eddie's circles firearms have always been regarded as intrinsically brutal and, somehow, not respectable. Greenspan knew better than anyone, of course, *that this did not go to the legal merits of the case, but just the fact the Scopelliti had a gun did not sit well with him.*

*All human beings assume that their tastes and feelings are normative — that is, that most "normal" people share them. Greenspan was worried that the jury would hold the mere possession of a weapon against Scopelliti. To some extent, Eddie had to deliberately suppress his own feelings not to hold it against Scopelliti that he owned a gun — and he feared that the members of the jury might not suppress their feelings. The possibility that many people on a jury might not have such feelings seemed remote to Greenspan. As far as he was concerned, the normal reaction to guns was to hate them.*

*Finally, most importantly, there was the emotional impact of the fact the David Sutton and Michael McRae were only seventeen years old. Greenspan kept saying that he was worried about the effect this would have on the jury, but (at least in Jonas's view) the truth was that it had a tremendous effect on Greenspan himself. He could not quite distance himself from the picture of the two kids lying on the floor of the shabby little convenience store. He kept going back to the photograph — Exhibit 9 — turning it over and over in his hand and, no doubt, turning it over in his mind. A father of two children himself, he grieved for the parents of the boys. He regarded their senseless deaths as a terrible tragedy. He could not escape the feeling that, in a jury room, even he would be tempted to somehow try and "put right" something that could never be put right again.*

*Intellectually, there was no doubt in Greenspan's mind that, on the evidence, finding Scopelliti guilty would be a grievous mistake. A guilty verdict would not be measured retribution but unthinking revenge: an angry, impotent reflex to fix blame, to punish someone, anyone, for what had happened. Yet, emotionally, he was not so sure.*

*Was it possible for the jury to look at that picture and do nothing? Fail to register its horror at two senseless deaths by some half-blame or compromise — say, a conviction for manslaughter? Was it possible for twelve ordinary people to understand that, in certain cases, no matter how great the tragedy, doing nothing was the only route to justice?*

*When it was the hardest thing to do nothing, would the jury have the courage to do the hardest thing?*

*Greenspan never raised his concerns in these terms. Then, when Jonas put to him the suggestion that follows, he emphatically denied it. But Jonas could never escape the feeling that the reason Greenspan found it so hard to believe that the jury would acquit Scopelliti was that, as a juror, he would not have found it easy to acquit Scopelliti himself.*

## NOTES

p.309, l.7: The other offences are: hijacking, sexual assault of any kind, forcible confinement, and hostage-taking. Murder of a peace officer or a prison worker is also first-degree murder.

p.309, l.28: Thus, a person is entitled to use deadly force where necessary to prevent the commission of a serious offence likely to cause immediate and serious injury, or to defend someone under his protection (a parent protecting a child, for example).

p.320, l.34: Dr. Russel LeRoy Fleming, in 1980 the Director of the Forensic Assessment Unit at Ontario's Penetanguishene Mental Health Centre for the criminally insane.

p.323, l.38: It happened to be one of my own cases, *R. v. Haines* (1977). By an interesting coincidence, it was heard in the same courtroom as Scopelliti's trial. My client, a businessman named John Haines, was acquitted in the shooting death of a man named "Pepper" Martin. Martin, who thought that his wife was involved with Haines, terrorized Haines in Haines's home for almost an entire night before being shot and killed by my client. The trial judge, Mr. Justice Henry, permitted evidence of violent incidents in Martin's past to be placed before the jury, including incidents not known to the defendant. His Lordship accepted my submission that such evidence would assist the jury in deciding whether or not Haines was telling the truth. This precedent created in my earlier trial, being unique in Canada, became of considerable importance in the Scopelliti case.

p.325, l.4: A journalist, Jerry Amernic, mentions the Scopelliti case in his 1984 book entitled *Victims: The Orphans of Justice*. In his book Amernic looks briefly at the trial from the point of view of the McRae and Sutton families. Amernic offers the following example of what he perceives as the court's bias in favour of the defence: "When admissibility of evidence was at issue, [Mr. Justice] Saunders ruled in favour of the defence nine times and in favour of the crown just twice." It may be necessary to point out for the benefit of all journalists who might suffer from similar misconceptions that courts do not attempt to achieve fairness by ruling in favour of both sides an equal number of times. Judges are obliged to rule in favour of whichever side happens to raise a valid point of law, no matter how often this may put one side ahead of the other.

*High-profile people attract pretenders. History is rich in examples of pretenders, a few of whom have attained considerable success. In ancient Russia, one "false Dmitri" actually managed to usurp the throne of Ivan the Terrible by pretending to be his deceased grandson (as everyone knows who has seen Moussorgsky's famous opera* Boris Godunov*), and when this false Dmitri was murdered a year later, a second false Dmitri raised an army of Cossacks and tried to march on Moscow. He has yet to have an opera written about him, though.*

*Returning quickly to the present after this brief historic and cultural excursion, it is perhaps reassuring to report that there has so far been only one false Greenspan.*

*Early in 1977 word got back to Eddie about a person, seen at parties and at other social events, who was supposedly working for Greenspan on an "exchange program" with the American criminal lawyer F. Lee Bailey's office. Knowing of no such person (and of no such exchange program, for that matter), Greenspan became mildly concerned. Inquiries yielded no result at that time, but a short while later Greenspan's office received a bill from a Los Angeles law firm for some work that, according to the bill, it had done at the request of someone from Greenspan's office. The work had to do with getting information about a person in Los Angeles.*

*Having requested no such work to be done, Greenspan called the police.*

*Eddie was not so much concerned with the amount of the legal bill as with the fact that a fraud artist was evidently walking around with some of the business cards and probably also the letterhead of Greenspan's law firm in his possession. Eddie did not like this one bit.*

*The constabulary started investigating, along with Greenspan's office. The trail seemed to lead to the client of a certain Toronto lawyer. The police asked the lawyer to please talk to his client and, if the client was involved, to tell him to stop. On the evidence of the man's possible involvement, that was as far as Greenspan was prepared to go.*

For a while things were quiet. Then, one Monday in December 1977, Eddie received a phone call at his office from the Chief (or possibly the Deputy Chief) of the Calgary police.

"Hello," said the caller. "Are you Edward Greenspan?"

"Yes, why?"

"I'm So-and-so from the Calgary police and you're under arrest."

"Oh, okay," said Eddie, thinking that it was a joke. "Would you like me to fly out to Calgary or wait for you here?"

"What were you doing Friday night?" asked the policeman.

Something in his tone suggested to Greenspan that this might not be entirely a joke.

"I was with my family," he said. "What is this all about?"

What it was all about turned out to be the following story:

Apparently a man had walked into the Keg restaurant in Calgary and had a long, friendly chat with the manager. Having introduced himself with a business card as the criminal lawyer Edward L. Greenspan from Toronto, the man sat in the manager's office for nearly two hours describing in detail the big banquet he wanted to throw at the Keg for some of his legal cronies in Alberta. It was to be a lavish affair and everything had to be done just right.

The Keg's manager was quite happy to get such a major catering job from a big Toronto lawyer. He was less happy when, at the conclusion of their discussion, the "lawyer" got up, pulled out a gun, pointed it at the manager's head, and robbed him of over $5000.

After the man left, the manager called the police. He told them that he had just been robbed by the lawyer Eddie Greenspan. He gave the police Eddie's business card. It seemed like a solid lead, so the investigating officers in Calgary issued a warrant for Greenspan's arrest.

However, before the warrant could get on the CPIC system, some bright supervisor (God bless him, Eddie was to say, whoever he was) displayed an unusual amount of initiative. He thought that there might be something fishy about a noted criminal lawyer robbing someone at gunpoint, having previously handed his victim his business card. Even ordinary robbers tend to be intelligent enough not to do that, let alone noted criminal lawyers. Before putting the arrest warrant on the wire, the supervisor sent it up to the office of the Calgary Chief of Police.

The Chief was also puzzled. He telephoned the lawyer Milt Harradence (now Mr. Justice Harradence of the Alberta Court of Appeal).

"Do you know Edward Greenspan, the lawyer, from Toronto?" asked the Chief.

"Yes," said Harradence.

"We have information that he was in Calgary yesterday and robbed the Keg's manager at gunpoint."

The Alberta lawyer laughed. "I don't think so, Chief," he said. "You see, whenever Eddie Greenspan comes to town to pull a robbery he always calls me first. He didn't call me this week."

"This Greenspan who did the robbery," said the Chief, "is described as a short, skinny fellow."

Whether or not Greenspan was much taller in 1977 than he is now, he certainly was much less skinny. No one who saw him would ever have decribed him as a "skinny fellow".

"If that's your identification evidence," said the future Mr. Justice Harradence, "I think even I could get him off."

After this legal opinion, the warrant for Greenspan's arrest never got on the CPIC. So, while the Calgary Chief might not have been quite serious about arresting Eddie, he did really want to speak to him to see if he had any idea about who might have been impersonating him. On the basis of their earlier investigation, Eddie was able to give the Calgary police some tips, eventually leading to a man named Tony Genovese. He was a man, as Greenspan put it later, "of half my size with twice the nerve".

Genovese, sometimes also known as Frank Lukes, had been involved in many armed robberies. Still, robbery was probably not the only thing Genovese wanted out of life. At the Keg, for instance, once he got inside the manager's office, he could have pulled his gun right away instead of chatting for nearly two hours. It is likely that Genovese enjoyed playing the role of Greenspan the lawyer as much as, or even more than, walking away with the manager's money.

Though he had threatened his victims with real guns, Genovese had a reputation as a con man rather than as a violent criminal — at least until, two or three years later, the gun found in his possession turned out to be the gun used in a Hudson's Bay store robbery in Toronto in which Ted Van Sluytman, a forty-year-old father of four, had been murdered when he tried to stop the fleeing bandits.

At Genovese's trial for second-degree murder arising out of the Hudson's Bay killing, Crown Attorney Michael Lynch suggested to Genovese that he was not even concerned with the trouble impersonating Greenspan in Calgary might have caused Eddie in 1977. Before Genovese could answer, his lawyer, Ross Mackay, objected. He probably *thought that Eddie had considered the story rather amusing and had been dining out on it ever since. "Why don't you call Greenspan," Mackay said to Michael Lynch, "and see if he's upset?"*

*"I'd be happy to," the Crown Attorney replied, but (apart from the fact that the issue was pretty irrelevant to the Hudson's Bay murder charge) he didn't risk calling Greenspan to testify about the matter. Imitation being the sincerest form of flattery, Lynch couldn't be quite sure that Eddie wouldn't view an investigation for robbery as a fair price for being considered worthy of impersonation two thousand miles from home.*

PART EIGHT

# JUST DESERTS

# 17. The Lions' Den

In the evening of September 28, 1966, a twenty-four-year-old Ontario man by the name of James Miller booked into a cheap hotel in Winnipeg, having driven there from Toronto with a friend named Rudy Couvreur. Both young men were broke. They had travelled to Manitoba in the belief that the police wanted to question them in Toronto in connection with a stolen-property offence. They both had minor criminal records — in the case of Miller mainly for taking cars for joy rides at fifteen and eighteen, as well as for receiving stolen property at the age of nineteen. He had, at various times, served a few months in jail.

The two young men were not exemplary citizens, but they were far from being hardened professional criminals. Miller had never been charged with a crime of violence. He was married, had a trade as a car-body repairman, and as a rule had always made his living working at ordinary jobs. In Winnipeg, too, he wanted to look for employment. However, neither he nor Couvreur had any money. Walking about the Main Street–Logan Avenue district after checking into their hotel, they noticed a small second-hand store at 208 Logan. It was just being closed by what appeared to be the sole proprietor, a grey-haired older man. They decided to return the next morning, enter the store, and see if Couvreur could distract the owner's attention long enough for Miller to grab "the cash box".

This was a Wednesday night. On Thursday, around 11:30 a.m., the two men walked back to the store. Couvreur asked the sixty-five-year-old owner, Ernest Rice, to show him a camera in the window. Meanwhile Miller, as planned, started approaching the counter behind which he hoped to find the money.

Despite his age, Mr. Rice was an observant and courageous man. He also happened to be strong. He noticed what was going on almost immediately, and started grappling with Couvreur to protect his store. It seemed obvious to Miller that Couvreur was getting the worst of the struggle, so he went to his friend's aid. Rice shoved him out of the way. Miller looked around for an object, and saw an iron bar. He picked it up and hit Rice across the shoulder. The older man did not even flinch, Miller thought, only threw a camera and tripod at him with one hand. With his other hand he continued holding Couvreur. Panicking, Miller hit him with the iron bar again and again, until finally Rice fell down.

The two men dragged the unconscious owner to the back of his store. They took his wallet, which contained about one hundred dollars in small bills. Then they left the store, padlocked the door from the outside, picked up their car from a nearby parking lot, and immediately drove out of town.

Ernest Rice was not discovered until about 2:30 in the afternoon when a neighbour saw the padlocked store and, becoming suspicious, called the police. They took the injured man to the hospital, from which he would not be released until February the following year. The iron bar wielded by Miller caused permanent brain damage, leaving Mr. Rice in a condition later described by Manitoba Court of Appeal as being "little more than a living vegetable".

However, it took nearly six years for any court to be in a position to comment on the matter. Miller and Couvreur were not apprehended for their crime until March 9, 1972. In the meantime something had happened to Miller which, while not unique, is not exactly an everyday occurrence. He had rehabilitated himself.

Miller was involved in a brutal, vicious crime, but he happened not to be a brutal, vicious person. He had the usual unfortunate beginnings, being placed in various foster homes after his father deserted his mother when he was about a year old. Eventually his mother found a new husband and Miller was reunited with her, but the stepfather turned out to be an alcoholic, which later caused the family to break up again. Probably more as a result of his unstable background than of any other factor, Miller ended up in an institution for juvenile delinquents at fifteen — that was after he had taken a car for a joy ride — and at the Bowmanville training school he formed some associations with boys far worse than himself. It was these friendships that continued to influence his life for a few more years, though to a diminishing degree.

In fact, after Miller married a girl named Edna-Anne — who came from a similarly unstable background but was a decent and level-headed person herself — the young couple's quarrels usually centred around Miller's friends, including Rudy Couvreur, who in Edna-Anne's view were leading Miller astray. At the time of the Winnipeg robbery Edna-Anne was expecting their second child. After Miller came back to Toronto she immediately noticed a change in him. (This may have been partly due to the shattering effect of his first violent crime, of which Edna-Anne knew nothing.) Miller still had a trial coming up in connection with an earlier offence after his return to Toronto, and he was sentenced to a few months in Burwash reformatory. However, according to Edna-Anne, when he emerged from jail in 1967 he literally turned over a new leaf.

Five years later, by the spring of 1972, Miller and his wife owned their own business — Miller Contracting — and were paying the mortgage on a house purchased a year earlier. They had even saved up enough money to help Edna-Anne's mother with the down payment on a new home. In Edna-Anne's opinion, her husband's attitude had changed "dramatically" in the last few years, and he had become "a responsible husband and devoted father". (By then the couple had three small children.)

Miller regularly worked twelve-hour days, seven days a week, doing such contracting work as painting, plumbing, brick-laying and eavestroughing. He first used an old truck and then, as business prospered, a later-model van. His customers — a pharmacist, a realtor, two or three small builders — expressed the highest opinions of his character and the quality of his work. One customer talked about a sum of cash inadvertently left behind in a building, which Miller had found and returned. Another expressed the view that "I have never found a more honest, conscientious, and congenial person to deal with." All confirmed that they would hire Miller again without the slightest hesitation.

Interestingly enough, as it turned out later, Couvreur appeared to have made a similar adjustment and had not been in any trouble with the law since the Winnipeg robbery.

The two men's arrest came about as a result of some personal quarrel involving one of them. In the afternoon of March 6 an angry woman gave a tip to the police in Toronto. They in turn got in touch with the Winnipeg police before the end of the day. Justice, asleep for nearly six years, woke up quickly. By 10:30 a.m. on March 9 Couvreur was arrested in Toronto. By 5:25 p.m. the same day Miller was placed under arrest. Both men were back in Winnipeg by Saturday, March 11, and by March 24 both had pleaded guilty to a charge of robbery in the City of Winnipeg Magistrates Court.

On April 7, Magistrate Wallace M. Darichuk, Q.C., sentenced James Miller, who wielded the iron bar, to fifteen years' imprisonment. Rudy Couvreur received a sentence of ten years.

It was at this stage that I became involved in the case, being retained by Miller to plead for a reduction of his sentence before the Manitoba Court of Appeal.

Even as a young lawyer with more self-confidence than experience, as I was in 1972, I did not think that the appeal would be a piece of cake. For one thing, the consequences of Miller's offence were much too grave. An elderly man had been terribly injured and was still not able, apparently, to walk without assistance. No court could or would overlook that.

For another thing, I knew from having appeared before Chief Justice George Gale's Court of Appeal in Ontario, when it included such legendary appeal court judges as Mr. Justice Aylesworth or Mr. Justice Schroeder, that courts of appeal are no picnic for young lawyers in any province.

Even so, it seemed to me that we had solid grounds for appealing a very harsh sentence. Upon his arrest, Miller confessed freely and immediately (as did Couvreur). Miller made no attempt to excuse or minimize his involvement, and he showed considerable remorse. "When we did this thing we had no intention of hurting anyone," he told the police. "We were in a fix for money and we thought that it would be no trouble to get a few dollars to keep moving — it was wrong and has bothered me for years. And I am truly sorry for it."

It was also evident that in the intervening six years he had changed his conduct completely. He had done as much as any man could to put his past behind him. He could obviously not undo his past — no man can — but he was doing his best for a future: a decent, law-abiding future for himself and for his family. Society had no need to protect itself from Miller any more. On the contrary, it had a greater interest in not crushing him (along with his wife and three children) so badly that he could never stand on his own feet again.

Miller's after-care service supervisor from the Ministry of Correctional Services said that he was "shocked" to hear of Miller's arrest for the violent Winnipeg robbery of 1972. He had kept in touch with

Miller after his release from jail and found his conduct and his family situation "very satisfactory". Without condoning his offence in any way, he expressed the view that Miller should be given "another chance".

None of this amounted to an argument, of course, that Miller should go free. However, there was a tremendous amount of case law indicating that confession and remorse, combined with a passage of time and a demonstrated successful effort at rehabilitation, were mitigating factors for the trial judge to take into account.

It was our view that Magistrate Darichuk had failed to do this. A fifteen-year sentence was pure retribution, with no consideration given at all, as required by our legal ideals and practice, to rehabilitation.

I understood that the judges sitting on the appeal were to be Chief Justice Freedman, Mr. Justice Guy, and, as he then was, Mr. Justice Dickson (now the Chief Justice of the Supreme Court of Canada). I arrived in Winnipeg a day early to slip, somewhat apprehensively, into the courtroom and watch them at work. I was very impressed, and said so to a friend, a bencher of the law society in Manitoba, when I met him for breakfast the next morning. "Seems like a fine court; civil, erudite, humane," I said. "I especially liked Sam Freedman."

"You won't have him today," my friend replied, ominously. "He's been taken ill."

"Oh? You sound as if I have problems. Who will I have?"

"Monnin."

I knew little about Mr. Justice (now Chief Justice) Monnin of the Manitoba Court of Appeal. "Bad?" I asked my friend.

He shrugged. I concluded that it meant bad. I had no inkling how bad until an hour later.

Appeal Court Justices Guy and Dickson entered the courtroom first, nodding politely in acknowledgement of my bow, in the usual civilized courtroom tradition. Then in came Mr. Justice Monnin.

He started yelling at me virtually from the first moment I opened my mouth. There was no question of letting me present my arguments. He wouldn't even let me sit down and surrender. "Pleading guilty is *mitigation*?" he shouted. "Chief Justice Gale says so? Well, you go back and tell your Chief Justice that this is not the law in Manitoba, and as long as I'm here it will never be the law in Manitoba!"

It was perhaps the only moment in my entire legal career when I actually felt sorry for myself. I felt even sorrier for my client, needless to say. The court's majority judgment rejecting the appeal (delivered by Mr. Justice Guy) echoed Mr. Justice Monnin's sentiments: "To argue or suggest," said the court, "that [the defendants'] lives have been relatively law abiding since the offence . . . [is] giving them good marks for not being caught immediately, and pleading guilty after the lengthy time it took to catch them."

I would have had serious doubts about the validity of my legal research and arguments, and perhaps about my entire career-choice as a lawyer, had it not been for the fact that Mr. Justice Brian Dickson disagreed with his fellow justices. In his dissenting judgment the future Chief Justice of Canada would have reduced Miller's fifteen-year sentence to six years. He was equally unhappy with lawyers' being swatted like insects in court, as he told me when he called me into his chambers to apologize for Mr. Justice Monnin's manners.

I managed a weak smile. "Well, it was an experience. His Lordship was the only person to actually make me miss Justices Aylesworth and Schroeder of Ontario."

Nine years passed. In view of my experience it was perhaps not surprising that when, in 1981, I returned to Winnipeg to argue the appeal of Robert Wilson — a maverick member of the Manitoba Legislature, convicted of importing and trafficking in marijuana — I kept delivering dire warnings to my associate counsel, Marc Rosenberg, about the dread Mr. Justice Monnin. I suppose I felt somewhat protective about Marc, a highly knowledgeable and scholarly young lawyer, who won his spurs in the perfectly civil atmosphere of the current Ontario Court of Appeal.

"It will be bad," I said to Rosenberg. "It will be something you could not have experienced before. By the time you came along, judges like Schroeder and Aylesworth were retired, so you have no reference points at all. I just want to make sure that you don't take it too much to heart."

The next day we stood in court facing Justices Monnin, O'Sullivan, and Huband. Rosenberg's hands never shake visibly, but looking at him I could tell that my warnings had not gone unheeded. His knuckles were just a touch whiter than usual, but he seemed prepared for all eventualities.

The proceedings began. After about an hour we took a brief recess. All I could do was to look at Marc apologetically, shake my head, and shrug my shoulders.

There was no way that a human being could have behaved with more consideration, with more exquisite politeness, with more careful attention or courtly solicitude, than Mr. Justice Monnin exhibited that morning. Rosenberg must have thought that I was crazy — and I couldn't blame him. To this day, whenever the Manitoba Court of Appeal comes into the conversation in any context, I notice Marc glancing at me with some suspicion.

The case of Robert Wilson raised a point far more important, however, than my experiences with Mr. Justice Monnin. Essentially, as in most appeals, the defendant's contention was that the trial judge, in this case Mr. Justice (now Chief Justice) Hewak of the Court of Queen's Bench, had made certain errors in law in his charge to the jury.

In particular, we argued that the trial judge had misdirected the jury on the law that deals with the dangers of convicting anyone on the uncorroborated evidence of a co-conspirator. He also failed to tell the jury that the evidence of this co-conspirator, whether believed or not, did little to implicate the accused; and he let in other evidence — namely, an intercepted telephone communication between a wife and her husband — that was privileged and therefore inadmissible under the Criminal Code.

These were important points. The case against Wilson had included lengthy testimony by a man named William Wright, a confessed accomplice and drug-trafficker, who received immunity in exchange for what he was saying in court. As discussed before with reference to Cecil Kirby, it is always in the interest of such people to implicate others. For this reason alone, juries must be warned to take any story that this type of witness may tell in court, unless confirmed by other evidence, with a grain of salt. Just as importantly, even if Wright was believed, it only proved that a drug ring existed, but not that Robert Wilson had anything to do with it. This fact was central to the defence's theory, yet the judge omitted to make it clear to the jury. As for the telephone conversation between a man named MacDonald and his wife, it was simply not admissible evidence. The jury — as the Supreme Court of Canada later confirmed in a different case — should never have heard it.

The Manitoba Court of Appeal agreed with these points — more or less. Speaking for the court, Mr. Justice O'Sullivan said: "I am satisfied there was in this case misdirection in the dilution of warning as to the danger of convicting on accomplice evidence and there was non-direction amounting to misdirection as to Wright's evidence and the theory of defence with respect to it." Mr. Justice O'Sullivan added that, considering Wright's evidence alone, "I would be inclined to reverse the verdict and order a new trial," and that in such case "there would be grounds for holding that the verdicts were unreasonable and unsafe."

As to the inadmissible telephone conversation, since the legal principle was then under consideration by the Supreme Court of Canada, Mr. Justice O'Sullivan simply stated: "I am not prepared to say whether counsel is right or wrong."

We happened to be right, as it turned out, but it would not have made any difference. Notwithstanding all legal errors in Wilson's trial, the Manitoba Court of Appeal confirmed his conviction — essentially because, on other evidence, the court believed that the jury would have reached the same verdict anyway. In coming to its decision the court relied on Section 613 of the Criminal Code, subsection (1)(b)(iii) of which provides that a conviction can stand in spite of certain errors in law at trial, if the appeal court believes that it would result in "no substantial wrong or miscarriage of justice".

I have always had a problem with Section 613(1)(b)(iii), even in my days as a law student. Did it imply that, while a substantial miscarriage of justice was to be avoided, a little miscarriage of justice was okay? Did it say that innocent people should have fair trials, but that it was all right for a person to be tried unfairly if an appeal court believed him to be guilty?

How was this possible, if in our system all people were presumed to be innocent? How could anyone tell who was guilty, unless he had been found guilty beyond a reasonable doubt *in a fair trial* first?

In this sense "fair" simply meant "according to law", as it could not mean anything else. Over the centuries, through a combination of precedent and legislation, we have developed a system of rules and procedures. We have developed them because long experience has shown them to be safe, just, and applicable to many cases. Together these rules constitute procedural law, and people must be tried in accordance with their requirements. There is no other way to try anyone fairly.

It has always seemed to me that procedural fairness — often called, mistakenly and disparagingly, "legal technicalities" by people who don't know any better (and even by people who ought to know better, such as some journalists) — is the very essence of the law. After all, we object to a lynching precisely because of its shortcomings as a *procedure*. It would not reassure us to know that the person we lynched did, in fact, steal a horse.

This was also the celebrated maxim of the American jurist Felix Frankfurter: "The history of liberty has largely been the history of observance of procedural safeguards." The late Alexander M. Bickel, Sterling Professor of Law at Yale University and one of the greatest legal scholars of the post-war years, was of the same opinion: "It is the premise of our legal order that its own complicated arrangements . . . are more important than any momentary objective. [Legal] technicalities are the stuff of law."

To argue that having come to a fair conclusion about an accused it should not bother us that we have been unfair to him in the process, because had we been fair to him we would have come to the same conclusion, is arguing backwards. We only know that a conclusion is fair by having reached it fairly. Otherwise we simply don't know whether it's a fair conclusion or not. An appeal court may *agree* with the verdict of a jury, but it cannot possibly know how that verdict was reached. It can only find out what went before a jury, in terms of evidence or instructions, and determine whether this was legally pure or tainted. If it was tainted, the job of the higher court is to reverse the verdict or to order a new trial.

True, there being few absolutes in life, some rules had to be developed to guard against truly insignificant errors interfering with well-substantiated findings. The original intent of Section 613(1)(b)(iii) was probably limited in scope to preventing very minor matters from resulting in the reversal of a sound verdict, thereby bringing the administration of justice into disrepute. No one could quarrel with that. The ability of higher courts to adjust results, whether in favour of an accused or against him, merely acknowledges and accommodates the frailties inherent in any system of human inquiry.

However, there is an immense leap from this to the practice that appears to have developed in the last twenty years. When I was an articling student in the Attorney General's Department in 1968, it was still a point of pride among Crown attorneys that throughout their careers they did not have to "argue Section 613" even once in order to have a conviction in a lower court upheld in the courts above. Having to plead that, while there might have been a *little* miscarriage of justice, it really wasn't substantial enough to disturb a guilty verdict, used to be regarded by prosecutors as a barely respectable, let alone routine, argument.

If older Crowns may have blotted their copybooks by relying on the argument even once, today's Crowns seem to blot theirs by not relying on it often enough. Section 613(1)(b)(iii) is being argued — and is being given effect to by our higher courts — as if it were the most ordinary matter in the world.

Far more than the odd stern, crotchety, snarling (or even truly abusive) judge, it is this development that can turn a court into a lions' den. Manners, on the whole, have much improved today in our halls of justice. But much as I like civility, I believe that the elevation of Section 613(1)(b)(iii) to a cure-all has proved to be a greater threat to the rule of law in Canada than the most ill-tempered judges ever were.

## NOTES

p.341, l.19: The Honourable John Bell Aylesworth was appointed to the Ontario Court of Appeal in 1946 and retired in 1972. The Honourable Walter Frank Schroeder was appointed to the High Court of Ontario in 1945 and to the Ontario Court of Appeal in 1955. He retired in 1975. In spite of their occasional impatience in criminal cases, they both were, and were regarded as, brilliant jurists.

p.342, l.9: There is a well-established body of case law indicating that remorse (*R. v. Wilmott*, 1967); confession (*R. v. Warner et al.*, 1946; *R. v. Doyle and 10 Others*, 1970); a plea of guilty (*R. v. Johnsons and Tremayne*, 1970; *R. v. Harper*, 1968); and rehabilitation (*R. v. Taylor*, 1984; *R. v. Cossette-Trudel*, 1979) are factors to be taken into account in imposing sentence.

Generally speaking, the theory of punishment rests on utilitarian principles. Courts are reluctant to impose a sentence solely as a matter of revenge or retribution. Where the accused pleads guilty, shows remorse, and has rehabilitated himself, there is no need for a lengthy penalty to deter or reform him or to protect the public. All that is required is a sentence which adequately reflects the need to deter others. In exceptional circumstances this can lead to the imposition of a sentence far below what would ordinarily be called for (*R. v. Humes*, 1978).

p.344, l.32: Since the Wilson case, the Supreme Court of Canada has substantially altered the accomplice rule. It is no longer mandatory for the judge to caution the jury about the danger of acting on the uncorroborated evidence of an accomplice, and to detail the evidence capable of being corroborated. The judge does, however, have to point out to the jury the particular dangers of evidence of someone like an accomplice, when the circumstances suggest that, as a matter of prudence, the jury should look for evidence that confirms the accomplice's story. (*Vetrovec v. The Queen*; *Gaja v. The Queen*, 1982).

p.344, l.39: *R. v. Jean and Piesinger*. See also *R. v. Lloyd and Lloyd*.

p.346, l.10: *McNabb v. U.S.*, 1943.

p.346, l.15: From *The Morality of Consent* by Alexander M. Bickel (Yale University Press, pp. 120-1). The full passages are worth noting. Commenting on the Supreme Court of the United States, Professor Bickel wrote: "The Warren Court took the greatest pride in cutting through legal technicalities, in piercing through procedure to substance. But legal technicalities are the stuff of law, and piercing through a particular substance to get to procedures suitable to many substances is in fact what the task of law most often is."

The Warren Court, of course, was usually "cutting through" procedural law for liberal purposes, but Professor Bickel had no more patience with those who would dispense with procedure for conservative aims. "It is ironic, but entirely natural," he wrote in the same essay, "that 'law-and-order' as a moral imperative should have clashed with the legal order. For the legal order, after all, is an accommodation. It cannot sustain the continuous assault of moral imperatives. . . . It is the premise of our legal order that its own complicated arrangements, although subject to evolutionary change, are more important than any momentary objective."

To put it simply, Bickel warned that if we play fast and loose with the law every time we have a moral objection to a result that observing the law may bring about, soon we'll have no law. It is a risk, unfortunately, that some "conservatives" as well as some "liberals" in our society are only too willing to take.

p.346, l.23: See also in Chapter 14 a case called *Giguere* to illustrate the impossibility of knowing what has or has not impressed a jury as decisive among the mass of information placed before it in a criminal trial. One may put before a jury several valid reasons for arriving at a certain result — all of which it may disregard, only to arrive at the same decision for the one invalid reason that was also in front of it. If so, the jury's decision will be unjustified, even though the same decision may have been justifiable if reached by a different route. (The same is true about major and minor reasons — a jury may reject a major reason and convict or acquit someone for a minor one — but this cannot be helped.) However, there should never be any *invalid* reasons allowed to go to a jury.

# 18. *The Rule of Men*

Roy McMahon was a pederast. He was a married man in his fifties when I first saw him in 1971. In so far as I can judge such things, he appeared to be quite ugly.

In spite of this, McMahon was a hit with young boys. He liked them, and, for some reason which I'm not qualified to analyse, many of them liked him. He had made sexual advances to boys for years, got caught, gone to jail, come out, and merrily continued as before. After serving a sentence for his last conviction, he was hired as a janitor in a church.

McMahon enjoyed his new job because of the Boy Scouts. He had worked his way through the Boy Scout troop and seemed to be halfway through the Cub Scouts when he was caught again and charged with indecent assualt.

Beyond whatever psychological damage he may have done to his victims, McMahon never hurt anyone. On the contrary, the evidence indicated that all the boys "consented" to his advances. McMahon was nice to them. The fact was, he *liked* young boys, and he simply enjoyed doing to them whatever one does to boys if one likes them in that way.

In a legal sense, of course, a child cannot consent to sexual advances; that's why I'm using inverted commas around the word. Acquiescing in the corrupting influence of an adult does not in any way amount to consent, but common sense suggests that it is still not in the same category as forcible assault.

In the early seventies, laying charges under the relatively new legislation for Dangerous Sexual Offenders was quite a popular thing to do. An order under that section meant an indeterminate sentence of preventive detention, to be reviewed periodically by the Parole Board. In theory, a person could be locked up forever, not for anything he did, but for something he might do at some future date. This was the section under which the Crown Attorney, Bob McGee, was planning to proceed with the charges against McMahon.

There was no question whatever that McMahon was a sexual offender — but was he dangerous? He never hurt, forced, or threatened his victims; he only cajoled, talked, or bribed them into letting him do whatever he did to them. What he then did to the boys was obviously unlawful (and even sick, in many people's opinion, including mine), but there was no evidence that it caused the boys any physical harm or mental anguish. At no time did McMahon show any sign of being "dangerous" in the ordinary meaning of the word.

McMahon may or may not have been the type of person contemplated by the Dangerous Sexual Offenders section of the Criminal Code. In any case, I was an eager young lawyer prepared to make lengthy constitutional arguments against the legislation, not under the Charter of Rights and Freedoms, because that did not exist in those days, but citing American law and the "Diefenbaker" Bill of Rights. I thought McMahon should simply be punished, like any criminal, for what he actually did (which was plenty). McGee, a wily and experienced prosecutor, glanced at the mass of lawbooks I was carrying under my arm, and agreed to my offer of a guilty plea on McMahon's behalf. As a result, the judge sentenced him to nine years in penitentiary but did not declare him to be a dangerous sexual offender.

For many years after that I lost sight of McMahon. He was up in Kingston Penitentiary, serving his time. Once in a while I did think about him, perhaps because he had a roguish sense of humour and his personality was not altogether unattractive. That may have been why some of his victims liked him, too. His case, in 1971, also happened to be my first "big" case in terms of the penal consequences involved.

In any event, a number of years later I happened to be in Kingston Penitentiary visiting another client. On my way out an older prisoner said hello to me.

"Roy McMahon," I said, recognizing him.

"Psst," he said, putting his finger to his lips. "Come with me for a minute. There's something I want to show you."

I followed him down the hall to his cell. Inside, the walls were absolutely plastered over with cut-outs from *Playboy* magazine. They were all glossy pictures of Playmates-of-the-Month, beautiful girls, complete with the most fearsome mammary developments.

I glanced questioningly at McMahon. He nudged me and winked. "Well, you know," he said. "Parole's coming up."

Another Roy incarcerated at Kingston, Roy Kully, a man in his early thirties, was a completely different type of human being. At any other historic period his strangeness would have been self-evident, but in the late sixties and early seventies the fashion of the times permitted some people to think of him (and perhaps Kully to think of himself) as just another "hippie". His weird lack of affect was a common cultural phenomenon in those days, and it allowed Kully to melt into the background, more or less. Being semi-comatose, even when not under the influence of drugs, was a kind of attitude assumed by other hippies. For Kully, however, it was the real thing. It expressed his essential being. To me he appeared to be the most unusual flower-child in Canada.

Unlike most other flower-children, when Kully woke up long enough to take notice of his surroundings, he usually did something vicious. The crime for which he had been sent to Kingston was raping and killing a five-year-old child. Once behind bars, however, his apparent passivity made him a kind of model prisoner. The prison system ( and, ultimately, the Parole Board) put a premium on "manageability", and Kully was highly manageable. When told to get up in prison, he would get up; when told to sit down, he would sit down. In jail, at least, Kully was being a good boy. Whatever psychiatric care might have done for him, in Kingston he did not seem to need, and was not receiving, any. What he got was points in the system for being easy to manage.

Soon Kully started getting certain privileges, and it was not unreasonable for him to expect to be paroled in a few years. However, just around the time that he became due for a parole hearing, some murder parolee in Vancouver went wrong. Whatever the details were, the newspapers made a fuss. Ever sensitive to media attention, the parole system temporarily shut down.

Kully was deeply hurt. He was a sensitive flower-child, after all. He stood apart in his personal sickness, but what he did share with other flower-children was a vague and perpetual sense of injustice. The larger society was being unfair again. *He* didn't do anything wrong, he felt; he was getting up and sitting down nicely as he was being told. He did his part of the bargain, yet now "the system" was depriving him of something to which it had earlier appeared to give him an entitlement. Society, as it seemed to Kully, was going back on its word. (Frankly, it was.) Kully started taking drugs, which are often available in prison.

Earlier Kully had established a friendship of sorts with a cultural prison-worker named Nancy Helwig. Having organized a theatrical production by prisoners, Helwig cast Kully in the title role of *The Dandy Lion*. The production was being mounted outside the prison walls, and during a rehearsal the sensitive star escaped. While at liberty, the Dandy Lion sexually assaulted a child in Cornwall and killed an elderly man in Chatham.

It was only after his recapture that I actually met Kully. There wasn't a great deal that could be done to defend him, but I became interested in his case. Without going into details, I rather doubted if he was fit to stand trial for his crime: he kept dozing off in the dock while the witnesses were testifying, with an irate judge (Mr. Justice Thompson) yelling: "Wake him up, wake him up!" At such times Kully would obligingly open his eyes for a few minutes, then fall back into his reverie again.

There was no way of knowing, of course, whether or not Kully would have waited patiently for his parole hearing even if the system hadn't temporarily shut down. Nor was it possible to know whether, had he been a parolee instead of an escapee, he might not have committed the same crimes on the outside. But the case-histories of both Kully and McMahon illustrate some fundamental points about our system of parole.

When a person is convicted of a crime and is sentenced to a period of incarceration, he passes from the court system to the parole system. This means that he is passed from an open legal system to a closed administrative system; from a system that operates in daylight to one that operates in the shadows. He is passed from a world of strict and reviewable legal procedures to a world of confidential memos and ever-changing bureaucratic edicts. To a considerable extent, he is passed from the rule of law to the rule of men.

When he passes from the bright halls of justice to the dark cellars of bureaucracy, the public may perceive him as passing into a liberal officialdom's care and favour. The prisoner perceives himself as passing into a senseless officialdom's caprice.

No human system is fully predictable; no system is entirely free from popular pressures. Courts can sometimes also be influenced by the vagaries of fashion. Advocates and judges can vary in skill or judgment; the finest legal minds are subject to individual quirks. The excellent criminal lawyer David (now The Honourable Judge)

Humphrey once chose to give a jury address which consisted of a single assertion that, if his client was guilty, he was a monkey's uncle. (He obviously wasn't, since his client was acquitted.) Still, courts are primarily ruled by case law and statute. They must hear arguments for both sides. Their decisions (and, just as important, their reasoning) can be reviewed by higher courts. Court proceedings are noted in public records: anybody can order up and read them. Judges (or juries) can never quite go off the deep end to the same extent that officials can. Relative to any administrative system, the justice system *is* highly predictable.

If administrative systems are much less predictable (even while being more rigid), it's not because bureaucrats are necessarily less fair, benevolent, or intelligent than judges or lawyers. Nor is it because they care less about the public interest, or about the welfare of the human beings in their charge. The sole reason is institutional: it is because officials operate behind closed doors and with an almost unfettered discretion. Compared to the courts, any bureaucracy will be — and will also appear to be — unfair and capricious.

Nevertheless, two-thirds (in certain cases up to five-sixths) of the actual time any prisoner spends in jail is determined by the bureaucracy of the parole system. When a judge sentences someone to nine years in prison, he will in fact only dispose of the next three years of that person's life. The other six years will be in the hands of prison and parole officials.

Under these circumstances it is not surprising that prisoners spend much of their time trying to learn (or guess) how to push the buttons of the parole system. It would be contrary to human nature for them to do otherwise. The likelihood that this aids their rehabilitation and reform is very small. What it is much more likely to develop is their manipulative skills and their cynicism about society and its institutions. In amusing instances this leads to an elderly pederast like McMahon sticking pin-up girls on the walls of his cell — but not all instances are equally amusing.

Generally, and especially since the mid-1970s, popular dissatisfaction with the operation of the parole system has centred around its perceived inadequacy to protect the public. As a rule, the media's favourite examples have been about cases where a person convicted of a violent offence (usually murder or rape) is released either "too early" or on some temporary-absence program, such as day parole.

In such cases, especially if the parolee has then eluded supervision, failed to return to custody, or, much worse, committed or attempted to commit a similar crime, there is a momentary wave of public indignation. The press makes editorial demands for the overhaul of the parole system, and sometimes Opposition members raise questions in Parliament.

Parole administrators ritually respond by explanations or apologies concerning the individual case, and by justifications concerning the system as a whole. However, another frequent response is to temporarily change the rules of the game. Parole officials often suspend certain programs for entire classes of prisoners, or turn down an individual application for parole (or for some other privilege) that, made only a week or a month earlier, would almost certainly have succeeded on its merits according to officialdom's earlier rules.

The impression of unfairness this creates is strengthened by the fact that, after the wave of public indignation has subsided, things often return to the status quo. The only losers are the prisoners caught in midstream.

The frustration, resentment, and *uncertainty* that this engenders in the prison population is not difficult to imagine. Nothing could be calculated to induce greater disillusionment and mistrust in society and its workings than the appearance of promises made and broken: promises on which some prisoners have relied in good faith, perhaps for the first time in their lives.

If criminals have one thing in common, it is their general tendency to feel ill done by; to view "straight" society as one that has never given them a fair shake. Most of them are devout injustice-collectors. This is the very perception, in fact, by which they justify their antisocial acts to themselves. Reinforcing this impression by administrative caprice is counter-productive, to use a mild expression. If reform and rehabilitation form any part of the goals of the penal system — and our highest courts have repeatedly confirmed that they do — any method that, instead of alleviating, reinforces the very suspicions and resentments in the minds of criminals that caused them to become criminals in the first place is probably the last method that we should employ.

Yet such methods are probably inherent in the nature of the parole system. Since it has no procedural or evidentiary rules comparable to the legal system's; since its procedures (with some exceptions) do not provide for representation, legal argument, or public scrutiny; since its decisions are usually unreviewed and unreviewable (and can therefore be no better, wiser, or fairer than the individual officials making them), this system cannot but disappoint the public on the one hand, and the prisoners it rules on the other. By its nature, whether it does or does not do justice, it cannot make justice be seen to be done.

Also by its nature, whether it delivers or fails to deliver to a given prisoner what he hopes from it, it cannot but increase his manipulative or cynical attitudes. Prisoners fully realize that parole is at least partly a management tool. It is often dispensed as a reward for good behaviour *in* prison, not in the expectation of reformed behaviour outside prison (after the supervisory period is over). To the extent that this is true, parole not only encourages dissimulation, but has a fundamentally different aim for its administrators than for the general public. Ordinary citizens are far less concerned with how hard or easy inmates are to manage in prison than with how hard or easy they will be to manage once they get out.

In otherwise open societies, all closed and arbitrary systems develop another special problem. Since such systems do not provide ordinary channels for representation and review, they become much too vulnerable to public pressure. A puff of popular wind can blow them every which way. By way of analogy, imagine a court system that does not allow a defendant to be heard or represented by a lawyer — but then might rescind a jury verdict if enough people oppose it in the newspapers. This, with only a slight exaggeration, describes institutions like the Parole Board.

In 1986-87 a multiple-rape-murderer named Henry Williams, dubbed the "Streetsville Dracula" by the press, was allowed a few unescorted spousal visits and temporary absences after serving about eleven years of a life sentence without eligibility for parole for twenty years. (I remembered Williams well, because he had been one of the witnesses in the 1974 trial of Peter Demeter for the murder of his wife. One of Williams' victims was killed on the other side of a ravine behind the garage in suburban Mississauga where the body of Christine Demeter had been discovered a few weeks earlier, and Demeter's senior counsel, Joseph B. Pomerant, wanted to canvass the question of whether or not Williams might have been responsible for Christine's murder as well.)

At any rate, when the newspapers learned about Williams' unescorted spousal visits, they raised a tremendous fuss. One of Williams' victims, a girl who survived and later became a police officer, wrote an open letter to the *Toronto Sun*. Within forty-eight hours Williams' privileges were suspended.

I have no views on whether or not the privileges of the Streetsville Dracula should have been suspended. Personally, I would say that it was an error to grant them in the first place. However, the privileges were no doubt granted for a reason, and that reason would not have been altered by anything that appeared in the press. If so, then from the point of procedural fairness, suspending Williams' privileges was worse than granting them initially. You cannot have a justice system in which the penal consequences of an individual's acts are decided by the newspapers. There is a great difference between public accountability and making decisions about someone's liberty at the whim of media attention.

It does not improve matters when bureaucrats, convinced that their original decision had been correct even if not propitious, quietly reinstate a measure after a period of lying low. This, too, has been a common practice of administrative bodies like the Parole Board. The trouble is, it builds neither respect nor confidence in the minds of their prisoner clients — or in the mind of the public. It is, at best, a temporary solution to a permanent problem.

What is really wrong with the parole system is seldom discussed in the press. Though hardly a day passes without some adverse comment or criticism, most of it is mistaken or beside the point. Parole administrators are quite right when they emphasize that the majority of parolees, or prisoners on temporary-absence programs, do not break the conditions of their parole (or abuse other privileges). They are quite right in saying that for an overall record of predicting accurately something as unpredictable as human behaviour the parole system comes second to none.

Nor, in a purely pragmatic sense, does it make any difference to a householder whether the burglar who breaks into his home is on parole or temporary absence — or has served every single day of his previous sentence. Keeping a prisoner in jail for the full term is no assurance that he will not commit a crime the minute he gets out (even though the matter is often discussed in the press as though no offender would ever break the law again if he were locked up for his full sentence).

Something quite different is wrong with the parole system. It is simply that it fosters the wrong values.

In prison, instead of helping to bring about actual rehabilitation, it puts a premium on "playing the game". Essentially the game consists of convincing the Parole Board that one has become "rehabilitated". Whether shrewd and experienced parole officials can see through it or not (they all claim they can, of course), the fact remains that prisoners concentrate harder on trying to con the Parole Board than on virtually anything else. Who can blame them, when two-thirds or more of their time inside depends on whether they succeed or not.

What is almost never written about is the stress this puts on prisoners of firmer character or with a more acute sense of human dignity, who find the parole game demeaning and refuse to go along with it. Some of the better people in prison, convicts of greater honesty or with stronger feelings of self-worth, who may not be as ready to kowtow or to dissimulate, may be incarcerated for this reason longer than others. In the worst position are those who maintain their innocence — and this includes those who are, in fact, innocent. An expression of "remorse" is often a key requirement of being paroled. People who do not feel remorseful about a crime they did not commit end up facing the awful choice of having to *pretend* that they are guilty or spending another number of years in prison.

In the outside society, the parole system fosters a sense of victimization on the part of the ordinary citizen. It is a feeling of being insufficiently protected — indeed, of being played for a sucker. It actually makes some law-abiding people believe that crime does pay and that criminals "can get away with it". It breeds in decent citizens a mistrust and cynicism about society and its institutions that is remarkably similar to the mistrust and cynicism of criminals. It is enough to open a newspaper almost any day to see some example of this. Reciting facts about the parole system or about recidivism rates, offering numbers, statistics, or flow charts, are powerless to counteract such feelings. Statistics simply don't address the objections involved. Ordinary people are afraid of a system in which faceless, nameless officials sitting behind closed doors can countermand judgments promulgated in open court. This, too, is a fact, and not facing it will not make it go away.

Though people in the street are mainly concerned with one side of the issue — namely, that parole officials may be too "soft" on criminals — their instincts should not be lightly dismissed by those whose concerns are different. The parole system does offend the principles of natural justice. Those principles demand that any process capable of determining people's liberty should be procedurally open, reviewable, predictable, and fair. This is fundamental — yet in its present form the parole system is on the whole procedurally closed, unreviewable, capricious, and arbitrary. It is ironic that we surround that part of the justice system that determines *one-third* of the potential penal consequences of an offence with the most elaborate safeguards, then leave without any safeguards the process that determines *two-thirds* of it.

Finally, in its present form the system fosters a sense of hypocrisy, coupled with a schizophrenic attitude, among the administrators of justice. Parole allows judges to sentence people to harsh or even crushing terms of penal servitude — but only as a symbolic gesture. Many of these sentences are not penalties that fit either the criminal or the crime (in fact, or even in the view of the people who impose them). However, we allow them to be pronounced in the knowledge that only a third or less of them will be spent in actual incarceration. We deceive no one, except ourselves and perhaps the public. We maintain that a certain punishment is a fitting sentence for a certain offence, but quickly deny it as soon as the convicted person steps outside the courtroom.

Why not, I suggest, sentence people to the actual terms we expect them to serve in jail? The usual answer is that such terms would seem inadequate for deterrence or for "denunciation" (that is, for registering society's disapproval of the crime) and that such sentences would not reassure ordinary citizens.

There is only one problem with this answer: the parole system reassures no one. If anything, it creates a profound feeling of disrespect for the administration of justice. It seems to me that people would be far more reassured by a three-year sentence than by the sight of someone sentenced to nine years back on the street in three years or less.

As for deterrence, most criminologists agree that the certainty of punishment is a greater deterrent than its severity — especially, one is tempted to add, when criminals know only too well that the punishment is not as severe as it appears.

Requiring convicts to serve the full terms of their sentences, incidentally, could only be contemplated if judges adjusted their sentencing practices accordingly. At present judges claim not to take the parole system into account when pronouncing sentence, but in fact a judge would have to come from Mars not to know that when he sentences someone to three or six or nine years, in the normal course of events it means that that person will spend one or two or three years in jail. Judges do not normally come from Mars, so they do take parole into account. In a system without parole they would have to be guided by the same understanding, acknowledged or otherwise.

Another argument advanced in support of a system of parole is that while a certain punishment may fit a crime, it may not fit a given criminal. The crime itself may call for a harsh sentence, but a particular individual convicted of it may be safely released much earlier. This argument has merit, but it does not answer the objections to the type of closed administrative system we have at present. Convicts who have a case for an early release could just as easily apply to the courts, where both they and society might enjoy the protection of a public procedure with all its ordinary safeguards, including legal representation for all parties involved.

While such an approach might create a hopeless bottleneck if immediately applied to all classes of crime, there would seem to be no reason why it should not be utilized for people accused of serious violent offences, beginning with murder.

There is no doubt in my mind that the crime of first-degree murder should be removed from the consideration of the Parole Board right away. This should be done both to safeguard society and to safeguard the rights of the prisoner applying for early release. It should be an open process, argued by submissions in front of a judge and jury according to the ordinary rules of evidence in all sentencing procedures, and reviewable by the higher courts. If for no other reason than public perception, parole for first-degree murderers should be considered in a forum where justice can be seen to be done.

## NOTES

p.351, l.28: McMahon was referred to me by Gary Siskind, my room-mate at law school. Gary became a real-estate lawyer and I never expected to receive a case from his practice, yet he was the first lawyer to send me a case. The place from which I did expect to receive referrals was my home town, Niagara Falls. I never got any.

p.353, l.25: Primarily such a person is passed on to the prison system, which after a passage of time and under certain conditions funnels him into the parole system. In spite of some overlapping aspects between the two systems, discussion of the prison system would require a separate chapter.

p.354, l.24: There are exceptions, notably when either legislation or a special condition of the penalty imposed by a judge specifies a minimum length of time a prisoner must serve before he becomes eligible for parole. Even in those cases, however, parole officials may determine a greater proportion of the actual time a prisoner spends in jail than the courts.

p.358, l.23: One of the most intriguing demonstrations of the problem that such insistence on "remorse" may cause occurred at the Supreme Court of Canada reference of Steven Truscott's case in 1966. Truscott had been convicted of murder in the death of a twelve-year-old girl named Lynne Harper in 1959 (Truscott himself being only fourteen at the time). Persistent public questions about Truscott's innocence resulted in a unique Supreme Court reference seven years later. At this proceeding, the Crown introduced a letter written by Truscott to parole officials, containing an expression of "remorse". This, the prosecution contended, amounted to a confession to murder. Truscott, of course, testified that he had simply been playing the "parole game"; he had meant to confess to nothing.

Another recent example is the case of Norman Fox, a man convicted in British Columbia of a charge of rape. For years after he became eligible for parole, the board failed to release him because Fox refused to show "remorse": he simply kept maintaining his innocence. As everyone found out several years later, Fox had an excellent reason. He *was* innocent; another man had committed the rape. Eventually Fox received a free pardon.

p.359, l.29: Another argument suggests that prisons would be difficult to manage without the incentives provided by the parole system. Apart from the fact that giving too much weight to management considerations makes the administrative tail wag the penal dog, I think the argument also fails on its merits. Incentives for good behaviour can take the form of privileges inside prison, such as better work-assignments, spousal visits, etc., while disincentives for not behaving can be the withdrawal of such privileges. Serious offences committed in prison, of course, can be dealt with through ordinary criminal procedures, exposing the unruly prisoner to a new conviction and additional time in jail.

p.360, l.34: Shortly after this chapter was completed in March 1987, the Canadian Sentencing Commission, headed by Saskatchewan Provincial Court Judge Omer Archambault, released its detailed and thoughtful study of problems of sentencing and parole. The Archambault Commission's recommendations, including its central recommendation about "real time" sentencing, as well as much of its analysis, coincide with the views sketched out in this chapter to a gratifying degree.

INTERLUDE: **FAST EDDIE**

*Greenspan is meticulously law-abiding in his private conduct, but his closest friends could not suggest that he is equally by-law-abiding. When it comes to parking, for instance, it's possible that Eddie did park his car legally once or twice in his life, but no one who knows him can remember any actual example.*

*In addition to municipal by-laws, Greenspan has had an uneasy coexistence with the Highway Traffic Act in general over the years. Not in all respects, because Eddie is a safe, experienced, and even considerate driver: he doesn't drink, doesn't run red lights, doesn't straddle lanes, and doesn't pull into traffic without looking. But neither does he carry a wallet. Since he doesn't, he never has any identification on him, and probably has no idea what a driver's licence or an ownership paper looks like.*

*The idea that his car's headlights ought to be balanced would enter Eddie's head just as little. The notion of Greenspan ever walking around a vehicle to see if things are in proper working order would strike those who know him as irresistibly funny. In fact, when it comes to automobiles, Eddie wouldn't know what to look for any more than the average society lady would. Actually this is an unfair slur on society ladies, because they may at least remember that a car needs gasoline to run, which Eddie doesn't. Being picked up by Greenspan in a car means spending prayerful moments hoping that the last few ounces of gas at the bottom of the tank will take one to the nearest gas station.*

*The Greenspan fleet — which for years has consisted of an old and somewhat battered Cadillac, a magnificent if quirky Checker cab, and an ancient Rolls-Royce — is being looked after by Suzy Greenspan. The Rolls (known affectionately as Roy's Rolls because it had previously been owned by the film producer Roy Krost) has caused Suzy to seriously consider becoming a licensed Rolls-Royce mechanic in her spare time. She gave up the idea on discovering that licensed mechanics couldn't keep Roy's Rolls rolling either.*

Eddie stays aloof from all such automotive exotica by sticking to the Cadillac, as a rule. Still, it was the unbalanced headlights of the Checker that caused a young policeman to stop him once on Yonge Street late at night. Naturally, Eddie did not have his wallet.

"Here's my licence," said George Jonas, who was riding in the front seat with Greenspan, to the officer. "Take down my particulars, and I'll vouch for who he is."

"Okay, so who is he?" said the young cop.

"His name is Edward Greenspan, and his home address is such and such," Jonas replied.

The policeman peered into Eddie's face. "That's right, too," he said. "That's exactly who he is. I recognize him. Wow!"

Saying this, the policeman started walking around the Checker, looking for any other possible irregularities. He checked the tail-lights; he asked Eddie to touch the brakes to see if the brake lights were working. Then he came back to the driver's side of the car.

"Well, Mr. Greenspan," he said severely, "you have no licence, no ownership, and no insurance papers on you, and your headlights are pointing all over the place. I'll give you a warning, and you've got forty-eight hours to have it all fixed and bring your car and your papers to the police station; otherwise you'll get a ticket. Okay?"

"Okay, officer," said Eddie. "Thanks and good night."

"Good night," replied the young policeman, then suddenly he pointed a finger at Greenspan. His face, very serious until then, broke into a sweet, triumphant smile. "I gotcha!" he yelled, walking away.

When it comes to moving violations, Eddie indulges in only one kind: speeding. More precisely, he never remembers to observe those totally unrealistic speed restrictions that exist in and around Toronto (as well as other cities) on four-lane highways next to empty fields or cemeteries. The speed limit in such places is continually enforced by radar checks, not as a measure of safety — the safest drivers will "speed" in these spots — but to produce revenue for the municipality's coffers. Even though Greenspan knows the location of these radar traps, having been caught in them many times before, he is unable to crawl by at legal but unreasonably slow speeds. For instance, during the period when he was living in North Toronto, Eddie would be caught almost every night in the same trap along an empty six-lane stretch of Bayview Avenue where the speed limit is set at an inexplicable 50 km/h. "Good evening, sir," the police officers would say, getting quite used to Eddie after a while. "Gee, I haven't seen you in twenty-four hours."

*Not every speeding-ticket cost Greenspan points, but several of them did. As a result, there was a period when his driver's licence was only a few points away from suspension. During this time it was an explicit part of his articling students' job description to keep their principal licensed and on the road by representing him in various traffic courts around Toronto. Greenspan chose to characterize this task as a part of their training. "I speed only for your good," he once told Guy Kay, before dispatching Kay — his student at the time — to do battle in yet another outpost of the traffic-court system.*

*Eventually, despite the yeoman efforts of several years of students, Greenspan was required to attend an interview and show cause why his licence should not be suspended.*

*Eddie was nervous about the interview. He knew that the authorities had the discretion to suspend his licence for three months, which, like most people, he would have found very inconvenient. While waiting for the interviewer, he could hear the voices of some of the other drivers telling their excuses. They ranged from one man who said that he needed his licence because his entire family was struck down by a disease of the vegetative nervous system and he alone had to feed thirty-eight or forty people, to another who insisted that all the radar guns were wrong and he had never exceeded the legal speed limit in his life.*

*Finally it was Greenspan's turn. He walked around the room-divider, to find himself face to face with a very attractive young woman.*

*"You have all these tickets for speeding," said the pretty interviewer to Eddie. "Why is that?"*

*"Because I get caught," replied Eddie, truthfully.*

*"What?" asked the woman, seeming genuinely puzzled.*

*"Well, you see," Greenspan explained. "I speed, and then the police catch me. If they didn't catch me I wouldn't have all these tickets, but they keep catching me, so that's why I have them."*

*"You mean," the interviewer said, "you're not going to give me an excuse?"*

*"Well, I'd be happy to," Eddie replied, "but I don't think I have any. You see, that's my problem."*

*The young lady was flabbergasted. "In five years of working here," she said, "you're the first person who hasn't come up with an excuse. You know, I think you may be the first honest person. I think I'll let you keep your licence."*

*Now it was Eddie's turn to look incredulous.*

"*Don't play with me,*" he pleaded. "*False hopes drive me crazy. I was very nervous about this interview.*"

"*You were nervous!*" said the woman. "*When I found out who I had to interview today, I was so nervous I couldn't sleep a wink all night.*"

# PART NINE

# ONE LAW FOR THE RICH

# 19. Going to Bat for the Pitcher

Some time in the fall of 1987 George Jonas was asked by a literary acquaintance if it was true that he was about to collaborate on a book "with a big lawyer". Jonas said, well, yes, with Eddie Greenspan. "Greenspan, eh, lawyer for the rich and famous," came the reply.

The man who made this remark spoke matter-of-factly, almost absent-mindedly; he wasn't trying to make any particular point. It was just a statement of what seemed obvious to him. For the moment, Jonas himself accepted the observation at face value. It struck him only later that it might be quite inaccurate.

No doubt there are some lawyers whose clientele consists chiefly, or at least significantly, of wealthy celebrities — but they are not likely to be criminal lawyers. At least, not in Canada. And if there are such criminal lawyers, Greenspan is not one of them.

When he first looked at a statistical breakdown of his cases from this point of view — sixty-two files initially selected for this book as being the most interesting or significant cases in his practice up to 1987 — Greenspan was somewhat surprised at the result himself. True, some of the people he had acted for were by now virtually household names — but only as a result of having been accused of notorious crimes. They had become "famous" solely as alleged or convicted criminals (or as innocent people justly exonerated). Their notoriety arose at the time of, and as a consequence of, their involvement with the law. They were famous cases, not famous people.

As for "rich", of the sixty-two cases exactly five were found to involve clients who could be called wealthy or socially prominent. About eight per cent. Of the ninety-two per cent left, another ten clients were professionals or businessmen, about as well off as thousands of other such persons in the phone book. Many of the remaining forty-seven cases involved working people, whether white- or blue-collar, salaried or self-employed.

The rest were Legal Aid clients.

*Though a few of Greenspan's clients had some local prominence or power — they included a small-town mayor, a publisher, a judge, a provincial politician, the owner of a well-known restaurant — not one, not even any of the wealthy clients, could be called a "celebrity" in any sense of the word. They were just solid citizens. "Well, another myth bites the dust," Greenspan remarked (rather regretfully as it seemed to Jonas).*

*There was only one exception. One real celebrity. For Greenspan, an avid if somewhat lapsed baseball fan, a very important celebrity indeed.*

I remember the day Ferguson Jenkins asked me (through the offices of CTV's vice-president, Marge Anthony) to act for him as his lawyer in a criminal matter. It was one of the most exciting days in my life. As it happened, it also turned out to be one of the most humiliating days.

The reason for my excitement was that Fergie Jenkins has always been one of my heroes. He was among the greatest pitchers in the history of major-league baseball; a rare Canadian star in this all-American game. In August 1980, Jenkins had 240 victories under his belt. He was on his way to having a genuine shot at winning 300 games — a number that would effectively guarantee his admission to baseball's Hall of Fame at Cooperstown among the likes of Babe Ruth and Ty Cobb. Representing someone like Jenkins brought me very close to the realization of my oldest, childhood fantasies.

As a kid I played first base myself. My favourite team was the Brooklyn Dodgers (I hated the Yankees in the manner of all true Dodger fans). The player I worshipped was Dodger slugger Duke Snider. When the Dodgers moved to Los Angeles, I went into mourning. For a while even at law school my friend Gary Siskind and I were betting money we didn't have on baseball games. Just meeting someone like Fergie Jenkins would have been a dream coming true for me.

Maybe as a mature adult one should be ashamed of having had such dreams, but why deny them? They are among the facts of my life.

However, it was also a fact that when I came to the big city I began moving in circles far removed from childhood heroes and sports preoccupations. My new friends were absorbed with political or social issues; with questions of law, literature, or philosophy. In terms of lifestyle or entertainment they were enjoying books, opera, exotic cars, travel, or fashion. Definitely not baseball. The intellectual or artistic types with whom I was associating in my off hours — Hungarian lyric poets, like George Jonas — don't usually go to baseball games; they don't even watch them on TV. I had no one with whom to share my exciting news.

The first person to humiliate me was the foreigner I married. When I phoned home to tell her that I had been retained by Ferguson Jenkins, she said:

"Who?"

"Jenkins. Fergie Jenkins. Jenkins, the baseball player."

There was a little silence.

"Come on, Suzy," I said, "Fergie *Jenkins*. The great pitcher, Jenkins? You know, Jenkins from the Texas Rangers?"

"Oh," Suzy replied. "That's nice." Then, after another little pause she said: "So, will you be home for dinner?"

The coming days cemented my friendship with the Toronto lawyer Michael Smith. He, almost alone in my entire social circle, didn't say "Who?" (or even "Whom?") to my exciting news. He alone knew and appreciated who Ferguson Jenkins was. I had been clearly moving with the wrong crowd.

The facts of the Jenkins case were as follows: On August 24, 1980, the Texas Rangers baseball team took a charter flight from the Dallas–Fort Worth airport to Toronto. When the plane landed here at a few minutes after 11 p.m., the members of the team picked up their luggage and were taken by bus to a hotel in downtown Toronto.

However, a few pieces of luggage, belonging to various people on the chartered flight, were mislaid at the airport. They did not come down on the baggage carousel. After waiting around for a while, those members of the club whose luggage was missing had to board the bus without their suitcases. Fergie Jenkins was one of them.

Bags being misplaced at airports is a common nuisance. In Toronto, when such unclaimed luggage is eventually found, the usual practice is to hand it over to Canada Customs at the airport. The customs people then open and examine all such luggage as a matter of routine.

Canada Customs opened Ferguson Jenkins' luggage the next day, on August 25. In it, they discovered a very small amount — three grams — of cocaine, along with similarly small amounts of hashish and marijuana. (The "street value" of the total was eventually estimated at five hundred dollars.) Two RCMP officers picked Jenkins up at Exhibition Stadium before 1 p.m., just as the game was about to begin. (They also picked up two other players and a club-house boy whose luggage had been similarly delayed.) Jenkins' hotel room had already been ransacked. At the airport, where he was taken next, Fergie told the officers that the luggage, and the drugs found in it, belonged to him.

The fans remained unaware of the drama behind the scenes. The game was played as scheduled — a bit of a yawner, with the Rangers walking over the Blue Jays 5-1. "The teams should have paid the spectators to attend" was how Alison Gordon described it in the *Toronto Star*.

Technically, since his flight originated in the United States, Jenkins could have been charged with importing narcotics, but there was no real danger that he would be. A charge of importing — with its draconian minimum penalty of seven years' imprisonment — is never laid against any person for such a minuscule quantity of drugs. The authorities may, however, as a kind of compromise, charge someone with "possession for the purpose of trafficking", even when the quantities involved — such as three grams — make it evident that the person could only have been bringing the drug into Canada for his own personal use. (When found inside the country, of course, the charge for such small amounts would always be simple possession.)

The practice of not wanting to expose a defendant to the risk of a seven-year sentence for a purely technical breach of inflexible "importing" laws shows much common sense on the part of prosecutors. However, I always hated the idea of the state's then turning around and charging someone with possession for the purpose of trafficking — a crime that the prosecution ought to know he did not commit. To my mind, even when based on lenient intentions (relative to the alternative) such a charge amounts to a false accusation.

The practice, incidentally, illustrates the inherent danger of rigid, minimum sentences for any crime. If we can trust judges to impose suitable penalties for such grave offences as manslaughter or violent robbery, it is difficult to see why Parliament cannot trust them to determine the right punishment for importing drugs. To say that a minimum penalty merely transfers this discretion from a judge to the Crown's office misses the point. Judges are impartial in the adversary process; prosecutors are not. Minimum penalties result in citizens' being pre-judged by officialdom rather than being judged by courts of law. The fact that at the present time they are pre-judged benevolently doesn't alter this. A memo from the Attorney General, written for some fashionable reason of social policy, could change charging practices in a single day — and the courts would be powerless to do anything about it. We'd see people going to jail for seven years for being caught coming through customs with one marijuana cigarette. This may not be the intention, but it is the consequence of all such legislation.

In any event, my first task as Jenkins' lawyer was to make sure that he would not have to face the totally unwarranted charge of possessing $500 worth of drugs "for the purpose of trafficking". Assuming we could get the Crown's agreement to this, it was equally vital that the prosecution should proceed against Jenkins by way of summary conviction rather than by indictment. This is always the Crown's choice in the case of such "hybrid offences" as possession of drugs, and I had to make sure within the first twenty-four hours that the prosecutor would make the right choice.

The difference was highly significant in the case of someone like Jenkins, a Canadian whose work in major-league baseball made it necessary for him to be able to enter the United States. It was one of the quirks of American immigration law that exactly the same offence, in this case possession of three grams of cocaine, would make Jenkins excludable from the United States if the Crown proceeded against him by way of indictment in this country, but not excludable if the Crown elected to proceed by way of summary conviction. A conviction under the first procedure would be the equivalent of a "felony" in the United States, while the second would only amount to a "misdemeanour". The Americans would let in a person convicted of a misdemeanour, but might not let in a convicted "felon".

For the Crown to proceed by way of summary conviction would still not have been enough to remove Jenkins from possible repercussions from the American immigration authorities. The maximum penalty for a first offence of simple possession in Canada was six months' imprisonment, a $1000 fine, or both. In practice, virtually no one was sentenced to prison for a first offence, but a judge might wish to make an example of someone with a $1000 fine. To qualify as a "misdemeanour" for U.S. immigration, a fine could not exceed $500.

What made it urgent to settle the question of the charge within twenty-four hours was that baseball in America is serious and sensitive business. Keeping the sport "clean" is one of the preoccupations of the Office of the Commissioner of Baseball. There was reason to fear that the baseball authorities might bring immediate sanctions against any player accused of a felony — just *accused*, never mind convicted. This was why an attempt had to be made to settle as much as could be settled right off the bat (as it were). The baseball authorities had to see that what Jenkins was being charged with was only a misdemeanour at worst.

For Ferguson Jenkins, thirty-eight years old at the time, the difference could mean being able or not being able to play two or three more full seasons of major-league baseball. In financial terms this difference could have amounted to well over a million dollars (Canadian), taking increments into account. More importantly, it could have meant the difference between having or not having a shot at 300 victories. One of the greatest black pitchers in the history of the game, the greatest Canadian player of all time, had a lot at stake for having been found with three grams of cocaine in his luggage.

Plea negotiations are an important and potentially beneficial part of the administration of justice. The process has been discussed in some detail in Chapter 6. Here I will touch on one additional aspect.

Like any other bargaining process, plea negotiations involve asking for something and offering something in exchange. In one sense, the bargaining is usually initiated by the police and the Crown. They often begin, as I have pointed out earlier, by laying a charge against an accused that is far more severe than the offence on which they wish to secure an eventual conviction (or far more severe than can really be supported by the facts and the evidence in a given case). This is the legal equivalent of an asking price.

The defendant is then expected to say: "Fine, what if I plead guilty to a lesser charge? This way I won't risk being convicted of the graver offence which you've cooked up, and you won't be put to the trouble of having to prove even the lesser charge against me."

As the next step, after some hemming and hawing, the prosecution agrees to this, having never considered the accused as being guilty of anything but the lesser charge anyway. (Or, sometimes, because the Crown lacks confidence that it could prove the defendant guilty of any charge at all.)

Though many people may be squeamish about seeing it described in such bald terms, this is one aspect of plea bargaining. It would work, too, because it has a certain crude efficiency, nor would it be necessarily unjust — if it were not for innocent people.

Innocent people upset the applecart. They may balk at pleading guilty to a "lesser charge" because they regard themselves as being guilty of nothing. As a result, ironically, it is sometimes people truly believing themselves to be innocent who end up facing the most serious charges in court.

Because of circumstances that never became part of the case, Jenkins was not, nor did he consider himself to be, guilty of any offence. Not even the offence of simple possession. This particular bargaining chip, therefore, was not available to me in the plea-negotiationg process. What I could offer the Crown Attorney, Ivan Bloom, was that the defence, after entering a plea of "not guilty", would agree to a set of facts. They would include the fact that the three grams of cocaine *were* in the luggage of Fergie Jenkins, and he had admitted to the RCMP officers that the drug belonged to him. Not contesting this, in spite of our "not guilty" plea, would almost certainly result in a finding of guilt on a charge of possession.

This was accepted by the Crown. In exchange, Bloom agreed to charge Jenkins with simple possesion only, and also to proceed by way of summary conviction against him. He would not, however, agree on a penalty (except for acknowledging that the offence did not call for a jail term). When it came to sentencing, the Crown would push for the maximum $1000 fine.

This, of course, still meant that Ferguson Jenkins' career would remain in jeopardy. For him, a fine of a thousand dollars could mean a million-dollar fine. It would also put an immensely gifted athlete's entire life of blameless behaviour and extraordinary efforts at risk for what was, at worst, one isolated lapse of judgment. Very few members of society would ever have to face such consequences for a single similar mistake.

Because of the politics, money, and social significance of major-league baseball in America, Jenkins was beginning to face grave consequences right after the charges were laid against him, and long before the trial that would determine his guilt or innocence began. Within six days of his arrest in Toronto, he was being called to an interview with Henry A. Fitzgibbon, Director of Security for Bowie K. Kuhn, the all-powerful Commissioner of Baseball in the United States. I flew to New York.

We entered the Commissioner's office at 75 Rockefeller Plaza in Manhattan on the morning of August 30, 1980. Jenkins and I were accompanied by Donald M. Fehr, General Counsel for the Major League Baseball Players Association. Fitzgibbon, along with two other members of Kuhn's staff, were waiting for us in the conference room. After a perfunctory greeting, Kuhn's investigator advised Jenkins that since a 1971 directive from the Commissioner's office issued to all baseball clubs, disciplinary action could be imposed on professional baseball employees found to have used or to have been in the possession of an illegal drug. Then Fitzgibbon began questioning Ferguson Jenkins.

Was he a citizen of the United States or Canada? Jenkins said that he was a Canadian. Which club was he employed by in the United States? Jenkins told him that he was employed by the Texas Rangers.

Did he attend a meeting at the Texas training camp on March 28 where players were told that using or possessing illegal drugs could result in disciplinary action? Jenkins replied in the affirmative.

Where was Jenkins residing, Fitzgibbon then asked, in Dallas, Texas, on August 24, 1980? Fergie gave him the address.

At this point Donald Fehr and I looked at each other. Where exactly was Fitzgibbon going? What exactly were the questions that Bowie Kuhn expected a player to answer — a person presumed to be innocent in both Canada and the United States, and entitled by law to say nothing to anyone?

We told Fitzgibbon that, to expedite matters, he should tell us the questions he proposed to ask Jenkins in advance, so that Fehr and I could see if we could advise our client to answer any of them. Fitzgibbon agreed. The questions he was proposing to ask Fergie are worth setting out in some detail:

Who else lived at his Texas address? If anyone, were they in the house when his bag was packed? Who else was in the house? Did anyone assist him in packing?

In Toronto, when did he learn that his bag hadn't arrived? Did he file a lost-luggage report? Did he talk to anyone about it? When did he first know the bag had been located? Did he authorize its going through customs? If he didn't, when did he first learn that illegal drugs had been located in it?

What did the arresting officers say to him, and what was his reply to them? Did he sign a statement? The Crown in Canada charges that illegal drugs were found in his bag: did he place such drugs in his bag? If not, did he have any idea how they got there? Did he know that possession of these drugs was illegal in Canada?

Then, if Fergie admitted possession, from whom did he get the drugs? Where? What did he pay? Had he ever done it before? Did he sell any? Did he give any to anyone? Had he ever had any drugs in his bag on prior road trips? Did he ever use any while playing a game?

If Fergie did not admit possession, could he think of anyone who for any reason would cause him this trouble? What would be the motives of such a person, and what would be his opportunities to place drugs in Fergie's bag?

Finally, had Jenkins ever had what he believed to be illegal drugs in his possession since he became a major-league player in 1965?

These were the main questions Bowie Kuhn, the Commissioner of Baseball, expected Jenkins to answer *before* his trial in Canada. Fehr and I could not believe our ears when we heard Fitzgibbon outlining them. Several of the answers might have required Jenkins to incriminate himself; any one of them could have been admissible against him in a criminal proceeding in Canada (or in the United States). He would have had to answer them under no privilege or safeguard whatever. It was a flagrant disregard of due process in the country that invented the term "due process".

I told Fitzgibbon flatly that I was advising my client not to answer any of his questions, except for the information that Fergie had never been previously arrested in his entire life on any charges either in the United States or in Canada. Then Jenkins, Fehr, and I got up and left the Commissioner's office.

Baseball Commissioner Bowie Kuhn's letter to Jenkins was dated eight days after this interview, on September 8, 1980:

Dear Mr. Jenkins,
    As you know from the interview with you conducted by my staff

on August 30th, this office has under investigation the events leading to your arrest in Toronto. . . . You declined to answer questions
. . . on the ground that to do so might prejudice the criminal case
pending against you in Canada. . . .

While I am, of course, disturbed by the pendency of drug charges
against you, I am prepared to defer further proceedings by this office
in that regard until they have been concluded.

However, since you have also declined to cooperate with this
office's investigation, and thus perhaps to exonerate yourself, I think
it is also fair that you should not be in uniform again until this matter
has been disposed of. . . . I am hopeful that your defence in the
Canadian proceeding will establish your innocence. Consistent with
that view, I am asking the Texas Club to continue your salary and
benefits in your absence, which should make it clear that my action
is in no sense intended to be punitive.

I would obviously reconsider your status if you were to agree at
any time to resume the interview and respond fully to interrogation.

Sincerely yours,

Bowie K. Kuhn

Talk about hardball. Kuhn spoke like the Queen in *Alice in Won-
derland*: sentence first, verdict later. I was especially outraged by the
effrontery of his suggestion that the act of suspending Jenkins with
full pay was not "intended to be punitive". What greater punishment
is there than suspending a player in mid-season? What's worse than
taking him out of the game and breaking his stride? This could apply
to any player, but especially to a player in his late thirties who may
have only two or three seasons of professional baseball left. It was
blighting the career of a great athlete with a stroke of the pen, not
for anything he might have done wrong — that hadn't been decided
yet by any court — but just for exercising his legal right (also his
constitutional right in the United States) of refusing to answer
anyone's questions before his trial.

Of course, Kuhn wasn't just "anyone". He was the Commissioner
of Baseball. Except that we believed he was doing something he had
no legal right to do. Like many autocratic, law-and-order people
before him, in my view Kuhn was showing contempt for the law
while casting himself as its protector.

In such situations it's often best to take off your gloves. I realized, however, that no matter what happened to Jenkins on the drug charges in Canada, he would have to live with Commissioner Kuhn for some time to come. He had to pitch in his ball park. It never serves a client to win a battle if it loses him the war, so I agreed with Major League Players Association counsel Donald Fehr's very proper and conciliatory plan to plead with Bowie Kuhn first, asking him to reconsider his decision. In a letter dated September 8, Fehr wrote to Kuhn that "As you know, the games a player loses by not being available to play cannot be made up to him — they are forever gone. Additionally, any action on your part would seem to indicate some prejudging of the matter, at least to the public, and might unintentionally adversely affect Mr. Jenkins, a result which I am sure you are striving to avoid." Dennis H. Asher, the Chatham, Ontario, lawyer handling Fergie's civil matters, also wrote to the Commissioner seeking some compromise.

The Czar of Baseball was not in a mood for conciliation or compromise. This left us with no choice. The next day, on September 9, the Players Association filed a grievance on Fergie's behalf. It called for his immediate reinstatement, "there being no just cause for the penalty imposed." Baseball's permanent arbitrator, University of Kansas Law Professor Raymond Goetz, agreed to the scheduling of a hearing for the evening of September 18, in Chicago, Illinois. Time was of the essence. The baseball season would end on October 5.

Meanwhile, of course, the press was having a field day. The initial charge against Jenkins, though widely reported, did not excite much comment in the media, but Kuhn's order of suspension did. This showed the validity of Donald Fehr's point about the highly prejudicial effects the Commissioner's order to bench Fergie would have on Jenkins before he could have his day in court. Since Bowie Kuhn was himself a lawyer, I simply said to *Sports Illustrated* when they called me: "It's taught at all law schools that a man has a right to remain silent. Kuhn must have missed that lesson."

On September 18 I flew to Chicago to testify before the arbitration panel. In addition to the Chairman, Professor Goetz, the panel included one representative of the Players Association bringing the grievance, and another from the Major League Baseball Player Relations Committee, Inc. — in essence, Commissioner Kuhn's office. The three men listened to the arguments. The gist of Kuhn's position was that (1) he had a duty to protect the image of baseball;

(2) he had the authority to make the decision that he made; and (3) there were several precedents supporting the view that if a defendant made the "hard choice" to answer his bosses' questions, even if it could be used against him at his trial later, it did not amount to denial of his constitutional right against self-incrimination.

It was the tough position of a tough guy. The position of a man with perhaps a little more power, and a little less understanding of fairness and decency, than he ought to have had. As it happened, Professor Goetz did not buy it. On September 22 he ordered Jenkins restored to active status with the Texas Rangers, effective immediately. The panel's reasons, along with the dissenting views of the representative of the Player Relations Committee, were released a few days later. Professor Goetz wrote:

> Even though Jenkins was allowed to pitch two games following his arrest and before his suspension, there is absolutely no evidence of any critical commentary by the press, by any organization of parents or educators, or by baseball fans — who might be expected to be quite vocal if something in baseball happened to displease them. This is probably due to the relatively light nature of the charge against Jenkins under Canadian law. . . .
>
> Can it really be supposed under present-day attitudes about matters of this kind that any significant number of baseball fans would withdraw their support if Jenkins were allowed to appear in uniform with the Rangers before he has had his day in court? [Such] an assumption about public reaction to this incident seems unwarranted. . . .
>
> Notwithstanding the Commissioner's legitimate interest in the potential problem of unlawful use of drugs by players . . . the Panel must conclude that under the circumstances of this case, Jenkins' refusal to answer the questions posed by Fitzgibbon was not unreasonable and did not provide just cause for the penalty assessed.

Bowie Kuhn did not wait to read Professor Goetz's reasons. On September 23, before the text of the panel's majority decision could be mimeographed and distributed, the Commissioner issued a press release. Kuhn was obviously angered. According to the press, it was the first time that a decision by the Commissioner had ever been overturned by an arbitrator. "In my judgement, the arbitrator's decision regarding Ferguson Jenkins is wrong," Kuhn announced to the media. "It does a grave disservice not only to those of us in sports administration, but to concerned parents and citizens everywhere."

Some voices in the press supported Kuhn. "The trouble with most arbitrators is that they are legal theoreticians," wrote Dick Young in the New York *News*. "Nowhere in the Constitution does it say that you should be in bed by midnight, but if a baseball manager or football coach wants it that way, then that's the way it should be, no matter what the arbitrator thinks." (I resisted the impulse to phone Young and tell him that Fergie would have been happy to be in bed by midnight, if Kuhn would have been satisfied with that.) Red Smith, writing in the *New York Times*, struck a far more pertinent note. "In lifting Ferguson Jenkins' suspension," he wrote, "Raymond Goetz, a law professor at the University of Kansas . . . repeated the rumor that in the eyes of the law a man was always innocent until proved guilty. Evidently the rumor hadn't reached the University of Virginia campus when Bowie Kuhn took his ticket there as a lawyer."

At this point we could leave the press to battle out the issue. Both Fergie and I had more important things to do. He, back in uniform again, was off to join the Rangers in Minnesota, ready to pitch against the Twins. I came back to Toronto to prepare for his trial, scheduled for December 18 in Provincial Court at Brampton, Ontario, before (as it turned out) His Honour Judge G. L. Young.

Since the Crown and the defence agreed on the facts, the judge would probably have no choice but to register a finding of guilt on a charge of simple possession against Fergie. For this reason the entire trial was likely to be about sentencing. Ivan Bloom for the prosecution had already indicated that he was going to ask for as large a fine as he could get under the law.

I made up my mind that the proper penalty in this case was an absolute discharge.

An absolute discharge would mean that, in spite of a finding of guilt, a defendant could walk out of court as if he had not been convicted at all. He would not acquire a criminal record of any kind, not even for a "misdemeanour".

I did not think that Ferguson Jenkins, any more than any other first offender, should have a criminal record for an offence of this nature. There was an interesting dilemma, however.

Jenkins was an outstanding athlete, a genuine major-league star. He was a winner of the Cy Young Award (1971) given to the best pitcher in the league. He had been named Pitcher of the Year by *The Sporting News* four times (1967,1971, 1972, and 1974). Jenkins was also, by all accounts, an exceptional human being. He was a recipient of this country's highest civilian decoration, the Order of Canada. I could have called an array of glittering international names to testify for him. The most prominent people, here or in America, would have been glad to offer character evidence on his behalf. But I couldn't help feeling that, rather than helping Fergie, this might somehow work against him.

Emphasizing Jenkins' great achievements, instead of bringing him the same result that any first offender on such a minor drug charge could reasonably hope for in 1980, might have the reverse effect on a court. It might create a feeling in the judge that he was being pressured, that he was asked to play favourites or to make an exception — when in fact the defence was asking him *not* to make an exception at all. I was only hoping for a judgment that would not put Jenkins in a worse position than it would any other first offender of previously impeccable character and blameless reputation.

I did not want Jenkins to be let off for being a great baseball star. I just didn't want him to be penalized for it.

At trial, Judge Young did make a finding of guilt against Fergie Jenkins. By that time I had decided not to call a single famous personality, a single celebrity. The witnesses offering evidence for Fergie would be four ordinary citizens. Four decent, public-spirited members of the small community in which he grew up, and which was still the permanent home of his family: Chatham, Ontario.

I did not expect these four witnesses to be particularly eloquent. I simply expected that they would tell Judge Young the facts. Tell him about the kind of a man Ferguson Jenkins was known to be by those who knew him best: his neighbours in his own community. In the end, this turned out to be the most eloquent testimony of all.

For instance, this was what Dr. Charles Keeley had to say: "This is the first time I've ever given a character witness in my entire career. I cancelled four cases this morning to come down here, because I felt it was so important that this man be represented by the community.

"I've looked after Fergie's family. His mother, I tended her in her final illness. And Fergie, just amazed me how he would come home and be there at the beck and call, even though he was involved in many campaigns at the time during the baseball season. This fellow's always available for any function, to raise money for any cause, and has always been most gracious about it."

"This may not be a fair question," I asked Dr. Keeley, "and his Honour has to decide this, but would it be in the interest of the public that he be given ... I suppose the best word is a break by this Court?"

"Yes," the doctor replied. "I think even in baseball you're allowed three strikes before you're out."

Ronald Hancock, a much younger man, president of the Kent Life Underwriters Association, described a fund-raising function for a local charity called Poor Boys Lunch at which Fergie took off his own cowboy boots, auctioned them off for a hundred and fifty dollars, then walked home in his stocking feet. "I'm fortunate," Hancock said. "I'm one of forty thousand people in Chatham that's been able to come here today. But I think you could probably go to almost any one of those forty thousand and they would probably give you the same testimony. . . . He's a super individual."

"I could not praise the gentleman enough for what he's done to help me with Senior Citizens, with our youth," said Douglas Allin, a former mayor of Chatham. And when I asked Gene Dziadura, a Chatham history teacher and one-time baseball player in the Chicago Cubs farm system, who later became a scout and had first scouted Jenkins for the Philadelphia Phillies, if people would think that the court was condoning Fergie's offence by giving him an absolute discharge, he had this to say:

"No, I don't. I don't think our community would look down upon the law, would look down upon Fergie as saying, 'This was easy for you. . . . ' I don't think so. I think they're genuinely feeling that Fergie is part of the community. A mistake has been made. And they want him to continue."

Ivan Bloom is a fair-minded prosecutor and he did what he had to do. I felt he was overreaching only once when, in cross-examining one of the defence witnesses, he started talking about the necessity for the penalty box in hockey games. But here we were not talking about giving someone two minutes for high-sticking. Here, as a penalty for a minor offence, we were talking about the potential for banishing someone from the game for life.

There wasn't any question of demanding privileged treatment for Fergie for being a major-league star, only a recognition that even an ordinary penalty, such as a fine, would have worse than ordinary consequences in his case. It was not a matter of punishing him less than anyone else, only of not punishing him more. "I'm not asking for leniency," I said to Judge Young in my final submissions. "I'm asking for a just result. . . . To suggest that the consequences are irrelevant, I would submit, would be ignoring a reality of sentencing that ought not to be ignored.

"My respectful submission is this. For some reason, the Commissioner of Baseball has a perception that is grossly in error about this case. . . . It is not beyond the realm of possibility that if a conviction is imposed by you, then that would lead to a suspension. It might symbolize something that the Commissioner would take as an opportunity to impose some additional punishment. If Jenkins is suspended, it will amount in his case to a banishment from the game of baseball.

"He is thirty-eight years of age. Given what he has done with his life, given the records to which he's so close, he will be denied the opportunity for a place in the sun, for a place in the legends of baseball.

"If you impose an absolute discharge, then you, the Court of this land, are telling the Commissioner of Baseball, for what it's worth to him, that the law of this country does in fact recognize all the circumstances of this case, all the circumstances of Fergie Jenkins' life, and is not prepared to impose a punishment that would bear no resemblance to the offence or to the man who has come before you. . . . I'm not trying to put Mr. Jenkins above the law. I'm not asking for special treatment. I'm asking for the consideration of the law, because the consequences that could flow to him would not be fair. And I don't think that any reasonable person could argue that they would be fair."

These were my final submissions, but of course they would have been useless to a judge without first establishing to his satisfaction that he was entitled to do in law what I was asking him to do. Contrary to popular belief, cases are not won by heartfelt pleas to a judge — or to a jury. They are at best icing on the cake of careful factual and legal research. In this instance, Judge Young was satisfied that the defence arguments had a solid basis in legislation and precedent. "It seems to me," he said in his judgment, "that a person who has conducted himself in such an exemplary manner that he is held in high account in his community, and indeed in his country, there comes a time when he is entitled to draw on that account. This is one of those occasions. Especially, and particularly, when the potential ramifications of a conviction would be so severe.

"I therefore find that it would not be contrary to the public interest to grant [an absolute] discharge."

No judge has ever more narrowly escaped being kissed on the cheek in open court by a defence lawyer than His Honour Gerry Young did after pronouncing judgment in his Brampton courtroom. But, as one of the great phrase-coiners of baseball remarked, it ain't over till it's over. The American immigration authorities were no longer a problem, but Fergie Jenkins' future was once again in the hands of Bowie Kuhn. No one could predict with any certainty how the Commissioner would react to the Canadian verdict.

The papers continued to speculate. While the overwhelming majority were sympathetic to Fergie, the odd exception, like Dick Young of the New York *News*, was urging Kuhn to suspend Jenkins for half a season. In the high-powered game of major-league baseball one couldn't be sure whether such opinions were independent suggestions, guesses, or planted reflections of decisions already made. However, strategy has always been a game for more than one player, and Bowie Kuhn wasn't playing alone. As a result, throughout the month of January 1981 the papers had reason to speculate a little more.

Jim Reeves, writing in the Fort Worth *Star-Telegram*, offered the view that "Greenspan . . . expects Kuhn to acknowledge the judgement of the Canadian court and agree that justice has been done. But if Kuhn decides more punishment is necessary, Greenspan seems more than willing to take up the challenge." The *Dallas Morning News* felt that "Now it appears to be a matter of getting Greenspan and Kuhn together. . . . According to Ranger sources, Kuhn has indicated that he wants to meet with Fergie and his [Toronto] attorney. . . . But apparently Greenspan has not been answering the Commissioner's telephone calls, which is a reversal of what happened in September, when Kuhn wouldn't return the calls of Greenspan."

Players Association counsel Donald Fehr wrote me a brief note after this particular piece appeared in the Dallas paper on January 15. It simply said: "Dear Ed: As we discussed, play out the string and see if it leads to a good result."

The string was for me to play hard to get. The good result, for Fehr at least, would have been almost anything Bowie Kuhn would do in response.

At this point one of those little byplays arose that are often part of intricate negotiations in a high-powered game. Fehr, a brilliant lawyer for whom I had developed much respect and a sense of personal affection in the preceding months, was naturally looking out for the interests of his client. That was his job.

Fehr's client was the Major League Baseball Players Association — Fergie's union, in effect. But my client was Fergie Jenkins himself. It was my job to look out for his interests. And, as it happens sometimes, at this juncture the interests of Jenkins and his union did not fully coincide any longer. In fact, they did not coincide at all.

Commissioner Kuhn and the Players Association had been engaged in something of a power struggle for years. Kuhn wanted to run baseball — in the best interests of the sport as he perceived it, but as *he* perceived it. Baseball was his fiefdom. He wanted no part of anybody else's perception. Except that, not surprisingly, the Players Association had some ideas of its own about the game of baseball and its best interests.

Kuhn considered the arbitrators' going against him in the Jenkins case a personal affront. He also viewed the result as a whittling away of some of his powers (which it probably was). Now that the court case was over, he might want to reassert the weight of his office by imposing a suspension on Jenkins, as he believed he had a right to do. He may, in fact, have had such a right — no one could tell until it was tested. And the Players Association believed that testing it was in the Association's best interest in the long run.

The problem was that the Players Association had a long run — but Fergie didn't. He was thirty-eight years old. For him, getting caught between a battle of giants and losing part of a season (or more) was putting his life's work at risk. It was risking his shot at 300 wins and maybe an election to the Baseball Hall of Fame.

I could not, in good conscience, advise him to take this chance. Whatever his union's best interests may have been, Fergie's best interest was to make a deal with Kuhn. For Fergie Jenkins, playing out the string that led to a good result (to use Fehr's expression) was to sue for a separate peace.

Quietly, without telling the Players Association of my intentions, I flew into New York. Without even checking into a hotel, I took a taxi to 75 Rockefeller Plaza and had a private meeting with Bowie Kuhn. The battle was won; to get the best result for my client, it was now time to make nice instead of picking another fight.

The result came in a press release from the Commissioner's office on February 5, 1981. There was to be no suspension. Fergie was going to contribute $10,000 to a drug-education program in Texas aimed at young children. He was also to make public appearances, both in person and on educational film clips, supporting the aims of drug-education programs, and expressing deep regret "for the mistake that led to my involvement in the drug charges that were recently disposed of in Canada."

In the press release the Commissioner said that he took into consideration the handling of the matter by Canadian authorities, along with "Mr. Jenkins' 19-year record of exemplary personal conduct as a professional player".

Now it was over. At our final meeting before his press release, Bowie Kuhn and I parted amicably. There was no question about Kuhn's sincere dedication to what he considered, no doubt often rightly, as best serving the cause of baseball. Nor was there any doubt in my mind — or in Fergie's, for that matter — that the use of psychoactive drugs is unlawful and pretty stupid. Almost as bad, in fact, as trying to deny a person's legal rights and immunities, or wiping out the results of a lifetime's outstanding athletic achievements for one single mistake.

There are several more things to be said about the Ferguson Jenkins story. First, as my friend the Toronto lawyer Gary Siskind pointed out recently, Jenkins most certainly belongs in the Baseball Hall of Fame. He finished his career with 284 victories and 3192 strike-outs, and had seven 20-win seasons. There are at present forty-four pitchers in the Hall of Fame, of whom only one had more strike-outs than Jenkins. His seven 20-win seasons would put Jenkins in a tie for thirteenth place; his winning percentage (.560) would tie him for thirty-fourth. Overall, he is among the top twenty pitchers in all of baseball's history. If his penultimate season had not been interrupted by the baseball players' strike, he might well have achieved his 300 wins. Not to elect Ferguson Jenkins to the Baseball Hall of Fame some day would appear to me, on the record, as unfair as the attempt to suspend him had been in the fall of 1980.

Going on to a completely different matter, a day after the verdict in Brampton I received a letter from a Toronto man. "As if there was ever any doubt, Ferguson Jenkins walked away from the charge of cocaine possession," he wrote, "for which we the common people would probably have been more seriously judged.

"I hasten to add that there is no doubt in my mind that due process of law was fully served [but] one cannot be other than totally cynical as he observes the circus-like performance of wealthy and powerful lawyers defending wealthy and prestigious clients, knowing the outcome is fully predetermined."

In so far as my correspondent's note reflects the honest if mistaken perception of some people, I think it deserves an answer.

First, if someone like Jenkins ends up paying ten thousand dollars plus substantial legal fees, in addition to many hours of donated time and a public apology, for a first offence of simple possession (for which any "common" first offender, pleading guilty *without* a lawyer, would receive a small fine at worst, but more probably a conditional discharge), the term "walking away" seems singularly misplaced. Even assuming that a man like Jenkins makes ten times more money than a "common" offender, his punishment — in financial terms alone, not counting the public humiliation or the risk to his life's work — would be at least a hundred times more severe.

Second, if the outcome of such cases were, as the letter-writer believes, "fully predetermined", I would be spending twelve-hour working days and sleepless nights for nothing. So would a lot of other lawyers, no more given to masochistic exercises than I. The cases of high-profile defendants, far from being predetermined in their favour, are generally judged less leniently than "common" cases, precisely to safeguard the justice system from the perception of people such as my correspondent, futile as the exercise may be.

Lastly, if once in a while — very rarely — a result should be achieved for a prominent defendant that *is* more lenient than other results in similar cases, it does not remain a privilege. On the contrary, it quickly becomes a precedent, setting new standards for all the cases that follow. Such precedents help other accused persons to get fairer sentences (or more reasonable charges) by putting an offence into perspective. In the case of Ferguson Jenkins, incidentally, there was no question of even that. The problem was the opposite: to make sure that he wasn't punished more severely than others simply for being more prominent.

One final note. In the spring of 1983 Fergie Jenkins was quoted in the *Wall Street Journal* as saying: "I know I didn't do anything wrong, but my lawyers told me that if I wanted to stay in baseball I'd have to bend, so I bent." I would have hoped that, having said this much, Fergie might have gone further. As his lawyer I can't. Only he is entitled to make all the circumstances public. Maybe he will, one day.


NOTES

p.371, l.3: Erroneously reported as four grams by the newspapers at the time.

p.372, l.14: In March 1987 the Canadian Sentencing Commission, headed by Judge Omer Archambault, recommended the abolition of minimum sentences. In a July 1987 decision, *Smith v. The Queen*, the Supreme Court of Canada struck down the seven-year minimum, because it constituted cruel and unusual punishment contrary to the Canadian Charter of Rights and Freedoms.

p.372, l.22: In Canada we have done away with the archaic terms of "felonies" and "misdemeanours" (although such terms are still used in many countries, particularly in the United States).

In our system, all criminal offences are classified as indictable, summary conviction, or "hybrid" (meaning indictable *or* summary, at the option of the prosecutor, as in the case of possession of narcotics). There are significant differences. Indictable offences usually carry much heavier penalties — as well as additional options as to mode of trial, including trial by jury. Summary-conviction offences — or hybrid offences where the Crown elects to proceed by way of summary conviction — are tried in provincial court, and most carry a maximum penalty of only six months' imprisonment.

p.380, l.37: Ordinarily, when an accused is found guilty he is convicted and has a criminal record. Where, however, the accused is given a discharge, no conviction is registered. Technically, he has no "criminal" record, only a record for a discharge.

# THE REAL GREENSPAN

*"About this book you're writing with Greenspan,"* an acquaintance asked George Jonas, *"is it an honest book? Will it tell about the real Eddie Greenspan?"*

Jonas shrugged, then pursed his lips. For good measure he also arched his eyebrows. There's nothing like body language when one can't answer a question. The book (so Jonas hoped and believed) was honest, but it wasn't Greenspan's autobiography. Nor was it a critical biography in any sense. It was simply a casebook and commentary about the life and times of a leading criminal lawyer in Canada, covering a twenty-year period. Still, the question was intriguing because it gave rise to a larger question.

Was it possible to portray the "real" Greenspan? Was it possible to portray the "real" anybody? In so far as "real" meant "full and complete", was it ever possible to fully portray all the complex elements that add up to a human being (except perhaps in fiction)?

Maybe; maybe not. Some serious biographers have certainly made a good stab at portraying their subjects fully and completely. But that wasn't what Jonas's acquaintance had in mind, because this isn't what "real" means in popular parlance. When people say "real", as a rule they only mean "private".

And that's where the question becomes silly. What is ever "unreal" about a person? The public side of someone's personality is not unreal; it's just easier to see. You wouldn't say that the invisible side of the moon is the "real" side. The side that is visible from the earth is no less real.

Yet when someone is in the public eye, when he is heard and seen on radio and television, when his picture and remarks are frequently published in the newspapers, most people assume that behind this official façade there must be a human being who, in some sense, is more real than his public persona. By now this belief has become a virtual cliché. Every magazine profile about a well-known personality offers to show readers the "real" So-and-so. It is a cultural assumption that *there is a real So-and-so who can be discovered and depicted if only a biographer digs long, low, and hard enough.*

*This is the sense in which the word "real" becomes meaningless. Why is Greenspan examining a witness or addressing a jury in court less real than Greenspan snoring at home on the couch? Why is Greenspan debating someone on camera or on a speaker's platform less real than Greenspan sitting white-knuckled as his jet is coming in to land? Used in this sense, "real" becomes a synonym for "mundane", a synonym for precisely those aspects of a person's being in which he most closely resembles many other persons. It's impossible to discover the essence of people at the very level on which they are the least distinguishable from one another. The Emperor Napoleon brushing his teeth would be very much like most other pudgy, middle-aged Corsicans brushing their teeth. Insisting on private glimpses, we have started to look for reality in the wrong place.*

*In fact, in our days we may have mistaken the lowest common denominator for reality. We may have read too much into the famous question from The Merchant of Venice. Sure, if you prick Shylock he bleeds, but how far do such allusions to common roots take us? If you prick an ant-eater it bleeds, but it doesn't follow that Shylock is an ant-eater. Obviously Greenspan, or So-and-so, is "human", but this discovery tells little more about them than the discovery that they are "mammals" or "vertebrates".*

*And when we insist on knowing about the "human" side of a prominent person, are we not just seeking reassurance? "See, Mabel, he gets horny, too; and look here where it says that he yells at his children!" Are we not confusing gossip with insight?*

*The truth, Jonas felt, was probably that there were several "real" Greenspans. Greenspan speaking about public issues or Greenspan addressing a jury were just as real as Greenspan in the bathtub — and a hell of a lot more interesting. In this sense, colleagues or law students who encountered Greenspan only in classroom or in court, who might never have had a private conversation with him over a cup of coffee, knew more about the "real" Greenspan than his aunts, uncles, and cousins. An attentive television viewer or newspaper reader may, in this sense, know more about the essence of any public person than his mother, wife, or children.*

*Anecdotes might be amusing, but depicting Greenspan merely in a series of anecdotes could mislead the reader in much the same way as overheard conversations could mislead an eavesdropper. In fact, at one time eavesdroppers were misled about Eddie and Suzy Greenspan precisely in this fashion. It happened in the mid-seventies.*

*There was a rumour that got back to both Eddie and Suzy over a period of months around that time: a rumour that was not only baseless but bizarre. It was that Suzy had left Eddie (or was at the point of leaving him) because she was moving to Orillia, Ontario, to set up a home for battered wives.*

*Modern marriages go on the rocks with boring regularity, so that was not the bizarre part of the rumour (unfounded as it happened to be in the case of Eddie and Suzy, whose union has been rock-solid not only for a modern but even for an old-fashioned marriage). Maybe even the word "battered" wasn't bizarre (though it was equally unfounded), because both Suzy and Eddie have volatile tempers and one could imagine them throwing soup tureens at each other in the heat of a fight (though Eddie would almost certainly miss). But setting up a group home? Suzy? And in Orillia?*

*Knowing Suzy Greenspan even casually is to know that, given a choice between setting up a group home and moving into a cave with an anaconda, she'd probably choose the latter. Suzy is simply not a group-home type of person. As for Orillia, if the deluge came and Orillia was the only dry place remaining on earth, Suzy would probably stay in the ark.*

*For the benefit of would-be gossips, in the unlikely event that Eddie and Suzy ever did split up, Suzy would almost certainly continue living in the family home, while Eddie would immediately move to a down-town apartment-hotel with twenty-four-hour room service. And if Suzy ever left Toronto, it would be to settle in a bigger city like Paris or New York — or at least a warmer one like Phoenix, Arizona. Definitely not a smaller, colder, and snowier one like Orillia.*

*In any case, just because it was so puzzling and so far off the mark, the Greenspans were racking their brains trying to figure out how such a weird rumour could possibly have gotten started. Finally, when an Ontario lawyer was charged with a drug offence, the coin dropped for Eddie.*

*Part of the evidence against the accused was a series of wiretapped conversations originating from the lawyers' lounge of the courthouse in Sault Ste. Marie, Ontario. The RCMP had apparently put a bug in the telephone, no doubt aiming to gather evidence only against the particu-*

lar lawyer who was eventually charged, but incidentally listening to the conversations of all the other lawyers using the lounge.

Eddie happened to have a court case in Sault Ste. Marie during the relevant time. In fact, he was defending the targeted lawyer in another matter. He did use the phone in the lawyers' lounge on several occasions. At one point he used it for a rip-roaring fight with Suzy — which originated in Eddie's not remembering to make room in his schedule for a celebration of his wife's birthday, then escalated, as usual, into Suzy's concern with Eddie's general working (as well as eating and smoking) habits. Eddie's health has always been one of Suzy's major concerns.

Suzy, who is nothing if not outspoken in a fight, has retained a few choice Arab phrases from her childhood in Morocco. She has been known to give vent to them in free English translation at moments she considers appropriate. In the Sault Ste. Marie conversation, Eddie recalled Suzy's using only one of her milder remarks — maybe she suggested that if Eddie's lifestyle led to his early demise, she, for her part, would "spit on his grave".

It was probably some such observation that was savoured by the RCMP officers listening to the wiretap tapes. By the time the rumour reached general circulation, it became Suzy setting up a home in Orillia for battered wives. (Why Orillia rather than Sault Ste. Marie? Who could tell?)

Whatever the process of transmutation was, it did little to brighten Greenspan's already dim views on wiretapping as an investigative tool. More to the point, the resulting rumour also illustrated the inadequacy of eavesdropping, candid-camera shots, and all other superficial devices to reveal the "real" person behind the public façade. The policemen or prosecutors who clicked their tongues or chuckled over the great battle on the wiretap may have believed that they had caught a glimpse of the "real" Greenspans. In fact, what they overheard was a single note of a rich and complex relationship — misinterpreted even at that. But then, most big lies are made up of little truths.

Greenspan anecdotes, singly or together, wouldn't add up to the "real" Greenspan". Description, however, is useful. For instance, in a critical biography Jonas might describe the fact that Greenspan never carries a watch or a pen, and generally has no change or matches in his pocket.

Why doesn't he? Certainly not because he has no need of jotting down things or knowing the time. Like everybody else, he'll want a quarter for a pay phone once in a while, and he will require a light more *often than most people.*

For this reason most people would find it inconvenient not to have a lighter or a pen in their pockets. Greenspan doesn't. He'd find it far more inconvenient to carry a pen. Also quite superfluous, having discovered that just by holding out his hand a pen will appear in it anyway. Why strap on a watch, when just pointing at his wrist and raising his eyebrows will cause someone in the vicinity to volunteer the time?

Greenspan's discovery is not new. Earls and princes have known it since antiquity. Aristocrats are conditioned from birth to the fact (a) that they are never alone, maybe not even in the most intimate moments of their lives, and (b) that the retinue of valets, footmen, stewards, secretaries, scribes, coachmen, and court jesters surrounding them at every moment has no other function, or indeed pleasure, than to tell them whatever they want to know or to place into their hands the objects they desire. For aristocrats this is in the nature of things, and it quite innocently and unconsciously shapes their personal habits.

But Greenspan, one might object, is not an aristocrat. He is a scrap-dealer's son from Niagara Falls. Nor was he born a prominent criminal lawyer: he used to be a penniless student. He helped to pay his way through school by such part-time jobs as collecting coins from municipal parking meters. Yet he never carried a watch. He didn't start holding out his hand for pens as he rose in the world: he has held out his hand ever since his friends can remember.

Greenspan's habits were not formed as a consequence of fame and fortune. On the contrary, one would be tempted to say that fame and fortune were the consequences of his habits. There are people other than aristocrats who never carry matches. There are people who, with all the unconscious innocence of an Italian duke, hold a cigarette between their fingers expecting it to be lit, and then watch the ashes grow on it in the knowledge that someone will soon show up with an ashtray to catch them.

Such people often become operatic divas (or prime ministers or captains of industry), whether they were born in a palace or a log cabin. (They may also, as Greenspan's friend Guy Kay remarked once, end up scouring ash-strewn apartments looking for matches.) They don't, of course, become operatic divas by this quality alone; to be an operatic diva one also needs a great voice and the willingness to study singing for fifteen years. But the finest talent is not likely to carry one to stardom unless one has this unconscious assumption of royalty as well. It need not specifically express itself in walking around without a watch, but however it is expressed, it's part of what people mean when they speak about "star quality". It distinguishes, often all by itself, leading actors from their equally gifted supporting cast.

The point is that the assumption must be unconscious. It must be innocent. It cannot be cultivated or learned. If someone tried to do it on purpose, it would probably work against him. It would only make that person seem pompous or ludicrous, while a born star always appears to be natural and at ease.

Such an assumption is more complex than mere self-centredness. Greenspan, like many other born stars, combines it with a keen awareness of others. Also, with a generosity that borders on the grandiose. He certainly notices other people, and he wants them all to be happy. He has a genuine interest in their happiness; he is the very opposite of a narrowly self-absorbed person. No one could appreciate more other people's qualities than Greenspan (if they impress him), and no one could pay more attention to other points of view (if they are well argued and seem valid to him). In fact, whenever he encounters top-notch individuals or opinions, Greenspan's first impulse, like a Medici prince's, is to hire the people and to adopt the views.

It's just that Greenspan does not accommodate himself to life. He expects life to accommodate itself to him — and, often enough, life obliges. When Greenspan clears his throat, others stop talking and look at him. It's not his doing: it just happens that way. When he finishes his coffee after a meal in a restaurant, he will rise, and others will generally rise with him whether they have finished their coffee or not. When, on the way out, he encounters an acquaintance at another table he may stop and chat with him, sometimes for as long as half an hour, innocently expecting everyone else to wait — and they generally do.

Some might object that this is just the result of Greenspan's being a noted criminal lawyer. The point is, it's not. When he cleared his throat, people stopped talking and looked at him long before he became noted — or even a lawyer.

Greenspan will behave the way he does within the limits, not necessarily of good manners, but certainly of good citizenship and professional conduct. In other words, albeit reluctantly, he will stop at red lights. He will not be late for court (just as the most temperamental diva seldom fails to be on stage when the curtain rises). Greenspan will wait on the law, as it were, but he will wait on nothing and no one else. At the same time, quite unconsciously, he will expect everyone else to wait on him.

*When this is called to his attention, Greenspan will go into a veritable tizzy of remorsefulness. He will attempt to make up for everything with extra doses of charm and generosity. Having others wait on him is the last thing he wants to do — he just doesn't quite know how else to live. The primacy of his schedule and convenience present themselves to him as a given. He finds the idea that his employees need the odd day off genuinely bewildering — though he'll give them a week when it's pointed out to him. He may stand immersed in a conversation with someone in the street oblivious to the fact that his wife has been waiting for him in the car for an hour — then, remembering, dash to the car and implore Suzy to think of a way in which he can make it up to her.*

*Suzy, to her credit, generally manages to come up with something.*

*Jeff Manishen, a criminal lawyer and former senior Crown Attorney in Hamilton, tells a story about the time he worked for Greenspan as an articling student. They were preparing a case in Eddie's office on a completely non-stop schedule. Jeff had hardly been able to go home to sleep for ten days running. The case was being heard in a town in Northern Ontario, and Jeff naturally accompanied his law principal. There followed another five-day period of no time off and little sleep while the case was being heard in court. Finally it was over. The jury acquitted, and Jeff got into Eddie's car for the long wintry drive back to Toronto.*

*After an hour's driving they ran into a snowstorm. It was a white-out. All Eddie and Jeff could do was to pull up at a roadside motel somewhere in the Northern Ontario bush. Next morning they found that the storm had still not abated. It was evidently going to continue all day, and they had no choice but to sit it out.*

*Eddie looked at Jeff. "Listen," he said, "you've been working pretty hard these last couple of weeks. Tell you what: take the day off."*

In such instances, of course, Greenspan is not unconscious of what he is doing; such cracks are simply his way of acknowledging his habits and apologizing for them. He is less apologetic about his habit of keeping everyone on more or less permanent stand-by. He may or may not have time for them, but he wants to make sure that they will always have time for him. This way he can keep his own schedule flexible while keeping everybody else's predictable, so that he can fit his associates into his timetable at a moment's notice as it suits him. For this reason, working with Greenspan is somewhat like working with the army. His colleagues have to be prepared to hurry up and wait.

On a private level, Greenspan often insists on seeing his friends even when he is much too tired to keep them company. He may fall asleep, but then again he may not. If he doesn't, he has the option of chatting with his friends; if he does, his friends have the option of watching him sleep.

Once, while doing a strenuous trial in Vancouver, Eddie had dinner with Jonas, who, having just flown in from Victoria, was on his way back to Toronto. Eddie could hardly keep his eyes open during the meal, but after dinner he insisted on Jonas's going back with him to his hotel instead of taking a cab straight to the airport. He pointed out that Jonas needed a shave — which was perfectly true — and that there was enough time for him to shave at the hotel before catching the red-eye special.

At the hotel Eddie lay on the bed and started telling his friend an amusing anecdote while Jonas was lathering his face in the bathroom. Eddie was just coming to the punch line: "And then the judge put the book on the table and he yelled at me, 'Mr. Greenspan . . . ' " when he stopped. Jonas waited for him to continue, but Eddie said nothing more. After a few seconds Jonas, somewhat concerned, looked out of the bathroom.

Greenspan was sound asleep. It was the first time Jonas had ever seen a man fall asleep, not while listening to someone else's anecdote, but while telling one himself. Jonas didn't think anyone could do that, but Greenspan did it. Not wanting to wake Eddie, Jonas finished shaving, left a note on the bed, picked up his briefcase, and tiptoed out of the room.

About six hours later, back in Toronto, Jonas was just coming through the door of his apartment when he heard the telephone ring. It was Eddie. "Anyway," he said to Jonas, making no reference to the six hours and two thousand miles that now separated them, "and then the judge put the book on the table and he yelled at me, 'Mr. Greenspan . . . ' "

If Greenspan were a car, he would be like a Formula One racing machine: his accelerator would either be pushed right to the floor or be fully released. He does not know the meaning of half-speed; his controls have no position between a furious work-pace and complete idleness. When working he's oblivious to his surroundings, but when at rest he requires sybaritic comfort. He can work through the night at an airport or a bus station, but won't sleep at a second-rate hotel.

A few years ago Eddie and his brother Brian were going to St.

Catharines, Ontario, to attend the funeral of a lawyer, an old family friend. As it happened, both Eddie and Brian were in the middle of exhausting and difficult trials at the time. They had hardly slept for days, and did not think that either of them would be safe behind the wheel of an automobile for the 100-odd mile return trip between St. Catharines and Toronto. They decided to rent a car and a driver.

Many large persons feel uncomfortable in cramped spaces, but Eddie, in addition, suffers from claustrophobia. He has to take a deep breath before getting into an elevator, and the experience makes him break out in a cold sweat. He can drive a small car if he has to, but he cannot sit in the back seat of even an ordinary car as a passenger. It simply makes him sick.

Very big cars, on the other hand, provide him with physical and spiritual comfort. They do not make him feel self-conscious at all. Eddie can sit in big cars with perfect ease.

"Okay, we'll take a stretch limousine," he said to Brian. "I'll phone my guy."

Brian Greenspan is in some respects very much like his older brother, but there are ways in which Brian and Eddie are light years apart. Taking stretch limousines to home-town funerals is one of them.

"Eddie, you're crazy," said Brian. "Everybody we know will be there from Welland and Niagara Falls. There is no way that I am going to pull up in a stretch limousine."

"All right," Eddie replied. "All right, all right. I appreciate your point; you don't have to belabour it. Tell you what we'll do. We'll rent two limousines. One will be a tiny little limousine with a tiny little driver. We'll have it follow our stretch limousine right to the outskirts of St. Catharines. Then we'll switch, and go to the funeral in the tiny little limousine. Happy?"

NOTE

p.395, l.29: Greenspan remembers the anecdote differently. He recalls that it happened to be Jeff's birthday, so he offered to give him a *night* off. He would never have offered, he says, to give a student an entire day.

PART TEN

# WHODUNIT

# 20. Some Time to Kill: A Murder Mystery

## 1. Spring, 1978

On May 16, 1978, Crown Attorney Michael Lynch stood up in court to say that the police had a strong circumstantial case against Lauralee Lorenz and her ex-lover, Gordon Allen, in the shooting death of Lauralee's husband, a Toronto lawyer named Bruce Lorenz.

Gordon Allen was my client. In the coming months, watching the evidence unfold against the two accused at the preliminary hearing, I would have disagreed with the Crown. I would have disagreed even if I hadn't been a defence lawyer acting for an accused. However, I might have conceded that (as Mr. Justice Holland put it in reply to the prosecutor's statement at Gordon Allen's bail hearing) "the Crown had *a* circumstantial case against Lauralee Lorenz and Gordon Allen." How strong it was, only time could tell.

That bail hearing in the spring of 1978 was the beginning of my involvement in possibly the most complex and intriguing murder case of my career as a criminal lawyer. It ranked with the *Demeter* and *Buxbaum* cases in notoriety at the time, and for mystery fans it might have outranked both as a genuine puzzle.

I will begin by outlining the story as it appeared to the investigators. The events of the first four days, March 20 to 23, 1978, were described to George Jonas and Barbara Amiel by the late Staff Sergeant Gerald Stevenson and Sergeant Robert McLean in 1979, shortly after Gordon Allen's trial for first-degree murder.

**Day one.** *The afternoon shift for Metro Toronto Homicide detectives Stevenson and McLean was busy but routine on Monday, March 20, 1978. Until about 6:30 p.m. they had been assisting another team of detectives investigating the shooting death of a black man, then they returned to their offices for some housekeeping chores. It was time for them, as McLean would say later, "to clean up the vaults", that is, to put* in order some court exhibits from earlier homicide investigations. There were many items to clean up because Stevenson and McLean were a crack team, perhaps the number one homicide team in Toronto during the late seventies. Among many other cases, they had recently concluded the famous "shoeshine boy" murder investigation: the homosexual torture-slaying of a young boy named Emanuel Jaques on Toronto's Yonge Street strip. Three of the four men convicted in that case (one man, defended by leading criminal lawyer Earl Levy, was acquitted) were coming up for sentencing in two days' time.

Stevenson and McLean were rather looking forward to attending the sentencing hearing in that case.

Around 8:20 p.m. the two detectives decided to break for the meal policemen call "lunch" at whatever time of the day it occurs. It wasn't so much that they were hungry, but they wanted to get away from the cleaning staff mopping the floor of their office. On their way out, the staff sergeant on the duty desk told them that a phone call had just been received from 41 Division at the city's east end: apparently a dead body had been found in a car in the parking lot at the St. Clair–Warden Avenue subway station. There was no immediate indication that the dead man was a murder victim, but 41 Division wanted to notify Homicide, just in case.

Stevenson nodded. They would have their meal, then see if anything developed. The officers at the scene could handle matters for now. They drove to a restaurant called Theodore's, where the steaks were good and inexpensive, then — after Stevenson phoned the duty desk from the restaurant and was told that no news had been received yet — the two officers drove to Intelligence Headquarters on Richmond Street to tie up some loose ends from their earlier case.

When they finished, Stevenson phoned the duty desk again. By then the body from the car in the parking lot had been removed to the morgue, and the news was that the morgue attendant had noticed what he thought was a bullet hole, which had apparently not been seen by the investigating officers or the coroner at the scene. The attendant had called Homicide, and the pathologist was also on his way.

Stevenson and McLean immediately drove to the morgue. The time was around 11 p.m.

The body being readied for the autopsy was that of a very tall — six-feet-five — man in his mid-thirties. The morgue attendant was right: the man appeared to have been shot just behind the left ear with a small-

*calibre bullet, which exited just in front of the right ear on the cheek. The entrance and exit wounds were both small, and they were partly hidden by the victim's hair and by what appeared to be a great deal of congealed blood on his head and face. It was not too surprising that the officers at the scene — Sergeants Gordon King and Patrick Tallon — and even the coroner, Dr. Paul Tepperman, who had pronounced the man dead, had not been able to see any sign of injury.*

*As the pathologist, Dr. MacDonald, began his post-mortem examination, Staff Sergeant Stevenson called 41 Division. He called in order to tell Tallon and King about the developments concerning the suspected bullet wound, and also to ascertain what the two officers had done up until that point. The time was 11:35 p.m.*

*As it turned out, King and Tallon had arrived at the parking lot a few minutes after 8 p.m., within about ten minutes of the police receiving a telephone call from the parking-lot attendant about a dead body in a car. (A man's legs sticking through a car window had been noticed by witnesses much earlier, between 6:30 and 6:45 p.m., but they thought that the man might have been a drunk or perhaps was working on something under the dashboard in the car. It was 7:30 before someone actually decided to take a closer look, then ran to call the parking-lot attendant.)*

*Though Sergeant Tallon phoned Homicide shortly after 8 p.m. just to keep them in the picture, he and King both felt that the conditions of the parking lot and the position of the body in the car were more consistent with an unfortunate accident than with foul play. March 20 was a dark, chilly night, with a mixture of rain and freezing drizzle. The parking lot was quite slippery. The body in the car was reclining in the driver's seat, with both legs hanging out the window. The head was resting on the console between the bucket seats, and one hand was clutching a blood-stained wad of paper tissue. There were many bloodstains in the interior of the car. The door on the driver's side was partly open, and the key was in the ignition. A briefcase and a newspaper were lying on the back seat. The victim wore a gold watch, and his wallet, containing over $200 in cash as well as a cheque and some credit cards, was still in his pocket. There was no weapon to be seen anywhere in or around the car.*

*These circumstances, coupled with the absence of any visible wound, made it quite possible that a commuter on his way home might have slipped on the icy parking lot and hit his head, then managed to crawl inside his car before he lost consciousness and died.*

Had Sergeants Tallon and King regarded the matter as anything but what police officers call a "sudden death" at this point, they would have requested Homicide to come and examine the car and the body at the scene before having them both removed. As it was, the police took some photographs and measurements, then had the 1976 Ford Mustang towed to the police garage and the body taken to the morgue. After that, the two sergeants proceeded to the townhouse in Toronto's east end which the driver's licence in the dead man's wallet gave as his address. They took along the victim's personal effects — his watch, glasses, wallet, the briefcase, a fountain pen — in order to give them to his next of kin. To his wife, probably, if Bruce Lorenz, the name on the victim's driver's licence, turned out to have been a married man.

Bruce Lorenz had been a married man. His wife, Lauralee, an attractive blonde woman in her early thirties, was at home with a girlfriend named Leanne Cooke when Tallon and King arrived at 10:35 p.m. The two women had been having dinner together. The officers duly carried out their sad duty of notifying the widow that her husband had died as a result of an unfortunate accident, gave her his personal effects, sat and talked with Lauralee and Leanne Cooke in the kitchen for about twenty minutes, then left the townhouse at around 11 p.m. They had still been talking to a neighbour when Staff Sergeant Stevenson's call from the morgue was relayed to them.

As Stevenson was to tell it later, he did not exactly berate his fellow officers for what they had done, but he did instruct them to go back immediately and retrieve Bruce Lorenz's personal effects from Lauralee. Whatever happened in the parking lot, a bullet wound in the head required that Bruce Lorenz's death be treated as a murder investigation. So Sergeant King returned to the townhouse and, without telling Lauralee anything more, took back the items he had left with her.

During the twenty minutes that Sergeants King and Tallon had spent with Lauralee in the kitchen right after notifying her of Bruce Lorenz's death, a distraught Mrs. Lorenz told the two policemen a number of things about her late husband. Though King and Tallon would later say that her manner appeared "unusual" to them in some respects, at the time they merely noted the information she gave them. This included the following:

1) Bruce Lorenz had been a real-estate lawyer. He had expected to find out that very morning if he was being made a partner in the law firm for which he worked, and was very depressed on discovering that he

*hadn't become a partner. He didn't even want to talk to his wife about it on the telephone. Lauralee told him to go and have a few drinks with his friends after work, and that she would keep his dinner for him.*

*2) It was Bruce Lorenz's first day back at the office after "a lovely holiday" he and his family had spent in Florida.*

*3) Bruce had a brother named Brian Koepke who was a police constable in Kitchener-Waterloo. (Bruce's original name had also been Koepke, but he had changed it on becoming a lawyer. Lorenz was his mother's maiden name.)*

As a result of this information, while Tallon continued talking with Lauralee, King had made a telephone call requesting the police to get in touch with Brian Koepke and ask him to phone his sister-in-law immediately on an urgent family matter. This routine courtesy was to acquire considerable significance later, though at the time none of the investigators could know or appreciate it.

Stevenson and McLean were just beginning to put together some background information about the dead man. Learning from Sergeant King that Lauralee's girlfriend, Leanne Cooke, had been having dinner with Lauralee that night, the officers' first move was to dispatch a police car for Leanne's husband, Glen Cooke. Mr. Cooke had been an acquaintance of Bruce Lorenz's, and the investigators wanted him to be brought to the morgue so he could officially identify the body.

Glen Cooke, as it happened, was an ex-policeman. It was he who first related some background information about Bruce Lorenz and his wife to Staff Sergeant Stevenson and Sergeant McLean.

The information was interesting. McLean would later say that "a soap opera couldn't be as strange as that." Essentially, Glen Cooke told the police that Bruce Lorenz and Lauralee had been married for some years and had two adopted children, but they were having marital difficulties and separated in the summer of 1975. Bruce moved out, and Lauralee and her children started living with a certain Gordon Allen, a man she had met some months earlier. Gordon and Lauralee purchased a house about a year later, in the spring of 1976, and they started a business together. However, the business did not prosper, and by the late spring of 1977 Lauralee had moved back with her husband, Bruce. Since that time they had been living together again. The two men in Lauralee's life, Bruce and Gordon, knew each other and were to all appearances on cordial terms.

As McLean would comment later: "This was a good one. Nothing *criminal, but worth looking at. Locating Gordon [Allen] became Number One on the hit parade."*

However, it was too early to take any steps in that direction on the night of March 20. After talking with Glen Cooke, the homicide team looked at the parking lot, examined the Mustang in the police garage, talked to Sergeants Tallon and King, made sure that whatever physical evidence was available would be collected and preserved for the forensic examiners, did the necessary paperwork, and went off duty at around 6 a.m.

**Day two.** The next afternoon, March 21, Stevenson and McLean visited the offices of Borden & Elliot, the large and very distinguished law firm that had employed Bruce Lorenz. After a talk with Mr. Elliot himself (whom the two detectives found rather awe-inspiring, along with the sombrely opulent decor of his firm's premises in downtown Toronto), Stevenson and McLean began interviewing the people who knew Bruce, including those who may have been the last ones to see him as he left the office building around 5:40 p.m. less than twenty-four hours before.

The first of these was a young woman named Christa Ahlers, a title-searcher at Borden & Elliot who actually walked with Bruce to the subway. She saw him buy a paper, then meet an acquaintance just as they were passing the turnstiles at the Osgoode subway station, where the public telephones are located. The man had been on the telephone, and Bruce greeted him by his first name (though Ahlers couldn't recall what the name might have been). The man hung up the phone immediately, returned Bruce's greeting, then stood chatting with him. Ahlers walked on to the platform, not wanting to intrude on the friendly conversation. She could hear nothing but the first two sentences as Bruce and his acquaintance followed some distance behind her. The stranger remarked that Bruce was looking tanned, and Bruce responded that he had just got back from Florida with the family.

On the platform Bruce waved good-bye to Ahlers and got into a northbound subway car with his friend.

Asked by Staff Sergeant Stevenson to describe the man, Ahlers responded that he was shorter than Bruce, but then most people were. She had no reason to look at him closely and she did not, but he appeared to be a rather heavyset man of about five feet eleven, wearing a full-length coat of some camel-type material. He had longish but well-groomed hair with, as far as she could recall, a red tinge.

A senior lawyer at Borden & Elliot, Robert (now Mr. Justice)

*Sutherland, also confirmed seeing a man on the subway with Bruce
Lorenz. His description, though equally sketchy, seemed to the officers
to coincide with Christa Ahlers' recollection of what the man looked
like. Sutherland saw this man and Lorenz changing platforms at the St.
George station, in mid-town Toronto, boarding the subway in the direction of Warden and St. Clair at the city's east end. The time was just
before 6 p.m.*

*These interviews took place in Mr. Elliot's private office. Also
present, besides the head of the firm and the two homicide investigators,
was a woman named Marilyn O'Brien, who had been Bruce Lorenz's
legal secretary for some years. Having worked for Bruce throughout the
period of his separation from Lauralee as well as their subsequent
reconciliation, she knew something about his private life. In fact, while
Lauralee had been living with Gordon Allen, Marilyn had seen Gordon
once or twice when he came to the office to consult Bruce on some
business matters. Lorenz, apparently, had done some legal work for his
estranged wife and Gordon Allen in connection with the business they
had been trying to establish during the year and a half Lauralee and
Gordon had been living together.*

*On hearing Christa Ahlers describe the unknown man in the subway,
Marilyn O'Brien looked up. "That's Gordon Allen," she said sponta-
neously, according to the recollection of the two detectives. Gordon
Allen's name, though Stevenson and McLean had heard it from Glen
Cooke the night before, had not come up in the conversation in Mr.
Elliot's office at all until that point. Sergeant McLean would later say
that "it was like a scene out of an Ellery Queen movie."*

*O'Brien mentioned one other thing the investigators found interest-
ing. She said that earlier in the day she had received a call from
Lauralee. Naturally distraught over Bruce's death, the two women were
crying for the first part of the conversation. Then Lauralee asked
Marilyn about Bruce's will. Apparently, after Lauralee and Bruce
separated in the summer of 1975, he had drawn up a new will excluding
Lauralee and the younger of his two adopted sons (who, in fact, had only
been adopted about one week before their separation) from his approximately $207,000 estate. However, some time after they got back
together, he had drawn up a new will which once again named Lauralee
as the principal beneficiary. A girl in the office typing-pool had just
finished typing the new will as Bruce was leaving for his vacation in
Florida. On March 20, his first day back, Marilyn had put the will on*

*his desk. Evidently he hadn't got around to signing it before he left the office on the evening he was murdered.*

*According to Marilyn, Lauralee sounded "incredulous" when she found out about this. "He hadn't signed it yet?" she allegedly asked the secretary on the phone.*

*Stevenson and McLean were to say later that, as they left the offices of Borden & Elliot on the afternoon of March 21, they still had an open mind about the case. They spent the rest of the day following up some leads about Lorenz's business deals to see if these might provide a clue to his murder. However, Stevenson also telephoned Lauralee to arrange an appointment with her for the twenty-third. As for Gordon Allen, in McLean's words they had "no doubt now [that] we gotta talk to this guy."*

***Day three.*** *On March 22, a Wednesday, Stevenson and McLean went to court in the morning to hear life-sentences being pronounced on the three killers of shoeshine boy Emanuel Jaques. After lunch the two investigators did a brief background check on Gordon Allen and found that the Orillia, Ontario, man worked as an insurance agent for his father's life-insurance business. He shared a house with a friend named James Round and Round's mother. He drove a silver Mazda. A few weeks earlier, in February, he had been arrested for impaired driving, which was his only police record of any kind.*

*Later in the day Lauralee's father phoned Staff Sergeant Stevenson to cancel his daughter's appointment with the police. Lauralee Lorenz, as McLean would say somewhat sarcastically later, apparently wanted to go up to her parents' cottage "to commune with nature".*

***Day four.*** *On March 23 Stevenson and McLean started working at 8 a.m. The vague leads concerning Lorenz's business dealings had petered out; in the two investigators' view, there was nothing there to follow up. So they asked the Ontario Provincial Police in Orillia to get Gordon Allen to come to their offices under some pretext connected with his impaired-driving charge; then they assigned an intelligence officer to drive up to Orillia and take some surreptitious photographs of Allen as he was arriving at the OPP station. The two homicide detectives also talked to the officer who had arrested Allen on the impaired-driving charge, and noted that his description of Gordon was similar to Christa Ahlers'.*

*Stevenson's plan was to show the surveillance photographs to Ahlers. If she identified them as being pictures of the man in the subway, it would be sufficient evidence for the investigators to ask a judge of the Supreme Court of Ontario to authorize a wiretap on Lauralee's and Gordon Allen's telephones.*

*Though the evidence was not yet remotely sufficient for laying a charge, the two homicide officers regarded Gordon Allen — along, possibly, with Lauralee — as not just the prime but the only suspects in the slaying of Bruce Lorenz by March 23, the fourth day of the investigation. Still, as Stevenson and McLean emphasized, their minds were not closed. They would certainly jump to no conclusion until they had talked to Gordon Allen in Orillia. "If we go up and talk to him," as Sergeant McLean explained later, "and he can verify his whereabouts on the day of the murder, then he's eliminated."*

*"And then," McLean added, "we're in real trouble. Because we have nowhere to go then."*

This thought must also have occurred to Gordon Allen and Lauralee Lorenz. They couldn't help realizing that with Bruce Lorenz's murder they had become natural suspects. Should the murder remained unsolved, the mere fact of their past relationship could have serious repercussions for them. The police might indeed have nowhere else to go.

Gordon and Lauralee reacted to this realization in the same manner as countless other people have before and since. On finding themselves in similar situations, innocent people, no less than guilty people, have become anxious and panic-stricken. As a result, they have tried to hide some facts from the police.

During the five weeks between Bruce Lorenz's death and their arrest for first-degree murder on April 26, 1978, both Lauralee and Gordon had several conversations with Staff Sergeant Stevenson and Sergeant McLean. In the course of these conversations the investigating officers came to believe, perhaps not unreasonably, that both Lauralee and Gordon attempted to create the false impression that their relationship was entirely a thing of the past. They freely admitted, of course, that they had lived as man and wife between the fall of 1975 and the spring of 1977, but they claimed that after Lauralee returned to her husband in April 1977, they considered their love affair to have come to an end. Gordon and

Lauralee said that they only maintained a fond, cordial relationship with each other. There were occasional contacts between them, they said — they had some business and tax affairs to wind down arising from their attempt to run a business together, which had ended in personal bankruptcy for both — but there was no continuing grand passion.

Lauralee specifically emphasized, to the police and to others, that Gordon would have no reason to harm Bruce Lorenz. Gordon, she said, fully accepted that she was deeply in love with Bruce, that she was making a go of her relationship with him once again, just as Bruce had earlier accepted her relationship with Gordon. The feelings between the two men were amicable.

However, in the investigators' opinion, this did not explain a number of the facts. It did not explain some 130 long-distance telephone calls logged between Gordon's house in Orillia and Lauralee's residence in Toronto between December 1977 and March 1978, including several calls between Orillia and Florida while the Lorenz family was holidaying there. It did not explain two telephone calls on the day of the murder itself, one made from Lauralee's home to Gordon Allen's office shortly after 9 a.m., and another made from Gordon Allen's home to Lauralee's house around 9:30 p.m. It especially did not explain why Lauralee had spent two weekends with Gordon *after* her return to Bruce, one in October 1977, and one in December 1977 — facts that Stevenson and McLean found out about during the five-week investigation between the murder and the arrest.

Nor did it explain, in the view of the police, the tone of some of the conversations between Lauralee and Gordon after March 26, the date on which Mr. Justice O'Driscoll authorized wiretaps to be placed on both of their telephones. (We will return to these conversations later.)

I knew next to nothing about the background of the case when Gordon Allen retained me to act for him after his arrest on April 26, 1978. I first saw Gordon in May in the Toronto East Detention Centre where he was being held pending his bail hearing. (Lauralee, who had retained the eminent lawyer and former Director of Crown Attorneys Clay Powell, was already free on bail. Her bail application had not been opposed by the Crown.)

The events of the next few weeks taught me yet another textbook lesson about why lawyers should never attempt to judge their clients' guilt or innocence in their own minds.

In our first interview Gordon Allen told me that on the day of Bruce Lorenz's death he had never left Orillia and that he had an alibi. He had explained, he said, the same thing to Stevenson and McLean both times he had talked to them prior to his arrest. I left the jail elated. If Allen was in Orillia at the relevant time, he couldn't have killed Bruce Lorenz in Toronto. At that point, if I had been in the habit of judging my clients, I would have concluded that Gordon Allen was innocent.

At Allen's bail hearing on May 16, I cross-examined Staff Sergeant Stevenson. On the basis of what my client had told me, I suggested to him that the evidence showed that Gordon Allen was in Orillia at the time of the murder on March 20. To my shock and dismay, the Staff Sergeant replied that the police had evidence that Gordon purchased gas at a service station in Toronto's west end around 7 p.m. on March 20. They had his credit-card receipt, with his car's licence number and his signature.

I carried on valiantly, trying not to show my horror. "If I were to tell you," I asked the Staff Sergeant, "that I have evidence that at exactly eight o'clock he was seen in Orillia, a trip that takes about an hour and a half, what would you say about that?"

"I'd have to dispute your evidence," Stevenson replied.

"Well, I guess we will sit here and dispute each other's evidence," said I, solid as a rock.

"There's not much doubt that he was in Toronto and he's denied being here," replied the police officer.

He sounded so calm and confident that I had the sinking feeling that he might be right. Still, I stuck to my guns.

"As far as I'm concerned, there is not much doubt he was in Orillia, so we're really about even right now."

Fortunately, at this point Mr. Justice Holland got tired of both of us and suggested that we move to some other area of cross-examination. Even more thankfully, at the end of the hearing he granted bail to my client. I immediately called Gordon to my office to discuss what Stevenson had said in the witness-box.

"You heard him," I said to Gordon. "Why would he say that you bought gas in Toronto?"

Gordon replied that "the mistake was obvious." He had been in

Toronto on Sunday, the night before the murder. He had filled up his car at the gas station, and since it was very late, the date must have been changed to the following day on the credit-card machine.

Once again I was thrilled. Had I been in the habit of judging my clients, I would have concluded in my mind that Gordon Allen was innocent. With Gordon's agreement, I confidently retained a private detective to acquire conclusive proof that Gordon had not been in Toronto on the evening of the murder.

My detective was a skilled man. In a few weeks he returned to me with documents that proved beyond the shadow of a doubt that Gordon Allen *had* been in Toronto on the evening of Bruce Lorenz's death. He *had* purchased gas in Toronto around the time of the murder. Our investigator proved this fact better than the police could ever have proved it.

If I had been in the habit of judging my clients, what would I have concluded at this point?

I called Allen into my office, and also called in my secretary and two articling students to emphasize the solemnity of the situation. In fact, I was furious.

"You've just spent $1500 of your own money," I said to my client, "to prove beyond any doubt that you *were* in Toronto buying gas at the time of the murder. For another $1500 I think our private investigator can prove beyond a reasonable doubt that you personally killed Bruce Lorenz. Would you like us to go ahead?"

Allen remained silent for several minutes. He was deeply upset. Finally he said that he had been afraid to tell me the truth because he thought that I might refuse to act for him knowing that he had, in fact, been in Toronto on the night of the murder.

Then he told us the following:

A couple of weeks before the murder he had met a young woman at a dance. She lived in Toronto at her parents' home, and Gordon had made a date with her for March 20. He was to come and phone her, then take her to coffee or dinner.

So, he drove to Toronto after work, arriving around 5:50 p.m. Needing gas, he filled up his car at the service station, and he paid with his credit card because he wanted to keep the receipt for his income tax. Then he telephoned his date from the lobby of a nearby hotel. She told him on the phone that she had forgotten about their arrangement and she couldn't disappoint her mother, who had already made dinner for her, but suggested that Gordon call her some other time. Allen said good-bye and drove back to Orillia, a distance of about eighty miles, arriving around 7:15 p.m.

"What is your date's name?" I asked.

Gordon looked pained. "I don't remember," he said.

"What's her phone number?"

"I don't know."

My secretary started laughing. Gordon Allen quickly added that the woman was related to someone in Orillia and that he would call me back with her name and number later that week. At this even my law students started snickering. I stood up, and told Gordon that he had better go home, think about his story, and make sure that it was the final one.

Gordon also stood up, visibly shaken. He was already in the doorway when suddenly the woman's name came to him. He told it to me, and asked if he should call her.

I'm afraid that I still spoke harshly. "You call no one," I said to Allen. "My investigator will get in touch with her. After I get his report, we will see."

Had I been in the habit of judging my clients, what could I possibly have concluded in my own mind after hearing the third version of Gordon Allen's story? Yet, had I concluded that he was guilty, I would have been wrong. My laughing secretary and my snickering law students *were* wrong. Because this time, as we soon discovered, Gordon Allen was telling the absolute truth.

## 2. Summer, 1978

The preliminary hearing of Gordon Allen and Lauralee Lorenz on a charge of first-degree murder started on June 26, 1978, before Provincial Court Judge S. G. Tinker. It ended on August 25, with both defendants being committed to stand trial on the charge. In those three months I discovered a number of additional things about the Crown's evidence, as well as about the manner in which the police had gone about investigating the case.

Briefly, it was the Crown's theory that Gordon and Lauralee, still obsessed with one another, decided to do away with Bruce Lorenz, then live happily ever after, presumably aided by Bruce's $207,000 estate, which Lauralee could expect to inherit by the terms of Bruce's revised will.

In this theory, the murder was planned by Lauralee and Gordon. On March 20 Lauralee told her lover about Bruce's schedule for the day when she called his Orillia office in the morning, then invited Leanne Cooke to come to her house for dinner to set up an alibi for herself. Gordon drove to Toronto, waited for Bruce to enter the subway at the Osgoode station after work at around 5:45, and rode up with him to the St. Clair–Warden Avenue station. Chatting with his intended victim, he walked Bruce to his Mustang in the north parking lot, waited until Bruce got into the car, then shot him behind the left ear. Having killed Bruce at the east end of Toronto, Gordon got back to his own car some time between 6:30 and 6:40, purchased gas at a service station in the west end of the city shortly after 7 p.m., and drove back to Orillia in time to be seen by various people there at around 8:30. Then, at 9:30 he called Lauralee at her home reporting that he had done the deed, just about an hour before Sergeants King and Tallon arrived with Bruce's personal effects.

What evidence could Crown Attorney Michael Lynch and his associate Bruce Scott lead in support of this theory?

For the defence team — consisting at that time of Clay Powell, assisted by his partner (at the time his law student) Paul Stern, acting for Lauralee Lorenz, and my partner Chris Buhr (then my articling student) and I acting for Gordon Allen — finding an answer to this question was, as it usually is, the primary task at the preliminary hearing.

The Crown presented evidence of frequent telephone contact between Gordon and Lauralee *after* her reconciliation with Bruce. It seemed to contrast with the impression both defendants sought to create after Bruce's murder, namely that their relationship had become a thing of the past. There was also the evidence of a woman, Evelyn Round — who with her son, James Round, shared Gordon Allen's house in Orillia — that Lauralee had spent at least one weekend there with Gordon in December 1977. This, too, could be interpreted as an attempt to mislead the investigation, since neither Lauralee nor Gordon told about it to the police. (Certainly Judge Tinker was to take this view. "If the evidence is true . . . then both accused are liars of some magnitude," he said later in his judgment at the end of the preliminary.)

There was the evidence of several wiretapped conversations between Gordon and Lauralee from March 26 until their arrest.

While they contained absolutely no admissions of guilt, they could be viewed, using Judge Tinker's words again, as being of "a highly circumspect nature, and not the type one would ordinarily identify with that of innocent persons."

One call, for instance, on March 27, made initially by Gordon's sister to the cottage of Lauralee's parents where Lauralee was staying with the children after Bruce's death, contained (among others) the following exchanges once Gordon got on the phone:

*Gordon:* Hi, how are you?
*Lauralee:* Fine.
*Gordon:* Guess what?
*Lauralee:* What?
*Gordon:* I love you.
*Lauralee:* Yeah. (Referring to his nephews and nieces) How are the, how are the kids?
*Gordon:* Very good. How are the kids?
*Lauralee:* Oh, everybody here is fine.

. . . . . . . . . . . . . . . . . . . . . . . . . . . . . . . . . . . . . . .

*Gordon:* Good. Ah, a . . . getting a lot of heat?
*Lauralee:* Pardon?
*Gordon:* Are you getting a lot of heat?
*Lauralee:* Oh yeah.
*Gordon:* Pretty severe?
*Lauralee:* No.
*Gordon:* No?
*Lauralee:* No.
*Gordon:* Are you sure?
*Lauralee:* Yeah.

. . . . . . . . . . . . . . . . . . . . . . . . . . . . . . . . . . . . . . .

*Gordon:* Is anyone concerned why I haven't got in touch?
*Lauralee:* I'm sorry I can't hear you.
*Gordon:* Is anyone concerned why I haven't got in touch or anything?
*Lauralee:* I can't say very much.
*Gordon:* Pardon?
*Lauralee:* You know.
*Gordon:* Your parents?
*Lauralee:* Yeah.

. . . . . . . . . . . . . . . . . . . . . . . . . . . . . . . . . . . . . . .

*Gordon:* Well, I've had some visitors.

*Lauralee:* I can't hear you.

*Gordon:* I had some visitors.

*Lauralee:* Yeah, I know.

*Gordon:* Pardon?

*Lauralee:* I said, I know.

*Gordon:* Oh, how did you know?

*Lauralee:* Well . . . they came to see me last night and, ah, you know, we've had that finished with, so . . .

*Gordon:* Pardon?

*Lauralee:* I said, you know, I don't know if a . . . you know, we just kinda talked . . . it was . . . They were very nice.

*Gordon:* Uh-huh, yeah. I got the old third.

. . . . . . . . . . . . . . . . . . . . . . . . . . . . . . . . . . . . . . . . . . .

*Gordon:* I was expecting you to call me from the cottage.

*Lauralee:* Oh, well, no.

*Gordon:* Pardon?

*Lauralee:* No . . . no.

*Gordon:* You didn't think it would be wise, eh?

*Lauralee:* No.

*Gordon:* I trust your judgment.

*Lauralee:* Pardon?

*Gordon:* I trust your judgment.

. . . . . . . . . . . . . . . . . . . . . . . . . . . . . . . . . . . . . . . . . . .

*Lauralee:* (sing-song voice) Well . . . just be careful.

*Gordon:* Pardon?

*Lauralee:* You know, don't lay anything on too thick, you know.

*Gordon:* I can't hear what you're saying.

*Lauralee:* Well, it's the best I can do right now.

*Gordon:* How about I call you Wednesday morning? Okay?

*Lauralee:* Yeah. . . . Okay. . . . Sure.

*Gordon:* Okay, and I won't say anything, you know, thick, apt to upset.

*Lauralee:* Pardon?

*Gordon:* And I won't say anything that's apt to upset.

This conversation occurred on the Sunday immediately following Staff Sergeant Stevenson's and Sergeant McLean's first interview with Gordon Allen in Orillia. (Stevenson and McLean were, obviously, "the visitors".) The March 27 call was not untypical of some subsequent calls, though it probably represented the Crown's wire-tap evidence at its highest — in other words, it was the most "incriminating". Still, in the view of the defence team, the exchange was as consistent with Lauralee trying to hide her not-quite-finished relationship with Gordon from her disapproving parents, in whose cottage she took Gordon's call, as with either of them trying to hide it from the authorities. In any event, it was as consistent with two people being terrified of their innocent contacts being misinterpreted in light of Bruce Lorenz's death as with two people guilty of murder. Still it undeniably was, as Judge Tinker put it, a "circumspect" conversation. (In the office we called it the "pardon me?" conspiracy, since Lauralee and Gordon were being so circumspect that they could hardly understand one another on the phone. Real conspirators rarely have this problem. To me, it was another indication of their innocence.)

The Crown had some identification evidence of Gordon as the man seen with Bruce Lorenz on the subway, but it was very, very weak. While the three witnesses who saw the man chatting with Bruce — Christa Ahlers, Robert Sutherland, and another lawyer, David Harley — could not eliminate Gordon Allen, neither could they identify him as being the man. Their description of the suspect did not fit Gordon in many important particulars. Gordon's hair, though it often acquired a reddish hue in the summer, was neither red nor blond, as the witnesses remembered the hair of the man they had seen. It was brown. It was brown on March 20, and it was described as brown on the police record of his arrest on April 26. His height was an even six feet, while the witnesses' description of the man in the subway ranged from five feet eight to five feet eleven. Most importantly, all three witnesses recalled the man as clean-shaven, while Gordon had a neat but highly noticeable moustache.

The police did not ask the witnesses to attend a line-up — not surprisingly, since they couldn't be counted on to pick Gordon out of a fair line-up, i.e., several men of similar age and build. This alone made their identification evidence suspect, but in the case of Christa Ahlers the police did something far worse.

After surveillance photographs were taken of Gordon in Orillia, Staff Sergeant Stevenson showed Ahlers five black-and-white prints of Gordon in different positions — Gordon alone, and no one else — asking her if she could pick any one of the photos as being of the man she had seen. Ahlers, a very honest witness, told Stevenson that one or two photographs could be the man, but that she wasn't certain and could make no positive identification. (As Judge Tinker would later remark in his judgment: "It did not help in effecting identification, and I am ignoring the item except to comment on what I consider to be unfair, unjustifiable procedure.")

When Stevenson and McLean talked to Gordon for the first time, on Saturday, March 25 (which was when Gordon told them that he had spent the day of the murder in Orillia), the homicide officers took away his brown corduroy winter coat. Gordon said that he had *not* been wearing that coat for the last couple of weeks because it was slightly damaged: it had one button and an epaulet missing. The officers also took a pair of pants, a jacket, a pair of shoes, and a light checkered spring coat which Gordon said he had been wearing on March 20. At the preliminary hearing Staff Sergeant Stevenson testified that, according to the forensic report, two faint smears were found on the corduroy coat, one on the outside sleeve and one inside the right pocket, and there was also a faint smear at the bottom of one of the trouser legs. These smears — according to the police — were "indications of human blood", though insufficient in quantity to be tested for blood-type. No blood was found on the rest of Gordon's clothes or shoes, but there was a similar, faint "indication" of human blood on the cover of a manual in the glove compartment of his Mazda automobile.

There were no identifiable fingerprints. There was no weapon found. The bullet that killed Bruce had been fired from a .22-calibre hand-gun or rifle. A single glove found inside the car on the floor did not appear to have been worn by a "secretor" — that is, a person whose blood-type could be determined from bodily fluids, such as saliva, semen, or sweat. Gordon was a type-A secretor, as the police determined from the saliva sample he voluntarily gave them at his first interview.

In total, this was very weak forensic evidence. It was especially weak because in this case the victim had bled copiously, and other evidence indicated that the killer had actually come into bodily contact with his blood-drenched victim (in the Crown's theory, while trying to drag him into the car so that his feet wouldn't be sticking out of the window). This evidence — which I will discuss in a moment — indicated that the killer, after shooting Lorenz on the driver's side, went around the car and tried to pull him all the way into the vehicle from the passenger's side. There were spots of blood on the ground at the back of the car as well as some blood smears on the exterior of the Mustang to support the theory.

A killer literally dripping blood as he ran around the car would be expected to have far more blood on his clothes than a couple of faint smears, insufficient for blood-typing (which meant that they might well have been Allen's own blood). If anybody's clothes were subjected to a forensic examination, such faint smears — from a nosebleed, insect bites, skinned knuckles, and the rest — might be routinely revealed.

Still, weak as it was, the phrase "indications of blood" carried a weight that laymen often attach to so-called scientific evidence. Such a phrase can impress a jury by its sound alone, and I knew that I would have to deal with it very emphatically at trial.

It was not necessary to rely on circumstantial evidence to know that the killer did, in fact, come into some contact with the body inside the vehicle. As it turned out, four people had actually seen him.

Richard Giovanetti was driving across the parking lot with his wife sitting beside him at 6:40 p.m. Another couple were sitting in the back seat. Giovanetti, as well as his three passengers, noticed a man leaning into a Mustang from the right side, and they could see another person lying across the driver's seat. The sight struck them as curious, but not sinister: it looked like a man assisting a sick or drunken friend, or perhaps both men trying to fix something underneath the dashboard. The Giovanettis thought little of it, until they heard a report of the murder on the radio the next day.

This was very important evidence for several reasons. First, the evidence of the Giovanettis and their friends showed that the killer's clothes would likely be heavily blood-stained. Second, their recollection of the time — 6:40 p.m. — gave a firm point from which all other relevant times could be calculated. Incidentally, the four people who had actually glimpsed the killer could not identify Gordon. The Crown did not even attempt to use them for this purpose. The best general description they could give of what they called a "fair-haired" individual was so vague as to fit most white males in the country between the ages of twenty-five and forty-five.

There was some other minor evidence which, though Judge Tinker took it into account for the purpose of committing Gordon and Lauralee to trial, did not unduly worry either Clay Powell or me. For instance, the observant Mrs. Evelyn Round testified that she had seen a book entitled *Murder* in the Orillia house that she and her son shared with Gordon, but that the book later disappeared. (Considering that in my house there are at least fifty books that have "Murder" in their title — and I can never lay my hands on the one that I'm looking for — I didn't think that this evidence would take the Crown very far even if the jury believed it.)

There was a remote-control device in Gordon Allen's closet, such as many people have for opening garage doors or turning on a TV set. Allen told the police that he was planning to use it for a model plane, but in court Staff Sergeant Stevenson voiced the suspicion that such a device could be used to detonate a car bomb, implying that it may be possessed by a man who has murder on his mind. Judge Tinker said that this evidence "was not satisfactorily explored . . . as to its possible uses." This was, I thought, putting it mildly: the device in itself was not evidence of anything. A remote control is every bit as capable of legitimate uses as of illegitimate ones — not to mention the fact that even the possession of such a single-purpose instrument as a bazooka would hardly be evidence against someone accused of having shot his victim with a small-calibre gun.

Next, Sergeant Tallon described his impression of Lauralee's behaviour as "unusual" when he and Sergeant King went to her home on March 20: she seemed hysterical to him even before the officers had said anything, yet when they told her that her husband had died as a result of an unfortunate accident, she did not want to know any of the details. Most other bereaved relatives would have asked questions at this point, in Sergeant Tallon's opinion. (This, too, meant next to nothing: people react to bad news in different ways, and many people might be very upset on seeing two policemen arrive at their door late at night even before the policemen tell them the bad news.)

Nor was it of much significance that Lauralee, as Judge Tinker put it, "sounded incredulous" when told by Marilyn O'Brien that Bruce had forgotten to sign his new will. Even if the jury accepted O'Brien's impression, a wife need not be culpably involved in her husband's death to be dismayed on finding that his only valid will would disinherit her and one of her two children.

Judge Tinker also noted that Bruce's colleagues thought that Bruce left the office in good spirits and "not in the depressed condition that [Lauralee] Lorenz stated he was in because of non-appointment to a partnership in the law firm." Though the Crown might argue that this was a deliberate attempt on Lauralee's part to mislead the police, it was highly unlikely that a jury would draw such an inference. Two conspirators, unless they left a weapon on the scene, could not even hope to create the suggestion of suicide. Under the circumstances of this case, it would be of no earthly use for Lauralee to lie about Bruce's being depressed. A much more logical inference was that Bruce simply tried not to show his disappointment in front of his colleagues. (The plain fact is that any lawyer passed over for a coveted partnership would almost certainly be depressed that day.)

There it was: the grand total of all the evidence the police had against Gordon and Lauralee *before* they arrested them. It was certainly not a strong circumstantial case at that point. It was a weak circumstantial case at best, in so far as it was a case at all. In the mysterious murder of a husband it may not be unreasonable to suspect the wife and her ex-lover — but in law, cases must be proved beyond a reasonable doubt, not beyond an unreasonable suspicion.

Staff Sergeant Stevenson and Sergeant McLean must have realized this themselves. This was probably why, at the moment of Gordon Allen's arrest, they resorted to a desperate attempt to extract a confession from the man they suspected.

The attempt was, in fact, more than desperate. Unfortunately, what the two homicide officers tried to do amounted to a criminal offence.

Throughout the investigation Stevenson and McLean employed ruses and guile in several legitimate ways. They put a body-pack on James Round in the hope that Gordon might make an incriminating statement to him. He didn't. Then the officers tried to create the illusion in the two suspects that they were in the clear. At one point Stevenson told Lauralee that the police now thought that Bruce's death was a result of some of his own business dealings, and it involved "a white man and a black man". Lauralee expressed some relief that her private life was no longer suspected, but that was all. On April 5 the officers returned Gordon Allen's clothes, telling him that he was "no longer a suspect". Gordon also expressed some relief, and reiterated that he had spent the day of the murder in Orillia. The police hoped that these methods might cause Lauralee or Gordon to make "a mistake" or say something on the wiretapped telephone that would provide evidence of culpability out of their own mouths, but no such thing happened. Next, Stevenson tried to confront Lauralee with a straight accusation. It resulted in nothing but a straight denial.

If at the end of five weeks the investigators could prove anything beyond a reasonable doubt, it was perhaps that the two suspects lied to them about the extent of their continuing emotional involvement with one another. This may have been consistent with a guilty conscience, but no more consistent than with an innocent anxiety. It fell far short of proof of murder.

So, as a last-ditch effort, the day before Gordon Allen's arrest, Stevenson and McLean prepared a false affidavit in Lauralee's name. In it, Lauralee purportedly swore that she and Gordon had been deeply in love, but Gordon remained obsessed with her after their separation. He had threatened to kill her husband. She had vainly tried to dissuade him because she was happy with Bruce again and wanted nothing more to do with Gordon. She did not come forward with this statement sooner because Gordon had also threatened her life and she feared for the safety of the children.

After arresting Gordon, Stevenson and McLean showed him their forgery. According to Stevenson's testimony at the preliminary hearing, Gordon read the forged affidavit, then looked out the window of the police car in which he was sitting with the two detectives.

"I didn't think she'd turn on me," he allegedly said after a pause.

"I think she's involved," Stevenson replied. "In my opinion, the woman you loved, did and still do, in my opinion, she put you up to it."

"Yes, I understand the point you're trying to make," was Gordon's alleged reply. "This is really heavy, but some of it is not true."

"Do you wish to tell us what's true and what isn't?" Stevenson testified he asked next.

"Here at the bottom," Gordon answered, "I never made any threats on her life, that's not true. Obsession and threats, that's heavy. I think I'd better get some counsel before I say anything more."

This meant that even the most desperate shot of the police

misfired: the forged affidavit did not result in a confession. (I did not think that Gordon's response would be admissible against him at his trial in any case, which in fact turned out to be the trial judge's ruling.) But, admissible or not, it was just a first utterance by a shocked, frightened human being at the moment of his arrest for murder. It was not an admission of guilt. When Lauralee supposedly swore that they "had been deeply in love" but that later Gordon "made threats on [her] life", it was not surprising for Gordon to respond that "some of it is not true." He'd have no reason to say that *all* of Lauralee's purported statement was false.

Then, however, Stevenson and McLean hit pay dirt.

When coming to arrest Gordon, Stevenson picked up a few pieces of paper that were lying in plain view on the coffee table in his living-room. Among them was the soon-to-be-famous credit-card receipt for six dollars and fifty cents' worth of gas purchased at the Pit Stop in Toronto on March 20. This was how the investigators found out, *after* arresting Gordon, that he had been in Toronto on the day of Bruce's murder, and that he had lied to them about being in Orillia.

This was bad for the defence. It immediately put the Crown's case on a different level. The gas receipt was proof of opportunity for Gordon to have committed the crime, and a jury could draw, from Gordon's denial that he had been in Toronto, an inference of consciousness of guilt.

The next piece of evidence only came to the attention of the police in June, well after the preliminary hearing had started. It came from Bruce Lorenz's brother, the Kitchener-Waterloo police officer Brian Koepke.

Apparently Brian Koepke, having been notified on March 20 at twenty minutes past 11 p.m. at his home in Kitchener to call his sister-in-law on an urgent family matter, responded immediately. After two tries he got through to Lauralee on the telephone. By that time Sergeants King and Tallon had left but, according to Koepke, in that phone conversation Lauralee told him that his brother Bruce had been fatally shot in the head.

This conversation between Koepke and Lauralee occurred at around 11:25. Bruce Lorenz had been dead for approximately five hours, but King and Tallon had still been treating the matter as an accidental death. Staff Sergeant Stevenson was just then in the process of confirming the existence of a bullet wound at the morgue.

He would not call 41 Division about it for another ten minutes. If Lauralee did say what Koepke testified she had said to him on the telephone, she could not have got the information from the police. The two officers who came to her house did not yet know that Lorenz had been shot. Even the pathologist, Dr. MacDonald, couldn't be quite certain: the autopsy had just then begun.

This was potentially devastating evidence. The defence could attack it on several grounds — among other things, because Koepke, who under the last will that Bruce Lorenz had actually signed was a beneficiary of his estate, was not an entirely disinterested witness. The fact that he appeared to come forward with the contents of his March 20 conversation with Lauralee only in June also made his evidence open to question. Alternatively, he might have made a mistake about the time of his call. Still, Constable Koepke was a believable witness, and it would certainly be open to the jurors to credit his story.

If they did, the conclusion they would almost inescapably have to draw from it was that Lauralee Lorenz knew, before anyone else but the killer could possibly have told her, that Bruce had been shot in the head. The only person to whom she was known to have spoken on the telephone before the police came to her door was Gordon Allen. As Judge Tinker put it at the end of the preliminary hearing: "In view of the evidence, *particularly in view of the telephone conversation of [Lauralee] Lorenz with the deceased's brother in Kitchener,* I am satisfied that a jury properly instructed could find the accused Gordon Allen guilty as charged . . . [and] I find as well so far as [Lauralee] Lorenz is concerned." (Emphasis added.)

Brian Koepke told the court one other thing at the preliminary hearing. His father had taken a .22 semi-automatic Remington rifle from his cottage to Bruce's home some time in November 1977. By that time, of course, Bruce had been reconciled with Lauralee and was sharing his home with her again. When, after Bruce's death, Koepke went to his brother's house to look for the rifle because their father wanted it back, the rifle was gone.

### 3. Fall, 1978

On August 26, at the end of the preliminary hearing, I made a somewhat unusual decision. By that time I knew that Gordon Allen was telling the truth about his reason for coming to Toronto on March 20. By then I had no doubt whatever that he did come to have a date with the girl whose name he couldn't immediately remember in my office. I believed that he lied about his trip to the police — just as he had lied to me — only because he had been afraid.

I couldn't blame him for being afraid. Instead of carrying out an objective investigation, the police appeared to be focusing on proving Gordon and Lauralee guilty of Bruce Lorenz's murder in a single-minded fashion. They failed to conduct a proper line-up; they showed a key witness five photographs of the same man, and finally they forged an affidavit to entrap Gordon. In my view, my client had an excellent reason to be frightened.

Normally, when a suspect has an alibi, it detracts from his credibility not to disclose it at the earliest possible opportunity to the police. The Crown is entitled to argue that his alibi has been recently concocted if the defendant brings it up for the first time at his trial. Also, the trial judge is so obliged to caution the jury.

In this case, Gordon had an excellent alibi — but I did not want him to disclose it to the authorities at this point. On the basis of how the police had conducted the investigation, I myself came to the view, just like Gordon, that telling the police everything could be dangerous.

Just before Judge Tinker made his formal committal at the preliminary hearing, I stood up and addressed the bench as follows:

> Your Honour, I would like to make a statement for the record with respect to the alibi evidence that will be led at trial by Gordon Allen.
>
> In my view of the police conduct in this case, [some of] which even your Honour called unfair and unjustified in your ruling, and the preparation and use of a false affidavit and an arrest that was not based on any new evidence, I am convinced that if I disclose the specifics of the alibi the police will do everything to demolish it. They will not examine it with any degree of dispassion or independence. So, for the record, *I* have made the decision to refuse to disclose the specifics of the alibi to the Crown. I tell your Honour, for the record, that I am in possession of that information and I will lead it at trial.

This created an entirely new ball game. The police would have no chance to intimidate or discredit the witness who was to be Gordon's alibi, yet the jury could not hold it against him that he did not disclose his alibi to the police. It was no longer his decision, but his lawyer's. If the jurors blamed anyone, they'd have to blame me — and I wasn't on trial. They could not say that Gordon's alibi was a recent fabrication.

I had an additional reason for playing it this way. The girl, whom I will call Heather in this account to save her from any further embarrassment, was a highly credible but very, very reluctant witness. It was precisely her reluctance that made Gordon Allen's story so obviously true.

Heather wasn't a friend of Gordon's; she was hardly even an acquaintance. She was a young, rather prim and straightforward girl who had met Gordon at a dance. She happened to meet him just at the time when she had had a tiff with her steady boyfriend, so when Gordon asked her for a date for March 20 she had said yes.

However, by the time Gordon came to Toronto, less than two weeks later, Heather and her boyfriend had made up. When my investigator got in touch with her, she and her boyfriend had already set a date to be married.

Not surprisingly, Heather's new husband-to-be was very reluctant to let his bride testify at Gordon Allen's trial.

Heather was very reluctant herself. Her involvement in the entire affair had been so marginal as to make it unfair that she should find herself on the witness stand in a murder trial on account of it. All Heather did was to agree to have coffee or maybe dinner with a personable young insurance agent she had met at a dance. But she did say yes, and Gordon took her up on it. He phoned her, as arranged, a few minutes before 6 p.m. on March 20. She was certain about the time because she had just got home from her computer-programming course, and she hadn't even had time to take her coat off when the phone rang. She did not want to go out with Gordon at all because she had made up with her boyfriend, but she did not tell that to Gordon. She just told him that she had forgotten their date and that her mother had already made dinner for her — exactly as Gordon reported the conversation.

There was no question in my mind that Heather was telling the truth. I was also quite sure that the jury would believe her: under the circumstances, why should anyone lie for a complete stranger? I only hoped that she would have the fortitude to go through the ordeal of testifying for someone she had only met once in her life, rather than take the easy way out and let an innocent person perhaps be convicted for murder. It was a tough decision for Heather — it would be for a lot of people — and I couldn't risk letting the police put the slightest pressure on her.

Heather's testimony would be essential for Gordon. Not only would it explain why he came to Toronto on March 20, but it would also prove that whoever Robert Sutherland saw changing platforms at the *St. George station* in Bruce Lorenz's company around 6 p.m. could not have been my client. Heather was quite certain about the time of Gordon's call. Gordon couldn't be calling her and standing on the subway platform with Bruce Lorenz at the same time.

After the preliminary ended in August, the next four months brought no new developments in the case. Both Gordon and Lauralee were free on bail, though under orders not to communicate with each other. The trial date was originally set for January 1979, but by mutual agreement Crown Attorney Michael Lynch and I postponed it until February 12. In January I had another trial coming up in Vancouver, and the Crown needed some more time to prepare. No doubt the investigation was still continuing.

The day after I left for Vancouver, on January 18, the police arrested Gordon Allen on charges of perjury, fabricating evidence, and attempting to pervert justice.

When Gordon swore an affidavit for his original bail hearing before Mr. Justice Holland, it included the statement that he held an MBA degree from the University of Western Ontario. This was not true. Gordon had attended some university courses, but he had acquired no degree. Like other people who exaggerate their academic qualifications at one point in their lives for business or social reasons — and there are many people who do that — he came to virtually believe it himself. It just became an automatic part of his curriculum. So, when setting out his particulars for his bail application, he included his imaginary degree as he had done on other occasions.

It was, technically, a false statement in a sworn document, but Gordon did not make it to mislead the court. A university degree would not have made the slightest difference to whether or not he would be admitted to bail. It had no more significance than someone making himself a year younger or an inch taller, having become accustomed to lie about his age or his height for reasons of personal vanity. That, too, would be a false statement in a sworn document, and just as immaterial in case of a bail application.

I considered the Crown's decision to look into Allen's bail affidavit eight months after it was made, then lay charges and proceed against him on this basis (and to do so on the very day that Michael Lynch knew I was going out of town on another trial), prejudicial, distasteful, and outrageous. Eventually I had occasion to say so in court. It simply wasn't fair ball either for the prosecution or for the police. Taking away a man's liberty for such a frivolous reason, and thereby depriving him of the opportunity to prepare for his defence three weeks before he was due to appear on the most serious charge in the Criminal Code, was just not fighting according to the Marquess of Queensberry rules.

Yet this was what the Crown did — and Judge Tinker refused to grant bail to Gordon on the new charges. He was still in custody when I got back into town from Vancouver on January 26 and immediately applied to have Judge Tinker's decision reviewed. Meanwhile I instructed my office to find examples of well-known people in the world who had exaggerated their academic background or accomplishments in a manner similar to Gordon Allen's. I knew there must be some, but to my pleasure and surprise Chris Buhr came up with an impressive list that included the famous American meteorologist Bob Harris (fake doctorate), Columbia Pictures mogul David Begelman (fake Yale degree), U.S. economics guru Eliot Janeway (fake Cornell degree), and even President Jimmy Carter, who had made certain claims about being a "nuclear physicist" (which he wasn't, really) and directing the Head Start program in the State of Georgia (which he didn't, quite). I presented my case in County Court to the late Judge John Greenwood, a very fair jurist and former prosecutor. Judge Greenwood agreed with the defence. "I can't think of something more trifling than the academic background of the accused," he said in a judgment granting Gordon Allen bail on the new perjury charges.

Naturally I was relieved — and when I discussed the matter with Chris Buhr and some other people from my office afterwards, we also concluded that the Crown's action showed a certain amount of desperation. Maybe the police wanted Gordon in jail so that they could body-pack some snitch — a common tactic — to see if they could trick Allen into making some incriminating statements. If so, it showed a significant lack of confidence on the eve of trial in the Crown's "strong circumstantial case".

We could also pat ourselves on the back for the defence team's decision not to disclose Gordon's alibi before the trial. The prosecution's latest move completely vindicated it. If the investigators (the very people who admitted to forging a sworn document to entrap Allen) would stoop to laying charges against him for exaggerating his schooling on a sworn document, what would they not stoop to in order to intimidate a key defence witness? I was confident that, in light of such harassment, the jury would understand our tactical move and not hold it against Gordon for a minute.

But even while we were congratulating ourselves, I felt depressed and anxious. Something was bothering me about the case, and I couldn't put my finger on it. There was something going on, something I should have been able to anticipate perhaps, but I couldn't and didn't. It worried me, but then I decided that it must be only nervous tension. Most lawyers feel tense as they are waiting for the main event and I'm no exception.

In retrospect, as I look back on those final days before the trial, it seems to me that even while thinking that the prosecution must be desperate, I did not realize how desperate it was. I did not understand it even when the day came, and with it a totally unexpected turn of events.

The Crown, in his opening gambit, captured my queen. More precisely, he forced me to exchange my queen for a pawn.

When that happened, I was terrified. I didn't see that my queen had been more of a liability than a defence, or that my opponent had opened up a gaping hole in his own ranks. Like a nervous chessplayer confronted with an unconventional move, far from seeing a chance for victory, I felt cornered and outmanoeuvred.

## 4. Spring, 1979

The trial, which was to begin in the Supreme Court of Ontario before Mr. Justice Allan Goodman and a jury on February 12, 1979, did not start on the appointed day. His Lordship was there at 10 a.m. on that Monday morning, and so were Gordon Allen, Chris Buhr, and I, but Crown Attorneys Michael Lynch and Bruce Scott were not in the courtroom. Neither were any members of the investigative police team.

The other people not present were Gordon's co-accused, Lauralee Lorenz, her lawyer, Clay Powell, and his law student, Paul Stern.

After waiting for several hours, Mr. Justice Goodman gave orders to locate the missing persons. For my part, I was perfectly happy to proceed without locating the Crown. As I told Mr. Justice Goodman (an eminent jurist, since elevated to the Ontario Court of Appeal), I liked the odds better.

It was late in the day before Michael Lynch and Clay Powell appeared, apologizing to the court and requesting that the case be put over by one day. They offered no explanation for their request and, after it was granted, immediately left the courtroom.

I developed a giant headache. It stayed with me for the next three months. I couldn't be absolutely certain what was happening at that point, but I could guess. So could Chris Buhr and the rest of my associates.

Lauralee Lorenz was jumping ship.

The next day, on February 13, Crown Attorney Michael Lynch announced that the prosecution was staying the charge of first-degree murder against Lauralee, but proposed to accept her guilty plea to a charge of accessory after the fact to murder. I objected to this — naturally, since such a plea would have prejudged the Crown's contention that Gordon Allen was a principal in a murder. A trial was about to be held precisely to determine whether this proposition was true or not. My argument was not settled law then, but one Supreme Court of Canada decision appeared to support it, and Mr. Justice Goodman agreed to remand Lauralee's plea until after the trial.

Once this was settled, Lauralee, neatly attired in a fur-and-leather overcoat, departed from the court on the arm of her attorney. My client, Chris Buhr, and I were left alone to read her "will-say" or proposed statement, a copy of which was provided to us at this point by the Crown.

Lauralee Lorenz was going to testify that on the day of Bruce

Lorenz's murder, at 6:30 in the evening, she had received a telephone call from Gordon Allen. According to Lauralee, Gordon had been panting heavily as though he had been running. First he said "Hi, how are you?" to her, then continued as follows:

"Guess what? I just shot your husband."

At that point (Lauralee was proposing to say) she screamed into the phone: "What did you say? What did you do?"

"I think I have killed your husband," Gordon supposedly replied, still breathing heavily. "God, Laura, all the blood . . . Jesus, there's some lady looking right at me."

According to Lauralee, she answered: "I don't want to talk to you," and hung up the telephone.

Unlike my client, I've never been in the habit of using the expression "That's heavy" but after reading Lauralee's will-say I very nearly did. It seemed like the only appropriate comment.

Lauralee seemed to contend that, totally unexpectedly, out of the blue, Gordon Allen shot her husband, then called and told her about it. She stated that she had "never encouraged Gordon to harm Bruce and never assisted him in any way." After he phoned her she did nothing, since "I was horrified by the call from Gordon and didn't want to believe it and didn't know what to do." Even when she learned about her husband's death later that night, Lauralee mentioned Gordon's call to no one, because "I was confused, upset, and afraid that if the police found out Gordon did it, I would be involved and that it would hurt my sons and my family." So she continued saying to the police that Gordon couldn't have done it, until she gradually and entirely "suppressed" the 6:30 telephone call into her "subconscious".

How did it emerge from her subconscious again? Well, Clay Powell was to testify later that he could see that something was troubling his client as he was preparing her to stand trial for first-degree murder. She had been having nightmares about the day of her husband's death, but they always stopped at a certain point, and then she could remember nothing. Since Lauralee couldn't tell her lawyer what was causing the turmoil in her psyche, Powell arranged for her to see Dr. Robert Coulthard, the head of Toronto's famous Clarke Institute of Psychiatry, who administered a Sodium Amytal ("truth serum") test to her in the morning of February 10, a Saturday, two days before her trial was to begin. By the afternoon of the same day the suppressed telephone call worked its way back into Lauralee's conscious mind again. She could now remember exactly what Gordon had said to her on March 20, at 6:30 p.m.

Since it was the truth — as she was to maintain later under oath — she wanted to tell it to the police. That was her only reason. She had no idea, she said, that it might help her in any way.

Clay Powell, however, being the excellent lawyer that he is, did realize that Lauralee's renewed ability to communicate with her subconscious might be of assistance in her legal difficulties. In the course of Sunday and Monday the deal with the Crown was struck. On Tuesday we were told about it, and by Wednesday, February 14, the court was ready to proceed with a trial for first-degree murder against Gordon Allen alone. As an unexpected Valentine's Day gift for her ex-lover, Lauralee was no longer a co-accused at his trial but a witness for the prosecution.

The defence had been dealt a new hand. After I got over the initial shock, my question became what, if anything, I could do with it. Was Lauralee's sweetheart deal with the Crown as great a calamity for Gordon as it appeared?

When I first realized what was happening to our case I could have cheerfully punched Clay Powell in the nose — but, on reflection, I couldn't blame him at all. As Lauralee's lawyer, it was his duty to get the best result he could for his client, and exchanging a potential life sentence without parole for twenty-five years for an accessory plea that, in the event of a conviction, was not likely to result in more than a few months in jail was a pretty spectacular result.

But what about the Crown? Was the deal a spectacular result for the prosecution?

Michael Lynch had decided to trade a circumstantial case against two defendants for a case of direct evidence against one of them. Was it because, as a good trial lawyer, Lynch did not have enough confidence in his circumstantial case? Or was it because Clay Powell, as a persuasive advocate and an experienced former Crown — a one-time director of all Crown attorneys — convinced Lynch that it was a good deal for the prosecution? Lauralee would give evidence of Gordon's alleged confession to murder (and as a bonus would also consent to the wiretapped conversations between herself and Gordon being admitted — evidence that might otherwise not be admissible against Gordon).

A case based on direct evidence, in the perception of most people, including some lawyers, appears to be stronger than a mere circumstantial case. Lauralee might not be a very credible witness, but so what? A jury would not have to believe her entire story about the struggle between her conscious and her subconscious. It would not have to believe that she knew nothing about Gordon's act beforehand, or that she never encouraged it. If a jury simply believed that, whatever Lauralee's own involvement, Gordon Allen did call her at 6:30 on March 20 to say that he had shot her husband, it would be enough to convict him. After all, Bruce Lorenz *was* shot on that date at around that time.

If Gordon Allen committed murder, he committed murder: it would be none of the jury's concern whether Lauralee had helped him or not. Even if the jurors disbelieved her protestations of innocence and found the idea of Lauralee's getting away with her part in a murder plot distasteful, their oath would oblige them to convict Gordon if they believed her evidence about his 6:30 phone call beyond a reasonable doubt.

But what, I thought, if the jurors didn't believe it?

What if the jurors retained a reasonable doubt, not only about the extent of Lauralee's own involvement, but about her entire story? What if they concluded that she might have invented it simply to save her own skin? She was at risk of going to prison for life, and she wanted to get out of it. People have lied for less. If the jury rejected Lauralee's evidence, what would be left of the Crown's case against Gordon Allen?

The full implications of the Crown's deal with Lauralee started dawning on me only after we selected the jury and the proceedings began. I rather suspected that Michael Lynch himself had not been able to analyse all the ramifications of his restructured case until then: after all, the sudden turn of events had come as a complete surprise for the Crown as well. It might have been only when Lynch started outlining the prosecution's proposed list of witnesses that the realization hit him. Certainly that's when I began to realize what had happened.

By staying the charges against Lauralee, the Crown had dropped part of its own "strong circumstantial case". The prosecution traded a number of high cards it might have had for one single card — and that card might not have been an ace. The Crown's best evidence that would have been admissible at Gordon and Lauralee's joint trial was no longer admissible against Gordon Allen alone.

Brian Koepke could no longer get on the witness stand to say that Lauralee had told him about Bruce's being shot in the head even before the police knew about it. Whatever Lauralee said to Koepke that night might have been evidence at the trial of the two accused tried together, but it was not evidence against Gordon.

Nor could Koepke testify that a Remington semi-automatic .22 rifle had disappeared from Lauralee and Bruce's home. Nothing connected Gordon either to the gun or to the house shared by Lauralee and Bruce. It was simply irrelevant in a trial of Gordon Allen alone. Whatever disappeared from Lauralee's home, in the absence of proof that Allen had ever been there, might have been evidence at the trial of the two accused tried together, but it was not evidence against Gordon.

Bruce Lorenz's secretary could not testify that Lauralee sounded surprised or dismayed on the telephone when she told her about Bruce's not having signed his new will. However Lauralee sounded to someone on the telephone, while it might have been evidence at the trial of the two accused tried together, was not evidence against Gordon.

Sergeant Tallon could not testify about what he thought was Lauralee's "unusual" behaviour when told about her husband's death. If Lauralee's behaviour was unusual, it might have been evidence at the trial of the two accused tried together, but it was not evidence against Gordon.

Once Lauralee was no longer a co-accused, whatever she might have known, said, or done had nothing to do with Gordon Allen at all. A person can only be tried on his own acts and words, or on the acts and words of an alleged fellow conspirator, but not on the acts and words of an uninvolved Crown witness. The Crown's best evidence in the case, the evidence of Constable Koepke — singled out as the most decisive by Judge Tinker in committing Lauralee and Gordon to stand trial together — was evidence against Lauralee. (Had Gordon Allen jumped ship by inventing some story, it would have been admissible against *her*.)

It was not admissible against Gordon.

After the legal arguments, watching Michael Lynch as Mr. Justice Goodman in a series of meticulous judgments excluded the choicest bits of the Crown's evidence, I couldn't help wondering if the prosecution did not begin to have regrets about rushing into a deal with Lauralee. Staff Sergeant Stevenson certainly looked to me as if he were ready to explode.

What evidence was there against Gordon alone? Well, there was still the statement of Mrs. Evelyn Round (who by the time the trial started had died of cancer) about a book entitled *Murder*. There was the remote-control device that could steer a model airplane or maybe set off a bomb. But no reasonable jury would convict on those two items: they were at best just icing without a cake.

There were the three eyewitnesses in the subway who couldn't eliminate Gordon as being the man with Bruce Lorenz — but couldn't identify him as the man either. It was hardly proof of guilt beyond a reasonable doubt.

There were the "indications of blood" on a brown corduroy coat — a coat that Gordon said he did not wear on March 20, and that, in the opinion of the witnesses who saw the man in the subway and the killer in the parking lot, did *not* resemble the coat of the suspect they had seen. Christa Ahlers saw a "camel-type" coat — definitely not corduroy, she said — and the people in the parking lot talked about a "light-coloured" coat. The rest of the witnesses simply didn't remember. Still, weak as it was, there was this forensic evidence. Dealing with the "indications of blood" on the coat, the pants, and the car manual would be important for the defence.

Finally, there was the credit-card receipt. The little slip that seemed to be the worst evidence against Gordon. The receipt that proved (a) that Gordon had been in Toronto, and (b) that he had lied about it to the police.

Except, as I was beginning to understand the Crown's case, the receipt proved one more thing. It proved that, on the prosecution's own theory, *Gordon Allen could not have killed Bruce Lorenz.* It was a physical impossibility.

The credit-card numbers established as a near-certainty that Gordon purchased the gas between 5:45 p.m. and 7:10 p.m. on that Monday. The Crown's own witnesses would confirm this. Two other Crown witnesses, a man named David Poidevin and another man named Larry Vanscoy, would establish that Gordon was back in

Orillia by around 8 p.m. If he had filled up his car at 5:45, he couldn't have been at the Osgoode subway station by 5:40 or even by 5:50 — you can't get from the west end of Toronto to the heart of downtown in five minutes. If he had purchased it at 7:10, he couldn't have made it back to Orillia by 8 p.m. Not unless he pushed the Mazda at 96 mph (154 km/h) all the way.

And if he had purchased the gas at any time in between, he couldn't have been the suspect on the subway or the killer of Bruce Lorenz. The Crown's theory postulated a triangle with three known points: the gas station in the west, the Osgoode station in the south, and the murder scene in the east. The three points were separated by a driving-time of about twenty minutes from one another. The man had to be on the subway roughly between 5:55 and 6:25 to get with Bruce from the Osgoode to the Warden station. The killer was still struggling to put the victim's body in the Mustang at 6:40 at the city's east end, seen by four of the Crown's witnesses. Gordon's car was never on the parking lot — the police carefully checked the licence numbers, of course — and the nearest legal parking spot was a seven-minute walk away. (In any case, his Mazda ought to have been parked around the Osgoode subway station, on the Crown's theory; he would have had to go back after the murder to retrieve it.) Even driving directly, he could hardly have made it from the scene of an east-end murder at 6:40 to a west-end gas station in twenty to twenty-five minutes, let alone back to Orillia by 8 p.m.

And if he was still struggling to pull Bruce's body back into the car at 6:40, "guess what?" He certainly couldn't have phoned Lauralee ten minutes *earlier* at 6:30.

Nor, as already mentioned, could he have phoned Heather for a date at 6 p.m. when he was supposed to be changing platforms with Bruce at the St. George subway station. On the Crown's own times, Gordon couldn't have made any of these phone calls (as I eventually pointed out in my address to the jury) unless he carried a phone in his shoe.

By proceeding against Gordon alone, the Crown also removed any suggestion of a credible motive. There was no evidence of a jealous passion, and while it may have made some sense for Gordon to kill Bruce Lorenz in a calculating conspiracy with Lauralee, it would have made very little sense for him to do it on his own and against her wishes. His chances of financial gain or for reconciliation with her under those circumstances would have been minimal.

Every witness is important in a trial, but I felt that in this trial four witnesses would be crucial. For the defence to succeed, I had to hurt two of the Crown's witnesses: Lauralee Lorenz and the forensic expert, a biologist named William Towstiak. At the same time I had to protect as much as I could two defence witnesses: Gordon Allen and his hoped-for date on that Monday, Heather.

The first of the four witnesses was Lauralee.

A former nurse from a respectable middle-class family, Lauralee Lorenz cut a cool, composed figure on the witness stand. Having watched her carefully during the *voir dires* and during her examination-in-chief, it seemed to me that she would know what she had to say to fulfil her end of the plea bargain. And say it she would, never using more words than necessary. She'd insist on even the least credible part of her story with a straight face. She would not be easily riled or rattled. She'd make no attempt to match wits with the examiner, or let her ego get in the way. She would know that she was there for a purpose, and try to accomplish it coldly and methodically. Mrs. Lorenz did not want to go to jail.

Lauralee was a difficult witness, but I thought that if she had one vulnerable point, it was her glance. She would probably not lose her temper with me verbally no matter how much I provoked her, but if I made her angry and then turned away, she might raise her eyes and look at my back.

When people were not facing Lauralee directly, she was capable of directing an icy, hate-filled glance at their backs that was truly heart-stopping. I had noticed it once or twice even during the preliminary hearing. I felt that if I could elicit it during my cross-examination, the jury could not fail to be disturbed by it. I asked Chris Buhr to watch her expression whenever I turned my back on her and signal me if the look came.

I actually managed to elicit Lauralee's special glance twice during my cross-examination. The first time was when I had caught her in a lie. During her direct examination by the Crown, she had tried to create the impression that, after she had left Bruce and lived with Gordon, neither man supported her. In fact, both did. Bruce gave her $1200 a month for a while. As for Gordon . . .

"You painted a picture for this jury," I said to Lauralee, "that

[Gordon] made no contribution. That is the evidence you gave, right?"

"Yes."

"You did not take a penny from Gordon Allen?"

"I believe he wrote me a couple of cheques for doing some typing," Lauralee replied.

"What was it, about fifty dollars?" I asked her. The folder in my hand had about $1300 worth of cancelled cheques from Gordon Allen to her for the month of October 1975 alone.

She glanced at me, sensing a trap. "I'm not sure," she said.

"Well, think about it, Mrs. Lorenz."

"But I did take a couple of cheques from Gordon, yes."

"Well, I want you to think about it for a minute," I said. "You gave a lot of evidence to this jury about how you paid for the house, and you paid for Gordon, and you got the next house, and you did this, and you did that. Did he give you fifty dollars? Seventy-five dollars? What did he give you for typing?"

"Maybe fifty dollars," she replied, after a tiny pause.

"Okay. So September, October, November, Gordon Allen gave you fifty dollars, right?"

"I'm not sure."

"Well, think back, Mrs. Lorenz. Sixty dollars?"

"Maybe fifty dollars, sixty dollars, twice."

I took one cancelled cheque out of the folder. "Well, let me show you a cheque made out to Lauralee Lorenz," I said. "That's your name, right?"

"That's correct."

"Signed by Gordon Allen — that's his name — on October 31, for three hundred and fifty dollars?"

"That's correct."

"Now, would that be closer to the total now?"

"Perhaps," Lauralee replied. "I told you before I couldn't remember."

It was just a small, small thing, but interesting to watch. "No, you said it was around fifty dollars," I said. "I'm bringing it up to three hundred and fifty dollars. Is that closer, yes?"

"Well, obviously the cheque is there, so he wrote it to me," she said coldly. Lauralee was not gracious in defeat.

"Now is that the total?" I asked.

"I am not sure what the total is."

"Well, you said it was around fifty dollars. It is now up to three hundred and fifty. Do you want to stop or go for more?"

"Is there any more?"

"You tell me. You tell the jury," I said. "Don't ask me questions."

"I don't know because I can't remember."

I took her up, cheque by cheque, to $1350. "Mrs. Lorenz," I said when I finished, "you painted a picture that you took $1200 a month from your husband because Gordon Allen contributed nothing. I submit to you you were painting the picture of a real martyr, weren't you?"

"No, sir."

"Hard-pressed woman?"

"No, sir." She spoke politely but her voice was getting tighter.

"Well, let me put this to you, Mrs. Lorenz, what you told Gordon Allen was that your husband was paying you nothing, and [Gordon] was giving you $1300 a month, and what you were doing was playing both ends against the middle, looking out for number one, Lauralee Lorenz."

"No, sir," she replied. At this point I turned my back on her and walked away, glancing at Chris Buhr who kept his eyes on the witness-box. After a second Chris nodded. Lauralee was staring at my back with a look of pure, icy hatred.

I watched the jury as I turned back. Without a doubt they had noticed her deadly glance. Some of the jurors looked shocked.

Lauralee was hurt in cross-examination even more when she did not flinch, did not react in any way, but stuck almost as if by rote to the most incredible parts of her story. For instance, according to Lauralee, her friend Leanne Cooke happened to go into the bathroom just before Gordon's alleged 6:30 phone call. The telephone was just outside the bathroom in Lauralee's home.

"And [Gordon] said, 'Guess what?' " I asked Lauralee as I took her through the conversation.

"That's correct."

"And did you guess what?"

"No."

"And if he had given you three guesses, would you have guessed what?"

"No."

"If he had given you a hundred guesses, would you have guessed what?"

"No, sir."

"And then he says, 'I think I've just killed your husband,' right?"

"That's correct."

"And you screamed, 'What did you say? What did you do?' Right?"

"That's correct," Lauralee replied stolidly.

"You screamed it, right?"

"Yes."

"And Mrs. Cooke is the thickness of a door away," I said. "She must have come out when you screamed it and said, 'Laura, what's the matter?' "

"No, sir," Lauralee said, her face set. It was evident that her mind was made up to brazen it through. One of the give-aways was that, whenever she decided to do that, she would call me "sir" with icy politeness. I glanced at the jurors, who were watching her intently.

"She didn't come out, did she?"

"No, sir."

"She didn't hear it, did she?"

"No, sir."

"So after Gordon says, 'I think I've killed your husband. Oh, God, Laura, all the blood,' and then, 'Jesus, there is some lady looking right at me' — what did you say?"

" 'I don't want to talk to you,' " Lauralee replied.

"I take it this is the first call of this nature that you have ever got in your life?"

"That's correct, sir."

"Wouldn't you be a little curious about this kind of call to the point where you'd like to find out a little more?"

"No, sir."

I paused, letting this answer sit with the jury for a second or two. Then I asked: "And then when you hung up, Leanne Cooke came out of the washroom, right?"

"I believe she walked in the room as I was hanging up, yes."

"A coincidence, correct?"

"Yes, sir," said Lauralee, still without batting an eye.

"What was the first thing you said to Leanne Cooke?"

"I didn't say anything to her."

"Well, she stayed with you until the police came and gave you news of your husband's death," I said. "Did you say nothing to her until the police came?"

Lauralee thought about that. "No," she said finally, "it was a little while later I said something to her."

"What?"

"I believe I told her I was going upstairs to get the boys ready for bed."

We continued in this vein for a while, with Lauralee refusing to see anything strange about the fact that after Gordon's supposed phone call she carried on as usual, with neither Leanne Cooke nor another girlfriend with whom she chatted for about fifteen minutes on the phone noticing a thing out of the ordinary. "You got a phone call 'Guess what? I think I have just killed your husband,' and you just put it out of your mind, right?" I asked her.

"I didn't want to believe I received it."

"You want the jury to believe that?"

"Yes, sir, because it is the truth," Lauralee replied, nodding like a schoolgirl for emphasis. This was fine with me; I just waited for about a minute to let it simmer with the jury. Nothing, in my experience, can antagonize twelve ordinary people more than a stubborn insistence on an obvious lie.

Lauralee's special glance stabbed me in the back the second time when I was cross-examining her about her subconscious. "You told a friend of yours on March 29 at 10:02 p.m.," I asked Lauralee, glancing at the logbook of police wiretaps in my hand, "that 'Gordon couldn't have done it. He has nothing to hide.' Right?"

"Yes, sir."

I paused. "Where was the 6:30 call now?"

"It wasn't there," Lauralee answered. "I don't know where it was. Somewhere in my mind, obviously."

"Where in your mind?"

"What part?" she asked. "Subconscious."

"Okay. It had gone from the conscious to the subconscious, right?"

"Yes," she replied. "I wasn't aware of [Gordon's] phone call, I don't believe, at that time."

I looked at her. "You got a phone call from Gordon," I asked, "on March 20 at 6:30 p.m., right?"

"Yes, sir."

"Were you conscious when you heard it?"

"Yes, sir."

"And it was in your conscious mind?"

"When I was talking on the phone, yes."

"And it was in your conscious mind when you got off the phone and spoke to Leanne Cooke, right?"

"I cannot say to you when it went from my conscious to my subconscious," said Lauralee. She spoke matter-of-factly, as if this were an everyday occurrence. When it's not convenient to face something, you repress it — she seemed to say — and then you recall it whenever it's convenient. Doesn't everybody?

"I'm having some difficulty, Mrs. Lorenz," I said to her. "You testified earlier that you consciously lied to the police. Were you hiding something in your subconscious or hiding something in your conscious mind?"

"Knowing what I know today and looking back on the first time that I saw the police," said Lauralee, noticing the problem that she was walking into just a touch too late, 'I . . . I lied to them, yes, because I didn't tell them about the 6:30 phone call."

"Which you knew about?"

"Which I know about now," she replied, trying to recover.

"You know about *now*?"

"Yes, sir."

"So, if we carry this on, you told countless people that Gordon didn't do it, right?"

"Yes, sir."

"You said to one of your friends on March 28 at 8:30 p.m. that Gordon wouldn't hurt a fly."

"Yes, sir."

"But your subconscious knew better, right?" When Lauralee didn't reply, I raised my voice. "Right?"

"You could put it that way."

"Well, no," I said, "*you're* putting it that way, right?"

"Yes. Part of my mind knew better, yes."

"Your conscious mind says Gordon couldn't hurt a fly. Your subconscious mind says he could hurt a fly."

"Yes, sir."

"Your conscious mind told another friend on March 29 at 10:14

a.m. that there is no conceivable reason for Gordon killing Bruce, that he would never do it. That was your conscious mind, right?"

"Yes, sir."

"But your subconscious mind knew better, right?"

"Yes, sir."

"And your conscious mind told your priest, Father Madden, that Gordon Allen would never do such a thing, right?"

"Correct."

"But your subconscious mind knew better, right?"

"Yes, sir."

"Your conscious mind told your parents that Gordon Allen wasn't capable of murder, right?"

"That's correct."

"But your subconscious mind knew better."

"Yes, sir."

Lauralee was hitting her stride. By this point she seemed almost comfortable in the position she had taken. She kept replying to my questions rather sweetly, as if to say: "That's my story, and you're stuck with it." It was time to elicit her special look, if I could. I waited for a second, then said:

"You told a catalogue of lies in your conscious mind about Gordon Allen, right?"

Lauralee didn't like the word "lies" and her voice became a little tighter.

"Yes, sir, I did."

"But the truth was in your subconscious mind?"

"That's correct."

"And subconscious minds don't lie."

"No, sir, I don't believe they do."

"Do you believe that," I asked her, "on your conscious level or on your subconscious level?"

A little pause. "Both," said Lauralee. I was watching her hands grip the rail of the witness-box.

"You told another friend on March 31 that you didn't have a clue about the death of your husband."

"That's correct."

"Right. That was your conscious mind that didn't have a clue; your subconscious mind knew it all, right?"

"I wouldn't say knew it all," Lauralee said, her voice rising. "It knew something that my conscious mind wasn't aware of."

I looked at her.

"Well, it knew enough to get you out of a first-degree-murder charge, didn't it?"

"It knew the truth — not enough — it knew the truth!" Now Lauralee's voice was shrill. I turned my back on her, saying as I walked away:

"But your subconscious mind wasn't talking to your conscious mind, right?"

This time I didn't even have to glance at Chris Buhr. I could *feel* the cold, thin blade of her fury stabbing me in the back. I paused at the defence table, taking my time, letting the jury take a long look at Lauralee Lorenz in the witness-box. The courtroom was silent for a full minute.

Then I turned to Mr. Justice Goodman. "My Lord," I said, "I notice it is five to one, and my conscious mind tells me I'm hungry."

The tension broke suddenly, with everyone beginning to move and whisper. "I would have thought it would be your stomach, Mr. Greenspan," his Lordship said, rising. "We will adjourn until 2:15." Everyone stood up, and after Mr. Justice Goodman and the jury left, people began to file out of the courtroom.

No one, I noticed, was looking at Lauralee.

I thought Lauralee had fatally wounded herself in cross-examination, but of course I couldn't be sure. I would probably not know it for certain until after the verdict was in. If the jury believed her subconscious beyond a reasonable doubt, it would *have* to convict Gordon: it was as simple as that. Someone did shoot Bruce Lorenz and, according to Lauralee, Gordon had confessed to her.

However, even if the jurors did not believe Lauralee's subconscious mind, or had a reasonable doubt about whether it was or wasn't any more truthful than her conscious mind (which, on her own evidence, had lied for eleven months), they might still convict Gordon on the remainder of the Crown's circumstantial case. The one witness, I felt, who could achieve this for the prosecution was William Towstiak.

Mr. Towstiak is a forensic biologist of some renown, and it was he who had tested Gordon's clothes for indications of blood at the Centre of Forensic Sciences in Toronto. In the jury's eyes he would be a detached, impartial scientist; if he said that Gordon's clothes and car manual were bloodstained following a bloody murder, the jury might conclude that Gordon had to be the killer. Towstiak was an experienced, professional witness; even his mid-European accent lent an air of authority to his pronouncements. In our scientific age, expert witnesses can be decisive in a jury trial. How could any layman question the word of a forensic biologist?

In this instance, the Crown attempted to use Towstiak for two purposes. First, to offer proof to the jury that Gordon had blood on his clothes. Second — trading on Towstiak's undoubted expertise as a scientist in the analysis of biological substances — to somehow create an aura of scientific certainty around the Crown's entire theory of the murder. Right down from the killer walking from the subway to the parking lot with Bruce — the Crown having contended, of course, that the man seen by witnesses on the subway in Bruce's company was Gordon Allen.

It was his willingness to lend himself to this task that got Mr. Towstiak into trouble first.

During the examination-in-chief, Michael Lynch gave his expert witness a long hypothetical question. It included the two men's walk from the subway; the manner in which Bruce Lorenz might have struggled or convulsed after being shot; even the question of the epaulet on Gordon's corduroy coat having been "torn" off. All of this might have fitted various bits and pieces in the Crown's theory, such as Gordon having some blood, but not too much blood, on his clothes, or the corduroy coat being damaged during some convulsive struggle with the dying Bruce Lorenz. (Also, of course, the corduroy coat *being* the coat worn by the killer, since Gordon's other topcoats did not have even any smears on them at all.)

The trouble was, none of these postulations had the remotest connection with forensic biology. Still, Towstiak responded enthusiastically to the Crown, saying: "This is precisely what I thought had happened."

It gave me a great opening in cross-examination right from the start.

"Mr. Towstiak," I said, "I want to first deal with the hypothetical that was put to you. You recall, sir, that it contained around twenty-one suppositions. Your answer was, 'This is precisely what I thought had happened,' right?"

Towstiak replied, somewhat testily, that he didn't count the number of suppositions, but that his "findings" were consistent with Mr.

Lynch's hypothetical, yes.

"I don't want to quarrel with you," I said, "but I have got down that you said exactly, 'This is precisely what I thought had happened,' right?"

"Yes, I said it."

"So, you said that, okay. Then let's go through it," I said, picking up my notes. "The first one is that the victim and the killer walked from the Warden Avenue subway to the parking lot. Is this precisely what you think happened?"

Michael Lynch saw where this was leading, and got to his feet. "Well, my Lord," he interjected, but Mr. Justice Goodman would have none of it. The prosecutor had opened a door and now his witness had to walk through it. "That is fair cross-examination, Mr. Lynch," his Lordship said.

Mr. Towstiak was getting a little defensive. "With respect to whether the killer and the deceased walked from the subway station or from the airport or from some hotel?" he asked. "Then, I did not consider that, so, therefore, if you want to be technical to that point, then this has to be excluded."

"Can I take it," I asked, "to avoid going through all of this, that everything up to and including the victim getting into the car, closing the driver's door, rolling down the window so he could speak to the killer, putting the keys in the ignition — all that is not part of what you say precisely in your view happened, right?"

"Probably," conceded Mr. Towstiak, "the word 'precisely' was not the one that suits in this the best."

After this rather inauspicious start for the Crown's expert witness, we spent the next hour dissecting Lynch's hypothetical that was supposedly "consistent" with Towstiak's "findings". Towstiak fought me every inch of the way, which was a credit to his persistence, if not his perspicacity. By insisting on matters in which he had no special qualifications and about which his guesses were no better than anyone's, he lessened his credibility with regard to areas in which he *was* an expert — which suited me just fine. Towstiak kept spinning theories about medical matters, or what a hypothetical killer would or would not do, undeterred by such comments from Mr. Justice Goodman as "This is a great detective story, but it really wasn't what you were asked, I don't think." He kept it up until I was able to drive the point home.

"You really have no idea what happened?" I asked him.

"I object." Michael Lynch stood up again.

"It is cross-examination, Mr. Lynch. The witness can look after himself," said his Lordship.

"The ideas that you are giving, Mr. Towstiak," I said, "are just the common-sense view of what must have happened. You didn't study this. You have got a BA from the University of Toronto and you are a biologist, right?"

"Sir, I don't think that you will find one man on this continent that went to university who has a degree in this field. That type of work — the knowledge in that type of work is gleaned through the experience, sir," replied Towstiak.

"I'm not quarrelling with the education you have had," I said, "but you are talking about things which are just your personal opinion and not based on any expertise. You are guessing."

"I have examined many, many homicide cases," the witness insisted, "and many scenes and many cars, and to that extent, I have testified in court, not only reporting strictly technical findings, but I was allowed in the Supreme Court in homicide cases to give my opinion as to what might have happened in these cases."

I did not doubt Mr. Towstiak's word for a minute. He had probably been allowed to do that. This is the very problem with the use of "expert" witnesses in our courts: they are frequently permitted, even encouraged, to play armchair detective. In this case I was grateful for it, because in a minute I had to tackle Mr. Towstiak on his own territory.

The Crown's biologist was going to testify that the faint smears on the sleeve of Gordon's corduroy topcoat and trouser leg were "indications of blood". In this field Mr. Towstiak was, indeed, an expert. Experts are rarely challenged on such findings. To the jury, unchallenged, the phrase would mean that the smears on Gordon's clothes were probably blood, and not just blood but probably human blood, and not just human blood but probably Bruce Lorenz's blood. The jurors could conclude that, therefore, Gordon had to be the killer.

But I did some research before the trial. I came to the view that the smears might not be blood at all.

The following is an abbreviated version of my cross-examination of Mr. Towstiak on this subject. It was central to the case for the defence.

"In reading your report," I said, "I note that when you examined the car you found 'human blood' on the driver's-side door."

"That is correct."

"But I notice when you are talking about the corduroy topcoat you use a different expression. You say: 'Indication of blood'. "

"That is correct."

"What do you mean by this?"

"By this, by taking this," replied Towstiak, "it means that what was found responded to the test in such a way as blood would respond."

"Human blood?"

"Blood, period," Towstiak said. "I didn't say this was blood. I only said 'indication of blood'. I am inclined to think it was blood, but technically speaking I cannot make a positive statement that this was blood."

This was, of course, an impeccable answer — technically speaking. On the basis of the tests he made, Towstiak couldn't say that the smears *were* blood. The problem was, he was saying so nevertheless. He could just as accurately have said that the smears were "indications" of many other things, but what he chose to say was "indications of blood".

Could I bring him to admit it?

"Well, sir," I said. "You did one test, right?"

"That's right."

"The phenolphthalein test? Did I pronounce it right?"

"You are right, yes."

"That's the only test you did. Very well, sir, let me . . ." I turned to walk to the defence table and pick up a textbook, noticing as I did so that Towstiak was bringing out a book from his own briefcase. "Oh, you're bringing a book out before I even get mine?"

Towstiak, the experienced witness, smiled. "I think it is a good idea for me to have one," he said.

"That evens out the odds," remarked Mr. Justice Goodman, amused.

"I take it you're familiar with *Taylor's Principles and Practices of Medical Jurisprudence* by Professor Keith Simpson?" I asked.

"Yes, I am, sir."

"It is a very highly respected book?"

"Yes, Professor Simpson is quite highly respected in this area."

"All right," I said. "Now this test you used, the phenolphthalein test, is, I suggest to you, not a specific test for blood."

"It is for indication of blood, sir."

"It is *not* a test for blood."

"I have to disagree with you, sir," replied Towstiak, "because it is generally used as a preliminary test for blood."

"Well, do you agree or disagree with what Professor Simpson says at page 265?" I started reading. " 'The phenolphthalein test depends on the presence in blood of a peroxidase and must be considered in its true character — that is, as a test for peroxidase — "

"That's perfectly correct, yes," Towstiak interrupted.

"Let me finish — *'and not a test for blood.'* " I paused, then continued reading. " 'It is well to remember this, for assertions are constantly being made that it is a definite test for blood.' " I looked at Towstiak. "Right?" I asked him.

"That is perfectly correct, yes," he replied with a tight smile. "But there is a slight qualification required . . ."

"There is no qualification in Simpson's book, right?" I said. "None. Read it."

"Yes. That is, this is perfectly all right."

"All right," I said. In the preceding months I had read all I could lay my hands on about the subject, so I felt on safe ground. "Peroxidase, which is all that the test you did can show, is present in a number of things . . . like apples?"

"Yes," said Towstiak.

"Apricots?"

"Cucumbers, garlic," he replied.

"Asparagus, beets, brussels sprouts," I continued, having memorized the list myself. "Onions, plums, tomatoes, milk, eggs, fish, blood, horseradish, yeast?"

"Yes, yes, that is correct."

"Right. So I am suggesting to you, sir, that what your test showed on that coat is an indication of many things, and *one* of them is blood."

"That is correct, sir. But, you see, the peroxidases from the other materials, they are not as stable as blood."

Here Towstiak explained that peroxidases from other substances can break down at various times, ranging from hours to weeks, but blood takes longer. This was quite true but also meaningless: a biologist would have no way of knowing whether or not the coat he examined had been in contact with some such substance an hour, a day, or a week before. "If there was a contact between this coat and some juice or whatever," Towstiak conceded, "then this could be that it reacted to the peroxidases, not necessarily from blood, but from whatever it was."

At this point Mr. Justice Goodman intervened.

"How many types of juices or vegetables or fruits?" he asked the witness.

"Most of them, your Lordship," said Towstiak, "would have . . ."

"Would have peroxidase?"

Towstiak agreed.

"And if any of these came into contact with the coat at the particular spot you tested, it would be reasonable to find that in your test?"

"That is correct, my Lord, providing . . ."

"Providing they were within a reasonable time," said his Lordship. "I presume if someone had eaten a plum before they picked up the coat and had plum juice on their coat, it would show up?"

"Could be," replied Towstiak.

"I suppose a more accurate report," asked Mr. Justice Goodman, "would be that some substance had come into contact with the coat which contained peroxidase and one of those various substances is blood?"

I carefully kept my mouth shut. This was far better than anything I could have expected. Should Mr. Justice Goodman elicit the final admission from the witness, it would carry even more weight with the jury.

"Would this be a fair statement?" his Lordship asked.

"Probably this is the way it should be put," said Mr. Towstiak unhappily; "however . . ."

"The way it *is* put," said Mr. Justice Goodman, "it just indicates blood but nothing else, but a fair way of putting it is that it indicates some substance which contains peroxidase and one of such substances is blood?"

The Crown's biologist gave up. "That probably would be the correct way to put it, sir," he said quietly.

After that, the forensic part of the Crown's circumstantial case was no longer a major threat. Later I wanted to say to the jury that if

Mr. Towstiak had ever analysed my jacket after I'd been to a McDonald's he'd have me down for the Texas Chainsaw Massacre. My wife, however, vetoed the line, so all I said to the jury was that if I had ever been subjected to a phenolphthalein test after eating a Big Mac, I would have ended up in the same prisoner's dock as Gordon Allen.

The battle was won, but the war was not yet over. After the Crown closed its case, Heather would have to testify about Gordon Allen's phone call to her on the day of Bruce's murder. It was vital evidence for the defence, but once I elicited it there was nothing for me to do but listen and make sure that she was not unfairly cross-examined on it by the Crown. If Michael Lynch could shake her testimony in a *fair* cross-examination, there was nothing I could do about it, of course.

Heather came and gave her evidence. The prosecutor cross-examined her fairly — and she remained unshaken.

Gordon Allen, according to this highly credible witness, phoned just before 6 p.m. on March 20, 1978, to take her out for a date right then and there, as prearranged. He did so about half an hour before, on the Crown's theory, he had murdered Bruce Lorenz.

If the jury believed Heather, what could it possibly conclude? Did Gordon shoot Lorenz just because, having been turned down for a date, he had some time to kill?

Then it was Gordon's turn on the witness stand.

In our system an accused person is not obliged to testify in his own defence. As discussed earlier in the *Goldman* case, no one is entitled to comment on, or draw an adverse inference from, a defendant's silence.

If he chooses to testify, however, he can be cross-examined on his evidence.

Cross-examination is a fearful weapon in the hands of a skilful lawyer. "The engine of truth," as cross-examination has been called, can also be the engine of deception or destruction. Innocent people can be made to appear guilty when cleverly or aggressively cross-examined. People of superb wit — as in the celebrated case of Oscar Wilde — can be reduced to silence by a seasoned cross-examiner.

Gordon Allen was not Oscar Wilde — very few people are. On the other hand, Michael Lynch was a very seasoned and capable Crown

Attorney. I had every hope by then that we might overcome the Crown's evidence against us, but ours would not be the first case to founder on a defendant's inability to withstand a good prosecutor's assault in the witness-box. From my own practice I remembered the *Giguere* case, outlined in an earlier chapter, where a jury would have acquitted the defendant if only he hadn't testified on his own behalf.

Yet, under the circumstances, it would have been unthinkable for Gordon Allen to exercise his right to silence. It was a strategy I never even considered, especially after Lauralee had turned Crown's evidence. The jury simply had to hear Gordon Allen proclaim his innocence. Legally they were not entitled to it, but as human beings they were. In any event, it was Gordon's own wish to face the jury and tell them that he did not kill Bruce Lorenz.

However, unlike police officers, experts, or professional criminals, Gordon Allen was not an experienced witness. Until his own preliminary hearing he had hardly ever set foot in a courtroom even as a spectator. I wanted to make sure that he did not go into the ring totally unprepared.

The trial had started on February 14; I expected Gordon to testify some time early in April. One evening late in March I took my client to an empty courtroom used during the day by a Royal Commission. Waiting for him in court were Chris Buhr, my secretary, and an old friend of mine, Harvey Strosberg, Q.C.

In my estimation, Harvey is one of the most effective cross-examiners in the country. The kindest of human beings in private life, as a civil-litigation lawyer Harvey is brutal. There is no other word to describe him. He is, of course, also exceptionally smart and meticulously prepared. He is never unfair as a cross-examiner, he doesn't hit below the belt, but he doesn't have to. His fairest punch can knock a witness flat. In 1979 Harvey also happened to be in top form, because as counsel to Mr. Justice Horace Krever's Commission of Inquiry into the confidentiality of medical records he had been cross-examining RCMP officers and lawyers every day for many months.

If Gordon could survive being cross-examined by Strosberg, I felt, he could survive anything. Minimally, he would have experienced the worst.

My friend Harvey managed to shock me as soon as we entered the courtroom. Gordon, of course, knew that he was going to be subjected to a "dress-rehearsal" by a tough cross-examiner. He knew that, to be worth while, the exercise could not be conducted with kid gloves. But he also knew that the lawyer facing him was one of my friends and a member of the defence team. He expected — and, frankly, so did I — that we would get down to brass tacks only after the usual social amenities.

However, for Harvey there is no such thing as a mock trial. When he plays, he plays for keeps. As soon as I introduced Gordon to him and Gordon extended his hand, Harvey threw a look at him that would have sent most people scurrying to their psychiatrists. Then, after a few seconds of awkward silence, Strosberg pointed to the witness-box:

"I don't shake hands with murderers, Mr. Allen," he said. "Kindly take your place on the witness stand."

At the end of Harvey Strosberg's cross-examination, my only hope was that Gordon Allen had learned from the experience. He probably had, but even so he came close to not surviving the real thing conducted by Michael Lynch.

A Crown Attorney is a lawyer and, as the late Judge Greenwood was in the habit of saying, "a lawyer's job is to win." A difficult, high-profile case arouses any lawyer's spirit in a special way, and the murder of Bruce Lorenz was a difficult, high-profile case.

Until Gordon Allen took the witness stand things had not gone too well for the prosecution. Right at the start the Crown traded a good part of its circumstantial case for the direct evidence of Lauralee's subconscious. What was left had been severely shaken by the prosecution's own theory of the murder: a theory that would have required Gordon to be in several different places at the same time. The Crown's case was also badly damaged by Heather's testimony and by the equivocal nature of the forensic evidence.

Michael Lynch was under a lot of pressure. Some of the police investigators had voiced their unhappiness about the deal the Crown had made with Lauralee. Destroying Gordon Allen on the witness stand would be Lynch's last shot in what looked like a losing battle, and he was determined to make it a good shot. (In his place, as a lawyer, I would have tried to do the same thing.)

Gordon Allen was a vulnerable witness because he was a human being. As with most other human beings, he had not led a blameless or saintly life. His first marriage had failed; he had taken up with another man's wife; his business had gone bankrupt. He pretended to have an MBA which he had not earned. Many people have worse episodes in their life histories, but very few have to account for them on a witness stand.

After Bruce's murder, Gordon Allen became frightened and he lied. He lied about having completely ended his relationship with Lauralee, and he lied about having been in Toronto on March 20. Many human beings tell worse lies even when they have less reason to be frightened, but not many have to answer for them under the shadow of a first-degree-murder charge.

Over four days, from the third until the sixth day of April, Gordon Allen was required to give an answer for everything that had ever gone wrong in his life to a skilled and relentless prosecutor. On the first day he faltered. He seemed cornered and ill at ease. If Lynch had ended his cross-examination after the first day, I don't know what the jury would have decided about Gordon.

The second day was even worse. Under the glaring searchlight that the Crown had turned on Gordon's character and history, every little crack seemed to gape like the Grand Canyon. "Is that another coincidence?" was the prosecutor's theme, and with detail piled upon detail it was indeed hard to see how a man could be hounded by so much misfortune without authoring it himself. Even though I knew that almost any man might be made to appear in this light if forced to explain his life to a jury by a hostile questioner, I was worried for my client.

There was nothing I could do to help him. Once a witness reaches the phase of being cross-examined, he cannot discuss his testimony with anyone until he has finished giving evidence. Not even with his own lawyer. The law did not permit me to give advice to Gordon at this point about anything at all.

As I walked across Toronto's City Hall Square at the end of the second day with my client, I knew that I had to make him pull himself together. Gordon was battered, and he seemed to be shrinking and giving up under the prosecutor's attack. I realized it was hard, but I felt that no matter how hard it was for him, he had to begin standing up to the Crown.

It happened to be one of the first beautiful days of spring. The afternoon sun was shining in a cloudless sky, and some passersby carried their topcoats over their arms. "Gordon," I said to my client, "you know I can't discuss your testimony with you. But I want you to look at the sky. I want you to look at these buildings and these people. I want you to look at them, because you're not going to see them for twenty-five years."

Afterwards some of my colleagues said that I was cruel and mistaken. Saying such a thing to a man under the worst pressure in his life could only shatter him completely. My colleagues might have been right, but I didn't know what else to say to Gordon, and I was not going to stand by and say nothing. It was his life and his innocence. He had to fight for both.

On the third day Gordon Allen rallied. I thought that he had fought the prosecutor to a draw.

On the fourth day, in my view, Gordon beat Michael Lynch cold. By the afternoon the Crown could do little but go over old ground. After four days the cross-examination ended on the following note:

"Well, Mr. Allen," said the Crown, "you have been under cross-examination since last Thursday, correct?"

"I believe so, yes, last Thursday," Gordon replied.

"I have put it to you on several different occasions that you murdered Bruce Lorenz, haven't I?"

"You certainly have and nothing could be farther from the truth, as you know by now."

"I put it to you," Lynch continued, "that I could cross-examine you forever and you will never, ever admit that you murdered Bruce Lorenz?"

I stood up. "What is the relevance of the question?" I asked.

"I have no idea. I have no idea," said Mr. Justice Goodman, but the Crown insisted:

"Correct or incorrect?"

"Absolutely," replied Gordon, "because of the fact I didn't kill Bruce Lorenz. I had no reason to kill him. I'm not capable of killing him and I didn't kill him and you know it."

"You had reason to kill Bruce Lorenz."

"I never had a reason to kill him and you know it."

"I don't know anything, Mr. Allen. I'm just asking you questions," said Lynch.

"Just look at the evidence and you will know."

"The jury will look at the evidence, Mr. Allen," Lynch replied. It looked as if he were about to continue, but then he changed his mind and turned to the bench. "Those are my questions," he said, walking back to the prosecution's table.

The defence rested. (I'm describing this out of sequence, actually, because Gordon Allen testified before Heather.) In any event, the prosecutor called no evidence in rebuttal. The trial was over.

While preparing my address to the jury, I only had to make one strategic decision. I wasn't sure how to deal with one question, and I delayed deciding it for quite some time.

Obviously, the defence contended that Lauralee was not telling the truth about Gordon Allen's 6:30 phone call. But, a jury might ask, why would she lie? I was under no obligation to explain her motive on Gordon's behalf — how could one person be expected to know why another person might lie? — but leaving the jury with no theory about it might have been dangerous.

Since Bruce Lorenz was murdered and Gordon did not do it, I could have suggested to the jury that Lauralee herself had something to do with her husband's murder. For her to blame Gordon, I could have said, was simply a way to avert suspicion from herself. In the end I decided against saying this for one simple reason. I did not believe that it was true.

What I said to the jury on April 17, 1979, was this:

This trial started on February 14, Valentine's day. Since that date we have heard from a lot of witnesses. But of all the evidence you've heard, I suggest that the only incredible, the only totally unbelievable piece of evidence is Lauralee Lorenz's claim of that 6:30 phone call.

She says it slipped from her conscious mind and she did not remember it until February 10 this year. That was four days after she'd read the Crown's brief — the case that Mr. Lynch intended to call against her. Four days after she became concerned that, no matter how innocent she was, she stood a good chance of being convicted.

Innocence may not be enough in a criminal trial involving circumstantial evidence. Her lawyer had told her that.

Now maybe if you're not Lauralee Lorenz and you're falsely accused of an offence you did not commit, you'd simply trust our criminal justice system to exonerate you. That's what Gordon Allen has done. That isn't what Lauralee Lorenz did.

What was the one thing she could do to take herself out of a first-degree-murder charge? She couldn't simply keep on saying: "I didn't do it and Gordon couldn't have done it." Saying that hadn't helped. She'd been saying it from the time the police had first questioned her. It just hadn't worked.

So, she couldn't keep saying that. She had to point the finger at someone. She had to do what the police had been demanding all along. Right from the first meeting, and at subsequent meetings. "You have the choice of being a witness or an accused," was what they had told her.

Not only had she been told what the police wanted, they'd even given her a script. Staff Sergeant Stevenson and Sergeant McLean prepared a forged affidavit. A lie, known by the police to be a lie, to show to Gordon Allen. She'd seen a copy of it at the preliminary hearing. That's where she got the foundation of her story from.

But she'd *told* everyone that she didn't do it, Gordon didn't do it, that they were both innocent. How could she change her story now and be believed?

You know how she did it. She looked up the word "subconscious" in the dictionary. Maybe she remembered it from her nursing education. And with the words "conscious" and "subconscious" in her vocabulary, she made up a story. To believe that evidence about her conscious and subconscious, you've got to be unconscious.

I say that that 6:30 phone call never happened. I say Lauralee Lorenz is completely and totally fabricating it for only one reason: to save herself at the expense of another human being. To sacrifice Gordon Allen, the man with whom she lived once, to save herself.

You may be asking yourselves what would bring a human being to do that to another. Consider this:

Lauralee is 33. Convicted of first-degree murder she'd be sentenced to life imprisonment — a minimum of 25 years in a penitentiary. She'd be 58 when she got out. The prison authorities wouldn't allow her her expensive clothing in the penitentiary. Her fur coat would sit in cold storage for a long time.

But most of all, there are her children. Lauralee loves her children: no one has ever doubted that. And in 25 years' time the younger child would be 28 and the older one would be 34. Adults, maybe with children of their own. And she'd never see them smile and she never hear them cry for 25 years.

25 years without her children. And she loves them more than anything in the world. It is safe to say she loves them more than she ever loved Gordon Allen.

When Lauralee was arrested she spent five or six days in the Detention Centre — and she couldn't stand it. The worst experience in her life, she said. But what is five days compared to 25 years?

Faced with a trial two days away, told by her lawyer that she might be convicted despite her innocence, she did the only thing Lauralee Lorenz is capable of doing in those circumstances. She lied. She tried to sink the man she'd sworn for a year was innocent to save herself. That's why she did it. It's that simple — and that terrifying.

Dealing with the rest of the Crown's case was, in a sense, much easier. In fact, by the end of the trial I concluded that the Crown's witnesses only helped Gordon Allen. This was what I said to the jury:

The prosecutor took seven weeks to complete his case. At the end of it he will stand before you and ask you to *disbelieve* part of it.

He will — he must — ask you to disbelieve his witness Leanne Cooke. [Cooke never heard the 6:30 call or Lauralee's scream. She testified that she didn't even go to the bathroom until after 7 p.m.]

He will — he must — ask you to disbelieve his witnesses the Giovanettis. [The people in the car on the Warden Avenue parking lot saw the killer at *6:40* trying to pull the victim inside the car, ten minutes after Gordon's alleged phone call to Lauralee.]

He will ask you to disbelieve David Poidevin and Larry Vanscoy, his witnesses who saw Gordon Allen in Orillia by 8 p.m. He will ask you to disbelieve his other witnesses David Harley and Robert Sutherland — they simply missed the moustache and confused the colour of the man's hair in the subway: that's what he has to say to you.

And I say to you that if you believe every single word of every Crown witness in the trial — except Lauralee Lorenz's 6:30 call — then, I submit, you must acquit. I invite you to believe every single witness that testified for the Crown, except Lauralee Lorenz. And you can believe every single word *she* says — except that 6:30 call.

Unless you believe her about that phone call, believe her beyond a reasonable doubt, to the point of moral certainty, I submit that you must acquit Gordon Allen.

Michael Lynch, in his strong, spirited address to the jury, put the emphasis on the string of what he called "coincidences" that had to occur to put Gordon Allen in his present predicament. Then Mr. Justice Goodman charged the jury at length and with meticulous fairness. To my mind, it was a model of what any trial judge's charge to the jury ought to be. (My only dilemma was that, having listened to his Lordship carefully, I could not easily see a defence appeal succeeding in the event of a conviction. On the other hand, I could not see a Crown appeal succeeding either in the event of an acquittal.)

And then, all we could do was to wait.

After a ten-week trial it took the jury two days to acquit Gordon Allen of first-degree murder. I certainly did not regard the verdict as a foregone conclusion, and after the jury addresses and Mr. Justice Goodman's charge to the jury I spent the next forty-eight hours, from Thursday afternoon to Saturday morning, in a complete daze. Waiting for the jury's final word was, as always, the worst time of the trial for me. I think it is for any lawyer — and if it is bad for lawyers, I have no idea how defendants can go through it. However, once Gordon's cross-examination had ended, I was only worried, not pessimistic. On the facts, I had every hope for an acquittal.

On the basis of the Crown's theory, Gordon Allen could not have murdered Bruce Lorenz. I felt that the evidence not only failed to prove him guilty beyond a reasonable doubt, but actually proved him innocent. The jury could only have convicted him on some stubborn speculation — to which no jury is entitled — that he must have killed Lorenz *somehow*, even if not the way in which the evidence and the Crown suggested it.

While it is illegitimate to speculate in a courtroom, it is quite legitimate to speculate in a book. Bruce Lorenz was undoubtedly killed. Since, on the evidence, it would have been physically impossible for Gordon to kill him, who did? Three possible answers occur to me (though there may well be additional possibilities).

First, even though there was no evidence (except for some vague hearsay) that Bruce Lorenz had had any business dealings or personal conflicts that could have resulted in his murder, it was also a fact that, after the first forty-eight hours, the police made no effort to investigate Bruce's life except in relation to Gordon and Lauralee. The investigators may have started with an open mind, but they closed it very quickly. In my opinion, they closed it as soon as they had heard Bruce's secretary exclaim that the man in the subway "must be" Gordon Allen. From that point on, or shortly after that point, the investigation concentrated on nothing but gathering evidence against Lauralee and Gordon — by hook or by crook. Other possibilities were simply not explored, but it would be rash to conclude that therefore they did not exist.

Second, there was some evidence that there were muggers operating on the deserted north parking lot where Lorenz had parked his Mustang. (Two women reported having been attacked in the preceding months, and some female customers would only park their cars in the south lot closer to the attendant's booth.) True, at six feet five and 200 pounds Lorenz was not a natural target for a professional mugger, but some crazy kid, armed and strung out on drugs, might have decided to take a chance. Then, frightened away by some passersby, he might have fled before robbing his victim. Such things have happened before.

Finally, hired assassins have been known to kill the wrong victim by mistake. Hit men are not very smart, and they frequently put bombs in the wrong car or torch the wrong garage. Admittedly, it is less common for hired killers to shoot the wrong man at close range, but it is not unheard of. Some support for this theory could be found in the method of Lorenz's death: a gangland-style assassination of a single bullet behind the ear. The absence of a weapon, fingerprints, or any other physical evidence connected with the killer, as well as the known fact that the assassin spent some time in the victim's car after shooting him, would also lend this scenario some support. It was only the Crown's assumption that the killer was trying to pull Lorenz's body into the car: he could just as easily have been looking for something that he thought would be in the victim's vehicle or on his person. If he couldn't find what he was looking for, such a killer would not take Lorenz's watch or wallet. An unidentified green car *was* reported speeding away from the parking lot around the relevant time.

All this is pure speculation, permissible only in a book. In court, lawyers, juries, and judges are not concerned with solving a crime, only with determining whether or not the accused is guilty of having committed it beyond a reasonable doubt. However, as armchair speculation, each of these three theories has some validity. On the evidence, Gordon Allen could not have killed Bruce Lorenz — and, as Sir Arthur Conan Doyle pointed out a long time ago, once you eliminate the impossible, whatever remains, however improbable, must be the truth.

As an epilogue, it may be of interest to note the following. On May 19, Attorney General Roy McMurtry announced that the Crown would not appeal Gordon's acquittal as it found "no errors of law by the trial judge which would, in the circumstances, merit an appeal." The Crown also declined to offer any evidence against Lauralee, whose guilty plea to a charge of being an accessory to murder after the fact had been remanded by Mr. Justice Goodman pending the outcome of the trial. On May 23 Michael Lynch dropped the charges against Lauralee, after which the case was dismissed by the trial judge. Lauralee's last appearance in court took less than three minutes. She left the building immediately for her parents' cottage, "totally and utterly relieved", according to the newspapers. About five months later, in an out-of-court settlement, she and her children reportedly received $175,000 from Bruce Lorenz's $207,000 estate.

Since the trial I have heard some people suggest that Clay Powell and I worked out together Lauralee's defection as a brilliant defence strategy to divide and defeat the Crown's case. Much as I would like to take credit for such foresight and shrewdness, I can't. Had it been a "strategy", the only person who could be credited with it would be Lauralee herself. If she had come up with it by design to *help* Gordon, she ought to have been a criminal lawyer. In fact, she would have made one of the greatest trial lawyers in history.

As an interesting sidelight to the case, after we heard about Lauralee's "truth serum" test, I decided to have Gordon undergo a combined truth serum and hypnosis test himself, just in case the Crown sought to admit Lauralee's test results as evidence. We even made sure that Gordon would receive twice as much Sodium Amytal as Lauralee did. Gordon, of course, passed his tests with flying colours, maintaining his innocence under both drugs and hypnosis. While I think very little of "truth serums" and hypnosis as vehicles for discovering the truth, whether administered to my own clients or to Crown witnesses, I must say that I was taken with one episode during the test. The doctor cut Gordon's hand while he was under hypnosis, suggesting to him that he would not bleed. Indeed, Gordon obediently refrained from bleeding. After being wakened, however, approximately half an hour later, he bled copiously from the same cut. I admit that I was impressed.

On June 26 Gordon Allen pleaded guilty and received an absolute discharge for including his mythical MBA into a sworn document at his bail hearing. A few days earlier, on June 22, Staff Sergeant Stevenson and Sergeant McLean were charged with the criminal offence of preparing and uttering a false affidavit in relation to the phony document they had concocted over Lauralee's forged signature at the time of Gordon's arrest. They pleaded not guilty. Less than six months later, on December 6, both policemen were convicted by a jury in Barrie, Ontario. Ironically, it was the only conviction by a jury in the Lorenz murder case.

The two homicide officers received an absolute discharge as well, but their careers suffered as a result of the conviction. Both Stevenson and McLean were dedicated policemen — and I happened to personally like them both, especially McLean — but this was not why I felt equivocal about what happened to them. I believed, and said at the time, that by charging them the authorities had turned them into scapegoats for getting caught at a practice that was not only condoned but encouraged by the police. Stevenson and McLean did not deny forging the affidavit: they admitted it almost proudly, regarding it as a clever ruse to catch the bad guy, something that police officers are entitled, and ought to be entitled, to do. I was certain that they did not arrive at this conclusion by themselves. On the contrary, it was a feeling fostered by the police — and even rewarded by the courts. If, for instance, Gordon *had* confessed as a result of the forgery, his confession (if otherwise ruled voluntary) might have been admissible against him as evidence. It would not have been excluded just because it was triggered by a criminal forgery, or as a practice that might bring the administration of justice into disrepute.

In view of this, I thought that the two officers were not treated very fairly. They were being punished for the sins of the authorities that condone such practices — as Robert McGee, a very honest and senior former Crown, now in private practice, pointed out to the newspapers at the time. For instance, had Stevenson and McLean simply put the word "Statement" instead of "Affidavit" on the same forgery, they might not have committed, technically, a criminal offence at all (according to one of their lawyers) — in which case their superiors who crucified them for their act might have applauded them instead. The policeman's lot is not a happy one.

I was more upset with Sergeant McLean's lawyer, John Hamilton, who, while trying to persuade Metro Toronto Council to pay his client's legal fees out of public funds, saw fit to characterize Gordon Allen as "a cold-blooded murderer". I was outraged that a criminal lawyer, of all people, would call a man found innocent by a jury of his peers a murderer, and expressed the view that I would expect this kind of comment only from someone without any knowledge of the law. The lawyer and author Jack Batten alluded to the incident in his 1982 book entitled *In Court*, saying that "other criminal lawyers rallied to Hamilton's cause, criticizing Greenspan among themselves for breaking an unwritten rule of the inner circle of criminal counsel by going public with a knock at one of their own."

Had Jack Batten called me for comment as well, he would have had another quote for his book. It would have been that I'm not overly moved by the unwritten rules of inner circles. I'm much more moved by the presumption of innocence. I'm much more moved by the verdict of a jury. I'm much more moved by the rule of law.

Having made such a ringing statement, I'd better add something for the sake of accuracy. I may not be moved by "inner circles", but nothing in my entire career has made me happier than a two-line note I received at the end of the Gordon Allen trial. It said: "Dear Ed: My sincere congratulations on a brilliant and thorough defence. I think I have some idea of the amount of hard work that contributed to your success." It was signed by Canada's greatest lawyer (and the subject, incidentally, of a recent biography by Jack Batten), John J. Robinette.

## NOTES

p.423, l.13: Staff Sergeant Stevenson and Sergeant McLean would later explain to George Jonas and Barbara Amiel that Constable Koepke had initially been interviewed only by the detectives at 41 Division. At that time, a few days after Bruce Lorenz's murder, Koepke did tell the officers what Lauralee had allegedly told him about his brother's being shot in the head, but the detectives were not sufficiently familiar with the case to understand the significance of the timing of Koepke's conversation with Lauralee.

p.429, l.30: *The Queen v. Vinette*. Ironically, some time later the Ontario Court of Appeal concluded in the case of *Regina v. McAvoy* that a person could be convicted of being an accessory regardless of whether a principal had been convicted of the offence or not. Had that been the law in this province in February 1979, Lauralee might have gotten her wish and been convicted of being an accessory after the fact to murder. She may owe her unblemished record solely to my misinterpretation of the law.

p.433, l.39: Strictly speaking, even at a joint trial of both accused, all this would have been evidence only against Lauralee Lorenz and not against Gordon Allen, but it would have been admissible evidence and the jury would have heard it. With Gordon being tried alone, the evidence became inadmissible. It simply couldn't come out at all.

p.434, l.9: Shortly before her death, Mrs. Round had testified at the preliminary hearing, and her evidence was read at trial.

p.450, l.36: Oscar Wilde, the brilliant Irish writer, spent two years in prison for homosexuality in the 1890s. As an absolute master at verbal fireworks Wilde expected (and was expected by London society) to demolish any lawyer daring to match wits with him at his trial. However, even the great writer and wit could not overcome the essential disadvantage of being cross-examined by a skilled advocate. Wilde ended his testimony with monosyllabic mumbles in the witness-box.

# Index